# Exploring England

Michael Jackson

MAYFLOWER

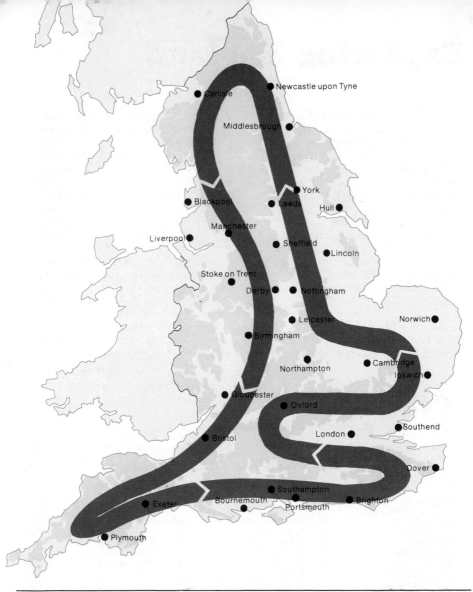

**Front cover:**
Warwick Castle, Warwickshire

A QUARTO BOOK

Published in the United States by
Mayflower Books Inc., New York
City 10022. Originally published in
England by William Collins and
Sons Ltd., London.

First published 1979.
© Copyright 1979 Quarto Ltd.

ISBN 0 8317 5773 6
Manufactured in Spain
by H. Fournier, S. A. - Vitoria

Library of Congress Cataloguing in
Publication Data

Jackson, Michael
Mayflower Guide to Exploring
England
Guidebook

This book was designed and
produced by Quarto Publishing
Limited, 32 Kingly Court,
London W1.
Consultant Editor:
Michael Jackson
Designer: Roger Daniels
Additional Text: David Hardy
Text Editors: Jane Struthers and
Philippa Algeo
Additional Research:
Patsy Bradbury
Additional Maps: Clive Hayball
Art Director: Robert Morley
Printed in England by
Loxley Brothers, Sheffield.

# Exploring England

In the last few years, the English Tourist Board has helped towns the length and breadth of the land to map both their city centres and their immediate countryside, as well as collating information on their attractions for the visitor. Now, with the publication of *Exploring England*, this material is available in a single volume.

*Exploring England* is edited and designed by a team which has for seven years acted as consultants to the Tourist Board in the production of town Miniguides and other publications. It has been compiled with the help of the Tourist Board, and of many towns.

Starting from London, *Exploring England* covers the whole country. It follows a route through the Thames Valley, across the Chilterns, East Anglia and the East Midlands, on through Yorkshire and the North East to the Scottish border, then south again down the West side of the country, making a circular tour which ends almost where it began.

En route, England is explored in manageable portions. Each segment of countryside is related to one or two towns which are known to have hotel space for visitors, and which also have Tourist Information Centres. Other towns which can usually accommodate visitors are identified as centres from which to explore.

*Exploring England* covers more towns than are commonly considered to be of pressing interest to the visitor. It does so because, in a small country like England, every town is near to interesting scenery.

Even the least promising town is full of surprises – indeed, every corner of England rewards exploration.

MICHAEL JACKSON

# Contents

# Exploring London:
# a week in the capital

London stretches for more than 35 miles up the river Thames, and in places extends for about 15 miles to either side. It is a cohesive metropolis, even though it is made up of more than 30 boroughs.

Even the Londoners themselves are unsure about their borough boundaries, but anyone can recognize the hundred or so little 'town centres' which represent the focal points of natural districts. Some of these districts have such individuality and character that they have been described as 'London villages'.

The term 'City of London' can cause confusion to the visitor. To the British, 'The City' is in this special case less of a geographical term than an omnibus journalistic description for the financial institutions which crowd into an easterly enclave of Central London. This is the original City of London, as settled and walled by the Romans, and it is only one mile

square. It retains the status of City, rich in pageantry, though the domain of the Lord Mayor of London does not extend into the metropolis around him.

Since the Norman Conquest, and especially since the Great Fire of 1666, London has been expanding in a westerly direction. Even in the 1600s, it was already reaching a mile up river to join hands with the City of Westminster. As an identifiable part of modern London, Westminster is an imposing four square miles of riverside, the seat of both Church and State. As an administrative area, the City of Westminster stretches away from the river by way of Charing Cross, Trafalgar Square, Leicester Square and Piccadilly Circus to embrace the famous shopping streets and theatre districts of Central London.

Having grown in this direction, London calls its centre 'The West End' – another confusion for the visitor.

Because of London's size and sprawl, the visitor can easily spend many a frustrating hour retracing footsteps back and forth from one side of town to the other. If the visit is just for a weekend, this can be ruinous, and it is an extravagant waste of time and money even in a fortnight's stay. It makes more sense to spend each day, or half-day, exploring one particular side of the capital, taking in sights and activities which are all reasonably near to each other. It doesn't really matter which area is visited on each day, though the following itinerary is built around certain fixed weekly events. There are more suggestions for each day than could possibly be followed, but the intention is to provide a choice.

'For children' includes many places which are also of interest to adults.

The cinemas mentioned are art houses, not general release theatres.

The Grenadier Guards . . . one of London's famous sights

4

# Saturday

**West London**, because Saturday is the day for both Portobello Road (best in the morning) and King's Road (best in the afternoon).

Take the Tube to Notting Hill Gate, walk down Pembridge Road, then follow the crowd when they turn left into *Portobello Road*. If you want to see the whole market, it can take all day. Antiques and junk appear first, then freaky shops and exotic greengroceries as Portobello stretches into the Caribbean neighbourhood of Golborne.

You'll pass the *Electric Cinema Club* (join just before buying your ticket), which has interesting movies in the evening. So has the *Gate Cinema*, back in Notting Hill. Plenty of eating places around Notting Hill Gate.

Full of colour and exotica . . . Portobello Road

**Afternoon alternatives:** Holland Park/Kensington High Street/Fulham Road, Chelsea/King's Road, Chelsea/Hammersmith/Shepherd's Bush/Kew Bridge.

A short walk down Notting Hill Gate, and a left turn, for a relaxing afternoon in *Holland Park*. The park has an *open-air theatre* in summer (tel 633 1707).

**For children:** Also in Holland Park, educative exhibitions and such like at the *Commonwealth Institute*.

From Notting Hill Gate, a tidy walk by the antique shops of Kensington Church Street, or bus 27, 28 or 31, or Tube to *Kensington High Street* for shopping there.

**For children:** There's always a good chance of model yachts on the Round Pond, and kite-flying in *Kensington Gardens* (Sundays, too). But leave the big museums in South Kensington for a weekday when they will be less busy.

From Notting Hill or Kensington High Street a 31 bus, or Tube to South Kensington, for *Fulham Road*: Shopping, restaurants, *soccer at Chelsea* and

interesting evening movies at the *Paris Pullman Cinema*, Drayton Gardens (tel 373 5898).

Still bus 31, or Tube to Sloane Square, for *King's Road*. The clothes and colour are at the Sloane Square end.

**For children:** Not far from Sloane Square, off King's Road, the *National Army Museum* (uniforms, guns, etc) adjoins the Royal 'Hospital', home of the *Chelsea Pensioners*.

From Notting Hill Gate, bus 27, or from Fulham or Chelsea bus 11, or Tube to Hammersmith: For summer evening drinks, *riverside pubs* near *Hammersmith Bridge* and dotted along the bank going further west; theatre, music and late films at *Riverside Studios Arts Centre* (tel 748 3354); also the *Lyric Theatre* (tel 748 3020 for information), with Edwardian plasterwork transferred into a new building; ethnic food at the *Polish Cultural Centre*, King Street. Across the river, Barnes village, with a famous *jazz pub*, The Bull.

From Notting Hill Gate, bus 12 or 88, or Tube to Shepherd's Bush for soccer at *Queen's Park Rangers*, a small *street market* with a Caribbean flavour, and

evening *pub-theatre* at The Bush Hotel.

**For children:** From Notting Hill Gate, bus 27 goes via Kensington High Street and Hammersmith further west to Kew Bridge for weekends-only *steam museum*, where the star attractions are enormous working beam-engines in a pumping station on the river. A couple of minutes away, Saturday afternoons in summer also provide a rare opportunity to see the *National Musical Museum*, in Brentford High Street. Older children will be fascinated by the Wurlitzer, pianola, musical boxes, etc.

Several interesting *houses* nearby, but phone to check opening hours: Chiswick House, with gardens by William Kent (tel 994 3299); Hogarth's House, home of the crusading illustrator (tel 570 7728); Boston Manor, Tudor and Jacobean, with parks and gardens (Saturdays only; tel 560 0617); Osterley Park, remodelled by Robert Adam (tel 560 3918); Syon House, with Capability Brown landscaping, conservatory, and garden centre (tel 560 0884).

# Sunday

**East London**, because Sunday is the day for Petticoat Lane and all the other East End markets. On Sundays, the rest of London can be sleepy and Sabbatarian, but that is no business of the East End's Jews and Moslems. Yiddish expressions colour the market spiel, Bengali sweetmeats brighten the back-street shops, and a carnival atmosphere shows that East End street-life thrives as ever it did when immigrants coming up the Thames had to settle here outside the City walls.

Get up as early as you possibly can. Take the Tube to Aldgate East, then walk along Whitechapel High Street to *Brick Lane* for antiques, furniture and endless bizarre junk, including inexplicable tangles of electrical equipment. Not much as you walk down the first half of the Lane, but look out for the architecture of *Fournier Street*, 16th- and 17th-century home of the Flemish silk-weaving industry here. Also the impressive new *Truman's brewery* building.

In Commercial Street, parallel to Brick Lane, is *Christ Church*, built by Wren's pupil Hawksmoor, and recently partly restored. There are two more Hawksmoor churches in the East End, at Stepney and Limehouse.

**For children:** At the far end of the Lane, in *Club Row* (Sclater Street), pets and exotic animals are sold, a scene which evokes memories of 'A Kid for Two Farthings', the story and film by East Ender Wolf Mankowitz.

If you are interested in silver, jewelry and coins, get up just as early but start from Liverpool Street Tube, and walk down Houndsditch to *Cutler Street* market.

Both of these markets are close to *Petticoat Lane* (Middlesex Street). Go there afterwards to hear the stallholders, and to eat shellfish from Tubby

Towering masts and yards . . . the Cutty Sark

Isaacs' stall if you can't wait for an almost-obligatory kosher lunch at *Blooms*, 90 Whitechapel High Street. There's always a queue at Blooms, but you can buy food to take out if you fancy a picnic.

**Afternoon alternatives:** Go back to town for *Speaker's Corner*, in Hyde Park, then explore Bayswater/Stay in the East End for two interesting museums/Go to St Katherine's Dock/Go to Greenwich.

From any of the markets, or from Liverpool Street Tube, it is fifteen minutes' walk, or a ride on almost any bus, down Shoreditch High Street to the *Geffrye Museum*, open from 2.00pm on Sundays, for rooms and furniture from the 16th century,

**For children:** A walk from the pet market in Club Row, or a bus 8 or 8A, or Tube to Bethnal Green for the collection of toys and dolls in the splendid local museum there. Apart from its considerable 'child-

6

hood' section, *Bethnal Green Museum* has costumes, Spitalfields silk, decorative arts, and sculpture, notably Rodin. Opens at 2.30pm on Sundays. First, join the East Enders for a picnic in nearby *Victoria Park*.

Or take the Tube to Tower Hill for a stroll around *St Katherine's Dock*, redeveloped as a yacht haven, and dotted with pubs, restaurants and extravagant tourist attractions.

**Afternoon in Greenwich:** A London 'must', with plenty for children. It doesn't have to be Sunday, but Greenwich Park and Blackheath offer a constitutional to walk off that filling lunch, or the riverside pubs the chance to have one. Try to arrive in time to see the observatory turret signalling 1.00pm Greenwich Mean Time. Remember, too, that on Sundays pubs shut for the afternoon at 2.00pm.

**How to get there:** The best way in which to sustain the feeling of the East End, and to sample the maritime quality of Greenwich, is to go by the river. During the week, call the London Tourist Board's River Boat number 730 4812 to check departures. If you have been to the markets in the morning, take the Tube from Liverpool Street to Tower Hill, and the boat from Tower Pier. From Central London, catch a boat at Westminster Pier or Charing Cross Pier. The journey will take between 30 minutes and an hour, and you will pass under Tower Bridge. The more conventional way in which to travel is by British Rail from Charing Cross or London Bridge to Maze Hill (Greenwich).

The sights of Greenwich all open to the public at 2.30pm on Sundays. It is possible to board and examine two vessels: *Gipsy Moth IV*, in which Sir Francis Chichester sailed round the world single-handed in 1966 (open in summer only); and the *Cutty Sark*, last of the great tea clippers, launched in 1869, and now a museum.

*Greenwich Church*, built by Hawksmoor, is a couple of minutes from the pier, on the hill which leads up to *Greenwich Park*, in and around which is a stunning array of architectural delights.

*The National Maritime Museum* is in a group of buildings centred on the *Queen's House*, a Palladian villa built by Inigo Jones for Queen Anne of Denmark. Nearby is the *Royal Naval College*, formerly Greenwich Hospital, largely designed by Wren, with additional work by Hawksmoor and Vanbrugh (who also built a castle-like folly in the park). The college is famous for its Painted Hall, and major orchestral concerts are occasionally held in its lavishly-designed chapel (tel 858 2154 for information). *The Old Royal Observatory*, with Wren's Flamsteed House, has the world's largest refracting telescope and, in the South Building, a modern *Planetarium*. The *Ranger's House*, built in 1688 and once the home of the Earl of Chesterfield, now houses a collection of English portraits. Classical concerts are sometimes held there (tel 348 1286).

There is sometimes Sunday *jazz* at the *Greenwich Theatre* (tel 858 7755), in a Victorian music-hall building. There are also a variety of attractions at the *Tramshed* (tel 854 3933).

The oddest attraction in Greenwich is a walk under the Thames by foot tunnel, starting in a red-brick domed building near the Cutty Sark. Once across the Thames, you can see Greenwich as Canaletto saw it, then say farewell to such Palladian splendour and return to the East End proper as represented by the 'Isle' of Dogs, in the heart of pubby dockland.

# Eating in London

English food is surprisingly hard to find in London (look out for the 'Taste of England' sticker), but variety is the spice of metropolitan eating. Restaurants of varied ethnicities offer good value all over the capital, and knowing Londoners like especially to eat in Soho for good value and genuine cuisine. Soho is also very convenient for the sightseer, shopper and theatre-goer, along with the adjoining 'villages' of Charlotte Street (close to Bloomsbury) and Covent Garden.

For a quick and filling snack, there are several *kosher 'nosh-bars'* in Great Windmill Street, Soho. Beef-on-rye and celebrity photographs on the walls.

Soho also has a thriving *Chinatown*, encircling Gerrard Street, where prices can be astonishingly low and the quality sometimes excellent. Unless you are Chinese or a New Yorker, you will never have seen such variety. Apart from Canton, Peking and Szechuan, there are restaurants specializing in noodles, Dim Sung snacks, duck, and wind-dried sausages.

Forming a cross with Soho's open market of Berwick Street and Rupert Street are the culinary delights of Brewer Street and Old Compton Street. The latter two streets have between them a smoked-fish snack-bar, a *Spanish* grocery shop and several excellent *Italian* food stores and restaurants. The Italian flavour intensifies in Frith Street, and restaurants get marginally more expensive there.

Up Frith Street and past Soho Square, this cosmopolitan neighbourhood tries to jump across Oxford Street, and lands among the *Greek* Cypriots of Charlotte Street, with lots of modestly-priced kebab houses and Zorba-esque noisiness.

Yet another change a block further north as the Cypriots give way to the *Indians* (in truth, Bangladeshis) around Whitfield Street.

# Monday

The City, because this has to be seen on a working day. To avoid the crush, start from the east and work west – the opposite direction to that taken by tour parties.

**For children:** Start at the *Tower of London*, which stands guard outside The City. Opens at 9.30am. Tower Hill Tube. Yeomen warders, Bloody Tower, ravens, Crown Jewels. At the Tower Gate there is a Tourist Information Centre which can tell you, among other things, whether any of the City's churches have lunchtime concerts on the day of your visit. Because The City is so small, the benefits of exploration on foot are easily enjoyed, though the first such excursion is the most arduous: A walk down Great Tower Street and Eastcheap, and 311 steps, lead to the top of Wren's hollow *Monument* and a superb view.

Along Gracechurch Street is *Leadenhall Market*, a delightful Victorian building with stalls selling poultry and a variety of other items.

As Gracechurch Street becomes Bishopsgate, Threadneedle Street runs off to the left, for the *Stock Exchange*. Public gallery at the corner of Threadneedle Street and Old Broad Street, open from 10.30am to 3.15pm. Further down Threadneedle Street, spare a glance for the *Bank of England*, which is not open to the public.

**For children:** A walk along Moorgate and to the left down London Wall leads to the *Museum of London*, which tells the story of The City in great style. Round the corner, just off St Martin's le Grand, in Angel Street, is the National *Postal Museum*, with a huge collection of stamps.

Ahead stands *St Paul's Cathedral*, the second largest Christian church in the world, built by Wren between 1675 and 1710, with its magnificent dome and Whispering Gallery.

World-famous . . . Fleet Street

The Cathedral opens at 7.45am, but the crypt and galleries are open only from 10.45am to 3.30pm.

Nearby in Newgate Street, on the site of the famous prison, is the Central Criminal Court, the *Old Bailey*, topped by the statue of Justice. Trials can be seen from the public gallery (no children under 14) from 10.30am until 4.00pm, with an hour for lunch at 1.00pm.

At the bottom of Ludgate Hill lies *Fleet Street*, synonymous with the newspaper industry. The newspapers themselves can be visited only by pre-arranged parties, but just off Fleet Street there is an interesting *Printing Library and Museum* in Bride Lane, and *Dr Johnson's House*, in Gough Square, can be visited between 11.00am and 5.30pm.

While you are in Fleet Street, have lunch at a newspapermen's pub. Suggestions: The Cheshire Cheese, with Johnsonian associations and excellent Burton beer, at 145 Fleet Street (tel 353 6170); The Cock, with Dickensian associations, 22 Fleet Street. The Punch, as in magazine, 99 Fleet Street; The Cartoonist, headquarters of their association, 76 Shoe Lane; The Printer's Devil, 98 Fetter Lane.

**From the Fleet Street area:** If you have had an early and filling lunch, and feel like a long walk, set off via Shoe Lane and Holborn Circus for the general street market at *Leather Lane* (11.00am to 3.00pm), a look at the *Hatton Garden* diamond district, and the stalls selling old books in Farringdon Road. The book market is in *Clerkenwell*, traditionally a printing-industry 'village', and a cradle of Socialism. Little remains as a reminder of the latter except the offices of the Communist 'Morning Star', and the Marx Memorial Library.

A more restful stroll would start at the top of Fleet Street, behind the *Law Courts*, pass by the *Old Curiosity Shop*, in Portsmouth Street, and pause in *Lincoln's Inn Fields* before crossing by Holborn Kingsway Tube station into Southampton Row and *Bloomsbury*, a 'village' of publishers and students.

Bloomsbury Street houses the *British Museum*, with its great Oriental collection (10.00am to 5.00pm), adjoining the *University of London*. Behind the university, in Woburn Square, is the superb collection of French Impressionists at the Courtauld Institute (10.00am to 5.00pm). In Upper Woburn Place is the *Jewish Museum*. (2.30pm to 5.00pm).

**For children:** Pollock's *Toy Museum*, Scala Street, Bloomsbury.

A third possibility is a walk from the top of Fleet Street past the rebuilt Wren church of *St Clement Danes* ('Oranges and Lemons' chime every three hours), round the Aldwych, right into Drury Lane, then left down Russell Street into *Covent Garden*, where the lovely buildings which once housed the fruit and vegetable market now have a new life as piazzas, cafés, galleries and craft shops, stretching across Long Acre, down Neal Street, in the direction of Soho and Bloomsbury.

# Tuesday

**Westminster:** With long-weekenders definitely gone, and Londoners safely at their work, midweek is the best time to do shopping and sightseeing in the middle of town. Shop during the first quiet hour or so, especially since the galleries and museums don't open until 10.00am. One, the *Photographers' Gallery*, at 8 Great Newport Street (near Leicester Square Tube station) doesn't open until 11.00am (Tuesdays to Saturdays).

On a grander scale, the West End has four major attractions within walking distance. The *National Gallery*, in Trafalgar Square, is next door to the *National Portrait Gallery*. Half a mile away, the *Royal Academy*, in Piccadilly, opens its doors to the public for important exhibitions (tel 734 9052), and rubs shoulders with the *Museum of Mankind*, in Burlington Gardens. Between the two is *Burlington Arcade*, an elegant thoroughfare with some expensive shops.

On Mondays and Tuesdays, there are sometimes *lunchtime recitals* at the church of *St Martin-in-the-Fields*, Trafalgar Square (tel 930 0089).

**For children:** Your whole day will have to take a different shape if you want to see the *Changing of the Guard*. On a fine day in July or August, enthusiasts have been known to start assembling at 6.00am, though nothing happens until 11.00am, by which time there can be 15,000 spectators.

From Trafalgar Square, walk down Whitehall to *Horse Guards'* Arch for the Changing of the Queen's Life Guard at 11.00am (lasts for 25 minutes). If there are crowds, abandon the idea, walk on, and see *Downing Street* instead. Also from Trafalgar Square, walk down The Mall for the changing of the guard outside *St James's Palace* at 11.15am, or all the way to *Buckingham Palace* for the popular ceremony there at 11.30am. It takes place inside the railings, and the public views from the outside. Times vary on special occasions, the changings are on alternate days in winter, and may be abandoned in wet weather. Details can be checked with the London Tourist Board (tel 730 0791) on the day.

A few minutes' walk from Horse Guards', or a stroll from either of the palaces by way of the delightful *St James's Park*, is *Westminster Abbey*, containing the Coronation chair and tombs and memorials of monarchs. Open 9.00am to 5.00pm.

Opposite are the *Houses of Parliament*, with separate and often lengthy queues at St Stephen's entrance to hear debates in the Commons and the Lords. There are conducted tours when the Houses are not sitting (tel 219 3000).

Walk down Victoria Street to the Roman Catholic *Westminster Cathedral*, an imposing Byzantine-style building. Despite its name, England's premier Roman Catholic church is almost in Victoria, not far from the railway station and Tube there.

On the Westminster embankment, not far from Pimlico Tube station, is the *Tate Gallery*, housing the nation's finest collection of 20th-century art, and a huge range of British masters dating back to the 1500s. *Lunch at the Tate*, because few public buildings have such good restaurants, but book during the summer (tel 821 1313).

**Afternoon in Kensington:** From the palaces of Westminster, walk or take a cab through *Hyde Park* to Kensington Gore to see the *Albert Memorial* and then the museums. From Victoria, Pimlico or elsewhere, take the Tube to South Kensington. On either side of Exhibition Road, Kensington has no less than four of London's major museums. The largest of these is the *Victoria and Albert*, a huge museum of decorative arts.

**For children:** The *Natural History Museum* is perennially popular; so is the *Science Museum*; and the lesser-known *Geological Museum* is gaining a great reputation for its simulated earthquakes. All of these museums open until 6.00pm on weekdays.

**Evening:** A concert at the *Royal Albert Hall*? Tel 589 8212. It's at the top of Exhibition Road.

Imposing . . . the Houses of Parliament

# Wednesday

**North London**, because Wednesday morning presents some midweek colour at Camden Passage – and provides a good example of the arty rejuvenation of the Inner London boroughs.

Take the Tube to The Angel, then walk along Islington High Street to *Camden Passage*. It's a pleasant market selling antiques and bric-à-brac, with one enclave dealing in silver. Although Wednesday and Saturday are the main days, coins may be found on Tuesday and second-hand books on Thursday and Friday. Parts of the market are covered, and parts in open paved areas, with book and print shops spilling into nearby streets, alongside boutiques, cafés and pubs.

To the other side of Upper Street and Liverpool Road is *Chapel Street Market*, which has been in business for more than a century supplying groceries and greengroceries to the people of Islington. In Chapel Street, there is also a shop selling the London working man's traditional hot snack: *eels, pie and mash*. The ethnicity of Islington would suggest as alternative lunches a pub stew washed down with Guinness, or a kebab in one of the local Turkish restaurants.

Georgian squares, crescents and terraces decorate Islington in what was described most accurately by 'The Observer' newspaper as 'a special blend of discreet elegance and disintegration'. A good example just behind Camden Passage is *Duncan Terrace*.

Walk back beyond The Angel to Roseberry Avenue for opera and ballet at *Sadler's Wells* (tel 837 1672). Under a trapdoor in the theatre is the well which Thomas Sadler discovered to make Islington briefly into a spa.

Opposite Camden Passage, on Islington Green, is an interesting art-house cinema: *The Screen on the Green*.

At 115 Upper Street, the King's Head *Pub and Theatre* offers lunch, music, and evening shows.

**For children:** Off Essex Road, in Dagmar Passage, Cross Street, the *Little Angel Marionette Theatre* (tel 226 1787) does weekday shows at 3.00pm in the school holidays, but is otherwise only open at weekends.

If you want exercise after a heavy lunch, take a tidy stroll up Essex Road and Canonbury Road, then through *New River Walk*, leading to St Paul's Road. New River Walk is a winding path with roses, pansies, weeping willows and a rather murky stream which once brought fresh water to London.

Close by is *Canonbury Tower*, a haunted 16th-century building the inhabitants of which have included Sir Francis Bacon and Oliver Goldsmith. Its lovely panelled rooms can be seen only by appointment in advance (tel 226 5111), though the *Tower Theatre* may have a show in the evening.

**Afternoon alternatives:** Regent's Park/Baker Street/ Hampstead/Highgate.

From behind Camden Passage, Duncan Terrace and Colebrook Row lead to *Regent's Canal* for towpath walks. In the

A bottle stall . . . Camden Passage

10

opposite direction, access to the towpath from Pentonville Road, Rodney Street and Muriel Street provides a long walk to *London Zoo* and *Regent's Park*. The Zoo (open until 6.00pm) can also be reached via Camden Town Tube and the 74 or 74B bus.

In the middle of the park, in the Inner Circle, an *Open Air Theatre* has performances on summer evenings (tel 486 2431), with an adjoining tent for light meals.

**For children:** Combine with the zoo a visit to the triple attraction of *Madame Tussaud's*, the *Planetarium* and a newer *Laser Show*, in a complex of buildings near Baker Street Tube.

For a look further north, take the Tube to Hampstead or Highgate, two delightful villages long famous as the home of London's fashionable intellectuals. These twin villages are set at either side of *Hampstead Heath*, with miles of lovely walks, and breathtaking views of Central London.

**For children:** three particular attractions, all in the same part of the Heath: *Whitestone Pond* for model boats; the Hampstead Scientific Society's small astronomical *observatory*, though it functions only on

Hampstead . . . a famous fashionable London 'village'

winter Saturday evenings (8.00pm to 10.00pm); and the deer enclosure and modest *zoo* at Golder's Hill.

Hampstead itself offers endless fascinating shops in its back streets, with lots of bookshops, and fashion in Heath Street. It also has a number of famous pubs: The Bull and Bush, North End Way (celebrated in song, and popular with fair folk at Bank Holidays); Jack Straw's Castle, North End Way (for Wat Tyler associations and view over the Heath); Spaniards Inn, Spaniards Road (16th-century, with rose-garden and aviary); The Flask, Flask Walk (arty, with good beer and malt whiskies); the Nag's Head, Heath Street (for beer enthusiasts).

*Keats' House*, in Keats Grove, can be visited. *Fenton House* (open Wednesdays to Saturdays) has occasional concerts and recitals, and a collection of keyboard instruments, furniture, needlework and porcelain (tel 435 3471).

*The Everyman Cinema*, near Hampstead Tube, is a very small art-house in a former var-

iety theatre – Noel Coward acted there. The cinema also has occasional concerts, and there are sometimes art exhibitions in the lobby.

**Highgate:** More shops, especially for antiques, in High Street and Archway Road, but fewer restaurants. Another popular pub called The Flask, with a Pell Mell court.

Highgate's most famous attraction is the tomb of *Karl Marx*, in the enormous cemetery in Swain's Lane. On the west side of the lane is an overgrown and crumbling continuation of gothic majesty, normally kept closed on account of vandals, but the subject of open days organized by the Friends of Highgate Cemetery.

An outstanding collection of *old masters* can be seen, and *poetry readings* and *recitals* occasionally heard at *Kenwood House* (Iveagh Bequest), on the Highgate Village side of the Heath. Major symphony concerts are held there on summer weekends (tel GLC Parks Dept 633 1707). Superb Adam interior, Orangery and lovely parkland.

## Entertainment

London's theatres and concert halls are listed in the two evening papers (**Standard** and **News**), and the whole range of entertainments receives an easy-to-follow, comprehensive listing, with potted reviews, in *Time Out* magazine, published every Thursday. *Time Out* lists local films, late movies, classical music, dance, jazz, rock, folk, poetry readings, children's events, and even political demonstrations. Its tourist-angled competitor **What's On** gives more coverage to such nightclubs as London can offer.

# Thursday

**Out of town,** because London is just too full of shoppers on Thursdays. In a throwback to the days of weekly pay-packets, Londoners choose this day to shop, and the West End stores oblige by opening until 8.00pm. Useful if you are imprisoned in an office from 9.00am until 5.00pm, but Thursday late opening attracts so many shoppers into town for a long session that pavements and Tube stations become battlefields. Visitors have the freedom to shop at less crowded, and better-tempered times, and should use it.

London is blessed like no other city with huge and numerous green spaces, and none are larger than the sequence of parklands around Wimbledon and Richmond. The first is very much a London 'village', with arty little shops and well-patronised pubs; the second a sizable country town on the Thames, just inside the metropolitan area. Both are lit-tle more than half an hour away by Tube.

**Wimbledon:** The tennis is in the last week of June and the first week of July, at the All-England Club, Church Road. During the rest of the year, go there to see a museum devoted to the sport (Tues-Sat).

**For children:** Wimbledon Common is the home of mythical creatures called Wombles, which also inhabit television sets. The 1,000-acre common also has a *windmill*, and an Iron

A multitude of pleasures . . . the river at Richmond

Age *fortification* misleadingly known as Caesar's Camp. Explore the common by *horse or pony*, hired from Hilcote Riding School, 24b High Street (tel 946 2520). A *toy exhibition* and *puppet museum* can be seen in Wimbledon, at Polka, 240 The Broadway (Mon-Fri).

**Evening:** The *Wimbledon Theatre*, in The Broadway (tel 946 5211) presents some ambitious productions. *Wimbledon Stadium*, in Plough Lane (tel 946 5361) mounts decidedly un-rural attractions such as greyhound racing (a favourite sport in London), speedway, stock cars, and League soccer. It also has a *solarium* which is open to the public during the day and in the evening.

**Richmond:** Ten miles of riverside with an unbroken towpath wind their way through this borough, from Kew by way of Twickenham to Hampton Court, with pleasures enough to fill a week rather than a day.

Go to Kew by Tube, and start with the Royal Botanic Gardens – 40,000 plant species, tropical greenhouses, a palm house, a pagoda, and even a palace. *Kew Gardens*, as they are popularly known, provide a fascinating and relaxing contrast after sightseeing in town.

From *Kew Green* walk down Ferry Lane for an exquisite *riverside walk* to the town of Richmond itself (it's quicker by Tube, but you miss a lot). Leave the river at *Richmond Bridge*, looking much as it did when Turner painted it, if you want to see the town.

Through the town, have lunch at one of several restaurants in Kew Road, or at the Orange Tree *Pub Theatre*, which sometimes has the bonus of a lunchtime performance.

*Richmond Theatre*, in an interesting 1899 building on the Green, presents touring shows and pre-West End runs (tel 940 0088).

There is sometimes *Open Air Theatre* at Marble Hill House, in Twickenham. This 18th-century Palladian villa, with early Georgian furniture and paintings, is open to the public (except Fridays). *Ham House*, a 17th-century building with early Georgian furnishings and a portrait gallery, is also open to the public (except Mondays).

There are interesting little shops in the streets around *Richmond Green*, with its pretty row of 18th-century 'Maids of Honour' houses. More small shops, too, on *Richmond Hill*, famous for its views. The Hill links the river with the Park.

**For children:** Room to roam in *Richmond Park*, with its herd of deer, and sharp-eyed glimpses of a fox, weasel or badger. The Maze at *Hampton Court*, palace of Henry VIII. 'England's most beautiful and interesting royal palace', according to historian Harold Hutchison.

**Tourist Information Centres:** At Old Richmond Town Hall, in Hill Street; and at 58–60 York Street, Twickenham. Tel 892 0032.

# Shopping: where to find what

The capital has countless, and competing, shopping thoroughfares. **Oxford Street** is the biggest, with the most department stores, middle-range prices, and some bargains. It is more than a mile long, with two **Marks and Spencers** and Oxford Circus in the middle.

Just behind Oxford Circus Tube station, to the left of the famous half-timbered **Liberty** store, is **Carnaby Street** — worth a glance, but strictly for teeny-boppers.

Off Oxford Street, just opposite Bond Street station, James Street leads to **Barrett Street antique market.**

**Bond Street** itself runs a block to the east of the Tube station. It starts as New Bond Street, and then becomes Old, but is chic and expensive all the way. Bond Street is just over half a mile long, running into Piccadilly (the broad thoroughfare, not the Circus).

**Piccadilly** has several noted establishments, including London's grandest grocers, **Fortnum and Mason**, where you can have a late breakfast or afternoon tea.

In the Piccadilly bus lane, pick up a number 14, 19 or 22 for the one-mile journey west to **Harrods**, in the stylish shopping territory formed by **Knightsbridge**, **Brompton Road** and **Sloane Street**.

This area still qualifies as West End, but a ¾-mile walk down Sloane Street (or take any bus) leads to Sloane Square and King's Road, Chelsea.

**King's Road** is very much for Saturday promenading in exotic plumage, and visits to the **Chelsea** **Antique Market** and **Antiquarius**. Most of the action takes place in the first mile, then the clothes shops dwindle in favour of antique shops and restaurants which are dotted along the road for the same distance again, until they finally get lost in residential Fulham, at Parson's Green.

The mantle of true fashion has been ceded by King's Road to nearby **Fulham Road**, which runs parallel. Full of ideas, interest and variety, plus plenty of eating places.

The third major shopping area in West London is some distance away, nearer to the big museums and Kensington Gardens. **Kensington High Street** (with its own Tube station of the Circle line) is a big, bustling thoroughfare of city-centre proportions. Apart from its shops, it has **Kensington Market**.

# Friday

**South London**, because it is too often forgotten, and because Bermondsey's New Caledonian antique market on Friday mornings is arguably the most genuine, and certainly the most challenging, of them all.

*Bermondsey* is a dealers' market, and the early birds are already there at first light, with torches in winter. Unless you can arrange an early cab, take the Tube to London Bridge and wake yourself up with a brisk half-mile walk down Bermondsey Street. Have a sustaining English fried breakfast at one of the market snack places.

Nearby *Borough Market*, centuries old, sells fruit and vegetables under the railway arches of London Bridge.

**For children:** Also underneath the arches are the slimy vaults of the *London Dungeon*, a medieval waxwork museum specialising in torture and horror. Opens at 10.00am, entrance at 34 Tooley Street. Nearby on the river, the cruiser *HMS Belfast* can be explored from 11.00 am. Visit the engine room and bridge, marvel at the D-day landings in a Naval exhibition. Opposite London Bridge station is Southwark Cathedral, dating from 1206, with a 16th-century tower and 19th-century nave.

Southwark is one of the oldest parts of London, having been settled by the Romans. One of its proudest buildings, also near the station, at 77 Borough High Street, is the surviving wing of *The George*, rebuilt after the Fire of London, and now the capital's only galleried inn. It was this style of inn, with a courtyard for strolling players, that inspired the Shakespearian 'wooden O', and gave birth to the English theatre. There are *performances of Shakespeare* at The George on summer weekends (tel 703 2917), but in the week you can still enjoy a pint and plate of cockles.

For early birds . . . Bermondsey Market

Walk down Borough High Street to the Elephant and Castle roundabout for more details on Southwark's history at the *Cuming Museum*, in Walworth Road, or head down St George's Road for the warning rumble of war . . .

**For children:** *The Imperial War Museum*, Lambeth Road, has British and German aircraft from both World Wars, a V2 rocket, and a sound-and-vision exhibit on life in the trenches.

After an early morning, take the Tube to *The Oval* for a snoozy summer's afternoon of cricket, or head further south to Dulwich village.

Take the Tube to Brixton, then bus 3 to Thurlow Park Road for the beautiful *Dulwich College Picture Gallery*, College Road. This was London's first public art gallery, and has works by Rembrandt, Rubens, Van Dyck, and a wide range of masters. Closed Mondays (tel 693 5254). Linger in Dulwich, a 'London village' before the idea was fashionable. London's last toll-gate, and lovely rhododendrons and azaleas in the park.

Imperial War Museum . . . exhibits from both World Wars

A tidy walk away, or a short ride on the bus 12, is the *Horniman Museum*, 100 London Road, Forest Hill, with a strange mixture of interesting attractions: 'magic' and religious dance masks and totems, early tools, in summer a 'working' glass beehive, and an ethnographic library, all in an Art Nouveau building.

**For children:** Bus 3 from Brixton, or bus 12, or a variety of other routes, including

British Rail, to *Crystal Palace*. Huge prehistoric monsters in plaster, boating lake, children's zoo, artificial ski slope in winter, swimming bath and England's biggest sports centre, with a huge range of facilities and events (tel 778 0131).

**Evening:** Stay in the South, but back towards town. South London was consciously given a share of the capital's cultural attractions when the riverside area near Waterloo station (Rail and Tube) was ordained in the 1950s as an arts complex. *The South Bank* was an attempt to make Central London cross the river, and it has in some measure succeeded.

Important art exhibitions, changing throughout the year, stay open until 8.00pm or later at the *Hayward Gallery* (tel 928 3144). You can buy a visitor's membership to the *National Film Theatre* (tel 928 3232), which has an agreeable bar and self-service restaurant. The *National Theatre*, with three productions running simultaneously, is a controversial and striking piece of modern architecture, with informal exhibitions and a bookstore (tel 928 2252). There is music at the *Purcell Room*, *Queen Elizabeth Hall* and *Royal Festival Hall* (all tel 928 3191).

## Finding a Hotel in London

Even if there were no tourists, London would be crowded, its streets tangled with the dialects and languages of half the world. Not only is it England's capital, and that of Britain, it is also the biggest city in Europe, and the mother of the Commonwealth. It entertains a lot of guests.

The tourist season now lasts the whole year, but it intensifies between April and October, and peaks in July and August. Avoid these months if you can, and book your hotel in advance.

If you live in another country, your own local office of the British Tourist Authority carries a leaflet called *100 Independent Hotels in London*, with an excellent map.

Alternatively, you can write, six weeks in advance, stating the price-range of hotel which you would find suitable, to the London Tourist Board, 26 Grosvenor Gardens, Victoria, London SW1W 0DU.

If you live in England, your local Tourist Information Centre, or any bookstore, should have a booklet called *Where to Stay in London*, published by the English Tourist Board.

If your visit is planned at such short notice that you arrive without a hotel, go immediately to the Tourist Information Centre at London (Heathrow) Airport or at Victoria railway station. They will book a room for you, at a fair price.

It is not essential to stay in Central London. The Inner London boroughs are all within easy reach of the centre, and public transport from them is fast and easy.

# Thames Valley

Barely beyond the borders of Greater London, Windsor and Eton face each other across the Thames. Another famous name, Ascot, manifests itself a few miles to the south.

Further up river are Maidenhead, a pleasant commuter town, Marlow, with its executive villas, and the little regatta town of Henley.

Like all of the counties which adjoin London, Berkshire is a place in which to live, and to take leisure, for those who otherwise spend their days in the capital. Its character changes, though, to the east.

In the middle of the county, Reading is a full-scale provincial town, beyond which country life becomes distinctly more agricultural. Along the river Kennet, Newbury has its famous racecourse and Hungerford is a pleasant town in which to stay or do a little fishing.

**Tourist Information Centres**
Central Library, St Ives Road, Maidenhead, Berkshire. (0628) 25657
Newbury District Council, Wharf Road, Newbury, Berkshire. (0635) 42400/44000
Civic Offices, Reading, Berkshire. (0734) 55911
Windsor Central Station, Windsor, Berkshire. (Windsor) 52010

## Windsor

As Versailles is to Paris, so Windsor is to London; so close as to be almost compulsory for the visitor from abroad. It is a largely Victorian town dominated by the great royal castle.

However, Church Street, behind the Guildhall contains mainly 17th- and 18th-century buildings, including Nell Gwynne's House, built in 1640 and the Old Kings Head, built 1525.

*Castle* The largest inhabited castle in the world, covering 13 acres, and the present queen's favourite residence. The building was founded by William the Conqueror in 1070 and first became a royal residence in the reign of Henry I. Additions to the building were made up to the time of Queen Victoria. Most of the castle visible from the river was built for George IV by Sir Jeffrey Wyatville. The *State Apartments*, dating from Edward III's reign, are open when the Queen is not in Official Residence, and include *Queen Mary's Dolls' House*, an exhibition of dolls and drawings by Holbein, Leonardo da Vinci and other artists. The *Albert Memorial Chapel* was built by Henry VIII but was converted into a shrine to the Prince Consort by Queen Victoria. *St George's Chapel* is vaulted and highly decorated. It is the Queen's place of worship when in residence here and is the burial place of royalty. The *Changing of the Castle Guard* can be seen daily at 10.25am. One mile from the Castle at *Frogmore Gardens* are the mausoleums of Queen Victoria's mother, and of Queen Victoria and Prince Albert.

*Guildhall* Completed by Sir Christopher Wren in 1689. The councillors insisted that the building was not safe without extra columns supporting the upper floor. Wren obliged, but ensured that the columns did not touch the ceiling, thereby

Windsor . . . compulsive

proving that the original structure had been sound.

*Household Cavalry Museum* Open Monday to Friday 10.00am to 5.00pm, Sunday 11.00am to 5.00pm.

*Brass Rubbing* Several brasses are available for rubbing in St John's Parish Church.

*Windsor Great Park* Includes the Savill Garden and the Valley Gardens. *The Savill Garden* was started in 1932 by Sir Eric Savill as a small water garden, and has since expanded to cover 35 acres of woodland. The garden contains a large collection of rhododendrons, trees, shrubs, and a large formal area of modern roses, herbaceous borders and alpine plants. Open March 1 to October 31 daily 10.00am to 6.00pm.

*Windsor Safari Park* Animals including lions, tigers, zebras, camels, llamas, baboons and giraffes roam wild in natural surroundings. There is also a children's farm and zoo, children's boating lake, a reptile house and an amusement park.

*Events* **Royal Windsor Horse Show**, in May; **Windsor Dog Show**, in June; **Royal Windsor Rose and Horticultural Show**, in July; **Windsor Festival**, in September/October.

## Eton

Britain's battles allegedly were won on the playing fields of Eton's world-famous public school. This claim cannot be proven beyond argument, but the school can be scrutinized. The 15th-century chapel contains some rare wall paintings dating from 1479. Open daily 2.00pm to 5.00pm during term-time, and 10.30am to 5.00pm during holidays. There are guided tours in the summer.

Many of the buildings in the High Street are very old, and consist mainly of antique and craft shops.

There are stocks outside the 15th-century Cockpit Restaurant where Charles II patronised cockfighting. A Victorian post-box stands nearby.

## Slough

Largely remembered, to its eternal chagrin, for John Betjeman's cruel invocation:
Come friendly bombs, and fall on Slough
It isn't fit for humans now.
The town is a light industrial centre.

## Maidenhead

A good base for touring the surrounding area. It is set on a beautiful stretch of the Thames, and Boulter's Lock, just upstream, has been a famous riverside spot since Edwardian days. It was mentioned in Jerome K. Jerome's Three Men On A Boat.

South of Maidenhead is a railway bridge built by Isambard Kingdom Brunel in 1838. It has the largest span of brick-work in the world at 128 ft.

1½ miles west of Maidenhead is the Courage Shire Horse Centre. There is a collection of shire horses, small animals and birds and a play-ground for children. Free dray rides are given. The stables contain a coach house, souvenir shop, display room and a static display of the ancient craft of barrel making. Open March to October daily except Monday 11.00am to 5.00pm.

A regatta is held at Maidenhead on the Saturday before the late summer Bank Holiday.

Cliveden, 3 miles upstream from Maidenhead, is an historic garden, with breathtaking views over the Cliveden Reach of the Thames. The house is now leased to Stamford University, but two rooms are open. Owned by the National Trust, the gardens are open March to November Wednesday to Sunday 11.00am to 6.30pm, house 2.30pm to 5.30pm.

## Marlow

Fishing in the Thames at Marlow was a favourite pastime of the 17th-century writer Izaak Walton. His book is celebrated in the name of The Compleat Angler Hotel, where the willow tree is said to have been planted by the Duke of Marlborough.

Mary Shelley wrote Frankenstein at a house in West Street and her husband wrote The Revolt of Islam there.

The local brewery is the purveyor of a typical English bitter much liked by beer-drinkers.

The outstanding feature of the town is the 19th-century suspension bridge.

## Henley

Best-known for the regatta which takes place every July.

Henley has an attractive 5-arched 18th-century bridge, timbered houses, including the 14th-century Chantry House and a square-towered Perpendicular church. The main street is Georgian.

On the river bank are Hambledon Lock and Mill and the 17th-century Fawley Court, now the Divine Mercy College.

Three miles north-west is Grey's Court, a Jacobean manor house set in gardens. There is a Tudor donkey wheel for raising well water and a collection of miniature rooms in the Cromwellian Stable. Owned by the National Trust, it is open March to September, house Monday, Wednesday and Friday 2.15pm to 6.00pm, miniature rooms and garden Monday to Saturday 2.15pm to 6.00pm.

## Reading

An industrial town on the river Kennet noted for its university. Jane Austen went to school in Reading, and Oscar Wilde wrote his Ballad of Reading Gaol and De Profundis during his imprisonment here.

The Museum of English Rural Life contains exhibitions depicting 19th- and early 20th-century agricultural life and history. Open Tuesday to Saturday 10.00am to 1.00pm, 2.00pm to 4.30pm.

Reading is a good centre from which to explore the river and the Berkshire Downs. Work on the Kennet and Avon Canal has cleared a 9-mile stretch of water from Reading to Tyle Mill Lock, with the canal navigable almost to Aldermaston.

The vineyards at Westbury Farm, Purley, are open to the public during weekend afternoons from July to September.

An Elizabethan mansion, Mapledurham House, north of Reading, contains fine 16th- to 18th-century portraits. Open Easter to October weekends 2.30pm to 5.30pm.

## Newbury

Famous as the home of the Newbury Race Course, where the Hennessey Gold Cup in November and the Schweppes Gold Trophy in February are among the annual attractions.

The remains of the house where Jack Newbury, founder of the town's fortunes, entertained Henry VII and Catherine of Aragon still stands in Northbrook Street. Jack Newbury also paid for the rebuilding of the church in the 16th century.

# Middle Thames

This balmy stretch of river was the inspiration of *The Wind in the Willows*; author Kenneth Grahame lived just north of Reading, in Pangbourne, which is still an attractive little town.

If he were alive today, he would find little to disturb his reveries along the middle Thames, as the river winds its way between the counties of Berkshire, Buckinghamshire and Oxfordshire.

Rich and peaceful countryside unfolds most of the way up river, by way of Goring and Wallingford to Abingdon, 25 miles further north. The countryside is best seen from the river, and boats can be hired at all of these places.

This is the river, too, of *Three Men in a Boat*. The author, Jerome K. Jerome, is buried in the village churchyard at Ewelme.

Away from the river, a few miles to the west, the Vale of the White Horse, running between the Lambourn Downs of Berkshire and the Oxfordshire Cotswolds.

The Vale is named after the white horse which is cut into the grassy slope of the Downs near Uffington.

Of all the white horses cut into the chalk hills of England, this is considered to be the finest. Its origins are in doubt, but it is close to an Iron Age site.

**Tourist Information Centres**
Civic Centre, Reading, Berkshire. (0734) 55911
8 Market Place, Abingdon, Oxfordshire. (0235) 22711

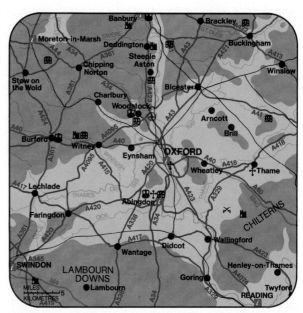

## Goring
This beautifully-sited small town owes its origins to its position. It stands on a narrow stretch of the Thames, with the Chiltern Hills to one side and the Lambourn Downs to the other.

Along these two ranges of hills ran, in prehistoric times, the *Icknield Way* and *Ridge Way* respectively. These two tracks, vestiges of which remain, were linked by a ford at Goring.

The enclosing hills can be seen at their most spectacular from the water at *Goring Gap*.

## Ipsden
Just off the river north of Goring, and on the *Icknield Way*, is Ipsden. This hamlet is the home of the *Wellplace Bird Farm*, with a wide variety of species.

Open daily in summer, Sundays in winter.

## Streatley
A very pretty and unspoiled small town on the opposite side of the river from Goring. It is noted for a shop which specializes in cheeses.

## Wallingford
Another one-time ford, further north and on the west side of the river. Wallingford is now a market town and riverside resort, with towpath walks. The town has some fine Georgian houses and timber-framed buildings. Its 17th-century town hall has paintings by Gainsborough.

## Ewelme
Apart from its association with Jerome K. Jerome, this pretty village, across the river from Wallingford, has a colourful history. Henry VIII spent his honeymoon with Catherine Howard at the local manor house.

## Dorchester
A pretty, little town at the meeting point of the Thames and the Thame, with half-timbered

houses and a beautiful late-Norman abbey.

## Long Wittenham
An attractive village, with hill walks. It is also worth visiting for the *Pendon Museum of Miniature Landscape and Transport*. This unusual museum shows countryside scenes in miniature. It also has railway relics from the early 19th century.

Open daily. Small admission charge.

## Steventon
A hamlet just south of Abingdon, notable for its *Priory Cottages*. These former monastic buildings are now a National Trust property. They may be visited on Wednesday afternoons.

Nearby is *Milton Manor*, with a splendid Strawberry Gothic library and chapel. The Manor has collections of teapots, musical boxes and visiting-card cases.

Open weekends (in the afternoon) and Bank Holidays, from early April until late September.

## Abingdon
A handsome, riverside market-town, with leather and brewing as its industries. Abingdon has remnants of a Benedictine abbey, and many other historic buildings.

There are two groups of surviving abbey buildings, not far from each other, both of which can be visited. One group is centred on the *Guildhall*, the other, in Thames Street, is now occupied by the *Unicorn Theatre*, which presents regular productions, often by amateur groups.

*The Guildhall* The main gateway to this group of buildings was the entrance to the abbey in the 15th century. It has both medieval and modern gargoyles.

The 12th-century abbey *hospital of St John* has been used as the local courtroom since 1560. A building dating back to 1733 is now used as the council chamber, complete with its fine display of paintings.

*The Roysse Room*, first used as the abbey almoner's hall and later as a school, now contains town relics and civic silverware.

The *abbey church of St Nicholas* is 12th-century, with a 15th-century tower.

*Thames Street* The main Unicorn Theatre building is a 14th-century hall.

The abbot's wine cellar and the offices of his treasurers were in the building known as *The Checker*. The wine cellar is a large, vaulted room, with a stone chimney of unusual design.

The *Long Gallery* retains its original 16th-century woodwork.

## Other historic buildings
*St Helen's Church* is of 8th-century origin, though the oldest surviving part is the tower, which was built around 1200. Most of the church is 15th- and 16th-century. It is unusual in that its breadth exceeds its length.

The superb *County Hall* built in 1682 with more than a hint of Wren's influence, now houses the *Borough Museum*. Exhibits include local fossil remains and Anglo-Saxon relics. Open daily.

The *Market Place* has been in use since 1050. Market Day is Monday.

The *Old Gaol*, built by prisoners in the Napoleonic Wars, has been converted into a *Sports Centre*.

This strange change from incarceration to recreation has brought with it a swimming pool, badminton, keep-fit equipment, snooker, a music room and theatre, and beautiful gardens.

Open daily from 9.00am to 9.00pm and sometimes later. Ring Abingdon 2271 for details.

*Events*
In a colourful ceremony, the residents of *Ock Street* elect their

Riverside setting . . . Abingdon

Napoleonic incarceration . . . 20th-century recreation

own Mayor for a day on the nearest Saturday to June 20. On this and other special occasions, it has apparently been known for hard buns to be thrown ceremonially from the roof of County Hall.

Abingdon entertains funfairs several times a year. The fixed annual dates are the very large two-day *Ock Fair*, in early October (usually the first Monday and Tuesday after the first Sunday of the month) and the *Runaway Fair*, also for two days, the following week.

These huge fairs once provided important casual employment in the town, and disgruntled workers were said to 'run away' on the second of the two occasions.

*Parks and gardens*
The Abbey House Grounds are a formal gardens and play area. *The Abbey Meadow* has a swimming pool, paddling pool, pitch-and-putt course, and putting green. *The Albert Park* has formal gardens, tennis courts and a bowling green.

*Sports*
Fishing in the Thames; summer boat trips on the river; a swimming pool; tennis courts, and golf courses.

**Didcot**
The Great Western Society Railway Museum This is probably Didcot's principal attraction for the visitor.

Although the museum opens only two days of the month, it offers the bonus of locomotives under steam on each of these occasions.

Opening days are the first and last Sundays of the month, from Easter to October, and Bank Holidays.

The museum is reached directly from Didcot railway station, where the main line west has a fork for Oxford and points north.

Because of its accessibility, Didcot provides the car-less with a useful starting point from which to explore the Vale.

In the immediate area of the town, however, views are unfortunately marred by Didcot power station.

**Wantage**
This quiet and pleasant market town is a useful base from which to explore the Vale. It is also interesting in its own right as the birthplace of Alfred the Great, and a statue of him stands in the town square.

A mile or two away, there is an Iron Age hill fort, close to the *Ridge Way* at Letcombe Bassett.

**Woolstone**
A small village further into the valley, from which a path leads to the Uffington white horse. Beyond the horse are the Iron Age ramparts of *Uffington 'Castle'*.

One and a half miles further west is a famous long barrow known as *Wayland's Smithy* after a Scandinavian hero.

**Faringdon**
This is said to have been Alfred's first capital, and was mentioned in the Domesday Book. Today, it is an agreeable market town, largely built in grey limestone.

Nearby is a folly built by Lord Berners in 1935 to relieve local unemployment.

Not far from Faringdon is *Kelmscott Manor*, where William Morris lived. This gabled Elizabethan Manor is open on the first Wednesday of each month, or by appointment with the Society of Antiquaries, in London (01-437 9954).

Red skies at night . . . Cookham

# Oxford

Such have been its gifts to the world that Oxford is a tangible piece of man's heritage. It is also an architectural set-piece, an elaborately-crafted city set down on a very large cushion of soft English countryside.

The city of 'dreaming spires' is even better remembered simply for its ambience: the soft colour of its stone, the tightly-packed city-centre which still somehow accommodates so much greenery, the subtle blend of bustle and quiet, the looping Thames (known in Oxford as the Isis) and the Cherwell, with college eights to watch, punts to hire and waterside walks.

Here, figures as diverse in English history as Raleigh and Rhodes, Wolsey and Wesley, Galsworthy and Tolkien dreamed their dreams.

Oxford has given Britain a cricket-team of Prime Ministers, and where they strolled in their formative years, the visitor can now roam – most colleges open their quadrangles and chapels in the afternoons.

One of the university's greatest benefactors was Lord Nuffield, the father of the British motor industry in its greatest days.

To the visitor, it is difficult to believe that this placid city remains a major motor-industry town. The only clue is in the prosperity of its well-served shopping centre.

Pork butchery is a local speciality. Oxford brawn (cold pressed pig's head) is a breakfast dish, and Oxford sausages are skinless, made from equal quantities of veal and pork.

Nor is any respectable English breakfast complete without Oxford marmalade, though the various Oxford college puddings are less easy to find.

**Tourist Information Centre**
St Aldates, Oxford, Oxfordshire.
(0865) 48707/49811
Accommodation Booking Service
operates daily all year. (0865)
40170

## The University

The heart of Oxford is dominated by its colleges. Within a square mile, the city has more than 600 buildings which are listed as being of architectural or historical interest.

That is to say nothing of such oddities as the famous door-knockers at *Brasenose* or the unusual sundial at *Corpus Christi*.

Sir Christopher Wren was a Fellow of All Souls, and he gave the city its *Sheldonian Theatre*, which is used for university functions and concerts.

The library at *Worcester College* contains original designs and drawings by Inigo Jones.

Altogether, there are 28 colleges, most of them within an easy walk of the High Street, and a visitor can easily see three or four in an afternoon.

Opening times of quadrangles and chapels are posted on college gates.

*Magdalen College* This is arguably the most beautiful. It has a lovely deer park, cloisters and chapel. The original buildings date from the 15th century.

Magdalen is also famous for its May morning celebrations. At dawn on May 1, the college choir sings from the top of Magdalen Tower.

*Merton College* (C3 on map over page) This has the oldest buildings, in which category is included the Mob Quad, and the oldest library in England built between 1371 and 1379.

Open daily except Wednesday and Sunday.

*Christ Church* (B3) The largest and richest of the colleges, it is known as 'The House.' In 1546, the college chapel became Oxford Cathedral.

The college hall has 17th-century fan-vaulting. The Tom Quad is Oxford's most impressive quadrangle.

*New College* (C2) The college has a magnificent chapel, usually with an exhibition of college treasures in the summer.

Dreaming spires . . . All Souls

It is notable for its fine gardens, containing parts of the medieval city wall. Cream teas are served in the hall during the summer.

*Worcester* (A2) and *St John's* (B2) Both colleges also have particularly beautiful gardens.

*The Old Bodleian Library* (Cat Street, C3) This is one of the world's great libraries, with more than three million books in its collection. The library, originally based on the collection of a diplomat, Sir Thomas Bodley, was opened in 1602. It has a 7th-century manuscript of the Acts of the Apostles used by the Venerable Bede, and a very extensive Oriental collection. There is a changing exhibition in the entrance.

An unusual building nearby is called the *Radcliffe Camera*, and is one of the university's reading rooms. It has an underground store holding 600,000 books.

## Museums and Art Galleries

*The Ashmolean Museum* (Beaumont Street, B2) One of Britain's finest museums and art galleries, its treasures include Michelangelo and Raphael drawings, pre-Raphaelite paintings, the unique Hope collection of engraved portraits, Paul de Lamerie's magnificent silver work, the Hill collection of musical instruments and Sir Arthur Evans' finds from Knossos. The museum was named after its founder, Elias Ashmole.

*Museum of Oxford* (St Aldates, B3) An exciting new museum, superbly displayed. It traces the history of Oxford from Norman times to its growth as an industrial city. Open weekdays except Monday.

*Museum of the History of Science* (Broad Street, C2) This museum has astronomical and navigational instruments, watches and clocks, telescopes and microscopes. Open weekdays.

*Museum of Modern Art* (Pembroke Street, B3) The changing exhibitions are devoted to young artists and local students. Open daily except Monday.

*Pitt Rivers Museum* (Park Road, B1) This houses a collection of ethnological artifacts from around the world, including some collected by Captain Cook. Open weekdays.

*Royal Greenjackets' Museum* (Slade Park TAVR Centre, Headington) Militaria of the former Oxfordshire and Buckinghamshire Light Infantry are on display here. Open weekdays except Saturday.

*Brass Rubbing* (Oxford Brass Rubbing Centre, University Church of St Mary the Virgin, High Street, C3) Rubbings can be taken from replicas of brasses from churches in the Oxford area. Open daily.

*Theatres* Playhouse (Beaumont Street, B2), (0865) 47133. New Theatre (George Street B2), (0865) 44544.

There are also many students and amateur productions in term-time, and these are advertised in *What's on in Oxford*.

*Tours of Oxford* start from the Oxford Information Centre (St Aldates, B3). Walking tours lasting two hours leave at 10.45am and 2.15pm in summer and at 2.00pm on Saturdays only in the winter.

*Views of the City* Carfax Tower (B3). 74 ft high. Open daily in summer.

St Mary the Virgin, High Street (C3). 88 ft high. Above the Brass Rubbing Centre. Open daily.

*Floodlighting* Many of the most beautiful buildings in Oxford are floodlit from dusk to 11.00pm. These include Magdalen Tower, Tom Tower, Oxford Cathedral, the Ashmolean Museum and St Mary Magdalen.

*Local events* University: Matriculation in autumn and Encaenia (degree-taking) in June, with a number of Degree

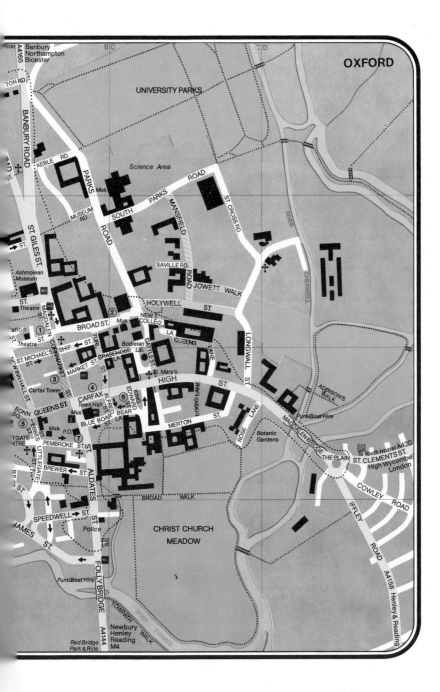

OXFORD

Days throughout the year. At the Encaenia there is a procession from the college of the present vice-chancellor to the Sheldonian Theatre and then back to the college. Rowing: The Spring Races (Torpids) in February; the great summer races (Eights Week) in May; Trial Eights in autumn, at which a crew is selected to compete against Cambridge in the annual Boat Race.

*Boating* Rowing boats and punts can be hired from the Folly Bridge Punt Station (B4). Punts can be hired from the Magdalen Bridge Punt Station (D3, down a ramp underneath Magdalen College Tower) or Cherwell Punt Station, off Bardwell Road. A steamer runs daily in summer from Folly Bridge to Abingdon.

## Riverside walks

*Christ Church Meadow* Walk through the meadow down to the Thames, and a circular route brings you back along a path to Merton College Cricket Grounds.

*The Botanic Garden* (High Street C3) Grassy lawns reach down to the Cherwell. Good views of punting.

*The Towpath* This path along the Thames is reached from an alley just south of Folly Bridge (B4). From the towpath you can watch the Eights racing or training.

*Addison's Walk* Reached from Magdalen College (D3), this follows a very beautiful stretch of the Cherwell. It is named after the essayist Addison, who was a Fellow of the College from 1698 to 1711.

*The University Parks* (C1) Often the scene of cricket matches, these border the Cherwell. This is a particularly peaceful part of Oxford.

A punting paradise . . . Oxford

# East Cotswolds

The Cotswold Hills are more commonly considered to be the property of Gloucestershire, further west, but they begin in this northern corner of Oxfordshire.

The small, old, country towns in northern Oxfordshire are sturdily built in the golden ironstone and limestone of the Cotswold ridge, and they bear the stamp of this hill region's medieval prosperity.

The country lanes in the foothills of the Cotswolds offer gentle walks, especially around villages like Adderbury (near Banbury) and Great Tew (further south).

Banbury also offers a useful base from which to visit several historic houses and castles.

Further south is Blenheim – one of the most famous of all the historic houses in England – and the city of Oxford.

**Tourist Information Centres**
St Aldates, Oxford, Oxfordshire.
(0865) 48707/49811
Borough House, Marlborough Road, Banbury, Oxfordshire.
(0295) 52535 ext 250

## Witney

The sheep which graze on the Cotswolds helped Witney establish a blanket-making industry for which it is still well-known. The wealth of the medieval wool merchants also contributed to some of the odd architectural flourishes in this handsome market town in the Winrush valley.

Nearby is *Minster Lovell Hall*, a 15th-century ruin in a delightful riverside setting. Open daily.

Between Witney and Woodstock are the Roman remains of *North Leigh Villa*. Open daily from April to September, and on Sunday afternoons.

## Burford

Also in the Winrush valley, this stylish little town in Cotswold stone is a good base from which to explore the hills.

Burford's *Tolsey Museum* has a Regency dolls' house and Old Corporation seals. Open daily from Easter to October.

Nearby is the *Cotswold Wildlife Park*, with animals, birds and reptiles from all over the world. The park also has a narrow-gauge railway and an adventure playground. Open daily. Small admission charge.

## Chipping Norton

A busy little town in the heart of the Oxfordshire Cotswolds. During the last week in June, Morris Men dance in the market square.

Nearby is the 17th-century *Chastleton House*. This fine Jacobean-style country house is known for its Flemish tapestries, many original furnishings and good plasterwork.

Open daily except Wednesday. Small admission charge.

A couple of miles further north, there are good views from the Bronze Age stone circle at Rollright.

## Banbury

Every English child learns the rhyme of Banbury Cross, and thus the name of the town has passed into folklore.

It is also famous for Banbury Cakes, one of England's oldest sweetmeats.

The cakes are still available, the cross was rebuilt in 1859, and the town's history can be traced further in *Banbury Museum* (closed Tuesdays).

Today, Banbury is a busy 20th-century town, most notable for its very large cattle market, held on Thursdays.

There is a sports day in early September, and a Michaelmas Fair.

Banbury is particularly useful as a base from which to visit the many historic houses, castles and sites in this part of England. *Compton Wynyates*, an outstanding Tudor mansion, is seven miles to the north-west of Banbury, just across the Warwickshire border in the direction of Stratford-upon-Avon.

It was built in a hillside setting between 1480 and 1520, and has a beautiful topiary garden. Open from Good Friday until September, on Tuesday, Wednesday, Thursday and Saturday afternoons. Open from 11.00am to 5.00pm on Sundays and Bank Holidays.

Two or three miles further

Churchill's birthplace . . . beautiful Blenheim

north is *Upton House*, a William-and-Mary mansion owned by the National Trust.

This is notable for its collection of paintings, including works by George Stubbs and Peter Bruegel.

There is also a collection of Sèvres porcelain.

Open May to September, Wednesday and Saturday afternoons; October to April, Wednesdays only.

Close by is *Edge Hill*, a ridge which was the site of the first battle in the Civil War.

The ridge can best be viewed from the landscaped terrace of the Italianate *Farnborough Hall*, another National Trust property two miles further north.

It contains Italian paintings and sculptures.

Open April to September, Wednesday and Saturday afternoons.

Three miles to the south of Banbury is *Broughton Castle*, built in 1306.

It is a beautiful moated castle, containing collections of armour and furniture, with interesting plaster ceilings, fireplaces and panelling.

The castle is the home of Lord and Lady Saye and Sele.

Open on Wednesdays and Bank Holidays between April 1 and September 30, and on Sunday afternoons during June, July and August.

*Deddington Castle*, six miles to the south of Banbury, was built in the 12th century. All that remains is the outer bailey, inner bailey and large earthworks. Open daily.

Nearby are the picturesque and unspoiled villages of Great Tew, Little Tew, Duns Tew and Nether Worton.

*Rousham House*, at Steeple Aston, nine miles south of Banbury, is a fine stately home with Civil War Associations.

Built in 1635, it has interesting pictures and furniture, and is set in acres of gardens which are open daily until dusk. The

The Butter Cross . . . Witney

gardens were landscaped by William Kent, and there is a remarkable dovecote.

Open on Wednesdays and Sundays from April until September and on Bank Holidays.

Nearby are attractive canal locks and boats at *Lower Heyford*.

**Bicester**

To the east of the Cotswolds, a centre for hunting and riding, with a 12th-century church and some 16th-century buildings.

To the south is the bleak and mysterious *Ot Moor*, crossed by a track which was once a Roman road.

**Woodstock**

Despite modern development, Woodstock is still a delight for its old buildings, from

the Anglo-Saxon period, late Tudor times, and the 18th century.

It is rich in history, with many royal links, and has Oxfordshire's *County Museum*.

Most of all, Woodstock is famous for *Blenheim Palace*. This was built as a gift from a grateful nation to the First Duke of Marlborough (John Churchill) to mark his victory over the French and Bavarians at the Battle of Blenheim in 1704.

It is a magnificent house by Sir John Vanbrugh, in more than 2,000 acres of parkland landscaped by Capability Brown.

Sir Winston Churchill was born there, and is buried a mile away at Bladon.

Open daily March 21 to end of October.

# The Chilterns

The popularity of this gentle range of hills is in part due to their accessibility and in part to their wooded beauty. With the fertile Vale of Aylesbury to the north and the Thames to the south, these chalk uplands describe a crescent through parts of Berkshire, Buckinghamshire in particular, and Bedfordshire, before fading out in Hertfordshire and Cambridgeshire.

The Buckinghamshire section is especially heavily wooded with beech trees. The wood known as Burnham Beeches, just to the south of Beaconsfield, is renowned for its beautiful walks.

## Buckingham

A quiet and interesting market town at the upper end of the restful Ouse valley.

Buckingham is sometimes also used as a base from which to explore the Chilterns, though it is 15 or 20 miles from the best hill country.

Buckingham has an interesting, partly-Norman Chantry chapel; *Castle House* has royal links; and the grounds of *Stowe House*, masterfully landscaped by William Kent, are open at Easter and in summer.

Several other historic houses lie in the triangle formed by Buckingham, Aylesbury and Thame.

## Aylesbury

A useful base from which to explore some of the most attractive Chiltern woodlands, which lie four or five miles to the south. The town is no longer England's greatest duck-farming centre, though Aylesbury duck still features on local menus.

The edible squirrel-tailed dormouse breeds in the area, but is no longer eaten.

At first approach, the town belongs emphatically to the 20th century, but its centre has many Tudor buildings, and the medieval *King's Head Inn* is owned by the National Trust.

The town also has the *Buckingham County Museum*, with exhibits on county crafts as well as local history. Open daily except Sunday. Admission free. *Dorton House* is a Jacobean mansion open from May to July on Saturday afternoons.

### Historic houses near Aylesbury

*Waddesdon Manor* In the village of the same name, it was built in chateau-style by Baron Ferdinand de Rothschild in the 19th century, and is set in 160 acres of National Trust land. It has a collection of paintings, including some by Gainsborough and Reynolds.

Open in the afternoons Wednesday to Sunday, from April to October.

*Claydon House* Set in the village of Middle Claydon, it was built by the Earl Of Verney. The house has Roccoco state rooms, a magnificent staircase, and mementoes of Florence Nightingale, whose sister married a former owner. Open daily except Monday. Small admission fee.

The village has as its immediate neighbours Steeple Claydon, East Claydon and Botolph Claydon.

All four villages were once manors belonging to the Earl of Verney, and together they form a particularly peaceful and attractive corner of Buckinghamshire.

Nearby is the pretty village of *Quainton*, with its haunted hill. The *Quainton Railway Society*

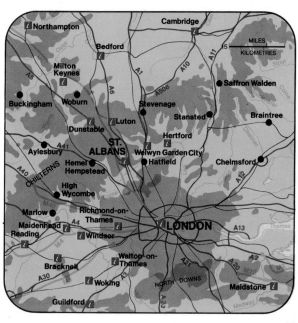

27

has working locomotives and rolling stock.

Also adjoining the Claydons is the thatchy little town of *Winslow*, with a Hall that was probably designed by Wren and a pub, The Bell, which is said to have been a haunt of Dick Turpin.

*Creslow Manor*, in the half-timbered village of Whit-church, was built about 1300, with a tower, mullioned windows, and a vaulted cellar. Today, it is a farmhouse.

**Thame**
Although this delightful market town is across the border in Oxfordshire, it is an ideal base from which to explore the Chilterns.

The eccentric John Fother-gill, author of the famous *Inn-keeper's Diary*, has long left the Spread Eagle, but the town still has plenty of hotel accommodation.

The unusually broad and long main street is full only at the September Agricultural Fair.

A short drive across the Vale of Aylesbury – no more than ten miles, whatever the route –

leads to the pretty village of Bledlow, and Chiltern walking country. From Bledlow, the Icknield Way runs across the Chilterns to Wain Hill, less than two miles away, with views across the wooded countryside, with its beeches, cherry trees and limes. Near Thame is the pretty little Rycote Chapel, a 15th-century building with medieval stalls and fine, late 17th-century rederos.

**High Wycombe**
A useful base from which to explore the Chilterns.

The beech forests of the region gave rise to a furniture-making trade which has in turn led to the industrialisation of this town, but there remains much of historical interest in the immediate vicinity.

*West Wycombe* This pretty National Trust village is the family seat of Sir Francis Dash-wood, the premier Baronet of Britain.

In the 18th century, the second Sir Francis and his *Hell Fire Club* were said to meet in a huge gilded ball on top of West Wycombe Church. They also met in West Wycombe caves,

which are open to the public. March to September, daily 11.00am to 6.00pm; October to February, weekends 1.00pm to 4.00pm.

*West Wycombe Park* is the family home, a Palladian mansion set in grounds landscaped by Capability Brown.

The house has interesting furnishings and fine ceilings. The grounds have garden temples.

Open Monday to Friday in June; every day except Saturday in July and August. 2.15pm to 6.00pm.

Nearby is *Hughenden Manor*, the home of Disraeli, containing his furniture, books and mementoes. A typical Victorian country mansion.

Open from March to November, Wednesdays to Fridays, 2.00pm to 6.00pm or dusk. Saturdays and Sundays 12.30pm to 6.00pm or dusk. Small admission charge.

**Beaconsfield**
This elegant town is a useful base from which to explore the Chilterns, and to visit Burnham beeches.

Within the town are Bekons-cot Gardens, containing a model village with a model railway. The gardens are open daily, and the trains run from Easter until October.

There are two places of historical interest nearby.

Three miles to the north-west is the village of Penn, which has associations with *William Penn*, founder of Pennsylvania. The church is of particular interest, and the village is typical of the country, with 17th-century cottages.

Four miles to the north-west is the village of Chalfont St Giles, where Milton completed *Paradise Lost* and began *Paradise Regained*. His home can be visited, and manuscripts can be seen.

Closed Tuesdays, and during some winter months.

Stowe Park . . . landscaped by Capability Brown

# St Albans

Not only is the small city of St Albans a base from which to explore the Chilterns and the countryside of Hertfordshire, it is also an important Roman site, and it has a Norman abbey which is noted for its medieval wall paintings.

St Alban himself was a Roman soldier who was executed for protecting a Christian fugitive. He thus became Britain's first Christian martyr.

The only English Pope, Nicholas Breakspear, was born locally and educated in St Albans. Today, the Breakspears are a brewing family.

For all its grander history, St Albans is particularly proud of its old inns, and the Tourist Information Centre produces a leaflet on pub lunches in the town.

St Albans is also the national headquarters of the Campaign for Real Ale, and the Barley Mow is a famous Real Ale pub.

**Tourist Information Centres**
37 Chequer Street, St Albans, Hertfordshire. (0727) 64511/2
The Marlowes, Hemel Hempstead, Hertfordshire. (0442) 64451

Roman remains . . . at Verulamium

## St Albans

At the edge of the busy shopping centre stands the abbey, which became a cathedral in 1877. Behind that, along a lane which passes the octagonal *Fighting Cocks* pub (built in 1600), is the Roman site of Verulamium, which also has its own adjoining museum.

*Verulamium* This important Roman town on the river Ver was first settled in AD 43. Little remains today, but large sections of the wall survive, and may be viewed daily between 10.00am and dusk.

A hypocaust (heating system) is preserved under cover on its original site as part of the *Verulamium Museum*, close to *St Michael's Church*. The museum has mosaics and an extensive collection of Roman relics.

From March to October, the museum is open from 10.00am to 5.30pm Monday to Saturday, and 2.00pm to 5.30pm Sundays. From November to February, it closes at 4.00pm.

A *Roman theatre*, the only extant example of its type in Britain, survives nearby in the estate of *Gorhambury House*, seat of the Earl of Verulam.

The house, built in 1777–84, opens on Thursdays in summer. Close by are the ruins of Francis Bacon's family home. It is possible that Bacon is buried in St Michael's Church.

*Cathedral* It was built by the Saxons on the supposed site of St Alban's martyrdom.

A shrine to St Alban remains, though the abbey was rebuilt by the Normans, and a great many additions have been made since, notably in the 13th century.

At one time it was the prime Benedictine abbey in England.

The building still includes bricks from the Roman site,

Once an abbey . . . now a cathedral

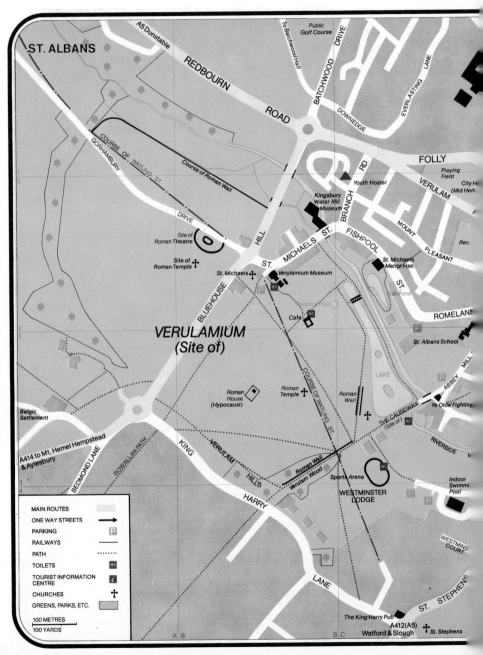

ST. ALBANS

VERULAMIUM
(Site of)

| MAIN ROUTES | |
| --- | --- |
| ONE WAY STREETS | ➞ |
| PARKING | P |
| RAILWAYS | |
| PATH | ········· |
| TOILETS | WC |
| TOURIST INFORMATION CENTRE | i |
| CHURCHES | ✝ |
| GREENS, PARKS, ETC. | |

100 METRES
100 YARDS

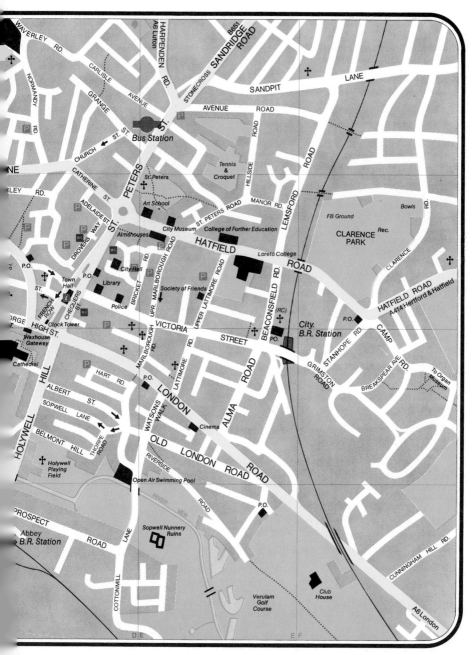

and, at 550 ft, is said to be the second longest church in Britain. As if this curious distinction were not enough, it also claims the longest nave, at 300 ft.

*City Museum* (Hatfield Road) The museum exhibits trades and crafts, plus natural history collection. Open daily except Sunday.

*Organ Museum* (Camp Road) This has a magnificent collection of fairground and dance-hall mechanical organs, plus other musical instruments. Open Sundays 2.00pm to 4.15pm except July and August.

*Kingsbury Water Mill* A fine example of a working water mill, over the river Ver, with its own museum. Open daily. Entrance off Fishpool Street.

*French Row* This little street off the market place has timber-framed houses from the 16th, 15th and perhaps 14th centuries. At the Fleur de Lys Inn, King John of France is said to have been kept prisoner. There are also interesting houses in *Fishpool Street*.

*Market* This is held on Wednesdays and Saturdays in the Market Place and St Peter's Street, which is the main shopping centre. *Early closing* Thursday.

*Entertainments* Abbey Theatre, Holywell Hill. Three-screen Odeon on London Road. Film theatre on Thursdays in City Hall. All types of concerts in City Hall. Concerts in Cathedral, and biennial International Organ Festival there.

*British Wildlife Zoo* in Verulamium Park. It also has a children's recreational area, an ornamental lake and *Abbey Orchard*. A recreation ground and gardens are also at *Clarence Park*.

*Rose Gardens* These are superb gardens owned by the Royal National Rose Society, at *Chiswell Green*, containing 30,000 plants of 1,600 varieties. Open June 17 to September 30, Monday to Saturday, 9.00am to 5.00pm, Sunday 2.00pm to 6.00pm.

*Historic house Salisbury Hall* is four miles south-east of the city, at London Colney. The prototype wartime *Mosquito aircraft* was designed and built there, and is now on display at Salisbury Hall with other warplanes. Open from Easter to September on Sunday afternoons and public holidays, and Thursday afternoons from July.

*Sports* St Albans City Football Club; two cricket pitches; hard-court tennis at Verulamium and Batchwood; grass courts in Clarence Park; putting greens; swimming; two golf-courses; some seasonal angling on the Grand Union Canal; running track.

## Watford

Markets on Tuesday, Friday and Saturday recall Watford's past importance to local agriculture, but today it is a printing-industry town, almost swallowed by Greater London. There are still quiet walks along the Grand Union Canal and the river Gade, and one or two rural attractions.

*Cassiobury Park* reaches from the centre of the town via Whippendell Woods to the open countryside. As well as a nature trail there are paddling pools and a miniature railway. One of the most attractive gardens in Hertfordshire is at *Cheslyn* where there are ornamental gardens, an aviary, a water garden and woodlands. Open daily except Tuesday and Thursday 10.00am to 5.00pm.

The *Watford Leisure Centre* in Woodside Park offers cricket, football, athletics, an artificial ski slope, golf, roller skating, bowling, tennis and putting.

*Sports* League football; tennis; bowling; indoor swimming.

*Events* Easter Gala; Whitsun Carnival; Watford Show, in September.

## Hemel Hempstead

Just a few miles from historic St Albans, and set in a pretty Chiltern Valley, is the attractive old town of Hemel Hempstead, which is rather less well known than its twin New Town.

Hemel Hempstead is a good base from which to explore the Chilterns, and its own local attractions include a 14th-century house called *Piccott's End*, with interesting wall-paintings. Open daily.

## Berkhamsted

Another attractive little town from which it is possible to explore the Chiltern's, with the bonus of the *Grand Union Canal*.

It has a ruined Norman castle, and the poet Cowper was born in the local rectory.

## Aldbury

A pretty village with a duck pond and stocks. Nearby is *Ashridge Park*, a beautiful woodland estate, owned by the National Trust, with a herd of red deer.

*Ashridge House*, a Gothic building, is not open to the public.

Within Ashridge Park is a monument to the Duke of Bridgwater (1736–1803), a pioneer of Britain's canal system.

Also in the park is *Ivinghoe Beacon*, which was lit in Elizabethan times to summon troops in case of invasion.

*Beacon Hill* (756 ft) affords splendid views.

## Tring

A small Chiltern town with Rothschild links.

The town's principal point of interest is its important *Zoological Museum*, which has an extensive collection ranging from stuffed animals to insects. Open daily.

There is a *National Nature Reserve* based on the four reservoirs to the immediate north of the town.

# Hertfordshire

Away from St Albans, as the Chilterns fade towards the flat lands of East Anglia, the green countryside of Hertfordshire is a forgotten pleasure.

This is a county for the traveller who enjoys the detour, and the exploration.

Charming little river valleys, wooded lanes, with beeches still much in evidence, and ancient villages. So much has survived, unspoiled, away from the New Towns and routes into London.

**Tourist Information Centres**
Vale House, Cowbridge, Hertford, Hertfordshire. (0992) 54977
Council Offices, The Campus, Welwyn Garden City, Hertfordshire. (96) 24411
Borough Council Offices, Stevenage, Hertfordshire. (0438) 56133

### Hertford

A pleasant county town dating back to pre-Roman Times, with the ruins of a *Norman castle*, a *Robert Adam Shire Hall*, and a *Victorian Corn Exchange*.

Boats can be hired on the river Lea, and there is trout and coarse fishing on the Lea and the Stort.

East Hertfordshire's history can be sampled in the *local museum* at Hertford. Open daily except Sunday.

Today, the area earns its living from salad crops, brewing and light industry.

Nearby is *Much Hadham*, where the sculptor Henry Moore works and lives. His studios are open to the public from May to September, Monday to Thursday, but by appointment only. Ring (027 984) 2566 to arrange a visit.

### Hatfield

A Georgian coaching town which has retained its charm despite much development and the birth of an adjoining New Town.

The old town has attractive houses, in Fore Street, and a 13th-century church.

Hatfield also has a clump of royal history: the *Old Palace* where Elizabeth lived as a child, and the superb Jacobean house built by her Secretary of State Robert Cecil, 1st Earl of Salisbury.

*Hatfield House*, home of the present Marquess of Salisbury contains royal mementoes, paintings, armour and tapestries. It is set in 1,500 acres of parkland.

Open March 25 to October 7, Tuesdays to Saturdays, 12.00pm to 5.00pm. Closed on Good Fridays.

### Welwyn

The old town lies on the north side of the pretty Mimram valley, seen by many travellers from the top of an elegant early railway viaduct. To the south is the 1920s Garden City.

Immediately to the east is *Bramfield Forest*, an area of woodland with nature trails. These forest walks can most easily be reached from the northern side of Bramfield village, where Thomas à Becket was once rector.

### Harpenden

A useful centre from which to explore. Harpenden has a sprawling green, with pleasant views, and is still an attractive town, despite being something of a London dormitory.

### Ayot St Lawrence

This small and restful village would be little known had it not been the chosen home of *George Bernard Shaw* for more than 40 years of his life in England.

(Another essayist, *Charles Lamb*, favoured the Hertfordshire countryside; he lived at Westmill, some miles to the north-east).

Shaw, who enjoyed cycling in the quiet lanes around Ayot, believed the village would bring him longevity. He lived to the age of 94, and his ashes were scattered in his garden.

Shaw's house has been pre-

Jacobean magnificence . . . Hatfield House

served as it was in his lifetime by the National Trust.

Open on Saturdays and Sundays in March, and daily (except Mondays and Tuesdays) from April to November. 11.00am to 1.00pm and 2.00pm to 6.00pm or dusk.

Also at Ayot St Lawrence is Lullingstone *Silk Farm*. This is a unique live exhibition, showing the production of silk from the silkworm egg to the reeled hank. Lullingstone has supplied silk to royalty for state occasions.

Open daily in summer except Saturdays.

Near to Ayot, along winding lanes, is *Codicote*, a lovely unspoiled Hertfordshire village.

### Knebworth
Set in delightful countryside, this modern town is best known for the nearby Tudor and Gothic mansion *Knebworth House* The house was originally built by Sir Robert Lytton in the early 1500s, but the exterior was remodelled by the 1st Lord Lytton in the 19th century. It is still in the hands of the same family.

Knebworth House has a fine collection of books, paintings, furniture and manuscripts. It stands in a country park, with picnic facilities, a steam railway and an adventure playground. 'Dickensian' banquets are held at the house.

Open March 24 to September 30, Tuesday to Sunday, and Bank Holidays. In October, Sundays only. Park, 11.00am to 6.00pm. House, 11.30am to 5.30pm.

### Stevenage
Yet another of Hertfordshire's New Towns, and again a base from which to explore. Although the town is new, it has an interesting local museum. Open daily.

The nearby *Aston Bury Manor House* is open on occasional summer afternoons. This 16th-century mansion is in a pretty, thatched village.

Another pretty village nearby is *Benington*, with the ruins of a moated Norman castle.

To the east is Westmill, where Charles Lamb's cottage is preserved but is not open to the public; the pretty and ancient village of Braughing; and Furneux Pelham, where the local church has windows by William Morris and Burne-Jones.

For those with more bibulous tastes, Furneux Pelham has its own brewery.

### Hitchin
An historic market town, with early 17th-century almshouses, interesting buildings in Sun Street, and a medieval church.

A very useful base from which to explore North Hertfordshire, Bedfordshire and Cambridgeshire.

Good views and Elizabethan beacon at Pegsdon, near Great Offley. The latter village has a team of Morris dancers.

Oughtonhead Common has interesting botany and ornithology.

The village of Ippollitts has a splendid 14th-century church devoted to St Hippolytus.

### Letchworth
Britain's first 'Garden City', built in 1903. There are changing art exhibitions at the *local museum*, as well as history of North Hertfordshire.

Nearby, on the road from Newham to Ashwell, is the site of an Iron Age hill fort at *Arbury Banks*.

Ashwell has a *folk museum*, open on Sunday afternoons from March to September.

The village has a church with the typical 'Hertfordshire spike' style of spire. Like several other Hertfordshire villages, it also has houses with decorative plasterwork, or pargeting, a style typical of East Anglia.

Heading off in the direction of East Anglia are the grassy remains of a Roman road.

Ayot St Lawrence . . . George Bernard Shaw's choice

# Bedfordshire

The landscape changes dramatically in Bedfordshire, from the Chiltern woodlands in the south to the flat pastures and water meadows of the Ouse valley in the north.

Even more dramatic is Bedfordshire's curious population of animal life, from exotic birds and rare deer to big game. No other county offers such a strange range of wildlife . . . or so many places at which unusual animals can be seen.

**Tourist Information Centres**
St Paul's Square, Bedford, Bedfordshire. (0234) 67422
Queensway Hall, Dunstable, Bedfordshire. (0582) 603326
25 George Street, Luton, Bedfordshire. (0582) 413237

A national attraction . . . Woburn

### Luton

Set in the upper reaches of the Lea Valley, in the heart of the Chilterns, Luton seems out of place as an important industrial town.

Since the 17th century, Luton has been famous for straw-plaiting and hat-making, but in the 20th century it has grown rapidly as a motor-industry town.

Like most business towns, it has modern hotels which are anxious for business at weekends.

It is a useful centre from which to explore the hills, and to see several nearby wildlife parks, and it does have its own stately home – *Luton Hoo* – with a famous art collection.

This includes works by Rembrandt and Titian, mementoes of the Russian Imperial family, 16th- and 17th-century jewels, porcelain and china.

The house was built by Robert Adam in 1768 and remodelled after a fire in 1843. The 1,500-acre park was land-scaped by Capability Brown.

Open Easter, then late April to October 1. Daily except Tuesdays and Fridays, 11.00am to 6.00pm. Afternoons only on Sundays and public holidays.

### Whipsnade

Six miles from Luton, this hamlet on the *Dunstable Downs* is famous for its parkland zoo of more than 500 acres, which has more than 2,000 animals and birds.

The rhinos can be seen from the *Whipsnade and Umfolozi steam railway*.

Open daily 10.00am to 7.00pm.

### Dunstable

This small town close to Luton provides a base from which to explore the Dunstable Downs. It is also the headquarters of the *London Gliding Club*, and flights can be arranged.

### Woburn

The village of Woburn, partly rebuilt in Georgian times after a fire, originally grew up around an abbey. After the Dissolution, it was given to the Dukes of Bedford.

The present Duke of Bedford opened his magnificently-appointed 18th-century home to the public, and it has become a nationally-known attraction.

*Woburn Abbey* has paintings by Canaletto, Rembrandt, Van Dyck and Gainsborough, and a fine collection of furniture and silver.

*Endangered species* of deer roam in the surrounding 3,000-acre park. Eleven varieties have been collected since the 11th Duke was enraged by the plight of the Père David's Deer, which has since become extinct in the wild.

*Big-game reserve* A 'Wild Animal Kingdom' is another part of the estate, with a large collection, including lions, tigers, bears and a dolphinarium.

The abbey and park close on winter Saturdays. In winter, the park closes in mid-afternoon.

### Ampthill

An historic town with a 300-acre great park which is open to the public.

35

The park is noted for its oaks, and an 18th-century cross marks the site where a castle once stood.

The house in the park, built by Lord Ashburnham in 1694, is not open to the public.

A mile north of Ampthill is the ruin of another 17th-century house which is said to have been the inspiration of John Bunyan's 'House Beautiful'.

**Elstow**

Bunyan was born in Harrowden, a mile to the east, but he subsequently lived in Elstow.

The village in Bunyan's day is recaptured by an exhibition at the 16th-century Moot Hall, on the green.

Behind the church of Saints Mary and Helen are parts of the cloisters of a nunnery founded by William the Conqueror's sister.

**Bedford**

The best base from which to explore the Ouse Valley, with its attractive river country, water-meadows and green landscape.

The Ouse enters the county from Buckinghamshire after passing through the market town of *Olney* (famous for its Shrove Tuesday pancake race).

It then winds itself around Bedfordshire villages like Harrold, Odell and Bletsoe (where *The Falcon* was a haunt of Thackeray).

Bedford has a *Bunyan Museum*, in Mill Street, with memorabilia and a world-famous collection of his work in more than 150 languages.

Open weekdays except Monday and Saturday.

*The Cecil Higgins Art Gallery*, in Castle Close, has a collection of water-colours, 18th- and 19th-century porcelain, glass, and furniture.

Open daily 11.00am to 5.00pm. Sundays 2.00pm to 3.00pm Closed Mondays.

*Rare birds*, including parakeets, snow geese and unusual pheasants (130 species in all) can be seen in eight acres of gardens at Stagsden, three miles to the west of Bedford. Open daily.

**Willington**

A village which was used as a river harbour by the conquering Danes. There is still evidence of the repair dock which they cut.

The village is equally well known for a huge and elaborate *dovecote* dating back to Tudor times, and a matching *stables*.

The dovecote is owned by the National Trust, and can be visited April to September by appointment.

**Sandy**

A pleasant town surrounded by market gardens, and a base from which to explore the area between Bedford and the beginnings of the Fens.

A mile from the town is a nature trail and the 104-acre Lodge bird sanctuary.

**Biggleswade**

A small brewing town, and another useful base from which to explore, with the headwaters of the Cam to the south.

Nearby is *Old Warden*, a mid-Victorian village of thatch and honey-coloured stone.

*Vintage aircraft* in working order are on display at the nearby airfield, and there are regular flying days in the summer. This unique collection also includes early cars, bicycles and carriages. Open daily 10.00am to 5.00pm.

Bunyan . . . still watching over Bedford

# Cambridge

For all its architectural similarities to Oxford, the city of Cambridge is distinguished by the larger scale of its colleges, its paler stone, and its geographical setting, with first the flat Fens and then the whole of East Anglia fanning out before it.

The first scholars came to Cambridge in 1209 . . . and modern times have seen the splitting of the atom by Rutherford, the work of Crick and Watson in establishing the Double Helix structure of DNA, and the age of Leavis.

Cambridge was once the only city of any size in the county which bears its name. Boundary changes have embraced Huntingdon and Peterborough but Cambridgeshire remains predominantly a rural county.

At the edge of Cambridge itself is Grantchester, 'lovely hamlet' of Rupert Brooke, and the county is dotted with villages in plaster, timber and brick.

To the north of the city, the landscape broadens into the water-laced Fens, where Hereward the Wake once hid. To the north-east, just across the Suffolk border, is Newmarket, headquarters of horse-racing in England.

**Tourist Information Centre**
Wheeler Street, Cambridge, Cambridgeshire. (0223) 58977/ 53363

## St Neots

An interesting market town, 17 miles west of Cambridge, which dates back to the 10th century.

A 15th-century Perpendicular church tower dominates the vast market square, which backs on to the Great Ouse. The church interior boasts magnificent roof carvings of animals, birds and angels.

## Wandlebury Camp

An Iron Age fort on the Gog Magog Hills, five miles southeast of Cambridge. The fort was rebuilt by the Iceni tribe of ancient Britons.

In 1956, an archaeological dig discovered the huge figure of an ancient goddess astride a strange beast. It was cut into the chalk. Wandlebury is also the starting point of a nature trail.

## Caxton

A picturesque village, seven miles west of the city, which has an attractive old coaching inn and a fine 15th-century pebble church.

## New Wimpole

The county's greatest mansion, *Wimpole Hall*, is to be found here, eight miles south-west of Cambridge. It was built by Sir Thomas Chichele around 1640, but was considerably altered in the 18th century.

## Newmarket

This famous town has been involved with horses and racing since the time of James I.

The King thought the place excellent for hunting, but it was his Scottish nobles who started the racing tradition. They found the Heath ideal for their two-horse races and today's major industry has grown from this small beginning.

Charles II was another royal racing enthusiast and the *Rowley Mile* course is named after his hack.

Needless to say, Nell Gwynn was also to be found in the town. Her house is in Palace Street, but is not open.

Visitors to Newmarket can watch the horses on their gallops and the *National Stud* is open to visitors in May and June, on Sundays and Bank Holidays from 2.00pm to 5.00pm. The stallions are paraded from 3.00pm to 3.30pm. The town is an ideal base for exploration.

## Cambridge

The town was an important centre long before the university. Its site marked the upper limit of navigability of the river Cam or Granta (the Roman name for the town). It was also a fording point for the Romans on their travels north.

## The University

The colleges can be visited. There are three tours daily, at 11.00am, 2.00pm and 3.00pm, starting at the Tourist Information Centre. To be sure of a place, it is advisable to book, in person, an hour before a tour. *Peterhouse*, founded in 1284, by Hugh de Balsam, Bishop of Ely, is the oldest-established college. Its more recent features include windows and decoration in the hall by the William Morris workshop.

*Christ's* was founded by Margaret Beaufort, mother of Henry VII (as was St John's). The mulberry tree under which Milton reputedly sat to write 'Lycidas' is here.

*Corpus Christi* has a distinguished 14th-century collegiate building in Old Court. The library boasts a fine collection of Anglo Saxon manuscripts left to it by Matthew Parker.

Christopher Wren designed the chapel of *Emmanuel*, where John Harvard was a pupil, before sailing to America in 1636.

*Jesus* College was once a con-

vent. The chapel windows are from the William Morris workshop.

The chapel at *King's* is a masterpiece of craftsmanship in stone, glass and wood. The *Adoration of the Magi*, by Rubens was presented to the college in 1962 and now forms the chapel altar-piece.

*Magdelene* houses Pepys's library in his original bookcases. Each book is propped to an equal height on a block of wood.

The chapel at *Pembroke* was Wren's first building. The fantastic silhouette of the 19th-century *St John's* building is known as the wedding cake. The chapel is the work of Sir George Gilbert Scott.

The Great Court at *Trinity* is the largest of its kind, and the library was designed by Wren. Visitors can go into the college courtyards, chapels, dining halls and some gardens at most times.

## Other historic buildings

*Great St Mary's Church* is 15th-century, with a 17th-century tower. It was originally called St Mary's-by-the-Market and there are still daily stalls (except Sunday) selling food, craft products and clothes outside.

Large congregations brought about the installation of galleries in the 18th century. Visitors can climb the tower, from which there are excellent views of the town and countryside.

The *Senate House* is an 18th-century creation of the architect James Gibbs. The university 'parliament' sits here every fortnight during term-time.

*The Church of the Holy Sepulchre* is one of the few circular churches in the country. A chancel and north aisle were added to the circular Norman nave in the 14th century. The whole building was restored in the 19th century.

*Stourbridge Chapel*, a mile east of the city centre, is a Norman

building which was once a leper hospital. Among the chapel's neighbours is the 13th-century Abbey Church.

## Museums

*The Fitzwilliam Museum*, in Trumpington Street, houses extensive Greek, Egyptian and Roman collections, in addition to illuminated manuscripts and a comprehensive display of English pottery and porcelain. Paintings include those by Titian, Rembrandt, Hogarth, Turner and Gainsborough. Its interior contains a wealth of marblework. Closed Mondays.

*Folk Museum*, 2–3 Castle Street, has a rich display of Cambridge's bygones. Closed Mondays.

*Scott Polar Research Institute*, Lensfield Road, is named after the great explorer. It is concerned with current polar discoveries and relics of past expeditions. Open weekdays. Closed Bank Holidays.

*Events* Cattle market every Monday at Hills Road; regatta, Saturday before Spring Bank Holiday; boat races; antiques fair in April; May Balls and madrigals on the river in June; Midsummer Fair in June; Cambridge Festival and Folk Festival in July.

*Sports* Rowing boats and punts at Mill Lane and Quayside; golf at Gog Magog and Bar Hill; swimming at Parkside (indoors), Abbey Pool and Jesus Green (open air); sports hall at Gonville Place.

The university cricket team plays a full list of fixtures against the First Class Counties, and there is a League soccer team.

*Gardens* The university Botanic Gardens at Trumpington Street cover more than 40 acres and are considered second only to those at Kew. Open daily, except Sunday. Gardens are open all day, plant-houses afternoon only.

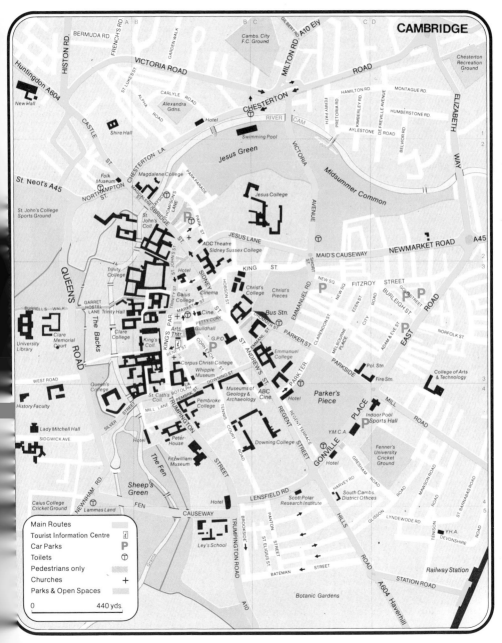

CAMBRIDGE

New Hall

Huntingdon A604

BERMUDA RD.
FRENCH'S RD.
HISTON RD.
GARDEN WALK
VICTORIA ROAD
Cambs. City F.C. Ground
MILTON RD.
GILBERT RD. A10 Ely
CHESTERTON ROAD
Chesterton Recreation Ground

CARLYLE ROAD
ALPHA ROAD
Alexandra Gdns.
ST. LUKE'S ST.
HAMILTON RD.
MONTAGUE RD.
PRETORIA RD.
DE FREVILLE AVENUE
HUMBERSTONE RD.
FERRY PATH
KIMBERLEY RD.
AYLESTONE RD.
BELVOIR RD.

CHESTERTON
RIVER CAM
Hotel
Swimming Pool
Jesus Green
VICTORIA AVENUE
Midsummer Common
ELIZABETH WAY

CASTLE ST.
Shire Hall
St. Neot's A45
St. John's College Sports Ground
Folk Museum
NORTHAMPTON ST.
Magdalene College
CHESTERTON LA.
MAGDALENE ST.
MAGDALENE BRIDGE
PARK PARADE
THOMPSON'S LA.
Jesus College
St. John's Coll.
PARK ST.
ADC Theatre
Sidney Sussex College
JESUS LANE
MAID'S CAUSEWAY
NEWMARKET ROAD A45

QUEEN'S ROAD
Trinity College
GARRET HOSTEL LANE
Trinity Hall
BURRELL'S WALK
University Library
Clare College
Clare Memorial Court
King's Coll.
The Backs
Caius College
SIDNEY ST.
ST. JOHN'S ST.
TRINITY ST.
KING'S PAR.
MARKET
Cinema
Arts Thtr.
Cine.
CORN EX.
Guildhall
G.P.O.
BENET ST.
Corpus Christi College
Whipple Museum
ST. ANDREW'S ST.
KING ST.
Christ's College
Christ's Pieces
EMMANUEL RD.
NEW SQ.
FITZROY STREET
GOLDWORTHY RD.
BURLEIGH ST.
NORFOLK ST.
EAST RD.
ADAM & EVE ST.
CLARENDON ST.
EDEN ST.
CITY RD.
MELBOURNE PLACE
NEW SQ.
Bus Stn.
PARKER ST.
Emmanuel College
PARKSIDE
Pol. Stn.
Fire Stn.
College of Arts & Technology

WEST ROAD
History Faculty
Queen's College
SILVER STREET
ST. CATH'S COLL.
PEMBROKE ST.
Pembroke College
TENNIS COURT ROAD
BOTOLPH ST.
DOWNING ST.
Museums of Geology & Archaeology
ABC Cine.
Hotel
REGENT STREET
PARK TER.
PARKER'S PIECE
GONVILLE PLACE
Indoor Pool Sports Hall
Y.M.C.A.
Fenner's University Cricket Ground
Hotel

Lady Mitchell Hall
SIDGWICK AVE.
NEWNHAM RD.
The Fen
Hotel
Peter House
Fitzwilliam Museum
TRUMPINGTON STREET
MILL LANE
REGENT TERRACE
Downing College
GRESHAM ROAD
MILL ROAD
TENISON RD.
MANOR RD.
ST. BARNABAS RD.

Caius College Cricket Ground
Lammas Land
Sheep's Green
FEN CAUSEWAY
Hotel
LENSFIELD RD.
Scott Polar Research Institute
South Cambs. District Offices
HARVEY RD.
GLISSON RD.
LYNDEWODE RD.
DEVONSHIRE
Y.H.A.

Ley's School
TRUMPINGTON ROAD
BROOKSIDE
ST. ELIGIUS ST.
PANTON STREET
BATEMAN STREET
HILLS ROAD
STATION ROAD
Railway Station

Botanic Gardens
A10
A604 Haverhill

### Key

|  |  |
|---|---|
| | Main Routes |
| i | Tourist Information Centre |
| P | Car Parks |
| ① | Toilets |
| | Pedestrians only |
| + | Churches |
| | Parks & Open Spaces |

0       440 yds.

# The Fens

The landscape might belong across the North Sea, in the Low Countries, and this Fenland illusion has been heightened by man's own intervention. Dutch experts were hired to drain the Fens in the 17th century, and windmills were used to pump the water.

Even the domestic architecture of the area displays its fair share of Dutch gables.

The thinly-scattered towns and villages are often on raised areas of land which were once islands.

The Isle of Ely is an example. It is no longer an island, and it is now the main town of the Fens, though it remains small and unspoiled. Ely can be seen from miles away in the shape of its beautiful cathedral, distinguished by a most unusual octagonal 'lantern' tower.

A larger cathedral city, Peterborough, stands on the northern fringe of the Fens, providing an excellent base for exploration. Peterborough's cathedral is a fine Norman monument, and the city retains a great deal of historical interest, despite its industrial development.

Between Ely and Peterborough lie the remarkable drainage canals known as the Old and New Bedford. Within this area is a notable windmill at Wicken, and a fine beam engine at Stretham.

The Fens have a large population of ducks and other water birds, and an abundance of wildlife which extends from otters to rare butterflies, coypus to spiders, freshwater fish to molluscs. Fenland reeds are still used for thatching and basketry, and the lush vegetation of the area is decorated in some places by wild orchids.

**Tourist Information Centres**
Council Offices, 24 St Mary's Street, Ely, Cambridgeshire. (0353) 3311
Town Hall, Peterborough, Cambridgeshire. (0733) 63141

## Ely

The town's name means Eel Island, and there are several explanations for its origin.

One story has it that eels were the staple diet of the islanders in Saxon times. Another says that St Dunstan turned the local monks into eels as a punishment for their sexual misdemeanours.

It was at Ely that Hereward the Wake held out against the Normans, and the town was

Roundhead representation . . . Cromwell House

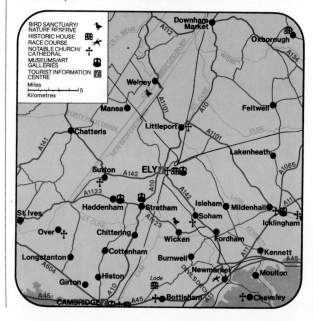

BIRD SANCTUARY/NATURE RESERVE
HISTORIC HOUSE
RACE COURSE
NOTABLE CHURCH/CATHEDRAL
MUSEUMS/ART GALLERIES
TOURIST INFORMATION CENTRE
Miles
Kilometres

Cromwell's home when he was MP for Cambridge.

The Ely of today is a small and captivating market town, as ever dominated by its cathedral. Each turning of the narrow streets seems to reveal some new cameo: the medieval gateways, the timbered houses, and the green parkland sweeping down to the Ouse.

### Swaffham Prior

This typical Fenland village has two churches in one churchyard, the curious result of parish amalgamation in the 17th century. One church is derelict, the other beautifully kept.

Nearby is the village of Lode, which takes its name from the Old English word meaning a navigable cut through swampland.

Three miles beyond is *Anglesey Abbey*, a 13th-century Augustinian foundation which was incorporated into a country house in the 17th century. The house and gardens are now run by the National Trust, and may be visited in the afternoon, except on Sundays.

### Soham

The 12th-century church has an awesome tower and ten-bell peal.

Just outside the village is *Wicken Fen Nature Reserve*, the only stretch of the washes to retain some of its primordial character, and with its windmill amid the marshes.

The nature reserve is open daily, except Thursdays.

Nearby is the *Old Beam Engine*, at Stretham, which can be visited daily.

### Huntingdon and Godmanchester

Godmanchester was an important crossroads in Roman times. It was here that the road from London to York crossed the road from Colchester to Chester.

Godmanchester was subse-quently outgrown by Huntingdon, to which it is linked by a causeway across a large meadow. Now, even Huntingdon has lost its status as a county town. It is, however, no less interesting for that.

Nor are its attractions limited to its agreeable location or its racecourse.

By a quirk of history, not only is the town the birthplace of Cromwell, the republican, it also has associations with Pepys, the Restoration diarist. Both men went to the same school, which is now the *Cromwell Museum* (open daily except Mondays).

Cromwell's great-grandfather built *Hinchingbrooke House* (open Sunday afternoons in summer). Ironically, this house subsequently came into the hands of the Earl of Sandwich, supporter of Charles II and patron of Pepys. The home of Pepys is nearby at Brampton, and can be viewed on application.

Given Cromwell's attitude towards the theatre, there is some irony in his grandfather's having owned the *George Inn* at Huntingdon.

The inn is laid out in the classical Tudor pattern, with galleries overlooking a courtyard in which plays can be per-formed. This arrangement was the precursor of the Shakespearian theatre layout.

### St Ives

This interesting little market town was once called Slepe. The name was changed to honour the building there in 1050 of a priory dedicated to St Ivo.

Well worth a visit is the 15th-century bridge which has a chapel in its centre bay.

Cromwell had a farm nearby and a statue of him stands in the marketplace.

### Stilton

Despite its name, this village on the edge of the Fens has never produced Stilton cheese.

The 17th-century *Bell-Inn* at Stilton was once a vital staging post on the Great North Road. The commercially-minded farmers of Leicestershire used the inn as a collection and delivery point for stagecoaches and their cheeses became known as Stilton.

### Peterborough

Recent archaeological research shows that this city has been an important settlement since the Iron and Bronze Ages, and was a Roman fortress guarding the River Nene.

Today it is a rapidly expand-

On the horizon . . . Ely Cathedral

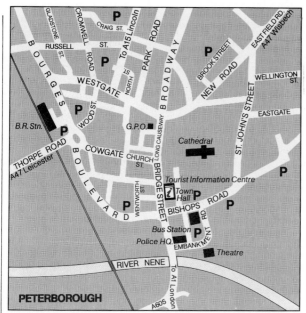

**PETERBOROUGH**

ing city and is an obvious centre from which to tour the surrounding region.

Catherine of Aragon is buried in the superb *Norman cathedral* and so was Mary Queen of Scots, although her remains were later moved to Westminster Abbey.

The first building on the site was a monastery, built in 656 by Paeda, King of Mercia. After being sacked and pillaged by Hereward and his Danish allies, the succeeding 10th-century building was destroyed by Saxons.

The present cathedral was begun in 1118. The Normans built their monument of local Barnack limestone. The massive columns sweep up to a roof with a magnificently-painted ceiling.

According to an epitaph, the gravedigger Robert Scarlett, who interred both of the unfortunate Queens, in his time buried twice as many people as the city's total population.

### Other historic buildings
*Longthorpe Tower* is a 14th-century building with early examples of secular wall-paintings.

Open daily.

The medieval *Church of St John the Baptist* has a fine peal of bells.

*The Guildhall* has an upper chamber dating from 1671 and the building is set in gardens which were once the market place.

It is not open to the public, and is used for storage only.

*Events* The National Heavy Horses Stallion Show, in May; the Royal Foxhound Show and East of England Show, in July; the Shire Foal Show, in September; Brudge Fair, in early October.

*Sports* Swimming pool; tennis courts; bowling greens; golf; sailing on the Nene and river boat trips every summer. A large sports stadium in the city offers most facilities. Peterborough United play professional soccer.

### Wisbech
This market town has been in existence since Roman times. The centre was rebuilt in Georgian times on a medieval plan.

Surrounded by bulb fields and orchards it is the market and business centre for the flourishing flower and fruit-growing trade.

Useful as a touring base, it also offers much to see in its own right.

It is the birthplace of Octavia Hill, one of the founders of the National Trust and it is appropriate that *Peckover House* (1723) on the North Brink, should now be a Trust property.

Open March to October, on Wednesdays, Thursdays, weekends and Bank Holiday Mondays, 2.00pm to 6.00pm.

*St Peter's Church*, reputedly built in 1111 has five bays of Norman arches and a pre-Reformation tower.

Medieval murals . . . Longthorpe Tower

# South Essex

It is possible, just, to enter East Anglia by Tube train from the heart of London. Having emerged from its tunnel under the capital, the Central Line continues eastwards past Epping Forest into the Roding Valley and a landscape with a clearly Anglian character.

This is rural Essex, and the countryside of the county can stake a healthy claim to being a part of East Anglia. Much of urban Essex, on the other hand, is an extension of London.

It is through this area, following the line of the Thames docklands, that the Londoner has traditionally beaten a path to his favourite seaside resort, Southend. Here, the estuary has widened and given way to sea coast.

Southend itself may be brash and breezy, the South's response to Blackpool, but its coastline reaches away to hidden creeks and wide salt-flats beloved of sea-birds.

Once again, Essex becomes a part of East Anglia.

**Tourist Information Centres**
Civic Centre, Victoria Avenue, Southend, Essex. (0702) 49451
Pier Hill, Southend, Essex. (0702) 44091

## The Roding Valley

The valley of the River Roding contains eight picturesque farming villages which lie among rich farmland. They have an 18th-century charm which has enchanted many people, including the Victorian novelist Anthony Trollope.

They are Abbess Roding, Aythorpe Roding, Beauchamp Roding, Berners Roding, High Roding, Leaden Roding, Margaret Roding and White Roding.

## Chelmsford

The county town of Essex, which has now become largely residential, with some light industry.

*Chelmsford and Essex Museum* This houses collections of Roman coins, local natural history, costumes and paintings.

Open weekdays 10.00am to 5.00pm, Sunday 2.00pm to 5.00pm.

The *Church of St Mary the Vir-*gin became a cathedral in 1914, and has a 15th-century tower.

In high summer *Chelmer Cruises* organise two-hour cruises on the Chelmer and Blackwater canal.

At nearby *Danbury Park* are woodlands and a lake with fishing and boating.

Chelmsford is a good base for touring the area.

Nearby at Felsted is 'Felstar' vineyard, where visits can be arranged during the late summer and autumn by appointment. Ring (024 534) 504.

## Great Dunmow

This town is perhaps best known for the 'Dunmow flitch', which is part of a ritual held every leap year. At the 'trial' a flitch of bacon is presented to any married couple 'who have not had a brawl in their home nor wished to be unmarried for the last 12 months and a day'.

This is an old Breton custom

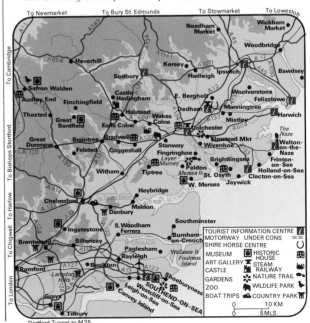

To Newmarket — To Bury St. Edmunds — To Stowmarket — To Lowestoft

Needham Market
Wickham Market
Woodbridge
Bawdsey

Haverhill — Kersey — Ipswich
Sudbury — Hadleigh
Safron Walden — Woolverstone — Felixstowe
Audley End — Finchingfield — Castle Hedingham — E. Bergholt — Manningtree — Harwich
Thaxted — Halstead — Dedham — Mistley
Great Bardfield — Wakes Colne — The Naze
Earls Colne — Colchester
Great Dunmow — Braintree — Bradwell — Stanway — Elmstead Mkt — Walton-on-the-Naze
Felsted — Coggeshall — Fingringhoe — Wivenhoe — Frinton-on-Sea
Layer Marney — Brightlingsea
Witham — Tiptree — Peldon — Holland-on-Sea
Mersea Is. — St. Osyth — Clacton-on-Sea
W. Mersea — Jaywick
Heybridge
Chelmsford — Maldon
Danbury
Southminster
Ingatestone — S. Woodham Ferrers — Burnham-on-Crouch
Brentwood — Billericay — CROUCH
Paglesham — Wallasea Is.
Romford — Rayleigh — Foulness Island
Basildon
Langdon Hills — Shoeburyness
Grays — Leigh-on-Sea — Westcliff-on-Sea — SOUTHEND-ON-SEA
Canvey Island
Tilbury

To Cambridge
To Bishops Stortford
To Chigwell / To Harlow
To London

Dartford Tunnel to M25

TOURIST INFORMATION CENTRE
MOTORWAY UNDER CONS
SHIRE HORSE CENTRE
MUSEUM — HISTORIC HOUSE
ART GALLERY — STEAM RAILWAY
CASTLE
GARDENS — NATURE TRAIL
ZOO — WILDLIFE PARK
BOAT TRIPS — COUNTRY PARK

0 — 10 KM
0 — 5 MLS

| | |
|---|---|
| MAIN ROUTES | TEN-PIN BOWLING |
| SHOPPING STREET | ATHLETICS |
| PEDESTRIANS ONLY PRECINCT | PUTTING |
| ONE WAY STREET | CRAZY GOLF |
| CHURCHES | TENNIS |
| TOILETS | CRICKET |
| CAR PARKS | FISHING |
| CINEMAS | TOURIST INFORMATION CENTRE |
| BOWLS | |

MILE  1/4  1/2
KILOMETRE  1/2

which was brought to Little Dunmow by the Fitzwalter family and revived in 1855 by the historical novelist Harrison Ainsworth.

## Saffron Walden

This town owes its name to its trade in saffron, although it was equally popular for its weaving.

*St Mary's Church* is the largest church in Essex, and has connections with the 12th century.

*Saffron Walden Museum* Displays include those of archaeology, geology and natural history. Open daily.

*Audley End House* A 17th-century house which was remodelled by Vanbrugh. Some Adam decoration was added later. Open mid-October to mid-March Sunday 11.00am to 3.30pm, Easter to October Tuesday to Saturday 10.00am to 5.30pm.

*Repell Ditches* 200 Saxon skeletons were discovered here in a large earthwork.

Just south of the town at Widdington is *Mole Hall Wildlife Park* which has the only Canadian otters breeding in England. Open daily 10.30am to dusk.

## Maldon

This town is one of the most unspoilt in Essex. The 13th-century *All Saints Church* has the only triangular tower in England. The town is famous for salt, and fishing boats and Thames barges cluster at its east end.

## Burnham-on-Crouch

Well known for yachting, oysters and sea-wall walks. The quay is a mass of bright colours from the colour-washed houses and there is a smell of ropes, tar and salt water in the air.

## Paglesham

Between the estuaries of the Roach and the Crouch lies this small village which was once a centre for smuggling lace, tobacco and spirits.

## Foulness Island

This is the largest island in the Thames estuary and has about 10,000 Brent geese on its marshes in the winter.

## Southend

This large and popular seaside resort was once a hamlet called the South End of Prittlewell. It has now joined with the towns of Leigh-on-Sea, Westcliff, Prittlewell and Thorpe Bay.

The seafront is seven miles long, with arcades, lights, and amusements. In the summer, a wide variety of fresh seafood can be bought from the many stalls.

Stretching a mile into the sea, Southend pier is the longest in the world, and those who don't feel energetic enough to walk to the end can take a train.

*Beecroft Art Gallery* As well as several permanent collections there are changing exhibitions. Open daily.

*Prittlewell Priory Museum* The priory was established in 1110 and is now a local, and natural, history museum. Open daily.

*Southchurch Hall* A 13th- to 14th-century timber-framed manor house set in beautiful gardens. Open daily in summer.

*Chalkwell Park* This is a memorial garden with a splendid rose garden, seasonal bedding displays and aviaries. There is tennis, cricket, hockey and football.

*Belfairs Park* The gardens are set in 320 acres of natural woodland with a nature reserve and trotting track. There is an 18-hole golf course and horse riding.

The *Cliffs Pavilion* is the top municipal entertainment centre of Essex.

*Local events* Easter Sports Festival; Multi-National Swimming Gala, in May; Vintage Bus Rally, in May; Vintage Bus Rally, in June; Carnival and Thames Barge Match, in August; Old Leigh Regatta, in September.

# North Essex

For many visitors from Continental Europe, the small port of Harwich provides a first glimpse of England.

Amid the tangle of boats, trucks and trains, most ports superficially look alike, but Harwich is worth a night's stay, less for its own few remnants of medieval times than for the surrounding countryside.

The town stands on a broad headland between the Blackwater estuary and the river Stour. This stretch of land remains typical of the Essex coastline, with its creeks, islands and flats, but it also has two or three resorts and, inland, an historic city of great interest.

Among the resorts, Clacton is very much the traditional English seaside town, popular with day-trippers from London. Frinton is altogether more genteel, and Walton-on-the-Naze is a rather smaller resort.

The historic city, and main town of the area, is Colchester. The city is best-known for its Roman history, though it also owes much to the Ancient Britons, the Romans, the Normans, and the Dutch.

Only the Norman nave remains . . . St Botolph's Priory

**Tourist Information Centres**
4 Trinity Street, Colchester, Essex. (0206) 46379
Parkeston Quay, Harwich, Essex. (Summer only) (025 55) 6139
Council House, Old Road, Frinton, Essex. (025 56) 2141
Publicity Hut, Lower Marine Parade, Dovercourt, Essex. (Summer only)
Town Hall, Station Road, Clacton, Essex. (0255) 25501

## Colchester

Old King Cole, the ancient British chieftain of nursery rhyme fame, ruled from Colchester. He was Shakespeare's Cymbeline. The Roman city was built by Claudius in AD 49–50, then sacked by the patriot Boadicea.

The Normans arrived in the 11th century and Cromwell besieged the town in 1648.

Colchester is a splendid base for touring.

*The Castle* This was built by William the Conqueror on the site of Claudius' temple, using stone from the Roman fort, and has the largest Norman keep in Europe.

It now houses the *Castle Museum*, which has an outstanding collection of Romano-British antiquities.

Open daily except Sundays.

*Town Hall* Designed by John Belcher and opened in 1902, this building is Italianate and elegant. The whole is topped by a bronze statue of Helena, mother of Constantine.

The most splendid room is the *Moot Hall*, where the annual *Oyster Feast* is held, and borough regalia is sometimes on display.

Open by arrangement.

*Jumbo* A Victorian water tower, not to be missed. It was named after an elephant sold to Barnum and Bailey's circus in 1882, the year the tower was built.

*St Botolph's Priory* The west front and part of the nave are all that remain of this great Norman church. Always accessible.

*University of Essex* Founded in 1961 and located in Wivenhoe Park. Visits by arrangement.

## Other places of historic interest

*Siege House*, pitted by bullets during the Civil War siege of 1648. Exterior always accessible.

*Dutch Quarter*, the district west of the castle where Flemish weavers made their homes in the 16th century.

*Bourne Mill*, rebuilt in 1591, may once have been a fishing lodge. It was certainly a finishing mill for baize, one of the cloths in which Colchester specializes. National Trust.

Open Wednesday, Thursday, Saturday and Sunday. Summer only.

*Oysters* The Oyster Feast is attended by invitation only, but there are plenty of opportunities to sample this famous gourmet treat.

Now that Portuguese and Pacific oysters have been introduced, the delicacy is available throughout the year. But the real local speciality can still only be had when there is an 'r' in the month.

Visitors can enjoy an al fresco meal at Mussett's Oysters, Coast Road, West Mersea, or the Colchester Oyster Fishery will arrange for parties to visit by boat and round off their trip with a meal. Telephone Rowhedge 2373.

*Events* Rowhedge Regatta, in May; Wivenhoe Regatta, in June; Rose Show and Carnival, in July; Military Tattoo in August; Oyster Feast in October.

*Sports* Swimming pool, tennis courts, golf club (temporary members welcome); motor racing at Marks Tey; Colchester United play League soccer.

**Fingringhoe**
Serious birdwatchers will not wish to miss *Fingringhoe Nature Reserve*, which lies outside this attractive little village.

Open Tuesdays to Saturdays, 9.00am to 4.00pm throughout the year.

**Coggeshall**
A medieval wool and lace town, with many fine old houses.

The most impressive is *Paycocke's*, the home of a wool merchant of 1500. The magnifi-

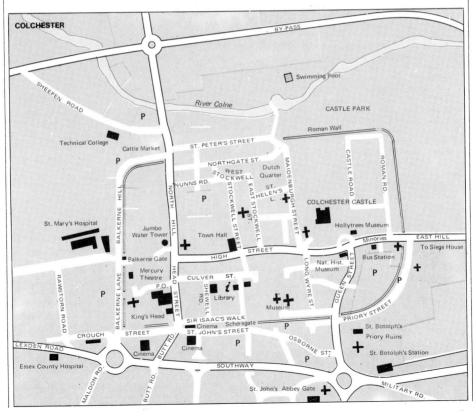

cent half-timbered house has a richly carved interior, National Trust. Open Wednesdays, Thursdays, Sundays and Bank Holiday Mondays, 2.00pm to 5.30pm March to September. Open weekends only in winter.

The nearby *Woolpack Hotel* is even older and the remains of a *12th-century abbey* can be found beside a stream.

## Clacton-on-Sea

A friendly, noisy popular resort of mainly Victorian and Edwardian buildings. It has the traditional British seaside trimmings of pier, pavilion, gardens and sandy beaches.

## Frinton-on-Sea

The more genteel version of the above. Neat and exclusive, Frinton came into being in the 1890s. It has excellent sands and sloping cliffs.

## Walton-on-the-Naze

Another paradise for bird-watchers, with broad salt marshes and islands. For the holidaymaker, it also has sands and an 800-ft pier. Sea fishing is first class.

## St Osyth

The priory here was founded by St Osyth in the 7th century, although the building dates from the 12th century. There is a gatehouse and beautiful gardens.

Gardens open Easter to September 10.00am to 5.30pm, apartments August 2.30pm to 4.30pm.

## Harwich

Charles II, the first Englishman to go to sea for pleasure rather than business, sailed from this medieval township. For some time it was the headquarters of the King's Navy.

The modern Harwich is a major ferry port, carrying cars and passengers to the Hook of Holland, Esbjerg, Bremerhaven, Hamburg, Zeebrugge and Kristiansand.

Key to Location Map **(Above)**

| Main A Roads | ▬ |
| B Roads | ― |
| Railways | ― |
| Towns with T.I.C. | *i* |

0                    5 Miles

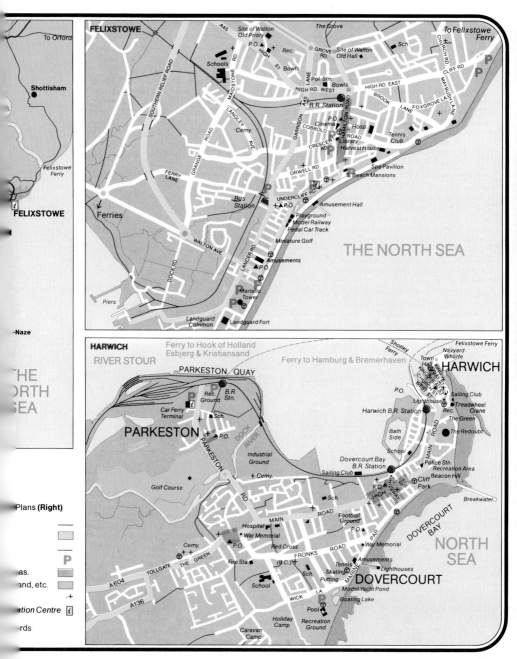

# South Suffolk

Harwich and Felixstowe describe themselves jointly as 'the haven ports' but they are, in fact, in different counties.

For all its cheery resort atmosphere, Felixstowe is also an entrance to the soft English countryside of Suffolk.

A few miles up the Orwell estuary, past the sailing barges at Pin Mill, stands the county's main town of Ipswich.

It is an unremarkable but perfectly agreeable town, and it offers an excellent base from which to explore the countryside made famous by two of England's outstanding landscape artists, Constable and Gainsborough.

Further inland are attractive medieval wool towns and villages like Kersey and Lavenham, still showing a prosperity which was once owed to immigrant Flemish weavers.

## Felixstowe (map p 49)
This cheerful seaside resort lies along the shallow curve of the beach, with houses rising on wooded slopes behind. The colourful and well-kept gardens and parks are a noted feature.

There are *sea and river cruises* and ferries cross the Orwell to Harwich.

Opportunities for *sea fishing* are plentiful, with skate and bass good catches in the summer, while cod is best in the autumn and winter.

*The Dooley* is a very old pub, with many doors, used by the revellers as fast exits whenever the Press Gangs and Revenue Men arrived.

*Events* Folk International, in May; Drama Festival, in June; East of England Tennis Championship, in July; Junior Open Tennis Championship, Felixstowe Carnival, Deben Regatta, in August; Fishing Festival, in October.

## Flatford Mill
This was the Constable family mill. Willy Lott's cottage, one of the painter's best-known subjects, has been beautifully preserved.

Unfortunately, the place is so popular that there are now one-way systems and souvenir shops – all of which is a long way from Constable's dreamy view.

However, once across the bridge, the visitor immediately steps back into the painter's world of tranquillity.

## Dedham
The 16th-century church here is featured in many of Constable's works. He is not the only artist to have graced the town, for Sir Alfred Munnings lived in *Castle House* where many of his canvases hang on view.

Open Wednesdays, Thursdays, weekends and Bank Holiday Mondays, 2.00pm to 5.00pm.

**Tourist Information Centre**
91 Undercliff Road West, Felixstowe, Suffolk (039 42) 2126/3303
Information Caravan, No 2 Dock Gate, Felixstowe Docks, Suffolk. (Summer only) (039 42) 78359
Sudbury Library, Market Hill, Sudbury, Suffolk. (078 73) 72092/76029
Countryside Centre, Duchy Barn, Dedham, Colchester. (0206) 323447
Town Hall, Princes Street, Ipswich, Suffolk. (0473) 55851

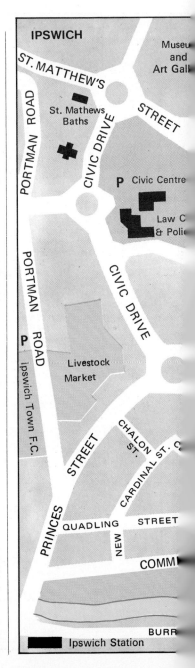

## East Bergholt
Constable's birthplace, this is a magnificent unspoilt village with grand houses and Elizabethan cottages. There are many splendid gardens and the grounds of the late Randolph Churchill's home are now the *Stour Garden Centre*.
Open daily, 10.00am to 5.00pm throughout the year.

## Hadleigh
The High Street of this peaceful and attractive town offers every variety of Suffolk architecture: timber, decorative and plain plasterwork. The Church Square is dominated by the 15th-century *Guildhall* (open Thursdays, 10.00am to 5.00pm, closed in August) and the *Deanery Tower*.

## Lavenham
An impressive Suffolk wool town. The 16th-century *Guildhall* has in its time been used as workhouse, almshouse and even prison. It is now in National Trust ownership.
Open March to November, 10.00am to 12.30pm and 2.00pm to 5.30pm.

Ancient frontage . . . **Ipswich**

## Ipswich (*map p 50*)
Originally a Saxon settlement on the river Orwell, Ipswich was an established trading port by the Middle Ages, and remains so today.
A renewed wave of prosperity in the Victorian era swept away much of the old town, but there are still many treasures. There are fine examples of pargeting – the patterned plasterwork which is at its best in East Anglia.
The Victorians gave the town a handsome legacy. One family left Christchurch Park, which is arguably the finest park in the centre of any provincial town.
In a county well known for its beer, it is appropriate that the county town should have its own brewery.
An ideal touring base.
*Ancient House* A Tudor house in Buttermarket with a secret chapel and Restoration pargeting. The Oak Room has impressive panelling, beams and a Jacobean mantelpiece. It is now a bookshop.
*Isaac Lord's* A Tudor merchant's house in Fore Street, with an inner courtyard leading to a private warehouse on the quay. The exterior only is viewable to the public.
*Wolsey's Gate* Cardinal Wolsey was born in Ipswich and founded what he hoped would be a great college. His fall from power ended those dreams and the brick gateway with its royal cypher is all that remains.
*Ipswich Museum* has interesting exhibits of Suffolk natural history, geology, ethnography, and archaeology. The art gallery houses modern prints and sculptures. Open daily.
*Christchurch Mansion* is a Tudor country house with period rooms, pottery, porcelain, and paintings from Gainsborough and Constable to Pissarro.
Open Monday to Saturday, 10.00am to 5.00pm (dusk in winter), Sunday 2.30pm to 4.30pm.

*Events* Suffolk Show, in May; Sports Festival, in September. *Sports* Two indoor and two outdoor swimming pools; speedway racing; tennis; greyhound racing. Ipswich Town soccer team emerged as a major force during the 1960s and 1970s.

## Sudbury
The entire area has a great artistic tradition and Thomas Gainsborough the painter was born here. A statue of him graces the market square. His father's house is now a museum.
Nearby is *Cavendish Manor*. There are ten acres of vineyards here which surround Nether Hall Manor House. Both are open to the public.
Vineyard open March to October daily 11.00am to 6.00pm, November to February 11.00am to 4.00pm. House open daily 11.00am to 5.30pm.

## Long Melford
This town is worth a visit to travel along the wide main thoroughfare, which must be one of the most outstanding in the county. It is flanked by eye-catching shops and houses, while *Holy Trinity* is the most impressive of Suffolk churches.
*Lady Chapel* was a school from 1669 to 1880 and there is still a multiplication table on a wall to remind one of those days.
A pleasing feature of Long Melford is the parkland and great manors, two of which are the Tudor Melford Hall, open end of March to end of September, Wednesdays, Thursdays, Sundays and Bank Holiday Mondays, 2.00pm to 6.00pm, and Kentwell Hall, open March to October, Wednesdays and Thursdays, 2.00pm to 6.00pm, plus Fridays, Saturdays and Bank Holiday Mondays between July and August.

# West Suffolk

At the heart of inland Suffolk is the old country town of Bury St Edmunds.

King Edmund of East Anglia, after whom the town is named, was crowned in about AD 850. He was a Christian and a peaceful man until he was persuaded to lead an army against the Danish invaders.

The unfortunate warrior was captured and decapitated. Legend says that a wolf led the English to his body and was found guarding the head. This would explain the representation of a wolf carrying a human head which appears on the crest of Bury's armorial bearings.

Thirty years after Edmund's death, his body was brought to Bury and a shrine built in his honour. This was incorporated by the Normans in their Abbey Church.

The site of the high altar is still discernible and it was here in 1214 that the barons of England met to swear their determination to force King John to ratify Magna Carta. This they achieved the following year.

Map legend:
- Railway
- Church
- Country Park
- Historic House
- Towns with T.I.C.
- Forestry Commission Land

**Tourist Information Centres**
Thinghoe House, Northgate Street, Bury St Edmunds, Suffolk (0284) 64667
Information Caravan, Abbey Gardens, Bury St Edmunds, Suffolk. Summer only. (0284) 63233.

## Stowmarket
A small market town with some light industry, it is worth a visit to see the *Museum of East Anglia Life*. This covers 29 acres, and incorporates *Abbey Hall*.

Its purpose is to preserve specimens of rural life and crafts and it has a growing collection of old farming implements, vehicles and machinery.

Open Mondays to Saturdays 10.00am to 5.00pm (dusk in winter). Sundays 2.30pm to 4.30pm. There is a special display of crafts every Saturday morning.

## Clare
This is a village which deserves to be seen on foot. It was once the scene of great outrage when the railway station went through the remains of *Clare Castle*. The station itself is now an abandoned ruin by the castle keep.

There is a 15th-century priest's house at the corner of the churchyard, while there are earthworks on Upper Common. Experts differ over these; some say the site is an Iron Age fort, others insist that it is a former Danish stronghold.

Clare College, Cambridge, takes its name from the Earl of Clare's family. A Benedictine priory once stood at nearby Stoke-by-Clare. Its remains are now a part of a school. The grounds are always open and the Priory may be visited by arrangement with the Prior.

## Cavendish
This is another picturesque stop, with a fascinating history.

It was the son of Sir John Cavendish, then Chief Justice, who stabbed Wat Tyler at Smithfield in 1381. A mob then stormed Cavendish.

The terrified Sir John hid all his valuables in the church belfry and fled. However, he got only as far as Lakenheath when he was seized and killed.

53

The scene is more peaceful these days and the air of unhurried ease is underlined by sloping greenery and a row of superbly maintained thatched cottages which sit in the shadow of the church.

## Bury St Edmunds

There are two distinct parts to this beautiful town. As in most medieval towns with a monastic foundation, there was a clear division between the abbey and the townspeople. This occasionally erupted into ugly riots.

The development of the town rather reinforced the division, for the business centre and the impressive public buildings all stand on the hill west of the abbey.

The first Norman abbot, who planned Bury, originally intended that the street should be a formal approach to the abbey, lining up with the altar. Later generations changed the emphasis so that the climb up the hill towards the newer part of the town passes what appear to be 'modern' houses of the 17th and 18th centuries. In reality these are considerably older buildings to which later, more fashionable, façades have been added.

On Angel Hill, the sloping plain by the abbey, is the *Angel Hotel* which is redolent with Dickensian memories. Mr Pickwick was staying here when he heard that the formidable Mrs Bardell was starting her famous breach of promise action against him.

In more recent years Bury has become the 'Baildon' of Norah Loft's romantic novels.

*Moyses Hall* This magnificent 12th-century house in *Butter Market* is one of the earliest stone domestic buildings in England.

In the 19th century it was destined to be converted into a fire station, but common sense prevailed.

It is an off-beat museum

Opulence . . . Ickworth House

which includes among the exhibits the death mask of William Corder, the Red Barn murderer of Maria Marten. It also has a book bound in his skin. Open Monday to Friday.

*Abbey ruins and gardens* These include a Norman gate, with a 12th-century campanile, the Decorated Abbey Gate, and the John Appleby Rose Garden.

*St Mary's Church* A perpendicular style building in Crown Street, it has an angel roof to the nave and a wagon roof to the chancel. The tomb of Mary Tudor, Henry VIII's sister, is also here. Outside is a wild, tree-shaded churchyard.

*Queen Anne House* This National Trust-owned building on Angel Hill houses an interesting collection of clocks and watches, dating from the 16th century. Open weekdays.

*Athenaeum* The undoubted social hub of Regency Bury, located on Angel Hill. Charles Dickens gave readings here, and stayed at the Angel Hotel next door.

*Corn Exchange* A fine Victorian building in Corn Hill. Its decorations are derived from farming and agriculture.

The best time to visit is on Wednesday mornings, before the market begins.

*Suffolk Regiment Museum* The history of this famous regiment from 1685–1959 is recorded and laid out here in Outer Risbygate Street.

Open Monday to Friday.

*Theatre Royal* Still offering entertainment to townspeople and visitors, this fine Regency theatre was built in 1819, by Wilkins, who also designed the National Gallery in London.

*Ickworth House* Three miles south-west of the town lies Lord Bristol's peculiar rotunda, set in a park landscaped by Capability Brown. It has an interesting collection of 17th- and 18th-century furniture.

Open end of March to end of October, not Mondays or Fridays, 2.00pm to 6.00pm.

*Thinghoe Hill* Named after the ancient Danish parliament, *thing-how*, this is situated north of Bury in the direction of Packenham and Ixworth.

*Sports* Bowls and tennis in Abbey Gardens; swimming, badminton etc in the Sports and Leisure Centre.

## Moulton

*Dalham Hall* was once the home of the Duke of Wellington. It was later bought by Cecil Rhodes as his retirement home, but he died before he was able to use it as such.

An attractive hamlet, boasting a packhorse bridge which is so narrow and humped, that modern traffic must avoid it and go through a ford which is often swirling with water.

Moulton is linked to Dalham and Lidgate by the river Kennet, which follows the border with Cambridgeshire.

## Packenham

This is well worth a visit to see the windmill which is in full working order.

It is open during the week by appointment. (Tel Packenham 30277).

A Roman fort north of Packenham guards the southern end of Peddlars Way.

# Suffolk Coast

The coastline of Suffolk has been attacked over the centuries not only by invaders from Continental Europe but also by the sea. Flooding and storms have swallowed entire towns. Because of erosion it is impossible to build a road along this shore and each little town and village has its own road off the main Ipswich-Lowestoft highway.

However, it is rewarding to take the minor road linking Woodbridge to Blythburgh, running through Theberton and Westleton on the way. This is an area of heather and pine and estuaries with only the wildfowl for company.

Aldeburgh is world-famous as the home of the late Sir Benjamin Britten and his Aldeburgh Festival, held each June at the Maltings at nearby Snape.

Yachtsmen will know it equally well – along with Southwold, Orford and Woodbridge – as a place where their skills will be fully tested. Thorpeness offers more tranquil waters with boats for hire on its mere.

The tides along this coastline continually alter the composition of its beaches, making it an outstanding place for beachcombing. Amber and cornelian are not infrequent finds along the ever-changing shore.

**Tourist Information Centre**
Esplanade, Lowestoft, Suffolk.
(0502) 65989

Woodbridge . . . a tangle of boats and nets

### Woodbridge
Yachts, motor cruisers and small sailboats are built in this lively little town. Only a mile away is the *Sutton Hoo ship burial* where the remains of a Saxon ship and its vast hoard of treasure were found in 1939.

### Orford
The castle keep, built by Henry II, has 18 sides with, not surprisingly, good views of the Ness and lighthouse. Open weekdays 9.30am to 7.00pm, Sundays 2.00pm to dusk.

Nearby in the river Butley are oyster beds. Other local delicacies are smoked salmon, eel and trout.

All visitors must pass the huge 14th-century gatehouse on the road into Orford. It is all that remains of Butley Priory.

### Aldeburgh
There is a mixture of architectural styles in this lively town, which expanded after the treacherous sea destroyed the medieval ship-building centre of Slaughdon.

The Rev George Crabbe lived in Slaughdon in the 19th century and it is on his collection of tales, *The Borough*, that Britten based his opera *Peter Grimes*.

Two miles north is *Thorpeness* with its disguised mock-Tudor water tower, known locally as The House in the Clouds.

### Snape
This is best-known to music lovers for the Maltings concert hall, which first housed Britten's Aldeburgh Festival in 1967.

The hall was destroyed by fire on the festival's first night in 1969, but such was Britten's determination and dedication to his creation, that it was completely rebuilt in time for the 1970 season.

It is widely used throughout the year for many musical and non-musical events.

### Wickham Market
The village meanders along the River Deben. Edward Fitz-

gerald, who translated *The Rubaiyat of Omar Khayyam*, is buried nearby. On his grave grows a rose bush which came from the grave of Omar Khayyam in Persia.

## Southwold
An elegant and attractive tiny town, sitting on the cliff top, it was a popular Victorian resort, and still retains an air of old-fashioned charm.

Times were more vigorous in the mid-16th century when Southwold was obliged to pay St Edmund's Abbey at Bury the annual sum of 25,000 herring. The town's prosperity has always depended on the sea.

Trade with the Low Countries over the centuries has left its mark on some of the local architecture.

The Battle of Sole Bay, between the Dutch and English fleets, took place just off the coast here, and is satisfyingly commemorated in the Broadside Ale produced by the superb local brewery.

Within easy reach are the bird sanctuaries of Minsmere and Westleton.

## Lowestoft and Oulton Broad
Lowestoft is exhilarating. Since the discovery of Dogger Bank in about 1665, Lowestoft has become a most important fishing port, even developing a unique style of trawler.

The harbour is used by cruising yachts, but Broads craft can come no further than Oulton Broad, a freshwater playground separated from the sea by a lock.

One of Lowestoft's two piers juts out south of the harbour mouth, and to the south of that is the sandy beach, backed by a traffic-free promenade.

The Ness, to the north of the town, is the most easterly point of England.

## Kessingland
This excellent wildlife park stands in very large woodland grounds near the Lowestoft Road. As well as the many animals, there are also aviaries and a children's zoo. Open daily, 10.00am to 6.00pm, or an hour before dusk. Closed in winter.

## Bungay
Those with a taste for the supernatural will immediately warm to this town, for its town sign is a castle, forked lightning and a mysterious black dog. The dog may represent Satan, who is said to haunt the lonely and forbidding coastal marshes.

Bungay Stone is believed to be a Druid relic more than 2,000 years old.

## Eye
A drowsy town with an interesting hostelry, *The White Lion*, which has a ballroom and gallery for the musicians.

The 15th-century church is noted for its 100-ft tower and its rood screen.

## Earl Soham
This picturesque village is worthy of attention for its contrasting but never clashing styles of period architecture.

A mile away at *Saxstead Cross* is the post-mill, revolving on a centre post. Visitors can climb a wide wooden ladder to inspect it.

Good views from all sides . . . Orford castle keep

# Norfolk

**The Norfolk Broads, a system of lakes linked by rivers, has become one of England's most popular holiday areas, especially among sailing enthusiasts and anglers.**

There are a dozen large broads, the longest of them stretching for four or five miles, and twelve smaller broads.

All of them were created by peat-digging in medieval times, and they are linked by the extensive system of rivers which flows through this flat area.

The obvious centre from which to explore the Broads is the county town, Norwich, one of the most noble among English cities. The best way to see it is on foot.

'A fine old city . . . view it from whatever side you will'. So said George Borrow in the early 19th century. If he would find little to persuade him to change his judgement.

The view from Mousehold Heath, where Ketts massed his doomed rebel peasants in 1549, still shows the old city clustered around the cathedral tower. On a warm day when the sky is blurred with summer heat, the view seems to come from an illustration to a medieval Book of Hours.

The 33 medieval churches within the old walls, the course taken by the walls themselves and the impregnable arm of the River Wensum show the old city very much as it used to be.

**Tourist Information Centre**
Augustine Steward House, Tombland, Norwich, Norfolk. (0603) 20679/23445
Information Kiosk, Hay Hill, Norwich, Norfolk. Open May to October.

## Norwich

Anyone interested in the social history of the city should take an evening stroll along the restored medieval cobbled street of *Elm Hill*, in the warm and friendly glow of lantern lamplight.

*Tombland*, once the scene of a Saxon market place, has two ornate gateways at the entrance to *Cathedral Close*.

*Cathedral of Holy Trinity* This Norman masterpiece has a nave and tower second to none, and its splendid spire is second only to that of Salisbury Cathedral.

The nave was built between 1096 and 1145, the transepts have no aisles and the choir has apsidal chapels. The spire, choir, clerestory, some windows and the vaulting are Perpendicular. The remains of the original Bishop's Throne are behind the high altar.

The grave of First World War heroine *Edith Cavell*, shot by the Germans, is outside in Life's Green.

*Strangers Hall* Late-medieval town house, fine costume and textile collection. Open weekdays.

*Augustine Steward House* This 16th-century building now houses the Tourist Information Centre.

It was built by the Deputy Mayor of Norwich, Augustine Steward, a sturdy citizen who rescued the Mayor from the clutches of Kett's rebels, and played a big part in quelling the uprising.

*Norwich Castle* Among its treasures are the Norwich School of Paintings, many of which were commissioned by wealthy 18th-century families, and the unique Norwich Snapdragon carried in Mayoral processions in the Middle Ages.

Open daily, 10.00am to 5.00pm.

*Guildhall* Built in 1407 of Norwich flintwork, it has for 500 years been the seat of local government, and was also a cloth market and a prison. It now accommodates the magistrate's court.

The Council chamber has a Tudor ceiling, a 15th-century stained glass window and a sword presented by Lord Nelson.

*Assembly Rooms* In the 18th and 19th centuries, fashionable society met here for the season during the Assizes. Now restored to its former stateliness, visitors can indulge in the ritual of afternoon tea where elegant ladies once flirted with their fans.

**Other historic buildings**
*Gurney Court*, home of Elizabeth Fry; the Octagon Chapel, where the non-

Elm Hill . . . restored medieval cobbles

57

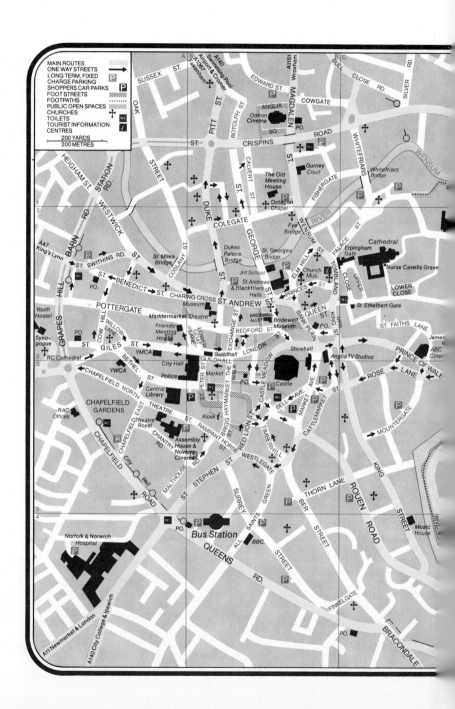

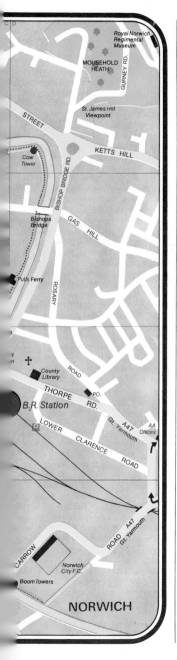

conformist philosophers and writers went to worship; the Georgian and medieval frontages of Colegate in 'Norwich Over the Water', once the fashionable area for merchants and businessmen, and now a fine example of blending old with new; Gentleman's Walk, where the Regency dandies used to take the air; St Giles Street, the dignified Georgian 'Harley Street' of Norwich; the Roman Catholic Cathedral, an imposing modern Gothic structure, built in 1884 to the design of George Gilbert Scott Junior; the City Walls, 14th-century flint-faced walls forming a four-mile barrier and river circuit of the medieval city.

*City Tours* A guided tour on foot in July and August, starting from the Tourist Information Centre at 2.30pm.

*Markets* General and provision market weekdays at the Market Place; main market days Wednesday and Saturday; livestock market Wednesday and Saturday in Hall Road.

*Sports* Indoor and outdoor swimming pools; tennis; squash; golf and bowls. The Norfolk County Cricket Club play at Lavenham cricket ground. Norwich City play League soccer.

*Boat Trips* There is an 18-mile river cruise aboard *Regal Lady*, from Thorpe Station, daily except Saturday, Spring Bank Holiday to September; the Victorian steam launch *Princess Margaret* makes daily trips on the River Yare, via Thorpe Island, Easter to September.

### Aylsham
This is worth a visit to see the Jacobean Blickling Hall.
Open daily, except Friday, April to October.

### Fakenham
This is a market town with some outstanding mansions around it.
The Tudor red-brick East

Barsham Manor is worth viewing from the outside, as is Raynham Hall, the home of agriculturalist Viscount Townshend who earned the nickname Turnip because of his enthusiastic growing of that vegetable. He also developed the system of crop rotation.
The hall is still in his descendants' hands.

### Great Witchingham
The parish church dates from the 13th century.
Outside the village is the *Norfork Wildlife Park*, which has otters, bears, deer and many other animals in natural surroundings.
Open daily, 10.30am to 6.00pm, or dusk.

### Thetford
The growth and expansion which have changed so many communities for the worse, have not altered the character of this old town. It has an attractive riverside setting on the Thet and Little Ouse and seems to have been an important Saxon settlement.
The Danes sacked and burned the town several times until they at last controlled East Anglia, and Canute made Thetford his capital.
After the Conquest, it became for a short time the East Anglian bishopric, until the see was removed to Norwich.
Other notable religious foundations, mainly the Priory, ensured the town's importance at least until the Dissolution of the Monasteries.
The great expansion of the Sixties altered only its size and it is now a most agreeable large town.
There are a number of interesting buildings and ruins to be seen, including the old *Bell Hotel*, the *King's House* (once a royal shooting lodge and now the council offices) and monastic remains.
The *Spring Walk* along the

59

river and the impressive *Castle Hill earthworks* should not be missed.

A bronze statue in front of the *King's House* recalls that Thomas Paine, that champion of American Independence, was born in Thetford.

*Kilverstone Wildlife Park* and *Thetford Forest* are nearby.

## Banham
This is worth a visit to see the *zoo*, which houses a rare breeding colony of woolly monkeys. Open daily.

## Earsham
*The Otter Trust* is quartered here and has a unique collection of otters from around the world. Open daily, March to November, 10.30am to 6.00pm.

## Wymondham
A 17th-century market cross is the centrepiece of this ancient town. For 500 years the Abbey church has been a monument to a dispute between the monks and their parishioners. When the monks built their octagonal tower, they also put up a wall to shield themselves and the high altar from the townspeople.

This so enraged the locals that they hit back by erecting the west tower – making sure that it was larger than the other.

In the 16th century Wymondham was the seat of a peasant's rebellion against encroachments on common land. Kett's Rebellion, led by Robert Kett, seized Norwich before finally being crushed. Retribution was massive and Kett was hanged in Norwich, his brother at Wymondham.

## Swaffham
A charming tale of two dreams is associated with the building of Swaffham's 16th-century church.

John Chapman, the Pedlar of Swaffham, is alleged to have gone to London to find a treas-

Golden fields of corn . . . Thetford

ure he saw in a dream. While on his journey, he met a man who said he had dreamed of treasure buried in Chapman's own garden. The pedlar hurried home to Swaffham and found his fortune under his own tree.

The money was used to build the church aisle.

## Downham Market
A hill town, it is the starting point for the roads which lead to Breckland and the Fen borders.

Nearby is Oxburgh Hall, a superb 15th-century moated house, with an 80-ft gate tower. The Bedingfield family have lived here for more than 500 years.

Open April to October only, Tuesdays, Wednesdays and Thursdays, 2.00pm to 6.00pm.

## Brandon
This is the home of England's oldest industry – flint knapping. In the Stone Age the flint weapons were hammered out of mined slabs. More recently Brandon supplied the flints to the British Army for the Napoleonic wars.

Even today, there is still a demand, now from America and Africa.

## Grime's Graves
Discovered in 1870, these craters are about 4,000 years old. Around 800 shafts were dug by the men of the late Stone Age and the discoverers found many mementoes of the time, including a chalk figure believed to be a fertility goddess. One pit is usually open.

# Norfolk Coast

Norfolk's coastline is yet another manifestation of this splendid county's personality, showing its rugged resistance to the battering of the North Sea. Much of the coastline is suitably armoured against the ceaseless attention of the waves. There are zigzag breakwaters, switchback promenades, sloping walls and concrete packed palisades.

This stretch of coast backing on to the Broads caters for almost every seaside holiday mood or need, from a bustling family resort, to quiet, away-from-everything fishing village and boating centre.

At the other end of the coast is the comparative tranquillity of the Wash, leading into Kings Lynn and then to Royal Sandringham. Great Yarmouth has some of the best herring to be found anywhere, and further up the coast crab and lobster are to be had in profusion, while Stiffkey has its cockles, known as Stewkey Blues.

All this can be found along the great stretch of unhurried coast road. It is a journey well worth taking.

## Tourist Information Centres

Department of Publicity, 14 Regent Street, Great Yarmouth, Norfolk. (0493) 4313/4
Marine Parade, Great Yarmouth, Norfolk. (Summer only) (0493) 2195
North Lodge Park, Cromer, Norfolk. (Summer only) (0263) 2497
Station Car Park, Station Road, Sheringham, Norfolk. (Summer only) (026 382) 4329
Le Strange Terrace, Hunstanton, Norfolk. (048 53) 2610
Town Hall, Saturday Market Place, King's Lynn, Norfolk. (0553) 61241

## Great Yarmouth and Gorleston

The sands at Great Yarmouth are lined by the Marine Parade, with its colourful gardens and countless attractions.

Neighbouring Gorleston pursues a quieter life, with flower gardens lining a wide promenade and old streets dating from when it was itself an important port.

The beaches outside town are unspoilt from Caister to Hemsby and Winterton. Cliffs shelter the sands at Scratby, California and Hopton.

Yarmouth's busy port is now the main service base for North Sea gas and oil exploration. Traces of the old walls around the town remain and there are guided walks round them on Wednesday evenings in July and August.

Within the walls are the Rows, although little now remains of this medieval town plan.

## Hickling

Hickling Broad is one of the widest stretches of water in the county. The pleasant little village is usually approached via the landing stage at the Pleasure Boat Inn.

Birdwatchers will find *Norfolk Naturalists' Trust* hides on the Broad. Telephone (0603) 25540 to arrange visits.

## Mundesley

An interesting holiday village, with quiet sands and secure bathing in the shallow waters. However, these have somehow managed to erode cliff, fields, houses and breakwaters over the last century.

*Paston Mill*, on Stow Hill, half a mile away, commands excellent views. Telephone (0263) 720798 to arrange visits.

## Cromer

A fishing village which became fashionable as a resort at the turn of the century. Breezy and

61

Stately Sandringham . . . royal residence

## Hunstanton

East Anglia's only west-facing resort, with a sandy beach backed by interesting red and white banded cliffs, caused by centuries of erosion.

Being 'around the corner' in the Wash, it is popular with all boating enthusiasts. The ozone is famous and is known as 'champagne air'.

Much of this coast is now a nature reserve.

Nearby is Nelson's birthplace, at *Burnham Thorpe*.

## Sandringham

This 7,000-acre estate is owned by the Royal Family and it takes in seven parishes. However, there is no village of Sandringham.

King Edward VII bought the estate in 1861, when he was Prince of Wales. There is a country park on the estate, which is open when none of the Royal Family is in residence.

## King's Lynn

This ancient market town entertained King John so royally that after his departure he died of a surfeit of lampreys. As if that were not bad enough, his following baggage train was wrecked crossing the Wash.

People are still looking for the treasure. It is easy to believe in treasure troves when confronted with such a town as King's Lynn: medieval streets crowd down by the quays, and merchants' houses with private warehouses present an air of continuing wealth.

Two *guildhalls* still function as a legacy of this mercantile prosperity.

One is the Council Office, with splendid regalia and a set of charters going back to the unfortunate King John. The other is now the home of the *King's Lynn Festival*.

It is thought that this is the only extant theatre in which *Shakespeare* appeared while he was one of Southampton's Players.

bright in the summer, Cromer stands on a cliff, by a sloping sandy beach.

Fishing boats work from the beach, as there is no harbour on this stretch of coast. The local crabs are memorable.

The lifeboat museum, *Cromer Museum*, is open daily.

There is also a zoo, open all the year round from 10.00am to dusk.

## Sheringham

The popular end of the town is Lower Sheringham, which became a resort at the end of the 19th century. High tide brings a ridge of pebbles, but the ebb tide washes them away to leave a stretch of magnificently clean sand.

Steam trains of the North Norfolk Railway operate from the town's old station and travel as far as Weybourne.

## Wells-next-to-Sea

A small, but delightful, old-fashioned port which still handles ships of up to 300 tons. A small fleet of whelk and shrimp boats operates from the harbour.

The town has many quaint streets, flint cottages and Georgian houses. Beautiful pine woods skirt the sandy beach and form part of a chain of local nature reserves.

It is not far to Holkham Hall, Walsingham Shrine, Binham Priory or the Warham Iron Age fort.

# Northamptonshire

'The county of spires and squires' survives as an apposite description of Northamptonshire. The county is particularly well blessed with elegant church-spires, and it retains more than a hint of the squirearchy.

The latter is evidenced by, among other things, the extent to which fox-hunting takes place in this part of England.

Much of the land in the county still belongs to private estates, including some villages, though they are perfectly accessible to the visitor. The only immediate sign that they are privately owned is their unspoiled quality.

This aspect of the county compensates for the recent growth of Northampton, an agreeable city, and the presence of industrial centres like Corby and Wellingborough.

Northamptonshire remains predominantly rural, especially in the northern corner, where there are wooded traces of the once-great Rockingham Forest.

The main centre in this area is Kettering, though the public-school town of Oundle is a pleasant centre from which to explore.

Whole chapters of English history, from the Wars of the Roses to the Civil War, were written in this county's green fields. Fotheringhay Castle, now only grassy remains, was where Richard III was born, and where Mary Queen of Scots was beheaded.

**Tourist Information Centres**
Information Centre, Public Library, Sheep Street, Kettering, Northamptonshire. (0536) 82143/85211
21 St Giles Street, Northampton, Northamptonshire. (0604) 34881 ext 404/537

## Northampton

An historic town, Northampton was originally an Ancient Briton settlement on Hunsbury Hill, and after Saxon and Roman occupations, William the Conqueror made it a garrison town due to its strategic position between Winchester and York.

In 1209 King John pledged the town and its castle as surety against the Magna Carta.

After most of the medieval buildings were destroyed by a fire in the 17th century, Northampton was rebuilt with one of the largest market squares in England.

Northampton sided with the Parliamentary cause during the Civil War and supplied shoes and books to Cromwell's men. In retribution Charles II ordered the destruction of the castle and town walls. However, by 1675 he seems to have mellowed in his attitude and helped the town with timber supplies after a fire destroyed most of the medieval buildings.

Northampton was rebuilt with a massive market square, one of the largest in England. The main shopping streets leading from it recall pre-fire prosperity: Gold Street, Silver Street. The Drapery, Sheep Street, Mercer's Row. Grosvenor Centre, with its new complex of shops and offices, is designed to blend with the elegant proportions of the Market Square.

*Central Museum and Art Gallery* A display of shoes through the ages is worth a visit. It includes shoes worn by Queen Victoria for her wedding, and the ballet shoes of Nijinsky and Margot Fonteyn. Also local archaeological finds, old and modern paintings.

Open daily except Sunday, 10.00am to 6.00pm.

*Abington Museum* A former manor house and once the home of Shakespeare's granddaughter, with displays of toys, pottery, and porcelain.

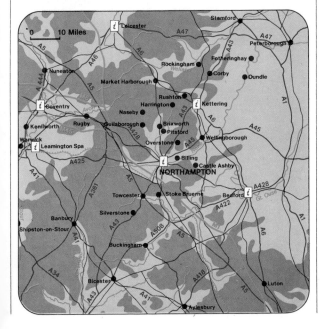

63

Open Monday to Saturday,
10.00am to 12.30pm and
2.00pm to 6.00pm, Sundays in
the summer 2.30pm to 5.00pm.
*Museum of the Northamptonshire
Regiment* This has a pictorial history of the regiment 1741–1960.
Open Monday to Friday,
9.00am to 12.30pm, 2.00pm to
5.00pm.
*Historic buildings Delapre Abbey,*
a house on site of the abbey
begun in the 16th century;
*Guildhall*, Victorian gothic built
in 1861, decorated with figures
from town history, *Eleanor
Cross*, on the London Road
south of the town, which is one
of three remaining crosses built
by Edward I in memory of his
queen, Eleanor.
*Factory visits* Shoe factories and
the power station, visits by
appointment. Daily tours of
Carlsberg Brewery, 9.30am
and 2.30pm.
*Sports* Indoor and outdoor
swimming; bowling; water-
skiing; boating; stock car racing; Northamptonshire County
Cricket; Rugby Union; Northampton Town play league
soccer.

**Silverstone**
This is best known to motor
racing enthusiasts for its racing
circuit, built on the site of a disused airfield. The *British Grand
Prix* is held here in odd-
numbered years.
The track is also used for
other motor and motor-cycling
events throughout the season.

**Towcester**
This town claims to be one of
the oldest in England. It has certainly been important since the
Romans built Watling Street.
The church, which dates from
the 13th century, has an interesting collection of chained books.
Dickens wrote of *The Saracen's Head* hostelry in *The Pickwick Papers*.

**Stoke Bruerne**
An ideal place for basing a

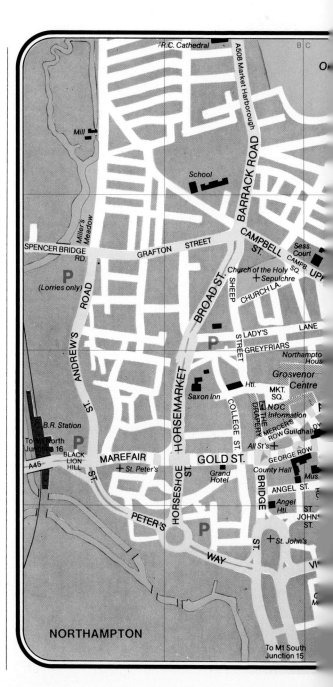

NORTHAMPTON

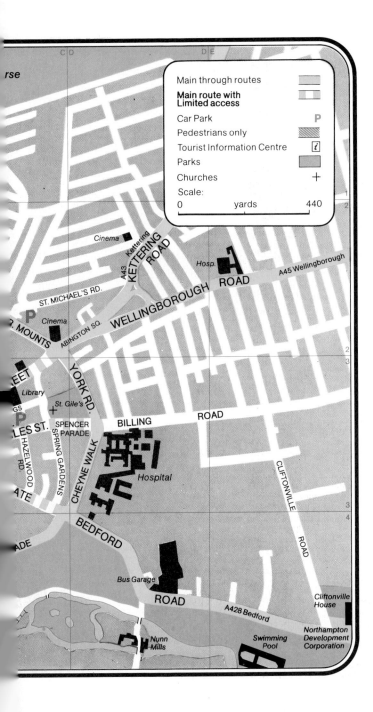

Main through routes
**Main route with
Limited access**
Car Park                                    P
Pedestrians only
Tourist Information Centre           [i]
Parks
Churches                                    +
Scale:
0                    yards              440

canal-cruising holiday. The Grand Union Canal runs through a mile-long tunnel from Stoke Bruerne and Blisworth.

In bygone days, this landlocked county relied on the canal network to transport grain, coal and many other goods to the ports. This history is illustrated in the Waterways Museum. Open daily, Easter to September, 10.00am to 6.00pm, October to Easter, closed Mondays, 10.00am to 4.00pm.

**Castle Ashby**
A hamlet with a superb Elizabethan country house, set in a magnificent park landscaped by Capability Brown.

The house was built in 1574 by the first Earl of Northampton, but the south front is attributed to Inigo Jones.

The castle has a collection of 15th- and 16th-century paintings. Open Easter weekend and then from April to September, Thursdays, Sundays and Bank Holidays, 2.00pm to 5.00pm.

**Guilsborough**
This small town is best known for Coton Manor Wildlife Garden.

This 17th-century manor house set in an old English garden has lakes, waterfalls, a water garden, ornamental cranes and flamingoes.

Open from Easter to October, Thursdays, Sundays and Bank Holidays, 2.00pm to 6.00pm, and on Wednesdays in July and August.

**Naseby**
This village was the site in 1645 of the battle in which Cromwell defeated Charles I to settle the Civil War. There is a stone column north of the village commemorating the battle.

Another monument south of the village marks what is believed to be the site of a decisive cavalry charge by Crom-

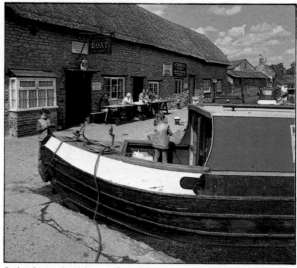
Perfect for canal cruising . . . Stoke Bruerne

well's forces. Relics of the battle can be seen in the village church.

**Oundle**
The River Nene surrounds this charming village on three sides. It is a marvellous centre for a boating holiday and craft can be hired from *Oundle Marina*.

*Cottestock Hall* has associations with the poet Dryden.

Open Easter weekend and the 1st and 3rd Sundays of the month from July to September. The gardens are open daily, April to September, 2.00pm to 7.00pm.

The town itself has many picturesque inns and cottages, in addition to its famous public school, and the Renaissance building Lyveden New Bield, open March to October, Wednesdays, Thursdays, weekends and Bank Holidays, 2.00pm to 6.00pm.

**Rockingham**
*Rockingham Castle* is the Chesney Wold in Dickens's *Bleak House*. It contains much fine furniture and a collection of paintings, including a portrait of Francis I of France, reputed to have donated it himself.

The castle was built by William the Conqueror and used as a fortress until the Middle Ages, but was very dilapidated by the end of the 15th century. Good Queen Bess gave it to the Lord Chief Justice and his son-in-law, Edward Watson, who restored it, and it has been in the same family ever since.

Open from Easter to September, Thursdays, Sundays, and Bank Holiday weekends, 2.00pm to 6.00pm.

**Rushton**
Visitors should see the *Triangular Lodge*, built by Sir Thomas Tresham to symbolize the Trinity. It has three gables, and the 33-ft long inscription around the building has 33 letters in each of its three sections.

It is believed to have been a meeting place of Guy Fawkes and his plotters.

Open daily, 9.30am to 5.30pm.

# Leicestershire

England's tiniest and quietest county, Rutland, was finally incorporated into Leicestershire in the early 1970s, though its sense of identity undoubtedly survives, as does its famous local brewery.

The Duke of Rutland's home is the splendid castle at Belvoir, which also gives its name to a famous hunt. The Belvoir hunt, like the Cottesmore and Quorn hunts, meets in the old Leicestershire town of Melton Mowbray. Hence Melton's famous hunt cake, though the town is even better known for its distinctive pork pie recipe. Both confections are readily available at local shops.

Much of the county comprises rolling agricultural country, though the landscape develops an unusual character in the area which was once the Charnwood Forest. This was a densely wooded area, but centuries of felling by charcoal-burners left behind a dramatic landscape of heather, gorse and outcrops of very old rock.

There are good views of this area at Beacon Hill and Bardon Hill, both near Ashby-de-la-Zouch.

Within the same part of the county, there is some coal-mining.

## Tourist Information Centres
Egerton Lodge, Wilton Road, Melton Mowbray, Leicestershire. (0664) 3662/5
Storer House, Wards End, Loughborough, Leicestershire. (0509) 30131/2
12 Bishop Street, Leicester, Leicestershire. (0533) 20644

## Leicester
An ancient cathedral and university city which grew with the hosiery and footwear trades.

The city has been developed considerably in the post-War period, though this has its compensations for the car-borne visitor.

There is a large number of multi-storey car parks in the centre, some of which operate a 'park and ride' system of shuttle buses ferrying visitors, shoppers and commuters to the central points of the city.

Overlooking the River Soar is a leisure park for walking and fishing, and pleasure craft can navigate the Soar from the Grand Union Canal to the Trent. The park was built around the area of the Norman castle, which is no longer standing.

*Guildhall* The 14th-century timbered building was used as the town hall until 1876. It contains a mayor's parlour, library and cells.

Open Monday to Saturday, 10.00am to 5.30pm, Sunday 2.00pm to 5.30pm.

*Clock Tower* A Victorian monument in the city centre, commemorating four Leicester benefactors – Simon de Montford, Gabriel Newton, William Wyggeston and Sir Thomas White.

*Castle Yard* The fine old Norman church of *St Mary de Castro* is situated here, where Henry VI was knighted. John Wesley once preached outside it.

*Roman Jewry Wall* One of Britain's most important relics, it houses Roman baths and an archaeological museum.

Open Monday to Saturday 10.00am to 5.30pm, Sunday 2.00pm to 5.30pm.

## Museums
*Belgrave Hall* An 18th-century country house containing coaches and agricultural equipment.

Open Monday to Saturday 10.00am to 5.30pm, Sunday 2.00pm to 5.30pm.

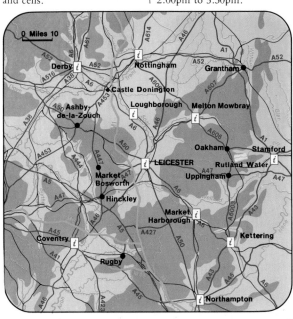

*The Magazine* A 14th-century gatehouse housing the museum of the 17th Foot Regiment.

Open Monday to Saturday 10.00am to 5.30pm, Sunday 2.00pm to 5.30pm.

*Leicester Museum and Art Gallery* Three centuries of British painting are on view here, including sporting artists. There are also exhibitions of ceramics, glass, silver, and natural history and geology. Open Monday to Saturday 10.00am to 5.30pm, Sunday 2.00pm to 5.30pm.

*Leicester Museum of Technology* Visitors can see four late 19th-century beam engines, and a collection of horse-drawn vehicles and motor cycles.

Open Monday to Saturday 10.00am to 5.30pm, Sunday 2.00pm to 5.30pm.

*Newarke House Museum* As well as collections of hosiery and knitwear, toys, games, clocks and musical instruments, there is an exhibition of Leicester's history since 1500

Open Monday to Saturday 10.00am to 5.30pm, Sunday 2.00pm to 5.30pm.

*Roger Wygston's House* Recently restored as a costume museum, this building is 15th-century, with an 18th-century frontage.

Open Monday to Saturday 10.00am to 5.30pm, Sunday 2.00pm to 5.30pm.

*Town Trail* A Guide is available from Tourist Information Centre.

*Market* Outside the Corn Exchange, every Wednesday, Friday and Saturday.

*Sports* Swimming pools; roller skating (winter only); boating; cycling; athletics; 18-hole municipal golf course; speedway; rugby union; Leicestershire County Cricket Club; Leicester City Football Club.

## Belvoir

As a visitor might expect, this village is dominated by the famous *Belvoir Castle*, the home of the Duke of Rutland, whose family have lived there since Henry VIII's reign.

The Rutland family collection includes paintings by Gainsborough and Holbein, in addition to Gobelein tapestries.

The castle also houses the regimental museum of the 17th and 21st Lancers.

Open March to September, Wednesday, Thursday and Saturday, 12.00 pm to 6.00pm, Sunday 2.00pm to 7.00pm.

## Uppingham

The town is best-known for its public school, situated in the centre, which seems to dominate everything else. The courtyards and quadrangles are 16th-century, but there are many later additions.

## Market Harborough

A market was first held in this pleasant small town as early as 1203, and today's traders still set out their stalls every Tuesday and Saturday. The specialist cattle market operates on Tuesdays.

The town's wealth of Georgian architecture has withstood the industrial development of recent years.

Market Harborough is worth visiting to see the 17th-century timbered grammar school building which stands above pavement level on wooden stilts, underneath which pedestrians can walk.

The town is an excellent centre for exploration of the region.

## Market Bosworth

The Domesday Book has a record of this small town built of stone.

There has been a market here since 1285, although the Dixie family have a royal charter allowing them to operate one of England's seven privately-owned markets.

The 14th-century church has many memorials to the family, who were the town's leading citizens after buying the local manor house in 1567.

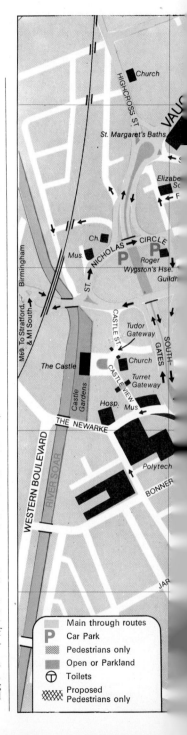

Main through routes

P Car Park

Pedestrians only

Open or Parkland

Toilets

Proposed Pedestrians only

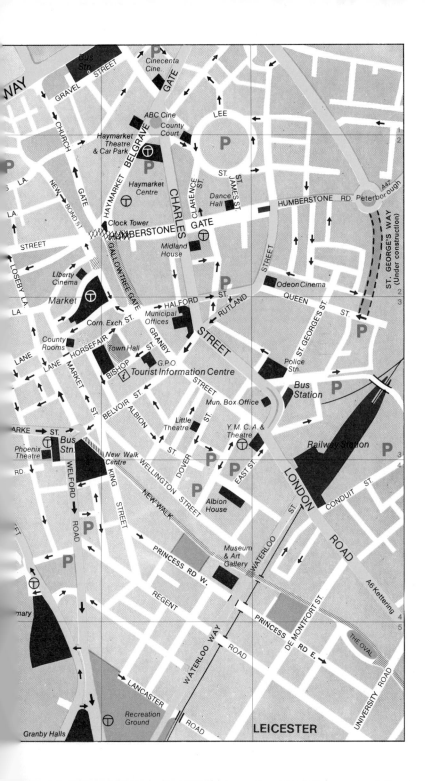

69

One mile south is *Bosworth Field*. In 1485 this was the scene of the decisive battle in the Wars of the Roses when Richard III was defeated and killed by Henry Tudor's forces, thus bringing to an end the Plantagenet dynasty.

The Richard III Society, which exists to prove the dead king innocent of the many foul deeds for which he is blamed, maintains a cairn over *Dick's Well*.

The information and exhibition centres are open throughout the summer from 2.00pm to 5.30pm and there are marked footpaths for those wishing to relive this significant incident in England's history.

## Oakham

This was the former county town of Rutland. It has many fine buildings and interesting relics of its past, including a set of stocks which sit in the well-preserved market square.

The walls of *Oakham Castle*, a 12th-century manor house, are decorated with horseshoes which have been paid as a toll by visiting peers since medieval times.

Open daily April to September 9.30am to 7.00pm, October to March 9.30am to 4.00pm.

## Melton Mowbray

This town has several gastronomic delights.

For more than 120 years the mounted gentry have eaten Melton Mowbray Hunt Cake, a fruit mixture laced with Jamaican rum.

The town is the capital of hunting Leicestershire, and is the meeting place of the Cottesmore, Belvoir and Quorn hunts. The latter traditionally contributes its Bacon Roll to the proceedings and it is usually given to the beaters.

Melton Mowbray gave its name to a pork pie, which is still baked with a hand-raised pastry crust.

Once away from the table there are recuperative walks along the banks of the River Eye.

Nearby is *Stapleford Park*, a 16th-century building which now has a lion reserve among its attractions. Open on summer Wednesdays, Thursdays and Sundays 2.30pm to 6.30pm.

By the large market square is a 15th-century house once owned by Anne of Cleves, one of Henry VIII's more fortunate ex-wives. But the visitor cannot long escape the town's culinary emphasis – the house is now a restaurant.

## Lutterworth

This town is better known to motorists as a motorway access point, but it is well worth turning off the M1 to see *Stanford Hall*, a late 17th-century house belonging to the Cave family.

It has collections of antiques, pictures, costumes, a motor cycle and car museum, a walled rose garden, nature trail, crafts centre and old forge.

Open on summer Thursdays, Saturdays and Sundays, 2.30pm to 6.00pm.

## Ashby-de-la-Zouch

The La Zouch family, from Brittany, took over this town from the Danes and left an indelible mark on its name. In the last century it was developed as a spa, but it has more than waters to commend it.

There are the ruins of the 15th-century *castle*, complete with underground passages. Mary Queen of Scots, James I and Charles II all stayed here.

Open daily, 9.30am to 5.30pm.

## Castle Donnington

This is the home of *Donnington Park Racing Car Museum*, with cars dating from 1911.

Open daily, 10.00am to 6.00pm.

A day in the country . . . Foxton Locks near Market Harborough

# Derbyshire

The county of Derbyshire embraces much of the Peak District, which was the first National Park in Britain.

The Peaks offer a wide variety of countryside to explore. The northern High or Dark Peaks, with their moorlands are good for climbing.

In the limestone uplands of the west, the White Peak area, is the stylish spa resort of Buxton.

The more tranquil central and southern areas have quiet rivers and warm red-brick cottages.

At nearby Longford, England's first cheese factory was set up in 1870, and the building can still be seen although the cheese is now made at Hartington.

Among the historic houses near Derby are Wingfield Manor where Mary Queen of Scots was captive, Hardwick Hall, once the home of Elizabeth, Countess of Shrewsbury, and Bolsover Castle.

### Ashbourne

This attractive market town, standing on the fringe of the Peaks, is the starting point of the Tissington nature trail which extends 13 miles.

Ashbourne's handsome parish church has a 212-ft spire which looks down upon many other fine buildings, including the 17th-century red-brick mansion where Dr Johnson visited his friend John Taylor.

### Chesterfield

This town in the Rother Valley is mock-Tudor almost from start to finish, apart from a few genuine examples in the market place.

*Revolution House*, in Old

All Saints . . . Chesterfield

**Tourist Information Centres**
13 Market Place, Ashbourne, Derbyshire. (033 55) 3666
St Ann's Well, The Crescent, Buxton, Derbyshire. (0298) 5106
Central Library, Corporation Street, Chesterfield, Derbyshire. (0246) 32047/32661
Reference Library, Central Library, The Strand, Derby, Derbyshire. (0332) 31111 ext 21856
Ilkeston Library, Market Place, Ilkeston, Derbyshire. (0602) 303361 ext 289

Abbeydale
Castleton
A625
Hathersage
A6
B606
Great Hucklow
Longshaw
A623
Eyam
A621
Tideswell
B6051
Buxton
A6
A619
Chesterfield
A54
A6
Chatsworth Hall
Bakewell
A515
Hardwick Hall
A6
A623
A632
Haddon Hall
A524
Hartington
Tissington
Matlock
A5012
Riber
A6
High Peak Trail
Middleton
Crich
A615
Wirksworth
A515
Alfreton
A623
Tissington
Ripley
A61
A610
Ashbourne
Alton Towers
Kedleston Hall
A52
Ilkeston
A515
Longford
DERBY
A52
Sudbury Hall
A516
A6
Elvaston Castle
Blithfield Hall
Burton upon Trent
A38
Melbourne Hall
East Midlands Airport

**10 Miles**

Whittington, is a 17th-century building with some interesting furniture.

However, the curiosity for which the town is best known is its parish church, All Saints, which has a crooked spire 228 ft high. Vulgar, but irresistible, tible, local legend has it that the spire twisted itself over to view the last virgin bride to cross the threshold – and that it will straighten itself when the next one does so!

### Crich

This hill town has excellent views, and a fascinating *Tramways Museum* containing 40 vehicles which date from 1874 to the post-War period. Some of the trams still run.

Open April to October weekends, 11.00am to 6.00pm, June to August, Tuesday to Thursday, 10.00am to 5.00pm.

### Wirksworth

Much of the novel *Adam Bede*, by George Eliot, is set in this small town, notable for stone houses and narrow streets. The 13th-century church contains the lid of a 9th-century Anglo Saxon coffin.

Beresford Dale . . . a High Peak near Hartington

### Tissington

This is the point at which the nature trail connects with the 17-mile High Peak Trail.

### Bakewell

There is much to see in this richly wooded valley town.

Nearby is *Chatsworth House*, the ultra-stately home of generations of Dukes of Devonshire. It was built from 1687 to 1707 and contains Reynolds and Rembrandt paintings. Outside there are red deer in the park and gardens landscaped by Capability Brown.

The town's *Old House Museum* houses a folk collection within its 15th-century walls. The ducal connections are strengthened by the *Bath House*, a brownstone building, built in 1697 for the Duke of Rutland.

The town has given its name to a delectable tart. It originated when a customer of the Rutland Arms ordered a strawberry tart. In error, the cook spread egg mixture on top of the jam instead of in the pastry.

Bakewell is a splendid centre for touring the Peaks.

### Buxton

One of the highest towns in England – 1,000 ft above sea level – and one of the oldest spas. The Duke of Devonshire established it as a popular resort in which to take the waters. At the end of the 18th century, he built the town's magnificent *Crescent* which was intended as a rival to fashionable Bath.

As an added bonus, the pale blue Buxton water is pleasant to drink, unlike that of most spas. Such resorts have lost much of their popularity today, but Buxton continues to bring in visitors because of its advantageous situation as a Peak centre.

Medieval manor house . . . Haddon Hall

## Glossop
The nearby Dinting Railway Centre has an operational steam engine and is open daily.

## Castleton
There is more below ground level than above it at this splendid village at the entrance to the Hope Valley. This is caving country, with such picturesquely-named places to explore as Peak Cavern, housing the Devil's Cavern, Roger's Rain House – where water pours unceasingly down the walls – and the Orchestral Chamber, which has remarkable acoustic properties.

At the top of Treak Cliff is the entrance to Blue John Mine, believed to be the only place in the world where the semi-precious mineral Blue John is found. This is a translucent variety of fluospar, prized for making ornaments since Roman times.

Jewellery and other items made from Blue John can be bought at the caverns and in the town. The caverns are quite safe and open to the public.

## Edale
An attractive village, it is set in craggy and spectacular National Trust land. This is fine walking country with many interesting routes.

One such is through Upper Booth to the slope known as Jacob's Ladder, on Edale Cross, concluding at Kinder Scout. At just over 2,000 ft, this is the

A Peak centre . . . Buxton

highest point in the Peak District. The surrounding land is *grouse-shooting* country. The season extends from August 12 to December 10 and prospective walkers can obtain information about access during this period from the Nag's Head Inn at Edale.

## Derby
This hill city is the home of a famous porcelain, of Rolls Royce aero engines, and of British Rail's high-speed train.

Having first been established as a Roman fort, Derby became a market centre in the 12th century, and in 1717 the country's first silk mill was set up on the River Derwent.

The advent of the Midland Railway in the 1840's established Derby as a freight and railway engineering centre.

With its fast rail links and proximity to the M1 and the East Midlands Airport, Derby is a good touring base.

*Derby Museum and Art Gallery* This contains important collections of Royal Crown Derby porcelain, a gallery of Joseph Wright's Derby paintings, local archaeology both domestic and

Towering for four centuries . . . Derby Cathedral

73

industrial, and a working scale model of the old Midland Railway.

Open Tuesday to Friday, 10.00am to 6.00pm, Saturday 10.00am to 5.00pm.

*Derby Museum of Industry and Technology* Housed in a restored silk mill on the river, this museum has a display of Rolls Royce aero engines and other local industries.

Open Tuesday to Friday, 10.00am to 5.45pm, Saturday 10.00am to 4.45pm.

## Churches

*Cathedral of All Saints* This has an early 16th-century tower, an 18th-century interior designed by James Gibbs with 20th-century windows and apse. The wrought iron chancel gates are by Robert Bakewell.

*St Mary's Chapel* A small 14th- and 15th-century restored church on an old river bridge.

*St Mary's Church* A fine specimen of Gothic Revival architecture, which was built by Pugin and completed in 1839.

*St Peter's Church* This is the only remaining medieval church in Derby, although it has been much restored.

*St Werburgh's Church* Dr Johnson was married here. It was partly rebuilt in the 19th-century and has a font cover by Bakewell.

*Old Inns* The Old Bell in Sadler Gate is a former coaching inn; The Dolphin, Queen Street, was first licensed in 1530; The Seven Stars, King Street, stands on the site of a monastery and has been licensed since 1680.

*Factory visit* Conducted tours of the Royal Crown Derby Porcelain Company and its museum each weekday by appointment. Telephone (0332) 47051.

*Sports* Swimming; soccer; athletics; badminton; squash; archery; three golf courses; newly-built municipal sports stadium; for spectators, Derbyshire County Cricket Club, and Derby County Football Club. (The Baseball Ground).

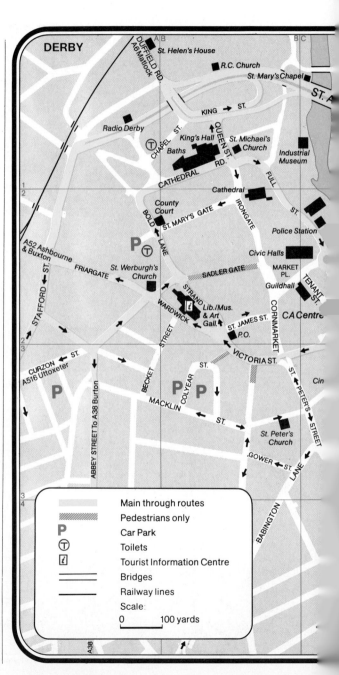

DERBY

St. Helen's House
R.C. Church
St. Mary's Chapel
DUFFIELD RD.
A6 Matlock
KING ST.
Radio Derby
CHAPEL ST.
King's Hall
Baths
QUEEN ST.
St. Michael's Church
Industrial Museum
CATHEDRAL RD.
FULL ST.
Cathedral
County Court
BOLD LANE
ST. MARY'S GATE
IRONGATE
Police Station
A52 Ashbourne & Buxton
FRIARGATE
St. Werburgh's Church
SADLER GATE
Civic Halls
MARKET PL.
Guildhall
TENANT ST.
STAFFORD ST.
STRAND
WARDWICK
Lib./Mus. & Art Gall.
ST. JAMES ST.
P.O.
CORNMARKET
CA Centre
CURZON ST.
A516 Uttoxeter
BECKET ST.
VICTORIA ST.
ST. PETER'S STREET
Cin
MACKLIN ST.
COLYEAR ST.
St. Peter's Church
ABBEY STREET To A38 Burton
GOWER ST.
LANE
BABINGTON
A38

Main through routes
Pedestrians only
P Car Park
T Toilets
i Tourist Information Centre
Bridges
Railway lines
Scale:
0    100 yards

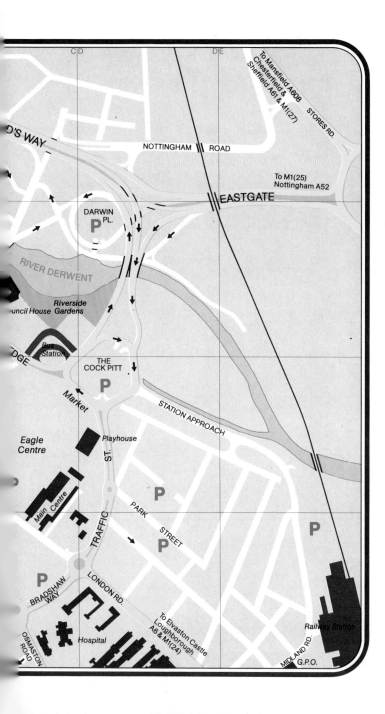

To Mansfield A608
Chesterfield &
Sheffield A61 & M1(27)

STORES RD.

NOTTINGHAM ROAD

To M1(25)
Nottingham A52

EASTGATE

DARWIN PL.
P

RIVER DERWENT

Riverside
Council House Gardens

D'S WAY

Bus Station

DGE

THE COCK PITT
P

Market

STATION APPROACH

Eagle Centre

Playhouse

ST.

Main Centre

P

TRAFFIC

PARK STREET

P

P

P

P

BRADSHAW WAY

LONDON RD.

OSMASTON ROAD

Hospital

To Elvaston Castle
Loughborough
A6 & M1(24)

Railway Station

MIDLAND RD.

G.P.O.

# Nottinghamshire

In the days when Robin Hood roamed Sherwood Forest, most of Nottinghamshire was under woodland. Today, only a few scraps of forest remain.

One of the most interesting stretches is near the village of Edwinstowe, where Robin is reputed to have married Maid Marian.

The colourful history of the county, more dramatic even than legend would suggest, has as its focus Nottingham castle, standing high over the centre of the county town. The castle adds greatly to the character of a city which is already one of England's most pleasant regional capitals.

William the Conqueror built the first Nottingham castle, but the fortifications were destroyed several times before the 17th-century version was restored about a hundred years ago.

Nottingham's historical role as a trading centre is evidenced by the huge autumn market, the Goose Fair, which survives as England's biggest funfair.

The city's importance grew with the industrial revolution, when the first of Arkwright's spinning machinery was set to work in the lace industry.

In more recent times, pharmaceuticals, tobacco and the manufacture of bicycles established themselves as major industries. Nottingham-built Raleigh racing bikes are among the most famous in Europe.

The industrial image of Nottingham has been graphically portrayed by Alan Sillitoe, in *Saturday Night and Sunday Morning*, and coal-mining country nearby inspired the genius of D. H. Lawrence.

### Tourist Information Centres
18 Milton Street, Nottingham, Nottinghamshire. (0602) 40661
The Ossington, Beast Market Hill, Newark-on-Trent, Nottinghamshire. (Summer only)
The Palace, Appletongate, Newark-on-Trent, Nottinghamshire. (Winter) (0636) 71156

## Nottingham

The county town provides an excellent centre from which to explore. Within the city itself, the castle is now open to visitors as Nottingham's civic museum and art gallery.

Set into the rock on which the castle stands is one of Nottingham's several historically interesting pubs. The *Trip to Jerusalem* is one of several claimants to the distinction of being England's oldest pub. It is said to have been the assembly point for an advance party of the Second Crusade, in 1189.

The sign outside this pub promises, confusingly, 'Home-brewed ales'. In fact, Home is the name of one of the city's three brewery companies, the others being the firm of Hardy and Hanson, and Shipstone's, the latter producing a superbly well-hopped bitter. Nottingham's beers, like those from further up the Trent valley, have been celebrated since the 1600s.

Sport and the arts have a strong tradition in the city. Notts County are the oldest Football League club in England, and Nottingham Forest also have a distinguished place in the history of soccer.

Nottinghamshire County Cricket Club's ground at Trent Bridge is one of the six where international Test matches are played and holds 40,000 people.

The Nottingham Playhouse, which opened in 1963, is one of the most modern theatres in Europe and has developed a fine reputation for drama.

*Wollaton Hall* Standing three miles outside Nottingham centre, this house was built by Sir Francis Willoughby from 1580–88. It was occupied by his descendants until 1925 and is now Nottingham's Museum of Natural History. The spacious grounds include a deer park, a golf course and lake. Open daily, 10.00am to 7.00pm or dusk.

Civic splendour . . . the Council House

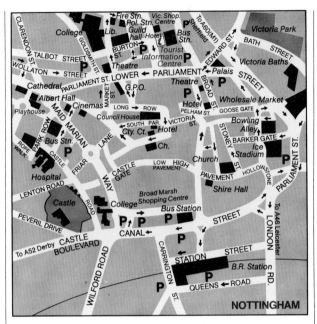

NOTTINGHAM

enhance the Chapter House columns.

Visitors should also see the 17th-century *Saracen's Head*, which is doubly distinctive. Not only is it the town's oldest inn, but it is also the place where Charles I gave himself up in 1646.

### Laxton

This village is an agricultural curiosity, for it is one of the few which still use the Middle Ages method of strip farming, in which the arable land is divided into three vast fields covering some 250 acres. One field is allowed to lie fallow each year, while the other two are split into strips among the farmers.

### Mansfield

Modern Mansfield is a heavily industrialized centre, ringed by collieries and hosiery and footwear factories.

Moves have been made to recover something of the old greenery, for the Sherwood Forest Golf Club is in a pine forest planted to disguise the coalmine slag heaps.

### Newstead Abbey

The Abbey was built for the Augustinians in 1170 as part of Henry II's reparations for the murder of Becket.

It became the home of the Byron family after the Dissolution in 1540 and they remained there until 1817. Lord Byron wrote 'Childe Harold' here.

The poet died in Greece, but his body was brought home to be buried at Hucknall Church, three miles away.

### Eastwood

This town is compulsory for all Lawrence lovers, as the great author was born here, at 8a Victoria Street, the fourth son of a coal miner.

It was in Eastwood that he set his early books, notably *Sons and Lovers*, regarded by many as his best work.

*Holme Pierrepont* Here is the National Water Sports Centre, five miles from the city. Opened in 1973, its extensive water areas include an international 2,000-metre course and separate lagoons for water-skiing and angling. These facilities are all set within a large country park with walks, picnic areas and a nature reserve.

Open daily, 8.45am to 9.30pm.
*Events* Nottingham Arts Festival, in June; Goose Fair, in October.

### Hawton

The village church has much of architectural interest, particularly the 15th-century tower and the 14th-century Easter sepulchre, which is thought to be one of the best in England.

### Newark-on-Trent

King John died in Newark Castle in 1219. The castle itself

was destroyed in the Civil War. After surviving three sieges, it fell to Cromwell's forces. However, the west wall is still there.

The town itself is no longer on the Trent, which now runs north of Newark. Instead, a canal section of the River Devon carries barge traffic. Newark has an attractive cobbled market place and two 14th-century inns which are certainly worth a visit.

### Southwell

The Minster, built between the 12th and 14th centuries, is the town's architectural pride. This superb Norman edifice has twin towers on its west face.

It is perhaps most famous for intricate stone carvings depicting different foliage such as maple, hawthorn, oak and vine. These carvings, known as the 'Leaves of Southwell' are by an unknown sculptor and they

# Lincolnshire

The triple towers of the Cathedral Church of St Mary dominate the city of Lincoln, and the countryside for miles around. Lincoln is by no means the biggest of cities, but in a county of small towns and villages, it is an unrivalled centre from which to explore.

The inland scenery of Lincoln is principally determined by two ranges of hills, running from north to south, almost the full length of this attractive county.

To the east are the Lincolnshire Wolds, an area of rolling chalk downs, broken by dry sheltered valleys.

Westward the land dips into the broad, flat acres of the Lincoln Clay Vale before rising again to a narrow finger of Jurassic limestone. This is known variously as Lincoln Edge, Lincoln Heath, or Lincoln Cliff.

In the south of the county are the Lincolnshire Fens, heart of the famous bulb-growing country. The most important towns here are Spalding and Boston.

## Stamford

An ancient town built of local yellow limestone. The Romans had a camp here, the Saxons developed it, and the Danes had the good taste to make it the capital of the Fens.

Later still the Normans built a castle, but today only traces of it remain. By the 12th century, Stamford had become an important wool centre and local cloth was much in demand all over Europe.

The ancient and attractive town makes an excellent centre on which to base exploration of the region.

## Bourne

The water in this market town is believed to be among the purest in England, and this would certainly account for the extensive watercress beds to be found here. Baron Burghley, who was Good Queen Bess's Lord High Treasurer, was born in the house which is now the *Burghley Arms Hotel*.

On a more up to date note, Bourne was also the home of BRM racing cars, which once dominated the Grand Prix scene.

## Spalding

This is the undoubted and colourful capital of Lincolnshire's bulb land. Predictably it was the Dutch who introduced the tulip some 65 years ago and the brick buildings ranged along either bank of the tidal River Welland show a strong Dutch influence.

Every year in late April and May, this quiet town is thronged as thousands of visitors tour the bulbfields.

Springfield Show Gardens hold a unique spring flower spectacular. More than 20 acres of gardens burst with over a million spring bulbs and flowers, and 30,000 trees and shrubs. During the summer 7,000 bush roses are on display.

There are also woodland walks, a lake and glasshouses.

The annual Flower Parade takes place in May.

Apart from the blooms, Spalding has much to offer the visitor and mixes old and new most agreeably.

*Ayscoughfree Hall,* which houses the Tourist Information Centre, is a restored 15th-century building, now the museum of ornithology, with exhibitions of wildlife. The hall is open Monday to Friday, while the gardens are open every day, 8.00am to sunset.

## Grantham

This one-time staging post on the Great North Road has, as might be expected, many picturesque inns. Among them is the Beehive which has the most appropriate inn sign – an actual hive of bees buzzing in the tree outside.

However, there are more reasons for visiting it than merely wishing to quench the thirst.

One of them is the 14th-century spire of *St Wulfram's Church* which looks down 281 feet on clusters of historic buildings. The church stands on the site of a Norman church and six pillars still remain.

Nearby is *Grantham House*, built in the 14th, enlarged in the 16th and extensively altered in the 18th century. Now owned by the National Trust.

Open April to September, Wednesday and Thursday, 2.00pm to 5.00pm.

## Lincoln

This beautiful city is graced by what many people regard as Britain's finest *cathedral*, a triple-towered architectural gem, built after an earthquake in 1185 wrecked an earlier church.

The third largest in the country, it stands on a limestone plateau in the middle of the city which was an important centre as long ago as Roman times. In 1068, William the Conqueror chose it as a site for a castle fortress and extensive remains can still be seen.

The cathedral, built between the 12th and 14th centuries stands 365 ft tall. It is built of the typical honey-coloured limestone of the region and appears to change its hue according to the light.

The general outline of the cathedral resembles that of Canterbury, but closer inspection reveals that it is very English in treatment. The best position from which to view the handsome west face is from the Observatory Tower of the *ruined castle*.

There are many Roman remains worthy of study, including the *Newport Arch* which is the old Roman settlement's north gate.

Steep cobbled streets lead down to the town and they are lined with medieval buildings, many of which are now antique shops.

In addition Lincoln boasts many Norman domestic buildings, such as the *Jew's House* and the *House of Aaron the Jew*. They were built around 1170 at a time when the Normans were trying to encourage the Jews to help finance trade.

The old racecourse was once the home of the *Lincolnshire Handicap*, the first big race of the flat racing season. It is now used only for the occasional point-to-point meeting.

The *Foosdyke Navigation Canal*, first created by the Romans, links the River Witham to the Trent. Its towpath offers a pleasant stroll up to the *Pyewipe Inn*.

Five miles south west is *Doddington Hall*, an Elizabethan manor house, containing collections of tapestries, china and furniture.

Further afield is *Tattershall Castle*, near Coningsby. It was built in the mid-15th century by the third Lord Cromwell, who was then Treasurer of England. The windows of the keep carry the coats of arms of previous owners. Open Monday to Saturday, 11.00am to 6.30pm, Sunday 1.00pm to 6.30pm.

### Skegness
A traditional English seaside resort, renowned for its good cheer and bracing 'sea breezes'.

The vast majority of its regular visitors come from the industrial heartlands of the Midlands.

Skegness is close to the Lincolnshire Wolds, which has been designated an area of outstanding natural beauty. Three miles south of the town is the *Gibraltar Point Nature Reserve*, on the tip of the east coast.

This is a field centre used by naturalists for the study of bird migration, and the ringing of migrant birds is all part of the work.

There is a visitor centre and hide, from which sand dunes, salt marshes and the seashore can be observed. Patient viewers may see kestrels and short-eared owls. Seals have been sighted on offshore sandbanks.

### Burgh le Marsh
A pre-Bronze Age axehead, one of only five discovered in Britain, was found in this village in the 1930's. The axehead is held by a local antiquary.

The village also has a *working windmill* and the giant sails dominate everything. A local school has renovated a mill outhouse and turned it into a windmill museum. Open daily.

### Alford
This town also has a five-sail windmill, but is less fortunate than Burgh le Marsh, for it does not now work.

This is perfect countryside for strollers, for there are pleasant lanes between the pretty villages of Ulceby, Skendleby and Claxby. Ulceby has an 18th-century manor house.

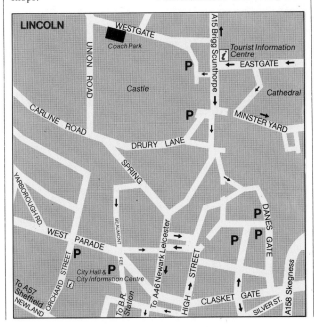

Mablethorpe . . . helter skelters, ferris wheels and sands

the natterjack toad, small and yellow-striped, which runs instead of the more usual hop.

Further along the coast, at Saltfleet Haven and right up to Donna Nook, the sea goes out so far at low tide that it can hardly be seen at all. Visitors should be careful of the mist which sweeps in from the sea.

### Cleethorpes
Only a century ago this was a tiny fishing village. Now it is a large resort town which attracts more than a million visitors each year during the short summer season. The wide sandy beach and safe bathing are typical of the Lincolnshire coast.

The promenade, in addition to being a good place to take the sea air, commands fascinating views of the big ships entering the Humber estuary.

Cleethorpes also has the largest open air swimming pool in Britain, a well-stocked zoo and a pier reaching 400 yards out to sea.

### Grimsby
The largest town on this stretch of coastline and one of the world's major fishing ports.

A fleet of 260 trawlers operate from the dock and they follow the shoals of fish inside the Arctic Circle for weeks at a time.

Apart from the bustle, noise and smells of the docks, Grimsby also has a restored 13th-century church.

### Thornton Abbey
The great castellated gatehouse to the ruined abbey stands north-west of Immingham and makes a strange contrast to the industrial and oil refinery skyline of Humberside.

It was built 600 years ago and has magnificent carved figures on the west front. The stone of the nearby farmhouses gives a clear indication of the use to which the abbey ruins were put after the Dissolution.

### Mablethorpe
Bungalows and huge caravan sites surround this quiet holiday centre. There are excellent sands and good, safe bathing extending all the way south to the twin town of Sutton on Sea, another favourite of caravanners.

### Louth
One of the most perfectly-preserved Georgian market towns imaginable, on the eastern edge of the Lincolnshire Wolds. Louth is well worth the drive in from the coast.

It has narrow winding streets, old houses, shops, and inns all in an attractive and interesting variety of Georgian and Victorian architecture.

The Perpendicular church of St James's has a 300-ft 16th-century spire and is a splendid example of late Gothic work.

For centuries Louth has been the busiest cattle market in the county, and this market is held on Fridays.

### Theddlethorpe St Helen
The grass-covered dunes here are a vital conservation area for

# South Yorkshire

With the Derbyshire Dales to the south, the Peak District to the west, the Pennines to the north, and rural Lincolnshire to the east, country delights surround the urban core of South Yorkshire. The southern part of Yorkshire has always had its own distinctive identity, with the Master Cutler city of Sheffield as its capital, and since the early 1970s it has been a county in its own right.

Among the big cities which have been redeveloped in the post-War period, Sheffield has achieved one of the most successful transformations. In contrast, some of the older urban landscape in South Yorkshire is worthy of attention from the viewpoint of industrial archaeology.

The metropolitan area of Sheffield includes one or two smaller towns, and there are two other important centres in the county.

One is Doncaster, well known to horse-racing and railway enthusiasts, but showing regrettably little for its Roman origins.

The other is Barnsley, always the heartland of Yorkshire chauvinism, and now the administrative centre.

**Tourist Information Centres**
Doncaster Central Library, Waterdale, Doncaster, South Yorkshire. (0302) 69123
Civic Information Office, Surrey Street, Sheffield, South Yorkshire. (0742) 734760

## Sheffield

The fourth city in England. Its prosperity has historically been based on steel, but has built up a thriving conference and tourist trade over the last few years. Sheffield is situated on a series of hills, and the Pennines are only a short distance away. The city boundaries encompass many square miles of Peak National Park which runs southwards to the Peak, itself only a few miles away.

It is this proximity to vast areas of outstanding beauty that makes Sheffield a natural centre for touring.

The area has been world-famous for its steel cutlery from the 16th century. This craftsmanship goes on today, while many examples of past achievements can be seen.

Since 1945 much of the city has been rebuilt, with a success far in advance of similar ventures elsewhere in England. Sheffield is justly proud of its superb new city heart and vast regional shopping centre.

It also has the Crucible theatre, one of the most modern playhouses in Britain, and some of Europe's largest nightclubs.

With 52 parks and recreation areas, the city can cater for almost any leisure pursuit. There is a round walk of 10 miles which takes visitors around the city's south and south-western suburbs, through parks, open spaces and shady woodland, offering magnificent views.

*Cathedral Church of St Peter and St Paul* The 12th-century foundation was replaced in the 15th century by the present Perpendicular-style building with its tower and crocketed spire.

*City Museum* An unmatched collection of cutlery from the 16th century to the present day is on display, along with the world's finest array of Old Sheffield Plate. There is also a general collection of natural history, geology, local archaeology and history.

Open weekdays, 10.00am to 5.00pm, Sunday 11.00am to 5.00pm.

*Bishop's House* A 15th-century timber-framed domestic building with additions dating from the 16th and 17th centuries.

Open weekdays 10.00am to 5.00pm, Sunday 11.00am to 5.00pm.

*Graves Art Gallery* English watercolours and European paintings are on show, including work by Murillo, Cézanne, Matisse, Ribera and Corot.

Open weekdays 10.00am to 5.00pm, Sunday 2.00pm to 5.00pm.

*Mappin Art Gallery* On display are British paintings of the 18th, 19th and 20th centuries, including Turner, Gainsborough, Constable and the pre-Raphaelites.

Open weekdays 10.00am to 5.00pm, Sunday 2.00pm to 5.00pm.

*Abbeydale Industrial Hamlet* Well worth a visit, it has an 18th-century scythe works with Huntsman's type crucible steel furnace, tilt-hammers, a grinding hull, a blowing machine, hand forges and workmen's cottages.

Open daily 10.00am to 5.00pm, with four special working days throughout the year.

*Shepherd Wheel* A Sheffield 'Little Mesters' water-powered grinding shop.

*Parks and woodland* Graves Park is the city's largest leisure space with 206 acres. It contains a nature trail, boating lake, two fishing lakes, bowling greens, tennis courts, a rose garden and a children's playground; Ladies Spring Wood, an excellent example of a natural Pennine oakwood; Ecclesall Woods, a bird sanctuary with oak, birch, holly, elm, and sweet chestnut trees and a bluebell wood; Whinfell Quarry Gardens have been created out of a disused quarry, with Whirlow Brook Park next door. This was landscaped in the 1920s and includes ponds, water gardens and rockeries; Botanical Gardens have Victorian, rock, woodland and heather gardens.

*Events* Lord Mayor's Parade, first Saturday in June; Annual Coal Board Brass Band Concert, in March; Christmas Illuminations, in December.

## Norton

Just south of Sheffield, this village is worth a call to see *The Oakes*, a Georgian House with old oak furniture, tapestries and a collection of dolls.

Open weekends and Bank Holidays 2.00pm to 6.00pm.

## Wortley Top Forge

Between Deepcar and Thurgoland, this is the only remaining ironworks of its kind in Britain still on its original site, with dams, sluices, hammers and waterwheels. Open Sunday 11.00am to 5.00pm.

## Maltby

The town is best-known for nearby *Roche Abbey*, a ruined 12th-century Cistercian building with the walls of the north and south transepts still standing to their full height. The extensive grounds were landscaped by Capability Brown.

Open weekdays 9.30am to 5.30pm, Sunday 2.00pm to 5.00pm.

## Tickhill

This little town stands just off the Great North Road. John of Gaunt was governor here when battles were fought around the castle, which is now private.

There is also the grandly-styled Perpendicular parish church of St Mary, which achieved its present eminence in the 14th century.

## Doncaster

This busy industrial town is of main interest to horse racing fans. Every autumn it becomes

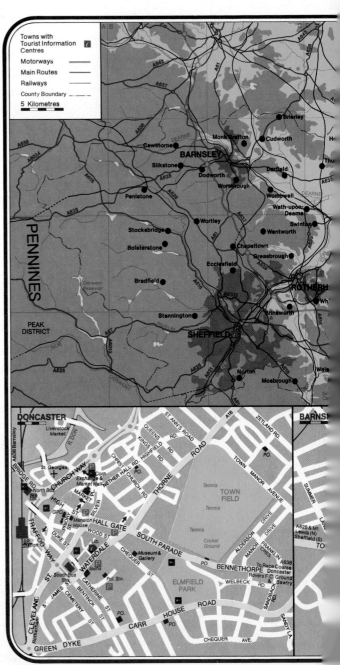

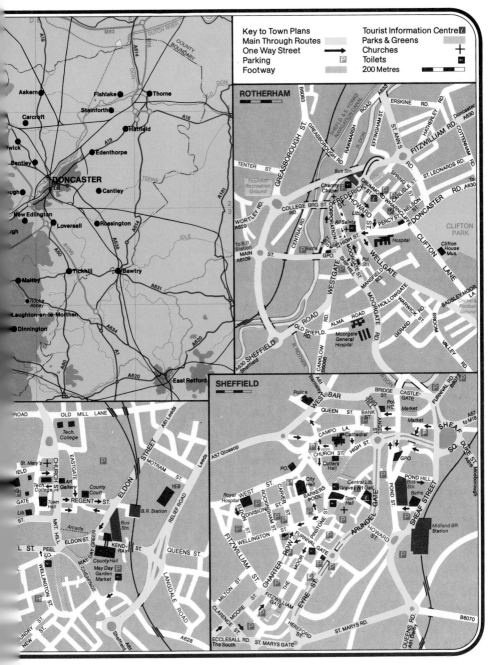

**Key to Town Plans**

- Main Through Routes
- One Way Street
- Parking **P**
- Footway
- Tourist Information Centre *i*
- Parks & Greens
- Churches
- Toilets
- 200 Metres

**ROTHERHAM**

**SHEFFIELD**

The Cornmill . . . Worsbrough near Barnsley

the mecca for followers of the Sport of Kings, for ever since 1776 the Town Moor race-course has been the home of the *St Leger*, the last great classic race of the season.

The course has a splendid 18th-century grandstand with Venetian windows, Tuscan columns and an Italianate tower.

## Barnsley (*map p 82*)

In his book *Goodbye to Yorkshire*, the Labour politician Roy Hattersley observes that, while in Sheffield the mores of Nottingham and the patois of Derbyshire 'clouded the clear stream of Yorkshire culture', Barnsley was 'heartland, not border country'.

The townspeople may tire of life under the sociologist's microscope, or in the comedian's script, but they are undaunted.

Surrounded by mining villages at the heart of the South Yorkshire coalfield, Barnsley still seeks to attract the visitor, offering him its own particular charms.

The superb local black pudding might be regarded with less levity by the Southern English if it were described as *blutwurst* or *boudin noir*, and it has won a few awards in Continental Europe.

The town's other gastronomic offering is the enormous Barnsley Chop, cut lengthwise across the saddle of lamb and roasted in the oven.

There are those celebrated townsfolk who argue that the Barnsley Chop is more truly a reference to a vicious kick popular with the town's once-famous soccer team.

Like many Northern industrial towns, Barnsley displays a keen interest in sport. Its soccer team may have seen more expansive times, but cricket remains a local obsession.

Another typically Northern theme is the open-air market. Barnsley's is open on Wednesday, Friday and Saturday.

It is a very large market, selling a wide variety of products, including local pork butchery, crockery bargains from Staffordshire, and wool textiles from Huddersfield. There is a small indoor market every day.

## Penistone

There is a barn at *Grunthwaite Hall*, north of the town, which has stood for 500 years. This immense half-timbered building is so big that it is said a young carpenter spent his seven-year apprenticeship making the wooden pegs that are still holding it together today.

## Wragby

A collection of 18th-century Swiss painted glass gives the tiny village church a charming glow. It stands in the grounds of *Nostell Priory*, a mansion built in the 18th century.

## Conisbrough Castle

Standing north-east of Rotherham, Conisbrough was the home of Athelstane in Sir Walter Scott's *Ivanhoe*. Its great white keep rises dramatically above the surrounding countryside. Open weekdays 9.30am to 5.00pm, Sunday 2.00pm to 5.30pm.

## Millstone Edge

This magnificent view over Derbyshire's Hope Valley is found just nine miles southwest of Sheffield. The viewpoint is called *The Surprise*.

## Rotherham (*map p 83*)

This industrial town, close to Sheffield, has several places of interest to the visitor.

It has three *markets* – the open market is held on Mondays, Fridays and Saturdays, and there is a daily covered market and a meat market.

*Clifton Park Museum* has a wide variety of exhibits, including collections of local geology, natural history, pottery, glass-making and of the discoveries from the Roman fort south-west of the town at Templeborough. There are also two period rooms – a late 18th-century parlour and a Victorian kitchen. Open weekdays, except Friday 10.00am to 6.00pm, Sunday 2.00pm to 4.00pm.

*Clifton Park* itself has a children's playground, nature trail, and extensive gardens and flower beds.

*Herringthorpe Leisure Centre* attracts many people from the surrounding areas and one of its facilities is a pool in a beach setting, with specially created waves. Open daily.

# West Yorkshire

The Wuthering Heights of Brontë Country are most easily reached by way of Bradford, a large city which is Yorkshire's wool-trade centre.

The Yorkshire Dales and the stately spa town of Harrogate are within the hinterland of Leeds, the county's main city and tailoring centre.

Yorkshire's other essay into gentility, the moorland resort of Ilkley, ironically celebrated in popular song, can be reached from either of these two adjoining cities.

The Pennine moorlands swoop down valleys lined with stone-built villages into two robust textile towns: Huddersfield (where fine worsted cloths are woven) and Halifax (where carpets are made). The cathedral city of Wakefield, West Yorkshire's administrative centre, completes a ring of main towns within which is contained the Heavy Woollen District.

In modern times, no region of England has produced as many novelists and playwrights, in generations which range from that of J. B. Priestley to that of David Storey. It is hardly surprising that the images of West Yorkshire are so graphically imprinted upon the popular imagination.

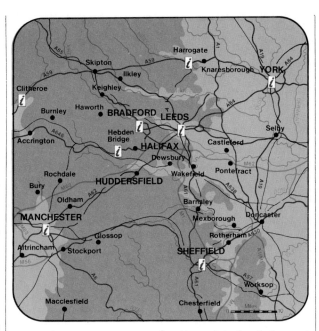

**Tourist Information Centres**
Central Library, Princes Way, Bradford, West Yorkshire. (0274) 33081
Mill Hey, Nr Keighley, Haworth, West Yorkshire. (0535) 42329
1 Bridge Gate, Hebden Bridge, West Yorkshire. (042 284) 3831
Central Library, Calverley Street, Leeds, West Yorkshire. (0532) 462453/4

## Haworth

The Brontës' famous parsonage sits on top of a steep hill. Also at the top is the *Black Bull Inn* where the unfortunate Branwell Brontë drank himself to death.

The parsonage, once the home of the Reverend Patrick Brontë and his gifted daughters, is now a museum.

Pilgrims to Haworth inevitably follow in the footsteps of Emily, Anne and Charlotte, by taking their favourite walk, a lonely two-mile route to the moors past Brontë Chair, a rock where they used to sit, and Brontë Waterfall.

It was to the waterfall that Charlotte came with her husband to mourn her sisters – and caught the cold which led to her death in 1855, less than a year after her marriage.

The Brontës are all buried at *Haworth Church*, with the exception of Anne who lies in St Mary's churchyard at Scarborough.

Haworth is also the home of the *Keighley and Worth Valley Railway Preservation Society*, which has an impressive collection of steam engines dating back to 1874.

Since 1968, the Society has operated the revived Worth Valley railway service, running the five trains between Keighley and Oxenhope.

The line was the setting for the film *The Railway Children*.

Open March 4 to October 29 weekends and Bank Holiday Mondays and Tuesdays, daily July and August, November 4 to February 26 weekends.

The Fleece pub in Main Street, known in its time to characters as dissimilar as Branwell Brontë and John Wesley, serves the superb, Keighley-brewed beers of Timothy Taylor.

## Hebden Bridge

Dramatically sited high in the Pennine moorlands, Hebden

Bridge is a particularly good example of the small Yorkshire mill town, with several interesting relics of the Calder Valley's industrial history.

In the town itself, there is a *pack-horse bridge* built in 1510, and a disused *canal aqueduct*. There are ruins of water-driven textile mills, in various states of preservation in the wooded country around the town. The best example is at *Hardcastle Crags*, and there are other ruins at Jumble Hole Clough, Colden Valley and Luddenden Dean.

Between Hebden Bridge and Hardcastle Crags is the village of *Heptonstall*, once a centre for hand-loom weaving. There are old weavers' cottages, a local museum, and the ruins of a 13th-century church. The local Wesleyan chapel, an octagonal building, dates from 1764. It is the oldest continually-used Methodist church in the world.

### Halifax

The folk museum of West Yorkshire is in Halifax, a hilly town built largely of millstone grit. The museum itself is in *Shibden Hall*, a 15th-century house equipped with 17th-century furniture.

Attached to the house is an 18th-century brewhouse, a dairy, and a barn with a collection of early agricultural implements and horse-drawn vehicles.

Shibden Hall is open from April to September, Monday to Saturday 11.00am to 7.00pm, Sundays 2.00pm to 5.00pm.

The pride of Halifax is the *Piece Hall market*. This colonnaded, three-storey building, dating from 1779, was originally the venue for the sale of 'pieces' by weavers in the local cottage industry. Now, it is the scene of an arts and crafts market.

The *market* is open on Tuesdays, Wednesdays, Fridays, Saturdays and some Sundays. Some stalls open only in the afternoons. An *open-air market* is held at the Piece Hall on Fridays and Saturdays, and a *museum* and *art gallery* there is open daily.

Just outside the town is a chimney-like folly, built in 1817, called the *Wainhouse Tower*.

Halifax has a Rugby League team and a League soccer team.

### Huddersfield

The Victorian pomp of this proud town is best represented by the Classical colonnades of its extraordinarily ambitious railway station, one of the most elaborate in provincial England.

The superb Victorian *Town Hall* also escaped a post-War epidemic of development. Like most buildings in the town, it is made from locally-quarried Yorkshire sandstone.

The Town Hall is the scene of three concerts a year by the *Huddersfield Choral Society*, but tickets are available only to subscribers. Music-lovers queue, sometimes through the night, for tickets to the Society's public performance of Handel's *Messiah* each Christmas.

A more accessible manifestation of the town's cultural interests is the festival of music and drama held in mid or late February each year at the Town Hall. This festival, which lasts for eight days, is named after its founder, a Mrs Sunderland.

Opposite the Town Hall, in considerable architectural contrast, is a fine 1930s *art gallery* and *library*. Outside the library, local ethnic groups (Black, Irish, Polish) sometimes present displays of music or dancing for summer Saturday shoppers.

Among the many famous brass bands which perform in or near the town is the *Brighouse and Rastrick*.

The town has two interesting parks. *Ravensknowle Park* has a small museum with Roman relics. The larger, Victorian *Greenhead Park* has a towering

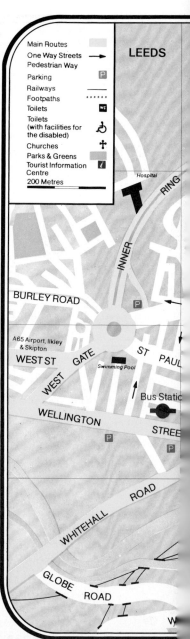

86

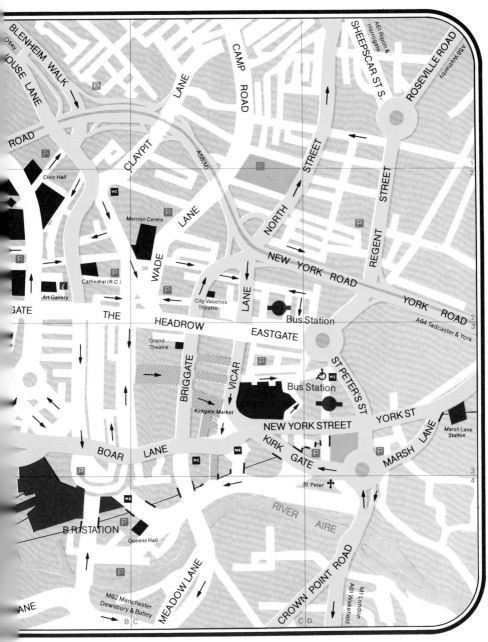

war memorial of 1920s design. A mock castle tower was built at the edge of the town to commemorate the jubilee of Queen Victoria.

The Rugby League was founded in Huddersfield, and the town also has a soccer team which can boast of great glories past. A large indoor sports centre includes covered bowling greens and swimming pools.

## Wakefield

Before the rise of Leeds and Bradford, this city was the county's clothing capital and its many Georgian houses echo that prosperous age.

The 13th-century *cathedral* has the tallest spire in Yorkshire at 247 ft and on the bridge over the Calder is one of only four medieval bridge chapels left in England.

This delicate structure dates back to the 14th century, but was heavily restored in the 19th.

## Pontefract

This town has a tragic and bloody history. In 1400 Richard II was murdered at the castle and later Roundheads and Royalists fought vicious and bitter battles around the walls.

Today the scene is more peaceful with well-kept flowerbeds around the ruins.

Open daily.

Those with a sweet tooth will know the town best for Pontefract cakes, round liquorice sweets which have been produced here since the 17th century, although the liquorice is no longer grown locally.

There is a racecourse on the north side of town.

## Leeds *(map p 86)*

The largest city in West Yorkshire, and one of the biggest in England, Leeds is a pleasant, cosmopolitan town.

There is an excellent *art gallery*, open daily except Sunday 10.00am to 6.00pm, and *Leeds*

*Art Library and Print Room* is open daily except Sunday 10.00am to 5.30pm.

Leeds is the home of the last remaining genuine music hall theatre in Britain, known as the *City Varieties*, and of one of the finest provincial theatres, the *Grand*.

Leeds has one of the best shopping centres in the North of England, with Victorian arcades in Briggate, and a famous indoor market.

For the drinking man, the city offers Brontë Liqueur, Tetley's Bitter, and a product called Black Beer which is unique in England. Black Beer is a malt extract, of minimal alcoholic content, which is allegedly derived from the brewing method used by Captain Cook when he landed in the Antipodes.

In fact, remarkably similar beers are produced in Brunswick, West Germany, and Bad Kostritz, East Germany. In Yorkshire, it is often drunk as a shandy with lemonade.

Every three years in September musicians come from all over the world to compete in the *International Pianoforte Competition*.

Headingley is the home of the *Yorkshire County Cricket Club*, and Leeds is the headquarters of Rugby League, and has three professional teams (Leeds, New Hunslet and Bramley). It also has one of Europe's most famous soccer teams.

There is a large, meandering public park at *Roundhay*, once a Royal hunting ground, with a large lake and Victorian follies.

Three miles north-west of the city centre is the 12th-century *Kirkstall Abbey* once inhabited by Cistercian monks, and now housing the folk museum.

Open weekdays 10.00am to 5.00pm, Sunday 2.00pm to 5.00pm.

*Temple Newsam House*, a mainly Jacobean building, enlarged in the 18th century, is

three miles east. It is now a museum, with grounds landscaped by Capability Brown, extending 935 acres. There are 40,000 rose trees in one corner.

## Bradford

A large, hilly, Victorian city on the edge of the moors, the birthplace of the Independent Labour Party and J. B. Priestley. Bradford has been excessively modernised, but retains its own distinctive character.

*The Bradford Industrial Museum* One of the most interesting museums in the area, this is housed in a four-storey spinning mill. The majority of the machines on display still work, and there is a gallery of old vehicles, including cars and tanks.

Open daily 10.00am to 5.00pm.

*Bolling Hall* Originally a 15th-century family home, it is now used to illustrate the domestic life of Western Yorkshire. It includes a collection of paintings, a display of 19th- and 20th-century toys, Chippendale furniture, a 'ghost room' and a display of local costume.

Open daily 10.00am to 5.00pm.

*Cartwright Memorial Hall*, Lister Park. This is now an art gallery, with a very comprehensive range of paintings, ranging from the works of Sir Joshua Reynolds to those of David Hockney, a son of Bradford.

Open daily 10.00am to 6.00pm.

*Tong Hall* Built in 1702, this Flemish brick building is the only one of the period to have been built in the area. Open weekends.

Bradford's three *markets* are very close together around John Street, and two are general while the third sells fish, meat and vegetables.

The *Richard Dunn Sports Centre* is on the edge of the city, at Odsal, and there is an open-air swimming pool in Lister Park.

# Yorkshire Dales

In the days when York was the capital of Northern England, monks went out from that city to find peace in the Dales, far from the world and its temptations.

The contemplative orders, the Augustine, Cistercian, Benedictine and Carthusian monks, built abbeys in the Dales, and several of their ruins rest still in celebrated peace.

The Yorkshire Dales, within which there is not a single town of any conspicuous size, spread themselves for more than 50 miles from north to south, and run almost as far from east to west.

The Dales are the valleys of rivers which run steeply down from the Pennine range through the wholly agricultural county of North Yorkshire, each of them gradually turning southwards to join the Ouse and then the Humber on the way to the sea.

In some places, the Dales have been scooped out of millstone grit, sandstone or greystone, but grey-white limestone is a particularly memorable visual theme.

## Tourist Information Centres
Royal Baths Assembly Rooms, Crescent Road, Harrogate, North Yorkshire. (0423) 65912
Town Hall, Ilkley, North Yorkshire. (0943) 2721
Market Place, Knaresborough, North Yorkshire.
Friary Gardens, Queens Road, Richmond, North Yorkshire. (Summer only) (0748) 3525
Swale House, Frenchgate, Richmond, North Yorkshire. (Winter only) (0748) 4221
Market Place, Ripon, North Yorkshire. (0765) 4625

### Harewood
*Harewood House*, the home of the Earl of Harewood, is open daily in the summer, and at weekends in the winter. The House and the village were designed by John Carr in the 18th century.

### Harrogate
The burghers of Harrogate eschew the term 'spa' for fear of seeming old-fangled, yet their town is one, in atmosphere as well as in fact. Perhaps they would prefer to describe it as a floral resort.

Spacious parks and gardens extend right into the centre of town, which is surrounded by 200 acres of grassland. This forms a horseshoe shape known as the *Stray*, and it is protected for all time against development by ancient charters.

The *Valley Gardens* lead to pathways through the pinewoods. The *Harlow Car Gardens* are the headquarters of the Northern Horticultural Society and are known internationally as a centre for experimental gardening.

Queen Mary was a regular visitor to the antique shops of Montpelier Parade, and they are still open for business. Sweet-toothed shoppers should not miss Harrogate toffee, or the town's distinctive rock.

There are many first-class hotels and other forms of accommodation near the town centre.

The famous Halle Orchestra gives weekly concerts during June, and the annual two-week *Harrogate Festival* is in August. This event attracts artists of international stature to the town's concert halls and theatres.

*Royal Pump Room Museum* In addition to the original sulphur well, there are collections of local historic and prehistoric material, and Victorian and Edwardian costumes.

Open weekdays 10.00am to

5.00pm, Sunday 2.00pm to 5.00pm, throughout the year, closed February.

*Tewit Well* The oldest medicinal spring in town, standing on the Stray. It has recently been restored.

*Events* Spring Flower Show, in April; Arts and Crafts Market, in May; Festival of Music, in June; Great Yorkshire Show, in July; Harrogate Festival, in August.

## Ilkley

The national anthem of Yorkshire is a song about a man who went courting on Ilkley Moor. Having neglected to wear a hat, he risked catching his death of cold, and causing the romance to end in tragedy.

This raucous lay does justice to the popularity of Ilkley's bracing moorland for Sunday afternoon walks, but it says little for the town's gentility as a Victorian spa and inland resort.

The town stands on the river Wharfe, and provides a useful base from which to visit *Bolton Abbey, Malham Cove,* and the attractive villages some miles further up this dale, like *Grassington* and *Kettlewell*.

In Ilkley itself, a 17th-century bridge over the Wharfe has been protected from traffic, and there is a church with interesting Saxon crosses.

The nearby moorlands offer fine views from the Iron Age or Bronze Age *'Swastika Stone'* or the *Cow and Calf Rocks*.

## Bolton Abbey

The 12th-century priory is now in ruins, but its nave has been repaired and lengthened and turned into the parish church.

The river Wharfe flows past the priory, and can be crossed half a mile north by stepping stones.

## Skipton

This bustling market town, high in the Dales, is a good base from which to explore.

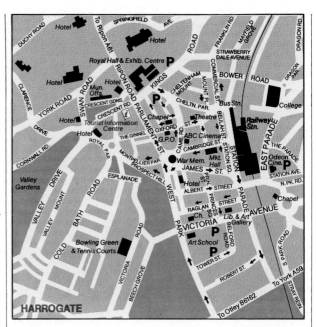

HARROGATE

*Clifford Castle* stands behind the partly 14th-century Holy Trinity church at the top of the High Street.

One gateway of the original Norman castle remains, the rest being mainly 14th- and 17th-century. Other features include the dungeons and a 'shell room' with walls decorated with seashells.

Open weekdays 10.00am to 7.00pm, Sundays 2.00pm to 7.00pm.

## Malham

One mile to the north of this village is the 240-ft limestone overhang of *Malham Cove*. Just over a mile to the east are the cliffs of *Gordale Scar*.

## Settle

A pleasant rural village amid Limestone Dales scenery.

The nearby *Victoria Cave* contains many Stone Age and Iron Age bones, of both animals and humans.

There is a 17th-century packhorse bridge at *Stainforth*, 2½ miles north, and there is a waterfall, underneath which the River Ribble cascades in waterfalls.

Like Skipton, it is set very high in the Dales, close to the Lancashire border.

## Ripon

This attractive market town is famous for its hornblower, the Wakeman, who still sounds his forest horn every night at nine.

Ripon's most interesting piece of secular architecture is the 13th-century *Wakeman's House* nearby, which is a timber-framed building housing a small museum. Open weekdays 10.00am to 6.00pm, Sundays 12.00pm to 4.00pm.

The *cathedral* dominates the town, and it was begun in the 12th century, on the site of an Anglo-Saxon church, the crypt of which still survives.

There is a cleanliness of line

and an economy of monuments in the cathedral which creates an illusion of space.

Only four miles south-west of Ripon is *Fountains Abbey*, a majestic ruin which may be the best-preserved in Britain.

It was founded in the 12th century by Cistercian monks, who with their canny and skilled trading in the wool market, made it one of the wealthiest in England. As a result of this prosperity, it was one of the first abbeys to be sold to Henry VIII in 1540.

The abbey ruins, which are floodlit at night, are best approached on foot, along the path leading nearly a mile through the grounds of Studley Park. Open Easter to October, daily 10.00am to 6.00pm.

*Newby Hall*, a few miles west of Ripon, was built in 1695 in the style of Sir Christopher Wren, but now of the original house only the centre block remains. There are extensive gardens. Open Easter to Whitsun Sunday and Bank Holidays. Whitsun to October Tuesdays, Wednesdays, Thursdays and Sundays.

### Bedale
A market has been held in the wide, cobbled main street since the 13th century. The town's 13th- and 14th-century church is one of the most imposing in the entire North Riding.

Three miles south is *Snape Castle*, a medieval and Tudor building partly ruined, which was the home of Catharine Parr, widow of Henry VIII.

### Knaresborough
Georgian houses line the narrow streets of this market town. Steep steps and alleys lead down to the river Nidd, curling around the sandstone cliff.

The ruins of the 14th-century castle crown the clifftop close to the market square. The ruins are open for inspection daily from Easter through to September.

On the opposite bank of the river paths lead through the beechwoods to the famous *Dropping Well* where drops of water turn objects hung there into stone.

There is even more to please students of the bizarre, for nearby is *Mother Shipton's Cave* where a legendary prophetess was reputedly born in July 1488.

Open daily 10.00am to 6.00pm.

She accurately predicted the development of aircraft, but it remains to be seen whether her assertion that the world will come to an end in 1981 is correct.

### Boroughbridge
This town is worth a pause to study a baffling legacy of early man. Standing a few hundred yards west of the town are three huge stone monoliths dating from 2000 to 1500 BC.

They are known as the Devil's Arrows, and the tallest is 30 ft high. No one has yet discovered why the stones were dragged 10 miles to their present site.

The remains of the Roman town of Isurium can be seen at Aldborough, a mile east of Boroughbridge.

### Northallerton
This medieval town is the administrative centre of North Yorkshire. *The Old Fleece*, a partly-medieval inn stands by the market cross. The church has a pinnacled 15th-century tower.

### Catterick
The Roman camp of Cateractonium was stationed here, and the town is still a military barracks. Catterick itself is a pleasant collection of greystone houses, and it even boasts a babbling brook and a pretty church.

### Richmond
The 11th-century castle overlooking the river Swale offers one of the most spectacular views of the whole region, across the dales through the Vale of York.

Richmond itself is one of the most pleasant towns in Yorkshire. The *market* takes place every Saturday in the market square, by Holy Trinity Church. The curfew is rung from here every night at nine.

Lovers of theatre and its history will be enchanted with the Georgian *Theatre Royal*, one of England's oldest surviving theatres. It was built in 1778, and although it was closed 60 years later, it was restored and re-opened in 1962.

Visitors to Richmond can also see the *Green Howards Regimental Museum*, open daily, 10.00am to 4.00pm.

Montpellier . . . a parade of antique shops at Harrogate

# York

With its city walls still intact, its magnificent Minster and its famous museums, York combines the role of ancient capital with that of market town.

In the heart of agricultural Yorkshire, it stood aloof when the Industrial Revolution was throwing up larger cities in other parts of the county. Chocolate, made by local Quakers, was industry enough for York.

However, mindful of its role as a Roman, Saxon and medieval capital, York made sure to remain at the crossroads when the Victorian railways were built. It still stands at the half-way mark on the London-Edinburgh line, has a magnificent station, and the National Railway Museum.

Yorkshire's three Ridings (from *thridings*, meaning thirds) meet at the walls of York. Yorkshiremen still prefer this 1,000-year-old division to the present arrangement of South Yorkshire, West Yorkshire, North Yorkshire and so on, and have been known to proclaim their preferences at the city walls on Yorkshire Day (August 1).

Whichever way Yorkshire is divided, each segment has its own county town, but also looks to York as the capital.

York's own immediate hinterland is defined by the valleys of the Ouse and the lower Derwent, with attractive market towns like Easingwold and Malton, and the abbey town of Selby.

**Tourist Information Centre**
De Grey Rooms, Exhibition Square, York, North Yorkshire. (0904) 21756

## York

York was fortified by the Romans, the Danes, and the Normans before becoming a wool centre in medieval times. The present-day walls are on Roman foundations, with medieval gates.

These four Bars, or gates, are Micklegate, Bootham, Monk and Walmgate Bars, and they still command the main streets. Any visit to York should include a walk along the three miles of walls that gird the ancient city and provide superb views.

York has been called the City of Churches, as there are 17 pre-Reformation churches within the city boundaries. However, there were 50 parish churches, two large abbeys and several other religious houses in the Middle Ages.

York is also one of Britain's most important horse racing centres and its racecourse holds meetings every month from May to October. The big race of the year is the *Ebor Handicap*, which attracts a top-class entry.

*Assembly Rooms* Built by public subscription in 1732 from designs by the Earl of Burlington, the Rooms were one of the most fashionable centres in Georgian England. Open June 1 to August 31 Monday to Friday 10.00am to 4.00pm.

*Castle Folk Museum* A series of period rooms and famous reconstructed streets, with cobbled streets and old-world shop fronts take visitors back to bygone days from Tudor to Edwardian times. There is a replica of a hansom cab, whose designer John Hansom was born in the city in 1803.

The museum also houses an 18th-century watermill and there are sections devoted to Yorkshire crafts, costume and military history. Open weekdays 9.30am to 4.30pm, Sundays 10.00am to 4.30pm.

*City Art Gallery* This is particu-

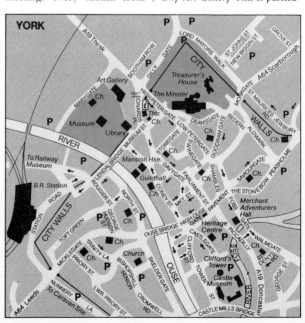

larly rich in Italian works, and there is an important collection of English and other European paintings, spanning 600 years. These include the famous Lycett Green Collection of European Old Masters. There are other collections of modern stoneware pottery, sculpture and engravings.

Open weekdays 10.00am to 5.00pm, Sundays 2.30pm to 5.00pm.

*Clifford's Tower* This unusual quatrefoil-shaped structure was built in the mid-13th century. The original Norman keep was destroyed by fire during the Jewish massacre of 1190.

Open weekdays 9.30am to 5.30pm, Sundays 2.30pm to 5.00pm.

*Guildhall* Built from 1447 to 1453 as the civic centre of York, the Guildhall was partly destroyed in an air raid in 1942. It has since been lovingly restored. The fine timbered roof and modern stained glass window is of particular interest.

Open May to September weekdays 9.00am to 5.00pm, Sundays 2.00pm to 5.00pm.

*Impressions Gallery of Photography* This unusual gallery is one of the few devoted entirely to photographic art.

Open Tuesday to Saturday 10.00am to 6.00pm, Sunday 2.00pm to 6.00pm July to August.

*Merchant Adventurers' Hall* One of the finest medieval guildhalls still standing in the city. It was built between 1357 and 1368.

*Merchant Taylors' Hall* The Hall was built in the second half of the 14th century and has a timbered roof. In the 17th and 18th centuries it was used as a theatre and plays were performed during Assize times.

*St William's College* Founded in 1461 to house the charity priests of the Minster, the college is now the home of York Convocation. It was here that Charles I set up his printing press in 1642.

*Treasurer's House* This building

The magnificent Mallard . . . National Railway Museum

*Crown Copyright, National Railway Museum*

stands on the site of the Roman Imperial barracks. The present House is mostly 17th-century, and it has a valuable collection of furniture and paintings.

Open Easter to October daily 10.30am to 6.00pm.

*York Minster* This Cathedral church of St Peter is the crowning glory of York. It has one of the greatest concentrations of medieval stained glass in Europe, and two of the most famous windows are the 'Five Sisters' in the north transept and the Great East Window, covering 2,000 square ft.

It is thought to be the largest area of medieval coloured glass in the world, and the panels tell the Bible story from the Creation to the Apocalypse.

The Minster is the fifth building to stand on the site, and it took 250 years to build, being completed and consecrated in 1472. It has recently been restored, at a cost of around £2,000,000.

*York Minster Undercroft* An unexpected and unique spin-off from the Minster's enormous restoration. It exposes to view the 20th-century engineering that has saved the magnificent edifice and reveals the sections of earlier cathedrals, together with the Saxon burial ground

and Roman legion headquarters once on the same site.

Open Monday to Saturday 10.00am to one hour before dusk.

*Yorkshire Museum* The museum is set in the grounds of St Mary's Abbey and is noted for collections of Roman antiques and medieval implements, in addition to sculpture, ceramics and natural history.

Open weekdays 10.00am to 5.00pm, Sunday 1.00pm to 5.00pm.

*National Railway Museum* This museum has a collection of historic locomotives, railway exhibits and relics from all over the country. The central display point is the Great Hall with its two turntables around which are grouped some 25 locomotives and 20 items of rolling stock. Visitors are not allowed to climb aboard the exhibits.

Open weekdays 10.00am to 6.00pm, Sunday 2.30pm to 6.00pm.

*York Story* This former 15th-century church of St Mary's, Castlegate, was restored as part of York's contribution to European Heritage Year.

It now houses an exhibition featuring colourful models of historic buildings with recorded conversations of the past and a

lively slide presentation.
Centuries of York are gathered here under one roof.

Open weekdays 10.00am to 5.00pm, Sunday 1.00pm to 5.00pm.

*Brass Rubbing* A wide selection of exact replicas moulded from original medieval brasses are displayed at two locations within the city walls. A charge, varying according to size, is made, but this includes all materials. Open weekdays 10.00am to 5.00pm, Sunday 12.30pm to 5.00pm.

*Archaeology* The York Archaeological Trust was established in 1972 to carry out excavations on city sites. The Trust is at work throughout the year and visitors are welcome to the sites. Details are available from the Tourist Information Centre.

*Arts Centre* Activities include experimental theatre, film shows, recitals, children's theatre and folk music.

*Boat Trips* Cruises along the Ouse start from points in the city centre. Most boats are equipped with public address systems and commentaries are given on the sights, including the 13th-century palace home of the Archbishop of York.

The boats operate from mid-March to September.

*Sport* In addition to the famous racecourse, there are excellent facilities for golf, fishing, hunting, riding, motor sport, swimming, rowing, gliding, cycling, tennis and bowls. Spectators can choose from Rugby League, cricket and soccer.

### Easingwold
This little market town still has some cobbled streets, and was built in red brick. The church was rebuilt in the 15th century.

Three miles to the east is *Crayke*, a straggly hilltop village with a church and a 15th-century castle.

From the top of the hill there is a marvellous view across the vale to York Minster.

### Selby
Dominating the main street of this old inland port is *Selby Abbey*, founded in the 11th century. It was restored after the central tower collapsed in 1690 and a fire broke out in 1906. It has a Norman doorway and some lovely 14th-century stained glass windows.

An 18th-century wooden tollbridge is still used by cars crossing the Ouse.

### Malton
There was a Roman camp here and it has been an important market town almost ever since. The market is held every Friday and Saturday.

*Castle Howard*, less than five miles south-west, is one of the finest houses in England. It was designed by Sir John Vanbrugh for the 3rd Earl of Carlisle.

Built between 1699 and 1726, it has an immense façade in a superb park, and can be seen for many miles around.

Open Easter to October daily, 1.00pm to 5.00pm.

There is a caravan and camping site here making it a good base for touring.

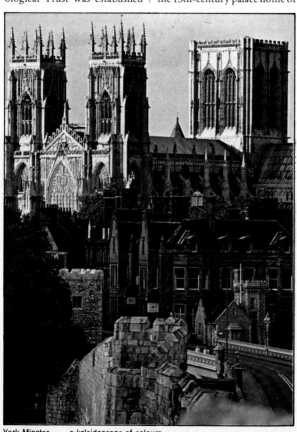

York Minster . . . a kaleidoscope of colours

# Humberside

Though the broad estuary of the river is one of Yorkshire's natural boundaries, the banks of the Humber have now been embraced into a county of their own. Thus, confusingly, an area which is popularly regarded as the eastern part of Yorkshire is officially known as the northern part of Humberside.

Within this area are the Yorkshire Wolds, a group of undulating chalk hills with some pleasant market towns; the flat Holderness peninsula, curling into a nature reserve at Spurn Head; the medieval Minster town of Beverley; and just one sizable city, the port of Hull.

A paddle-steamer crosses the Humber from Hull to New Holland, though its future must be in some doubt with the building of the world's largest single-span bridge a few miles up river at Brough.

## Hull

Kingston upon Hull is the city's official name, bestowed on it by Edward I in 1293. Its trade, particularly in wool, grew and flourished and eventually this meeting place between the rivers Hull and Humber became the third seaport in Britain.

The *Docks Museum* has interesting exhibits relating to all aspects of sea fishing and shipping and is open weekdays 10.00am to 5.00pm, Sunday 2.30pm to 4.30pm.

Hull also has *Wilberforce House*, the birthplace of the anti-slavery campaigner William Wilberforce. This Elizabethan mansion is open weekdays 10.00am to 5.00pm, Sunday 2.30pm to 4.30pm.

The city has two Rugby teams, Hull and Hull Kingston Rovers, and a professional soccer team.

## Spurn Head

This is a 3½-mile sliver of land curving in a hook shape into the Humber's mouth. In places it is only a few yards wide, but each year the silt carried down the river lengthens it by a yard. It is owned by the Yorkshire Naturalists' Trust and is a refuge for migrating birds.

Waders and terns can all be found here and visitors can drive their cars as far as the lighthouse. They must then attack the last half-mile on foot.

## Hedon

The 12th-century church is known as King of Holderness and boasts one of the finest towers in Yorkshire.

## Sproatley

This is a straggling village in the very heart of Holderness. A mile away is *Burton Constable Hall*, with its collections of furniture and paintings, and dolls museum. The house and grounds were landscaped by Capability Brown.

Open daily, Easter to September.

## Tourist Information Centres

The Hall, Lairgate, Beverley, Humberside. (0482) 882255
The Floral Hall, Hornsea, Humberside. (040 12) 2919
Central Library, Albion Street, Hull, Humberside. (0482) 223344
Corporation Road, King George Dock, Hedon Road, Hull, Humberside. (0482) 702118

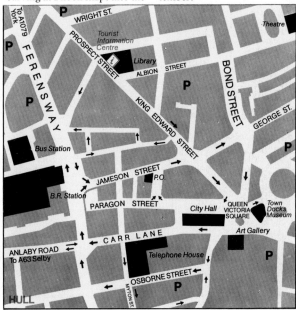

Humberside . . . the call of the sea

## Patrington
The village church has the proportions of a small cathedral and is known as the Queen of Holderness. It dates from the 14th century and its spire can be seen for miles.

## Hornsea
A popular holiday town which, like most of the east coast, can boast a fine sandy beach. Behind this pleasure area lies the old village with its interesting houses and narrow lanes.

One of these leads to Hornsea Mere, the largest freshwater lake in Yorkshire. The Mere is the sole survivor of the many lakes formed in Holderness by the melting glaciers at the end of the Ice Age.

The Hornsea end has boating facilities, but at the western end a nature reserve guards the undergrowth and its plentiful wildlife.

## Great Driffield,
A typical Yorkshire market town, known as the capital of the Wolds.

Little Driffield, which is nearby, is the burial place of Alchfred, a King of Northumbria, who died here in 705.

## Burton Agnes
This is thought by many to be the prettiest village in the Wolds. Certainly the grouping together of vicarage, church and hall make a most pleasing sight.

Beside the church stands the Elizabethan *Burton Agnes Hall*, with its beautiful red-brick chimneys. Inside is a fine collection of Impressionist paintings.

Open May 1 to October 15 daily except Saturday 1.45pm to 5.00pm.

Five miles to the west are the *Dane's Graves*, where traces of a large Iron Age burial ground can be seen.

## Sledmere
This is the seat of the Sykes family, who began to tame the wasteland of the Wolds 200 years ago. *Sledmere House* was rebuilt after it burned down in 1911.

Open May 16 to October 15 daily except Monday or Friday 1.30pm to 5.30pm.

It is not possible to go far in these parts without encountering a monument to one of the Sykes clan. The most impressive is two miles from the village at Garton Hill – a single spire rising from the fields to honour the memory of Sir Tatton Sykes, the 19th-century farmer and pugilist.

## Kirkham Priory
A 12th-century Augustinian foundation, it nestles beside the river Derwent between the Wolds and the Howardian Hills. All that remains is a peaceful ruin in a wooded valley.

Open weekdays 9.30am to 5.30pm, Sunday 2.00pm to 5.30pm.

## Beverley
This is one of the most gracious towns in all of England, with interesting architecture.

This small town has the 14th-century St Mary's Church at one end of the main street and the twin-towered Gothic Minster from the 13th century at the other. Few other places can be so architecturally blessed.

Between these are narrow streets and market squares, graced by houses built during the prosperous heyday of the wool trade.

The 15th-century red-brick North Bar is the sole survivor of five medieval gates.

## Goodmanham
One of the earliest Christian sites in Britain, its Norman church was built on the grounds of the pagan temple of Coifi, the high priest.

He was converted to Christianity in AD 627 by the efforts of Paulinus and Edwin, the Northumbrian King. This event is depicted in a stained glass window in the present church.

# North York Moors

The moors of North Yorkshire are wild and beautiful, coated in heather, and forming a dramatic National Park.

They are bordered in the south by the pleasant Vale of Pickering and in the north by the Cleveland Hills from which the river Esk runs to the sea at Whitby.

Man has been here since the Bronze and Iron Ages, and evidence of his early beginnings can still be seen. The Cleveland Road, running along the western rim of the moor, was a prehistoric highway.

Walkers of today can follow virtually the same route by taking part of the Cleveland Way, a trail extending some 100 miles.

There is also a Roman road to follow through Wheeldale Moor, but the most forbidding and desolate trail is the Lyke Wake Walk, across the heart of the moors where it is easy to believe that no man has ever set foot before.

But the moors are not entirely inhospitable. Two superb waterfalls can be seen – Falling Foss, at the hamlet of Littlebeck, and at Mallyan Spout, near Goathland.

The marriage of the North Yorkshire moorland with the sea is one of the surprises of the area, for this spectacular countryside culminates in an equally impressive coastline.

Boulby and Ravenscar, the highest cliffs in England, are just a small part of a coast that extends down through such villages as Staithes and Robin Hood's Bay, to the major resorts of Whitby, Scarborough, Filey and Bridlington.

### Tourist Information Centres

Garrison Street, Bridlington, Humberside. (Summer only) (0262) 73474/79626

The Spa, Bridlington, Humberside. (Winter only) (0262) 78255/6/7

John Street, Filey, North Yorkshire. (0723) 512204

Chapel Beck Gallery, 10/12 Fountain Street, Guisborough, Cleveland. (028 73) 35240

North York Moors Railway, The Station, Pickering, Yorkshire. (0751) 72508

St Nicholas Cliff, Scarborough, North Yorkshire. (0723) 72261

New Quay Road, Whitby, North Yorkshire. (0947) 2674

### Pickering

An attractive town south of the moors, it has a ruined 12th-century *castle* and a church with some 15th-century frescoes.

The castle is open weekdays 9.30am to 5.30pm, Sunday 2.00pm to 4.00pm.

The *North Yorkshire Moor steam railway* runs 18 miles along a scenic moorland route from Grosmont to Pickering, through the beautiful Newton Dale. The service operates every day from mid-June to September and is closed on Mondays and Fridays from Easter to mid-June and from mid-September to mid-October.

Two miles east of Pickering is another rural treat, the village of *Thornton Dale* which slopes down to a roadside stream of clear water. Just outside the village are the forests leading to the upper Derwent valley.

### Hemsley

This is an ideal centre for a short or long exploration of the surrounding countryside. An attractive town, it sits beneath the moorland's southern rim, and has a market every Friday.

The 12th-century ruined *castle* is believed to have been built by Walter l'Espec, the founder of *Rievaulx Abbey*. The *Cleveland Way* begins at the castle and leads directly to the abbey. The castle is open weekdays 9.30am to 5.30pm, Sundays 2.00pm to 4.00pm.

Rievaulx is pronounced 'Reevo' and is taken from Rye Vallis, the valley of the river Rye.

The abbey was founded in 1131 and was the first Cistercian house in the north of England. It is certainly one of the finest monastic ruins to be found.

### Hutton-le-Hole

This village is a showpiece, ringed by moors and standing at the meeting place of two becks.

The *Ryedale Folk Museum* houses a fascinating collection

Now a shell . . . Whitby Abbey

97

of exhibits illustrating the way of life of ordinary folk from prehistoric to Victorian times.

There are unique reconstructions, including an Elizabethan glass furnace, a medieval longhouse and an Elizabethan manor house. Open daily, from Easter to October 2.00pm to 5.30pm, July and August 11.00am to 5.30pm.

## Rosedale Abbey
This is the principal village in Rosedale which runs for seven miles. The inscription above the church porch reads *omnia vanitas* – all is vanity – and it would be easy to understand if the inhabitants of this charming spot were to be vain about it.

In the churchyard visitors can find some stones of the 12th-century Cistercian nunnery, from which the village derives its name.

## Osmotherley
The starting place of the formidable *Lyke Wake Walk*, named after an ancient Cleveland song about a dead man's soul passing over Whinny Moor.

Anyone wishing to qualify for membership of the Lyke Wake Walk club, which meets at Osmotherley, must make the 40-mile journey through heather, bracken and bog to Ravenscar within 24 hours.

## Great Ayton
Captain James Cook, the discoverer of Australia, went to school in this pretty village.

The school now houses a Cook *museum*, open daily 10.00am to 6.30pm.

The cottage where he lived is now thousands of miles away, having been shipped stone by stone to Australia.

In its place is an obelisk made from rocks imported from Point Hicks, the first part of Australia sighted by Cook on his voyage of discovery from 1768 to 1771.

Whitby . . . an historic harbour

## Guisborough
There is a craggy ruin of a 12th-century priory near the grounds of Guisborough Hall, with its moorland views.

## Staithes
This is an ancient fishing village with a picturesque harbour and cliffs plunging into the waves.

Cook worked here as a grocer's apprentice before the call of the sea lured him away.

The shop has long been washed away, but the cottage where he lived still stands.

Two miles west at the end of Cowbar Lane is *Boulby Cliff* – which at 700 ft, is the highest perpendicular cliff in England.

## Runswick
At the end of a wide sandy bay is this interesting village. The remains of a Roman lighthouse can be seen at *Kettle Ness*.

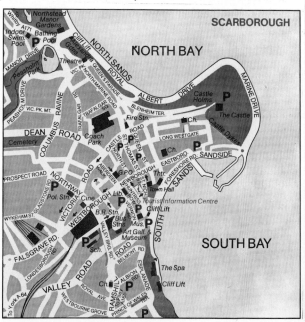

## Whitby

This historic fishing port straddles the mouth of the river Esk, Yorkshire's only salmon river.

On the headland above the river are the ruins of *Whitby Abbey*, built in the 13th century. Not all the damage is due to old age, for the Germans shelled part of it in 1914.

The first Abbey was founded by St Hilda in the 7th century on land given by King Oswy of Northumbria. It was the home of Caedmon, the first English Christian poet and a monument to him stands in St Mary's churchyard.

It was from Whitby in 1768 that Captain Cook left on his journey to Tahiti via Cape Horn. His ship *Endeavour* was built at Whitby Harbour, where there is now a modern yard building fishing boats and pleasure craft.

Cook lived in a house in Grape Lane, and a plaque on the wall marks the spot.

From a Viking settlement . . . to a seaside town

## Robin Hood's Bay

This charming village was once the haunt of smugglers and is now equally popular with artists, for the coastal views are unequalled.

An attractive jumble of cobbled yards, footworn steps and spray-soaked houses seem to cling precariously to the cliff as they tumble down to the shore. The sea has already claimed many houses and others are likely to follow.

A *Roman lighthouse* once stood on the southern headland at Ravenscar. The site is now occupied by a hotel that does not need to boast about its sea view.

## Scarborough

This brash and breezy seaside town is almost all things to all holidaymakers. It is at the same time a fishing village, a spa and an historic site.

There are two bays, separated by the headland on which stands the 12th-century ruins of *Scarborough Castle*. Open weekdays 9.30am to 5.30pm, Sunday 2.00pm to 5.00pm.

Colourwash houses tumble down to the old harbour where drifters, trawlers and pleasure boats nose in and out alongside the covered fish market.

There has been a town here for more than 1,000 years. It has grown from a Viking settlement to a North Sea port and later from a fashionable spa into the bustling playground of the north-east that it is today.

*Wood End Museum* The former home of the Sitwell family, it has collections of natural history, in addition to a conservatory and aquarium.

Open weekdays 10.00am to 1.00pm, 2.00pm to 5.00pm, Sunday 2.00pm to 5.00pm, closed Sundays in winter.

*St Mary's Church* Anne Brontë is buried in the adjoining yard of this 12th-century church.

## Filey

Thunderous breakers smash on to the rocky ridge of *Filey Brigg*. The sands of *Filey Bay* are much more peaceful, sweeping round towards *Flamborough Head*.

The town, which also has a major holiday camp, is still a pleasant mixture of an old fishing town and a modern resort.

## Bridlington

The old town is a mile inland from the beaches and amusements and is well worth exploring.

It has a priory church, founded during the reign of Henry I, and the massive *Bayle Gate*, once part of the priory building, now houses a museum. Open April to October, Thursday 2.00pm to 4.00pm.

The Georgian mansion, Sewerby Hall, stands north-east of the town. Its park and zoo is open daily 9.00am to dusk.

# Teesdale

The Tees is born high on fells which rise to more than 2,000 feet.

At Cauldron Snout the waters tumble through eight cataracts, descending some 200 feet. Downstream at High Force, the waters drop over falls protected by steeply wooded banks. For all the craggy language, its villages are tranquil, as evidenced by Middleton in Teesdale, Ronaldkirk, and Cotherstone, where a local cheese is made.

Still in the heart of moorland country, the market town of Barnard Castle provides an excellent base for exploration.

For a good dozen miles more, the river passes through countryside, forming the border between Yorkshire and County Durham.

Only when it has entered the new county of Cleveland does the Tees meet its own cluster of industrial towns – Darlington and Stockton, of railway fame, and Middlesbrough, a large industrial centre of 20th-century origins.

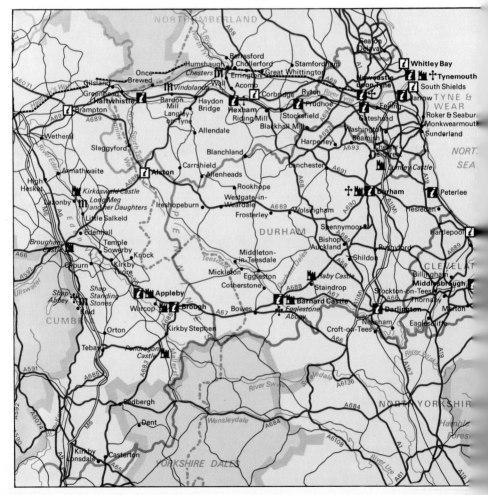

### Redcar

This is a pleasant resort with wide sandy beaches.

The town's shipping and fishing museum, *Zetland Museum*, vividly illustrates the close association with the sea.

Open Monday to Saturday, 10.00am to 5.30pm.

### Saltburn

Saltburn was founded in 1862 and has interesting period quality. It was originally a dry town although there are now plenty of pubs.

The pier was severely damaged by bad weather and only half of it remains. There is a cliff funicular railway to carry people up and down the 300-ft Huntcliff.

A miniature railway runs through the gorge.

### Middlesbrough

A major port for the Durham coalfield. It is a useful centre from which to explore the pretty hill country nearby.

Students of the life of Captain James Cook should visit Middlesbrough's *Central Library* which has the largest biographical collection relating to this great explorer.

Open Monday to Friday, 10.00am to 7.00pm, Saturday 10.00am to 4.00pm.

*Municipal Art Gallery* Temporary exhibitions and a small permanent collection of paintings. Open weekdays.

The famous *Transporter* bridge links Middlesbrough and Stockton across the River Tees. The bridge itself moves and can carry up to twelve vehicles or 600 people at a time.

It was built in 1911 and designed by the Cleveland Bridge Company. It has a total span of 850 ft and stretches 570 ft across the water between the tower centres.

The overall height of the bridge is 225 ft and 2,600 tons of steel were used in its construction.

Middlesbrough's League soccer team plays at Ayresome Park, which has also been the scene of the Newport Jazz Festival's British performances.

Just outside the town at Coulby Newham is *Newham Grange Leisure Farm* featuring many rare breeds of farm animals, an interpretive and audio-visual display, an agricultural museum and a nature trail.

Open daily 10.00am to 6.00pm or dusk.

South of the town stands gracious *Ormesby Hall*. The Manor of Ormesby was purchased in 1600 from Ralph Rokeby by James Pennyman.

It was the new owner who commissioned the impressive low quadrangular building that survives today. The features of the original Jacobean house have been lost in its conversion into the kitchen wing of the Georgian Hall.

One remarkable door remains, on which can be seen a magnificently carved family crest. Open May to September, Wednesday and Sunday, 2.00pm to 6.00pm.

### Darlington

This was the birthplace of the railway. Indeed the town's North Road Station is now a museum dedicated to the memory of steam pioneer George Stephenson and the Stockton and Darlington and North Eastern Railway.

Stephenson's early steam engine Locomotion stands on the main platform. There are

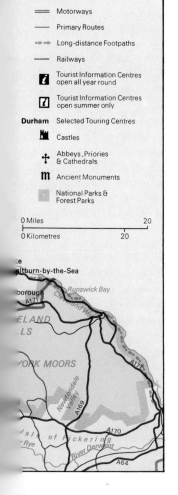

Motorways

Primary Routes

Long-distance Footpaths

Railways

Tourist Information Centres open all year round

Tourist Information Centres open summer only

**Durham** Selected Touring Centres

Castles

Abbeys, Priories & Cathedrals

Ancient Monuments

National Parks & Forest Parks

0 Miles                    20

0 Kilometres              20

The Tees . . . flowing past Barnard Castle

many other locomotives, including the Derwent.

Open Easter to September weekdays 10.00am to 5.00pm, Sunday 2.00pm to 5.00pm. Telephone (0325) 60532 to arrange winter visits.

Visitors venturing outside the station should seek out *St Cuthbert's Church*, which is an outstanding example of Early English architecture.

Only five miles north-west is *Heighington*, the village that perches on a 450-ft high escarpment.

## Stockton

This town has the broadest High Street in England and every Wednesday and Saturday an open-air market is held there.

*The Church of St Thomas* was designed with the help of Sir Christopher Wren and completed in 1712.

At Eaglescliff, *Preston Hall Museum* in Preston Park has collections of armoury, pottery, toys and some period rooms.

Open Easter to September weekdays, 10.30am to 6.00pm, Sunday 1.00pm to 6.00pm. October to Easter 10.30am to 6.00pm, Sunday 2.00pm to 6.00pm.

## Barnard Castle

This attractive market town is a useful base for touring Teesdale and the upper dales of west Durham.

The castle itself is now a ruin,

but in its great days stood guard over a crossing point on the River Tees. It was founded in the 13th century by the Baliol family, who later became better known as the founders of Baliol College, Oxford.

In 1630, the castle was despoiled by Henry Vane to provide materials for his own castle at Raby.

The town boasts one of the finest museums in Britain, *Bowes Museum*, housed in an impressive French Chateau-style building.

It was begun in 1869 to house the collections formed by John Bowes, son of the 10th Earl of Strathmore, and those of his French wife Josephine.

The museum has 40 rooms and galleries. The original collections were European, but the acquisitions of the last 100 years have been mainly British.

Among the European treasures are works by El Greco, Goya and Canaletto. Also on view are collections of English and French furniture, porcelain, tapestries, embroideries, regional archaeology and folk life, and there is a children's gallery.

Open daily, 10.00am to 5.00pm.

The nearby village of Bowes has the ruins of a 12th-century keep.

## Staindrop

The battlements of *Raby Castle* and its surrounding ancient deer

park are on the outskirts of this village.

The castle which had a hall where 700 knights could meet, is mainly 14th-century, with additions in the 18th and 19th centuries.

Open Easter to September daily except Friday.

Staindrop itself has a long rectangular village green, a feature of many mid-Durham villages.

## Middleton in Teesdale

This pleasant town sits on the hillside above the Tees, and is ideal as a centre for exploration of the *High Force* and *Cauldron Snout* waterfalls and the Durham moors beyond.

High Force is one of the most celebrated places in Teesdale. A stroll through rich pine and beech woods leads to this 70-ft fall waterfall over steep cliffs.

It is known to freeze solid in a hard winter and is seen at its full beauty after rain.

The mighty Cauldron Snout, four miles to the west, is England's highest waterfall. The water here crashes 200 ft down a rocky staircase. It can only be reached after a 2½-mile drive to Langdon Beck, and then a walk of another mile.

On the way is *Cow Green Reservoir* nature trail which has some rare alpine plants.

Pony trekking expeditions and tuition for beginners are catered for in Middleton.

## Hamsterley Forest

There are 5,000 acres of Forestry Commission land open here for motoring and walking. Routes have been laid out, along with car parks, camping sites and picnic spots in the fields by Bedburn Beck.

This beautiful forest is rich in spruce, pine, larch and hemlock trees. However, it does have a practical use, for the wood is marketed for paper, chipboard, fencing and, inevitably in a mining county, pit props.

# County Durham

Set high on a rocky hill, entwined by the placid River Wear, with its magnificent Norman cathedral, its castle and its university, Durham is one of the most attractive cities in England.

Its qualities are less widely known than those of cities like Bath, Chester or York, and it is therefore marginally less overcrowded than they are, even in summer.

Durham is an ancient county town, but it is suffixed by no shire. Since it was once a County Palatinate, a prefix is preferred. The style sounds Irish, but County Durham it remains.

For all its historical and scenic interest, the city is perhaps better known as the scene of the celebrated Miners' Gala, held in July. This day of parades, bands, beer-drinking, and speeches by Labour Party leaders, is one of the most important events in the socialist calendar.

The city of Durham has no coal mines. County Durham has many, but they are concentrated in the east. To the west lies some of the most rugged moorland scenery in the Pennines.

## Tourist Information Centres
13 Claypath, Durham, County Durham. (0385) 3720
Central Library, Prince Consort Road, Gateshead, Tyne and Wear. (0632) 773478
Jarrow Hall, Church Bank, Jarrow, Tyne and Wear. (0632) 892106

## Bishop Auckland
This has been the country seat of the bishops of Durham since the 12th century. The town grew outside the gates of the castle, still the official residence of the bishop.

The village of Escomb, a mile away, has the oldest intact Saxon church in England.

## Durham
For many a traveller, the city of Durham has been seen but not visited. From the main London – Edinburgh railway line, it appears like a faintly Gothic backdrop. Many trains even have the manners to stop in the station for a moment before hurrying on to Newcastle and points north.

The traveller's entrance from the M1 is less spectacular, but equally easy, and a short drive through the outer districts leads to the heart of the city.

*Durham Cathedral* Considered by its admirers to be the finest Norman building in Europe. It was reputedly founded as a shrine for St Cuthbert when the monks carrying his coffin from Lindisfarne paused to rest and then mysteriously found the body too heavy to move again.

The vast and beautiful building was begun in 1903 by Bishop William of Calais and the Norman part was completed by 1133.

Described by Sir Walter Scott as 'Half church of God, half castle 'gainst the Scot', the cathedral gives an impression of immense, lofty strength.

It has many outstanding features: a superb screen behind the high altar, the tomb of the Venerable Bede, illuminated manuscripts from the 8th century, and a 12th-century sanctuary knocker.

During the Civil War, the cathedral was used by the Puritans as a prison for the Scots.

*Castle* Until 1836, the bishops of Durham had unique powers; they were lay rulers in addition to being religious leaders.

As a Palatinate, Durham could have its own army, nobility, coinage and courts.

The castle, built around 1070, was the seat of the Prince Bishops for nearly 800 years, and the bishop still uses it on occasion.

It was originally the site of a Saxon church built in AD 995, but none of it now remains. The oldest surviving parts are the tiny Norman crypt chapel and the Norman archway in the *Tunstall Gallery*.

The castle is now used as a hall of residence for Durham University, but guided tours are available. Open weekdays July to September, 10.00am to 12.00pm, 2.00pm to 4.30pm, Sunday 2.00pm to 4.30pm. Monday, Wednesday and Saturday, 2.00pm to 4.30pm the rest of the year.

*Silver Street* This has retained much of its medieval character, with its Tudor fronted shops. It is worth exploring, along with Saddler Street and North Bailey, and the quaint alleyways (vennels) which leave them to dart around corners to the river.

Number 43 Saddler Street is the entrance to a former Georgian theatre.

*Other historic buildings* Old Elvet Bridge, built 1160, some medieval buildings remain; Tithe Barn, Hallgate Street, medieval, once belonged to the Priory; Guildhall, dates from 1754. Admission on application to the janitor (0385) 67130 ext 101; Corn Mill, Riverbanks, originally belonged to the bishops; Count's House, Riverbanks, a small folly near site of house where Polish dwarf, Count Borulawski lived; Watergate, arch erected in 1778; Quaker Burial Ground, off Claypath; Kepier Hospital, river banks near Gilesgate, medieval arch and buildings. Exterior only.

*Gulbenkian Museum* This is

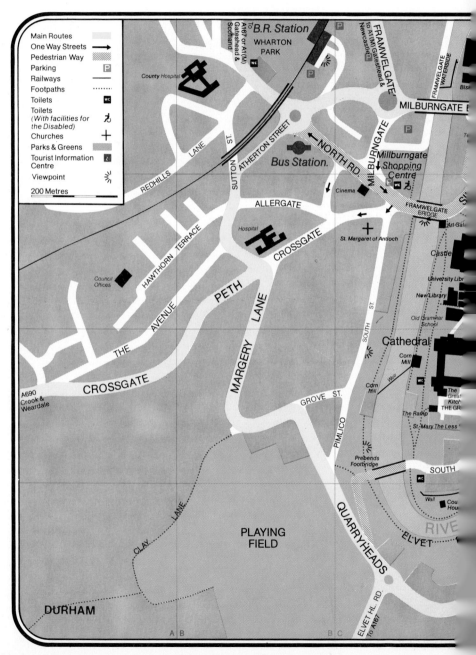

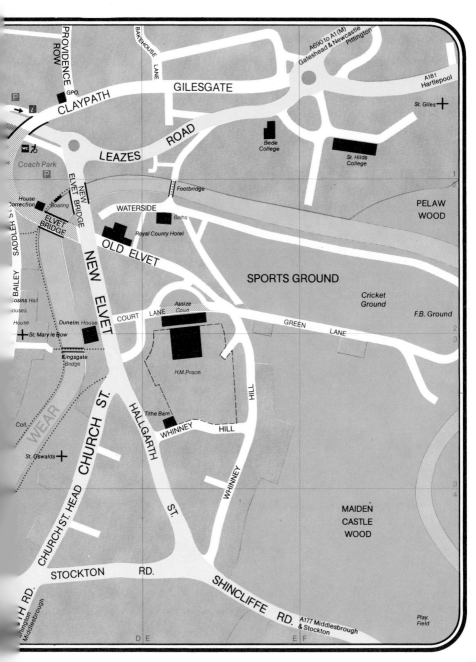

Drums . . . from Durham's regiment

the only museum in Britain devoted to Eastern art. Exhibits include Egyptian and Chinese antiquities. Open weekdays 9.30am to 1.00pm, 2.15pm to 5.00pm, Sunday 2.15pm to 5.00pm. Closed weekends from Christmas to Easter.

*Durham Light Infantry Museum and Arts Centre* Uniforms, medals and illustrations tell the 200-year history of the county regiment. There are constantly changing exhibitions in upper gallery. Open Tuesday to Saturday, 10.00am to 5.00pm, Sunday 2.00pm to 5.00pm.

*Sports* Swimming; ice skating; tennis; putting; boating; golf; cricket.

*Events* Durham Regatta and Antique Fair, in June; Miner's Gala, third Saturday in July; Folk Festival and City Carnival, in August; Music Festival, in October and November.

### Chester le Street

Lions and giraffes now roam free at the *Lambton Pleasure Park*. In addition to the many animals, there are picnic areas and children's amusements.

The *North of England Open Air Museum* is nearby at Beamish. This 200-acre site has exhibits representing the social and industrial development of the region.

The buildings include a row of cottages, farmstead, railway and colliery, all of which have

been restored and rebuilt. There are also working trams and a Victorian pub. Open Easter to September daily except Monday 10.00am to 5.00pm. Reduced hours in winter, ring (0207) 33580 for details.

### Sunderland

Once the biggest town in County Durham, Sunderland now finds itself the junior partner to Newcastle in the county of Tyne and Wear. In an area famous for shipbuilding, Sunderland is known especially for its Doxford marine engines.

*Monkwearmouth Station*, by the big iron bridge, has been converted into a museum of rail and local transport. Open daily.

Also in town is the *National Museum of Music Hall*, commemorating the great days of vaudeville theatre with costume, play bills and programmes. Open weekdays.

On the outskirts of town, the shipyards give way to miles of wide sandy beaches at Roker and Seaburn, the twin holiday resorts.

Southwards along the coast is Ryhope, with its *Engines Museum* which has two-beam engines of 1868, restored and working to illustrate aspects of water pumping. Open Monday to Saturday 10.00am to 6.00pm.

Sunderland's League soccer team, which plays at Roker Park, has a history alive with colour and heroics.

### Marsden

Marsden Bay lies at the foot of sheer cliff, pockmarked with caves and arches. Just offshore is the impressive Marsden Rock, a vast tower of limestone, with a natural archway.

The rock is a noted nesting place for seabirds, including gulls, cormorants and kittiwakes.

Just up the coast is South Shields, a town with a double life. On one side it has fish

quays, warehouses and factories, and on the other, the sandy beaches and amusements of the typical English seaside resort.

### Jarrow

Although this town is renowned for its hunger march, there is only a plaque on the wall of the Town Hall to commemorate the event.

The Venerable Bede wrote his history of the English church at *Jarrow Monastery*, part of which, the Saxon *St Paul's Church* is still standing.

The 15th-century Jarrow Hall houses many finds from this site, and also has a craft shop and temporary exhibits of local crafts and photography. Open daily except Monday.

### Washington

This is the ancestral home of George Washington. The 17th-century *Washington Old Hall* was the family home and it has been restored with the help of American funds.

*Washington Waterfowl Park* has more than 1,500 birds of 100 species. The park covers 103 acres.

Open June to August daily 9.30am to 8.00pm, September to May daily 9.30am to 5.30pm.

Students of industrial history should not miss *Washington 'F' Pit*, preserved on its original site, with winder house, steam winding engine and headstock in working order. Open Monday to Friday 10.00am to 12.00pm, weekends 2.00pm to 4.00pm.

### Causey Arch

The first single-span stone bridge, dating from 1727, spans Beamish Burn just north of Stanley. The bridge is 105 ft long and 85 ft high.

### Blanchland

A charming and beautifully preserved village. It was planned early in the 18th century.

# Newcastle upon Tyne

With the elegant shopping streets of Grainger, Dobson and Clayton, with six bridges side by side across the river Tyne, proud Newcastle is the last city before the Scottish border.

As such, it watches over the 50-odd miles of often-wild Northumberland countryside, and perceives itself as capital of the five or six northernmost English counties.

Half an hour's ride away by a once-pioneering and now ageing electric railway (to become a pioneering Metro system in the 1980s) are Newcastle's own coastal resorts.

In the opposite direction, Hadrian's Wall climbs into the Pennine moorlands, interrupted only by attractive little towns like Hexham (20 miles from Newcastle) and Haltwhistle.

A dozen miles up the A1, the market town of Morpeth – with its Vanbrugh town hall – is a base for exploration in the Wansbeck valley.

**Newcastle upon Tyne**
In the 1830s, Newcastle was graced with one of the finest town centres in the land. For this, succeeding generations can give thanks to three men of vision.

They were builder Richard Grainger, architect John Dobson, and town clerk John Clayton. Between them they redeveloped the centre replacing it with the broad elegance of Grainger Street and Grey Street.

Dobson also designed the magnificent *Central Station*, standing on 17 acres with two miles of platforms. Queen Victoria opened it in 1850.

Such a grand station is appropriate to a region which pioneered railways, and which since early Victorian times has manifested an insatiable appetite for engineering projects, civil and otherwise.

Every one of the thoroughbred steam trains which plied the London-Edinburgh run was at some time or other photographed amid the railway lines which converge to cross the river Tyne by the *King Edward Bridge*.

Until the King Edward was built in 1906, trains from the South had to reverse into Newcastle by way of the dramatic *High Level Bridge*, built by Robert Stephenson in 1849.

The High Level is a two-tier bridge, with a road on the lower deck and a railway on top. It stands as a remarkable example of early cast-iron bridge-building, and it still carries trains, on the routes between Newcastle and the other main towns of the North-East. From the High Level, passengers can see the 82 ft keep of the Norman Castle, built in 1172, which gave the city its name.

The famous structure which is most commonly used as a visual symbol of Newcastle was built as the *New Tyne Bridge* in 1928. This soaring parabola was constructed from Teesside steel

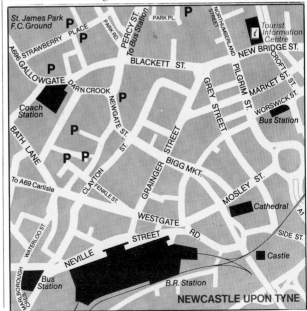

NEWCASTLE UPON TYNE

as a prototype for the Sydney Harbour Bridge, in 1928. It is usually known simply as the Tyne Bridge, occasionally prefixed as 'Great', and carries much of the road traffic from the South.

Another road crossing, the *Redheugh Bridge*, was built in 1871 and rebuilt in 1901, but is of less interesting design.

The lowest of the Tyne's bridges is pivoted in the middle of the river, at quayside level. In the centre of the span is a control cabin of maritime appearance, from which the bridge can be swung through 90 degrees so that vessels may pass. The *Swing Bridge*, on the site of a Roman crossing point, was built in 1876.

The newest of the bridges was built in 1978 as part of the Metro system. These six bridges stand in parallel, all within sight of each other, each of them taking traffic into the heart of the city. Another bridge was built a few miles up river, at Scotswood, in 1967.

In addition to the stalls and market cries, there are steep stone steps to explore between the 17th-century timber warehouses.

These lead to the castle enclosure and Black Gate, which was built around 1247.

Beyond this the street names sound echoes of the past – Bigg Market, Cloth Market and Groat Market.

At the junction of the three stands the Church of St Nicholas. Until it became a cathedral in 1882, this medieval building was the fourth-largest parish church in the country.

Nationally-known Newcastle Brown Ale is misnamed, being no more than copper-coloured. It is also somewhat stronger, and far less sweet, than the type of beer which is commonly accepted as brown ale. The same brewer's unusual Amber Ale, and the rival Vaux's strong Double Maxim

together represent a style of beer which is unique to the North-East.

The beer-drinker with socio-political interests will wish to sample the products of the Federation Brewery in Newcastle, which is owned by the working men's clubs of the North-East. These beers are exported to London for consumption in the House of Commons bar.

The Royal Shakespeare Company have made Newcastle a home away from home with long seasons each year at the Theatre Royal.

There are several night clubs on Tyneside, and music hall is revived at Balmbras theatre restaurant.

In June the vast expanses of Town Moor are filled with the largest travelling funfair in the world. This is the traditional accompaniment to Race Week, when the Northumberland Plate – the Pitman's Derby – is run at Gosforth Park racecourse.

What is left of Hadrian's Wall, which once extended 73 miles across England, starts at Denton on the outskirts of Newcastle.

*Local dishes* include Singing Hinnies, a type of griddle scone ('Hinny' is a friendly form of address); Pan Haggerty, a hotpot of potatoes, onions and grated cheese; and leek pudding. Leek-growing, for competitive shows, is a local obsession.

## Museums and Art Galleries

*Hancock Museum* One of the finest natural history museums in England.

Open Monday to Saturday 10.00am to 5.00pm, Sunday from Easter to September 2.00pm to 5.00pm.

*University Museum of Antiquities* Displays of prehistoric, Roman and Anglo Saxon exhibits, and scale models of Hadrian's Wall.

Open Monday to Saturday 10.00am to 5.00pm.

*Science Museum* There are exhibits showing the history and development of engineering, mining, transport and shipbuilding. Open April to September weekdays 10.00am to 6.00pm, Sunday 2.00pm to 5.00pm, October to March weekdays 10.00am to 4.30pm, Sunday 1.30pm to 4.30pm.

*National Bagpipe Museum* A unique collection of more than 100 sets of pipes from many countries.

Open Wednesday to Friday 12.00pm to 4.00pm, Saturday from Easter to September 10.00am to 4.00pm, October to March 9.00am to 1.00pm.

*Keep Museum* The garrison room in the basement was used as the county jail until 1812.

Open Easter to September Tuesday to Saturday 10.00am to 4.30pm Monday 2.00pm to 3.30pm, October to March Tuesday to Saturday 10.00am to 4.30pm Monday 2.00pm to 3.30pm.

*University Greek Museum* Greek and Etruscan art and archaeology. Open Monday to Friday 10.00am to 4.30pm.

*Laing Art Gallery and Museum* British oil paintings from the 17th century onwards, and displays of armour, costumes and local history.

Open Monday, Wednesday, Friday, Saturday 10.00am to 6.00pm, Tuesday and Thursday 10.00am to 8.00pm. Sunday 2.30pm to 5.30pm.

*Hatton Gallery* Italian and other paintings, 14th-century sculpture and drawings. Open term-time only Monday to Friday 10.00am to 6.00pm, Saturday 10.00am to 5.00pm.

*Armstrong Bridge* (over Jesmond Dene) Open air exhibition by Northumbrian artists. Sundays Easter to November.

*Pentangle Gallery* (Percy Street) Permanent exhibition by Northumbrian artists.

Open Tuesday to Friday 10.30am to 4.00pm, Saturday 10.30am to 6.00pm.

Elegance . . . the Central Arcade, Newcastle

Newcastle's League soccer team has a glorious history.

Across the river at Gateshead is the famous *Gateshead Stadium*, which has an all-weather synthetic athletics track. There is a tuft-turf football pitch and an indoor sports hall is being built. Jogging sessions are open to the public Monday to Friday 12.00pm to 2.00pm.

The Stadium is also the home of both the Gateshead and the Saltwell Harriers.

There are several greyhound tracks on Tyneside, and miner's welfare clubs organise whippet-racing.

### Wallsend
The eastern end of Hadrian's wall. It is also a major shipbuilding centre, from which was launched the liner Mauretania in 1907.

### Killingworth
This was the home of railway pioneer George Stephenson, while he was still brakesman and engineer at the local pit in the early 1800s.

The town has since then moved into a new community with many award-winning building designs.

An outstanding feature is the man-made lake created from a section of badly drained land.

It is said to be after George Stephenson that the people of Tyneside are known as Geordies.

### Ponteland
Worth visiting in this town is the *Blackbird Inn*, which was once a fortified manor house belonging to the De Valence family, the medieval lords of the manor.

The bar is in the 600-year-old tunnel-vaulted basement. It has a superb stone fireplace.

### Tynemouth
A small holiday resort on the Tyne estuary, boasting wide sandy beaches and dramatic views of the shipyards and river.

The High Street is lined by elegant 18th-century houses and beyond it is a moat and a

ruined gateway to the 11th-century priory.

The priory was founded by Benedictines on the site of a 7th-century Saxon building which was destroyed by the rampaging Danes in AD 865.

### Whitley Bay
A busy seaside resort two miles north of Tynemouth. Whitley Bay has its full share of the sandy beaches which are such a dependable feature of this coastline, a vast amusement park, golf, boating, swimming and sea fishing.

At low tide, strollers can cross the causeway at the north end of the bay to *St Mary's Island* with its lighthouse and cottages.

### Seaton Sluice
A charming little harbour. Its name came from a sluice which was built to remove sand washed in by the tides.

Coal was once shipped from the tiny port, built in the late 17th century by Sir Ralph Delaval, but the scene is much more peaceful now.

Seaton Delaval Hall, designed by Vanbrugh in 1720 for the Delaval family is a mile inland. The Hall is now the venue of medieval banquets.

### Morpeth
A pleasant market town on the River Wansbeck, with a town hall built by Vanburgh in 1714, and a 15th-century clock tower that once did duty as the town jail, and still strikes a curfew each evening.

A feature of the town is the number of bridges which cross the river, in addition to a path of stepping stones.

The huge battlement tower by the Great North Road is not the castle, as many people believe, but merely the local police station.

The Norman castle is a private residence and stands on a hill overlooking the river.

# The Roman Wall

The Roman wall, built by the Emperor Hadrian in AD 122, runs for 73 miles across the width of the battle-scarred north country to Bowness-on-Solway.

The wall was the furthest frontier of the Roman Empire, with a garrison of 5,500 cavalry and 13,000 infantry keeping vigil against attacks from the barbaric north.

Some surviving stretches are nearly 14 ft high, and the finest can be found between Chollerford and Gilsland. The mighty wall is at its most spectacular along the rim of Whin Sill Crags above the waters of Crag Lough.

Important remains of the Roman occupation can be inspected at Housesteads, Chesters, Corstopitum and Vindolanda.

The beautiful abbey town of Hexham is the ideal base from which to explore this fascinating area, from south of the wall, up through the Northumberland National Park and the edge of the Kielder Forest.

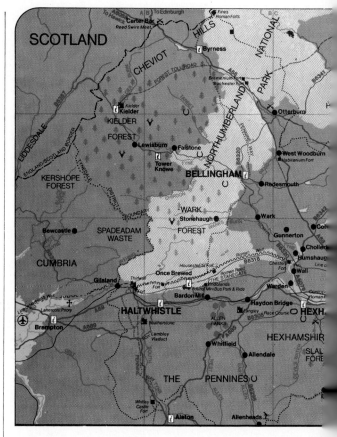

**Tourist Information Centres**
Council Offices, Bellingham, Northumberland. (066 02) 238
Vicars Pele Tower, Corbridge, Northumberland. (043 471) 2815
Council Offices, Sycamore Street, Haltwhistle, Northumberland. (049 82) 351
Manor Office, Hexham, Northumberland. (0434) 5225
Council Offices, South Road, Prudhoe, Northumberland. (0661) 32281

## Corbridge

An appealing small riverside market town which has grown up near the Roman camp at Corstopitum.

It has a 17th-century bridge, an old market square and a complex system of streets lined with charming stone-built houses, antique shops and a craft workshop.

*St Andrews Church* is the most important Anglo Saxon survival in Northumberland, after the crypt at Hexham.

Next door to the church is the Vicar's Pele, a fine example of Northumbrian Pele tower where, in the 18th century, people took refuge from raiders.

This tower now houses the local Tourist Information Centre.

To the south-west, Devil's Water flows through the woods, past ruined *Dilston Castle*.

*Corstopitum Roman camp* The remains of a Roman town and supply base. Excavations on display include granaries, portico columns and the site of what was probably the regional headquarters. The museum has Roman pottery, sculpture,

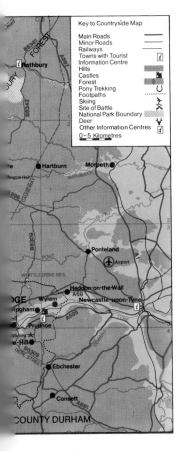

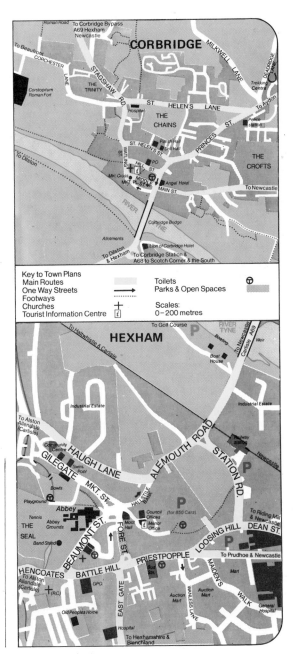

inscribed stones and small objects. Open weekdays 9.30am to 5.30pm. Sunday 2.00pm to 5.30pm.

### Hexham

A picturesque old town on a terrace overlooking the Tyne and set among hills and moors.

Hexham has flourished since Saxon days and was once the centre of the tanning and leather industry. It is now a lively market town, dominated by its beautiful abbey, with its fine Anglo Saxon crypt.

Among its many treasures are the *Frith Stool* or *St Wilfred's*

*Chair* – the seat of bishops and the throne of the old Northumbrian Kings – Bishop Acca's cross, dating from AD 740, a Saxon font and splendid misericords.

Other important buildings include the 14th-century *Moot Hall*, which was the gatehouse of a castle, and which now houses exhibitions. The 14th-century Manor Office was the town jail until 1824 and is now the area's principal Tourist Information Centre.

It is also a museum depicting the life and times of the turbulent Borderlands.

### Allendale

In hard winters, this is a popular skiing resort, set on a steep cliff 1,400 ft above sea level.

At New Year, in a ceremony dating back to pagan times, the men of the town carry barrels of blazing tar on their heads to a bonfire in the market place.

There are many pleasant strolls along the riverside, one of which leads past the mouth of Beaumont Level, the tunnel entrance to what was once a lead mine.

### Chollerford

The site of Chesters Fort (Cilurnum), one of the major forts of the entire Roman wall. It occupies a six-acre area and was a garrison for 500 cavalry in the second century.

Visible remains include defences, barrack blocks, stables, the Commandant's house and baths, and the regimental baths. It lies in the grounds of an 18th-century mansion. Open weekdays 9.30am to 5.30pm, Sunday 2.00pm. to 5.30pm.

On the opposite bank of the Tyne a Roman bridge abutment can be seen. A museum houses the Clayton collection of items excavated from local Roman forts, including altars and sculpture. Open weekdays 9.30am to 5.30pm, Sunday 2.00pm to 5.30pm.

### Twice Brewed

The most spectacular viewpoint along the wall, with an opportunity to walk three miles east to Housesteads, considered one of the finest Roman forts.

Housesteads (Vercovicium), which lies on a five-acre site, once housed 1,000 infantrymen. The remains of walls, gateways, headquarters, granaries and turrets can be seen.

Open weekdays 9.30am to 5.30pm, Sunday 2.00pm to 5.30pm.

### Bardon Mill

The Roman frontier fort and civil settlement of Vindolanda lies north of Bardon Mill. Exposed remains include gateways, towers and headquarter buildings and bath house. A large museum houses notable finds from recent excavations.

The site and museum are open daily, 10.00am to 5.00pm.

### Haltwhistle

A pleasant small town in the South Tyne valley, where Cow Burn flows down from Greenlee Lough.

Haltwhistle is an ideal centre from which to explore the Wall Country and the North Pennines.

The towerless Holy Cross church dates from 1200 and is hidden away behind the market place. To the west is *Gilsland* with its numerous Roman remains.

### Bellingham

A friendly small town near the moors and the forests of the Border country.

*St Cuthbert's church* has a unique stone roof, barrel-vaulted with hexagonal stone ribs. A winding path behind the churchyard leads to a well with waters supposed to have healing powers.

Just north of the town is a pleasant walk up the steep valley of Hareshaw Burn, to *Hareshaw Lynn*, one of Northumberland's well-known waterfalls.

The Pennine Way passes through the town.

### Kielder Forest

Fifty years ago, Kielder was a moorland wilderness. Since then the Forestry Commission have planted trees on its 145,000 acres.

The spruce, larch and pine now provide not only a beautiful sight, but shelter for an expanding community of deer, badgers, otters, red squirrels and foxes.

There are tracks through the forest and recommended points for viewing the wildlife.

Nearby Lewisburn has a natural history museum, depicting the wildlife and human activity of the Upper North Tyne.

Roman remains . . . Hadrian's Wall

# Border Country

Beyond the Wall, the echoes of border war intensify. For centuries, this wild, hill country was the scene of bloody battle between the English and the Scots.

The Cheviot Hills form a massive natural border between the two countries.

This imposing barrier is further strengthened by the broad waters of the river Tweed, watched over by the border town of Berwick.

Since Berwick is on the northern side of the river, it has been claimed by Scotland as often as England. Having changed hands 13 times, it is currently English. Thus the town of Berwick is in the English county of Northumberland, while the county of Berwickshire has been lost to Scotland.

Berwick is a fortified town, and no part of England has as many castles as can be found along a coastline which was once perilously handy for the Vikings and other Northern European invaders.

As if the man-made scenery were not majestic enough, the coastline itself has been declared an Area of Outstanding Natural Beauty.

Warkworth Castle . . . the towering keep

### Tourist Information Centres
The Shambles, Northumberland Hall, Alnwick, Northumberland. (0665) 3120
Castlegate Car Park, Berwick upon Tweed, Northumberland. (0289) 7187
United Auto Services Ltd, Malting Yard, High Street, Rothbury, Northumberland. (0669) 20358
Main Car Park, Seafield Road, Seahouses, Northumberland. (0665) 720774
Padgepool Place Car Park, Wooler, Northumberland. (066 82) 602

## Warkworth
The name of Harry Hotspur has been spread far and wide by Shakespeare's *Henry IV*. Hotspur was the nickname of Sir Henry Percy, an important figure in British history and a Northumbrian hero, who was born at Warkworth Castle.

Warkworth was for centuries one of the most important castles in the North, and it remains a dramatic sight, towering over the village.

Nikolaus Pevsner wrote of it, 'Warkworth must be approached from the north. With its bridge, its bridge-tower, then a short street at an angle and then the main street up a hill to the towering, sharply cut block of the keep is one of the most exciting sequences of views one can have in England.'

A few miles from the village is a superb sandy beach with safe swimming.

## Alnwick
This has been a stronghold of the Percy family since 1309, and its *castle* is now the home of the Duke and Duchess of Northumberland. It was restored by the 18th-century Duke after standing as a ruin for 200 years following the Border wars.

Four miles south-east is *Alnmouth* which boasts one of the oldest golf courses in England, dating from 1869.

Only eight miles north is *Chillingham Castle Park*, which is the home of a unique herd of wild white cattle which have roamed the 600-acre park for centuries.

These cattle are the only remaining descendants of the prehistoric oxen which once inhabited England.

Open daily, except Tuesday, from Easter to September, 1.30pm to 4.30pm.

## Craster
A fishing village renowned for its superb kippers. Herring are brought ashore from the North Sea and transformed by smoking over oak-chips.

A short walk along the coast leads to Dunstanburgh Castle. These 14th-century ruins stand on top of 100-ft cliffs.

Open April to September daily 2.00pm to 6.00pm.

113

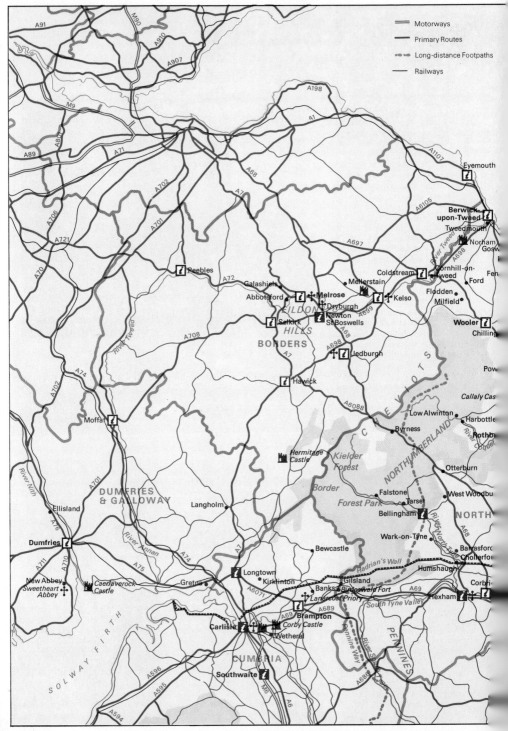

Motorways
Primary Routes
Long-distance Footpaths
Railways

A91

M90

A910

A907

A89

M9

A80

A71

A89

A702

A706

A721

A70

A74

A702

A701

A7

A68

A198

A1

A697

A6105

A1107

Eyemouth

Berwick-upon-Tweed

Tweedmouth

Norham
Gosw

Coldstream

Cornhill-on-Tweed

Ford

Fen

Peebles

Galashiels

Abbotsford

Mellerstain

Flodden
Milfield

Melrose

Dryburgh

Newton
St Boswells

Kelso

Wooler

Chillingh

A72

Selkirk

EILDON
HILLS

BORDERS

A699

A68

A708

A7

A698

Jedburgh

Pow

Hawick

Callaly Cas

A6088

Low Alwinton

Harbottle

Byrness

Rothb

C
H
E
V
I
O
T
S

Moffat

Hermitage
Castle

Kielder
Forest

Otterburn

N
O
R
T
H
U
M
B
E
R
L
A
N
D

River Tweed

River Coquet

Border
Forest Park

Falstone

Tarset

West Woodbu

DUMFRIES
& GALLOWAY

Langholm

Bellingham

NORTH

River Nith

Ellisland

A76

Wark-on-Tyne

Barrasford
Chollerfor

Bewcastle

A68

Humshaugh

Dumfries

A711

A710

A74

A7

Longtown

Kirklinton

Hadrian's Wall

Corbri

New Abbey
Sweetheart
Abbey

Caerlaverock
Castle

Gretna

A6071

Banks

Birdoswald Fort

Lanercost Priory

A69

Hexham

SOLWAY FIRTH

Carlisle

A69

Brampton

Corby Castle

Wetheral

A689

South Tyne Valley

River North Tyne

CUMBRIA

A596

Southwaite

A595

M6

A6

Pennine Way

River S

PENNINES

A594

River Annan

A75

A7

A6071

114

Holy Island

Farne Islands

nburgh
Belford

Seahouses

Beadnell

Chathill

Embleton

glingham

Dunstanburgh

Craster

wick

Alnmouth

Warkworth

Amble

nkburn
ory   Felton

**NORTH SEA**

Ashington

Newbiggin-
by-the-Sea

Morpeth

ND

nington

Blyth

rdham

am

A69

HAM

A690

## Bamburgh
The mighty stone castle, once
the seat of Northumbria's first
kings, dominates this unspoilt
resort.

Open April to September
2.00pm to 6.00pm.

The village has a *museum*
devoted to the heroic Grace
Darling, daughter of the local
lighthouse-keeper. With her
father she rowed out one
stormy night in 1838 to rescue
five people from a wrecked
steamboat.

Open April to October
11.00am to 7.00pm.

## Holy Island (Lindisfarne)
It looks as though it came from
a medieval fairy-tale, but Lindisfarne belonged first to Christian history.

Missionaries from Iona settled on the island in the 7th century, and it was from this retreat
that St Cuthbert helped make
Northumbria one of England's
first Christian kingdoms.

The *priory* was rebuilt in
1082, and its ruins share the
island with a small *Elizabethan
castle* which rises steeply from a
spike of rock.

Depending upon the wea-
ther, Holy Island can be romantic, dramatic or eerie. Its character has attracted the attentions
of a number of film-makers,
including Roman Polanski.

This island and the *Farnes*, to
the immediate south, are noted
for their sea-birds, including
puffins, kittiwakes and terns.
The Farne Islands are the only
breeding grounds of the grey
seal on the east coast of England.

At low tide, it is possible to
drive across a causeway from
the mainland at Beal to Holy
Island, though it is essential to
adhere to the times set out on a
notice-board there to avoid
being cut off by the tide.

Ferry services run to the
Farnes from *Seahouses*, a popular fishing village and weekend
resort.

## Rothbury
A very busy small market town
in Coquetdale, dignified by
Victorian stone houses and
shops on the green by the river.

## Berwick upon Tweed
England's northernmost point
on the river Tweed. A 15-arch
stone bridge was built across the
river in 1611 by order of James
I, connecting the town to
Tweedmouth.

The Elizabethan town walls
are the best preserved example
of this type of fortification in
Europe, and a two-mile walk
leads visitors around the top
from which there are views
along the Tweed.

*Church of the Holy Trinity* A
17th-century church built by
John Young, with no tower.

The 18th-century Town Hall
has a jail on the upper floor,
from which prisoners were
taken to the ships which
despatched them to the penal
colony of Botany Bay.

To arrange visits to the jail,
ring 0289 6332.

## Norham
This secluded village was once
the home of the Bishop of Lindisfarne and its Norman castle,
high on the rocks, was a favourite target of Scottish armies.

Open weekdays 9.30am to
5.30pm. Sunday 2.00pm to
5.30pm.

Norham is noted for its
ceremony of *Blessing the Nets*,
which takes place at midnight
on February 14 when the salmon fishing season opens.

## Flodden Field
A short walk south of the village of *Branxton* leads visitors to
the scene of the worst carnage in
the bloody history of Border
warfare. Between 9,000 and
16,000 soldiers were killed
before the battle went to the
English.

A simple monument near the
battlefield reads, 'To the brave
of both nations'.

# Solway and Eden

Just as England protects its border on one flank with the Cheviot Hills and the river Tweed, so it girds the other with the Cumbrian mountains and the Solway Firth, beyond which lie the Scottish hills of Dumfries and Galloway.

The word 'firth' is the Scottish cousin of the Scandinavian 'fjord'. England has estuaries, but Scotland has firths – great, wide channels hacked out of the coastline – and the first of these is the Solway, which forces the two countries apart.

The Solway Firth, more than 20 miles wide in parts, has a broad, sandy coastline, magnificent sunsets over the mountains, and a notable winter population of wild geese.

The Firth is never quite an estuary, since it is fed by more than a dozen rivers, but its deepest inlet on the English side meets the river Eden, upon which stands the border city of Carlisle.

Inland, the Vale of Eden stretches for many miles, to towns like Appleby-in-Westmorland and Kirkby Stephen, with beautiful walking country in the North Pennines.

**Tourist Information Centres**
Holm Cultram Abbey, Abbey Town, Cumbria. (096 56) 654
32/34 Main Street, Brampton, Cumbria. (069 77) 2685
Old Town Hall, Carlisle, Cumbria. (0228) 25396/25517
17 Swan Street, Longtown, Cumbria. (022 879) 201
Central Garage, Waver Street, Silloth, Cumbria. (0965) 31276
M6 Service Area, Southwaite, Cumbria. (069 93) 445

## Silloth (map p 121)

This unusual and tiny resort is a delightful base from which to explore the unspoilt coastline of the Solway.

Silloth is known for its broad, empty sands, its pleasant, grassy dunes, and its views of the Scottish coast and hills. The town is mid-Victorian.

## Allonby

South of Silloth and the Drigg Dunes lies this small, attractive, seaside town in the centre of Allonby Bay. Sandy beaches and swimming have made it a favoured holiday resort. Allonby shares with Silloth views both out to sea and inland to the fells of the Cumbrian Mountains.

## Bewcastle

An historically-interesting village in a remote corner of England.

In the churchyard of the village of Bewcastle is a fine, 7th-century Anglo-Saxon stone cross with Runic decoration. Close to the village is the six-acre site of a Roman fort, an outpost of Hadrian's Wall. Nearby are four ruined pele towers – 14th- and 15th-century rectangular fortified residences which are common to this part of England and Scotland.

## Lanercost

This tiny village deserves a visit to see the red sandstone priory founded around 1166. It was repeatedly attacked by the Scots between 1296 and 1346, but the nave has been restored as the parish church.

Weekly services are held after dark by candlelight. The setting of the church near the river Irthing is magnificent.

## Brampton

This sandstone town stands on a tributary of the river Irthing. It boasts a ruined Norman church built on the site of a Roman fort.

Two miles south-west is a

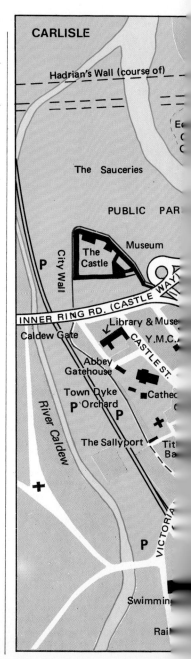

CARLISLE

Hadrian's Wall (course of)

The Sauceries

PUBLIC PAR

Museum

City Wall

The Castle

INNER RING RD. (CASTLE WAY)

Caldew Gate

Library & Muse

Y.M.C.

Abbey Gatehouse

CASTLE ST.

Town Dyke Orchard

River Caldew

The Sallyport

VICTORIA

Swimmin

Rai

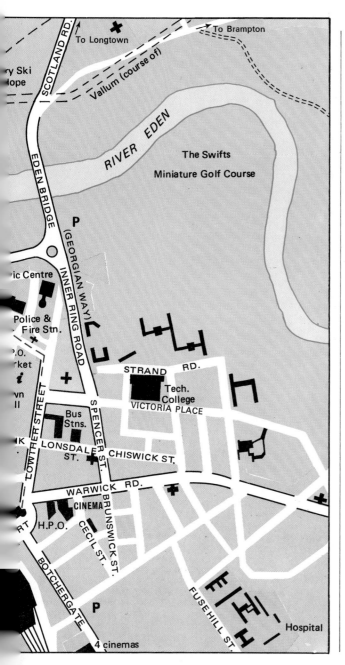

quarry near the river Gelt which still shows the inscriptions scratched there by Roman workers.

## Carlisle

When William Rufus reclaimed Carlisle from Scotland in 1092 he built the present castle and city walls. The fortifications did not deter the Scots, and many battles ensued. The argument over the nationality of the town was finally settled in 1745 when Carlisle was last captured for England during the Jacobite rising.

The city's Celtic name *Caer-Luel* means the town that belonged to the local lord *Caer*. In Roman times it was called Luguvalium, and the city's museum is rich in Roman remains.

In the 12th century the church that was to become Carlisle's impressive cathedral was begun, and the earlier grey stone buildings were complemented by additions in red sandstone. The castle was added to first by a Scottish king, David I, in the 12th century, and then by Henry VIII. A fine market cross was built in 1682, and an 18th-century building formed the Town Hall and is now the Tourist Information Centre.

Throughout its chequered history the town remained an important agricultural centre. During the 19th-century expansion of industry in Britain Carlisle placed itself firmly on the commercial map, and it remains today one of the important railway centres of the North.

*Carlisle Castle and the Border Regiment Museum* The museum is housed in the castle keep and both are open from May to September daily 9.30am to 7.00pm, March, April and October daily 9.30am to 5.30pm.

*Cathedral* A church became Carlisle's cathedral in 1133 and the tower was added in 1401. It has a very fine east window and

Carlisle Castle

there are beautiful misericords under the seats of the 11th-century choir stalls. The Prior's Room has an exceptional, medieval decorated ceiling which was recently restored.

Open May to September daily, Cathedral 7.30am to 8.30pm; Prior's Room 10.00am to 8.00pm, October to April 7.30am to 6.30pm; Prior's Room 2.00pm to 5.00pm.

*Tullie House Museum and Art Gallery* A 17th-century Jacobean mansion with an extensive collection of Hadrian's Wall remains. Open April to September, Monday to Friday, 9.00am to 7.00pm, Saturday 9.00am to 5.00pm; October to March, Monday to Saturday 9.00am to 5.00pm; all Bank Holidays and Sundays 2.00pm to 5.00pm.

*The Citadel* An 1807 renovation of Stefan von Haschenparg's 1541 southern gateway to the old walled city. It now houses the Crown Court.

*Carlisle Cross* For centuries this has been the spot from which *Carlisle Great Fair* has been proclaimed at 8.00am, every August 26.

*City Walks* These are guided walks around the most interesting points of Carlisle. The walks take in the cathedral, the castle and visit the walls through the older streets of the city.

The remaining sections of the fortifications are at West Walls (including Sally Port), Devonshire Walk (including the Richard III or Tile Tower) and by Castle Way at the West Tower interchange. This last section was excavated in 1973.

The walks leave from the Crown and Mitre Hotel in Town Hall Square every evening at 8.00pm in the summer.

*Sports* Swimming; tennis; squash; dry ski slope; bowling; athletics; salmon and trout fishing; golf; cricket; horse-racing; Carlisle United professional soccer.

**Penrith**

Half-way up the Vale of Eden, which separates the Cumbrian Mountains from the Pennine Hills, and near the river Eamont, which flows down from the lake Ullswater, lies the market town of Penrith

The striking beauty of the landscape is enhanced by Penrith's buildings, many of which have been constructed from red sandstone.

The 14th-century castle ruins and the 18th-century church of St Andrew, with its Norman tower and other antiquities, are worth visiting, while the Lowther Wildlife Country Park has rare breeds of cattle, deer and cranes to be seen.

On Easter Monday the local tradition is a 'pace egg' race in which painted, hard-boiled eggs are rolled down a hill.

**Langwathby**

The *Little Salkeld Corn Mill*, Little Salkeld grinds corn in the traditional way and it is possible to buy flour or bread or stop for afternoon tea. Open to the public at certain times.

Ring (076 881) 523 for more details.

**Alston**

Reputed to be the highest market town in England, Alston now offers visitors an ideal base from which to set out on walks over the fells of the Pennines and across the Vale of Eden to the Cumbrian Mountains.

**Appleby**

This pretty little village is famous for the horse fair which is held every June. Local farmers as well as gipsies from all over Britain meet to trade their horses.

The town itself has many Norman ruins. The *castle* has a Norman keep. *St Lawrence Church* is a part-Norman construction. The church was rebuilt in the 17th century and contains the tomb of Lady Anne Clifford, who was responsible for many works of charity in this market town.

Appleby is an excellent centre for walking holidays, and the *Woodland Nature Trail* takes a route past more than 20 tree species.

# Northern Lakes

As the Solway opens out to the sea, it runs close to the Lake District and the Cumbrian Mountains.

Coast, lakes and mountains can all be explored from the same base. Useful centres from which to roam are Maryport, on the coast; Cockermouth, a few miles inland; or Keswick, in the heart of the hills.

From any of these towns, the full range of countryside can be seen within a radius of ten or 20 miles.

Though this part of Cumbria has long stretches of unspoiled, sandy beaches, the coastal towns offer a highly-individualistic mixture of fishing village, Georgiana, and isolated, sometimes overgrown, Industrial Revolution.

The northern lakes include Bassenthwaite, Derwent Water and Thirlmere. Among the mountains are Skiddaw, Latrigg (1,203ft), Castle Head (529ft) and Friar's Crag.

**Tourist Information Centres**
Riverside Car Park, Cockermouth, Cumbria. (0900) 822634
Moot Hall, Market Square, Keswick, Cumbria. (Summer only) (0596) 72645
Council Offices, Main Street, Keswick, Cumbria. (Winter only)
Maryport Maritime Museum, 1 Senhouse Street, Maryport, Cumbria. (090 081) 3738
Carnegie Theatre and Arts Centre, Finkle Street, Workington, Cumbria. (0900) 2122

**Maryport** (*map p 120*)
An 18th-century industrial village, parts of which today are overgrown.

The town was named after the wife of the local squire, who developed it as a coal port, but the pits have long since closed, and now the dock is used only by fishermen and weekend sailors.

The *Maritime Museum* is open October to Easter Tuesday to Saturday 10.00am to 12.00pm, 2.00pm to 4.00pm, Easter to September weekdays 10.00am to 5.00pm, Sunday 2.00pm to 5.00pm.

Just outside Maryport are the remains of an important *Roman camp* overlooking the sea. This was part of the defensive complex that guarded the flanks of Hadrian's wall.

There is a golf course on the seafront.

**Workington** (*map p 121*)
Cumbria's second town. Workington stands at the mouth of the river Derwent, and grew during the Industrial Revolution as a coal and iron town.

Ambitious and imaginative reclamation projects have provided the town with leisure facilities.

There are traces of the *Roman fort* of Gabrosentum overlooking the harbour.

*Workington Hall*, now a ruin, was a 14th-century *pele tower* which gave shelter to Mary Queen of Scots when she fled from Scotland in 1586.

*St Michael's Church* has fragments of 8th-century crosses and a Norman arch, while *St John's* was designed by Inigo Jones.

The *Helena Thompson Museum*, at Parkend House, has *costumes and ceramics* as well as local memorabilia.

Open Tuesday to Saturday 10.00am to 12.00pm, 2.00pm to 4.00pm.

Workington has a professional Rugby League team.

**Cockermouth** (*map p 120*)
The birthplace of the poet William Wordsworth in 1770. *Wordsworth's House* is open Easter to October 31 weekdays 10.00am to 5.30pm, Sunday 2.00pm to 5.30pm.

Cockermouth is a rural town with a broad, handsome main street, Georgian squares and a ruined *castle* dating from 1134.

The town is known for salmon fishing on the Cocker and Derwent, views of Skiddaw and walks in the Vale of Lorton. The nearby lakes include Lowes Water, Crummock Water, and Bassenthwaite.

The tiny local brewery produces an excellent bitter beer. *Moorland Close*, only 1½ miles south of Cockermouth, is the farmhouse birthplace in 1764 of Fletcher Christian who led the famous Mutiny on the Bounty. It is here, legend says, that he returned from the Pitcairn Islands to spend the rest of his life in hiding.

**Keswick** (*map p 120*)
Magnificently situated between Skiddaw and Derwent Water, with Helvellyn, Scafell, Great Gable, Bassenthwaite Lake, Thirlmere and the Borrowdale valley all within walking distance, Keswick is an extremely popular centre for such activities as climbing, walking, pony-trekking, boating, fishing and swimming.

The Saturday market, in the shadow of its unique Moot Hall, dates from 1276.

The poet Robert Southey lived at Greta Hall just north of the square and his tomb is in the churchyard at nearby Great Crosthwaite. This church was founded in 1175 with consecration crosses dating from 1553.

The *Fitz Park Museum and Art Gallery* in Fitz Park houses mineral and rock specimens, manuscripts of Wordsworth, Southey, Ruskin and Hugh Walpole, and a scale model of the Lake District.

119

Open September to June weekdays 10.00am to 12.00pm, 2.00pm to 5.00pm, July and August 10.00am to 12.00pm, 2.00pm to 7.00pm.
*Castle Head* is half a mile south of Keswick and those climbing all its 529 ft will be rewarded with breathtaking views of Derwent Water and Bassenthwaite Lake.

Two miles south of Keswick is the picturesque village of *Watendlath*, where Hugh Walpole set his novel *Judith Paris*.

## Thirlmere

This 3¾-mile lake is now a reservoir and the best views of it are from the minor road on the west side.

Castle Rock of Triermain and Raven Crag are regarded by climbers as the best targets bordering this water.

## Buttermere

It is possible to walk right around this lake which is hemmed in by mountains. At one point the walk goes through a tunnel in the cliff, but otherwise it is a ramble through pine trees and bracken. It's a delightful walk, but noisy and crowded in season.

Buttermere village, north of the lake, leads to the waterfalls of *Sourmilk Gill*.

Further north-west is *Crummock Water*, while south is *Scale Force*, at 100 ft the highest waterfall in the Lake District.

## Caldbeck

The home of the huntsman John Peel, born in 1776. He would have remained just a local character if a friend had not celebrated his exploits by writing *D'ye Ken John Peel* to the tune of a traditional Cumberland air.

Peel was immortalized by the song. A six-footer, he was addicted to hunting and kept his own pack of hounds so that he could go off in pursuit when he pleased. His grave is in Caldbeck churchyard.

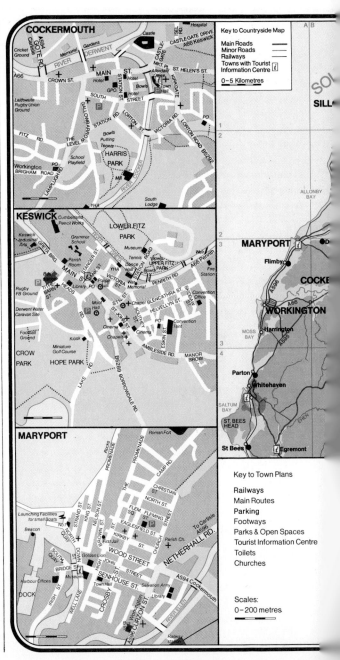

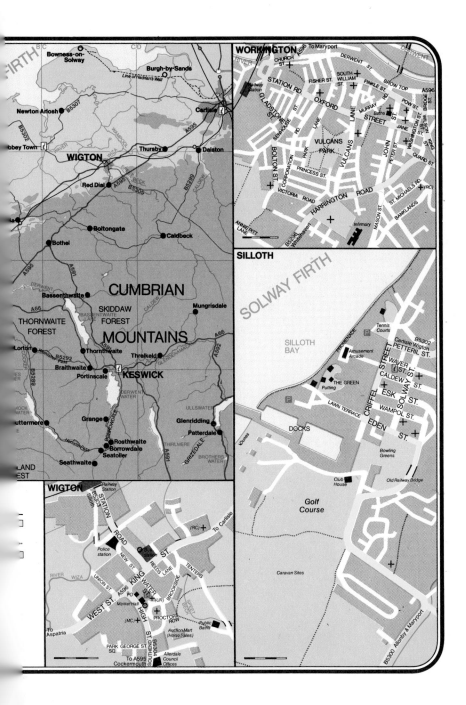

**FIRTH**

Bowness-on-Solway

Burgh-by-Sands

Line of Hadrian's Wall

Newton Arlosh — B5307

Abbey Town

WAVER

Carlisle

A595

**WIGTON**

Thursby

Dalston

Red Dial — A595 — B5305

B5299

CALDEW

Boltongate

Caldbeck

Bothel

**CUMBRIAN**

A66

Bassenthwaite

SKIDDAW FOREST

Mungrisdale

THORNTHWAITE FOREST

BASSENTHWAITE LAKE

**MOUNTAINS**

Lorton — B5292 Pass

Thornthwaite

Threlkeld

Braithwaite

Portinscale

**KESWICK**

DERWENT WATER

Buttermere

Grange

Glenridding

Patterdale

Rosthwaite

Borrowdale

Seatoller

THIRLMERE

Seathwaite

GRIZEDALE

BROTHERS WATER

ULLSWATER

**WORKINGTON**

To Maryport

RIVER DERWENT

CHURCH ST.

DERWENT ST.

Railway Station

STATION RD

FISHER ST.

SOUTH WILLIAM ST.

BROW TOP — A596

GLADSTONE

OXFORD

BRIDGE ST.

POW ST.

KING ST.

Baths

JANE ST.

WASHINGTON ST.

SEYMOUR ST.

PARK LANE

STREET

MURRAY RD

JOHN ST.

PETER ST.

QUARD ST.

BOLTON ST.

**VULCANS PARK**

VULCANS LANE

CORPORATION RD

PRINCESS ST.

HARRINGTON ROAD

ST. MICHAELS RD (RC)

VICTORIA ROAD

MASON ST.

BANKLANDS

ANNIE PITT LANE

B5292

Whitehaven

Infirmary

**SILLOTH**

**SOLWAY FIRTH**

SILLOTH BAY

Tennis Courts

PROMENADE

Carlisle Wigton — B5302

PETTERIL ST.

WAVER ST.

STREET

Amusement Arcade

THE GREEN

Putting

CALDEW ST.

SOLWAY ST.

CRIFFEL ST.

ESK ST.

WAMPOL ST.

LAWN TERRACE

**EDEN ST.**

DOCKS

Bowling Greens

Old Railway Bridge

Club House

*Golf Course*

Caravan Sites

B5300 Allonby & Maryport

**WIGTON**

Railway Station

STATION ROAD

B5305 Silloth

Police station

NEW ST.

Bus Station

(RC)

To Carlisle

UNION ST.

A596 KING WATER ST.

REEDS LANE

TENTERS

PO

HIGH ST.

PROCTORS ROW

BROOKSIDE

SPEET BECK

**WEST ST.**

Market Hall

(MC)

RIVER WIZA

Public Baths

Auction Mart (Horse Sales)

PARK GEORGE ST.

SQ. ST.

B5304 ST. JOHNS

Allerdale Council Offices

To Aspatria

To A595 Cockermouth

# Cumbrian Coast

The middle stretch of the Cumbrian coast sharpens into a headland at St Bees, where there is a nature reserve, then recedes sandily towards the Furness peninsula. This coastal strip is known as Copeland after the forest which lies behind it.

Copeland's main town is Whitehaven, noted for its Georgian architecture and American associations. Further south, the coastal village of Ravenglass is a delightful centre from which to explore lovely Eskdale. The beginning of the exploration can be carried out by narrow-gauge steam railway.

Inland lies England's deepest lake, Wast Water, and the country's highest mountain, Scafell Pike (3,210ft). South of the Esk and beyond the smaller river Annas is Black Combe (1,970ft). On a fine day it is possible from the top of Black Combe to see Scotland, the Isle of Man, Ireland (the Mountains of Mourne) and Wales (Snowdon).

## Tourist Information Centres
Lowes Court Gallery, 12-13 Main Street, Egremont, Cumbria. (0946) 820693
The Folk Museum, St Georges Road, Millom, Cumbria. (0657) 2555
Car Park, Ravenglass and Eskdale Railway Station, Ravenglass, Cumbria. (065 77) 278
Market Place, Whitehaven, Cumbria. (0946) 5678

## Whitehaven
This Wren-style town offers the most surprising and cohesive example of Cumbria's elegant and often faintly incongruous architecture.

In the 17th and 18th century, before its industrial growth, Whitehaven was one of Britain's most important ports, ranking with Liverpool and Bristol. It was the trade with the Americas which led to the use of rum in several local recipes.

During this period, the town was developed in a Wren-inspired style by the wealthy local Lowther family. Despite the growth of shipbuilding, coal and chemical industries, much of Georgian and Victorian architectural interest has been preserved.

The Copeland Council has published the *Whitehaven Walkabout* which includes all the outstanding architecture of the town.

Whitehaven has a professional Rugby League team.

Two miles north at Moresby is *Rosehill Theatre*, used for drama and chamber music. A local silkmill owner, Sir Nicholas Sekers, founded it in 1959, and the red silk interior was designed by Sir Oliver Messel.

*Whitehaven Museum and Art Gallery* Local history museum and changing exhibitions.

Open Monday to Saturday 10.00am to 5.00pm.

*Whitehaven Castle* Once the home of the Lowther family, this is now a hospital. The Castle Park consists of 13 acres of natural park and woodland.

*Somerset House* A fine 18th-century building, housing the council offices.

*St James' Church* One of the finest Georgian interiors in Cumbria, designed by Carlisle Spedding.

*St Nicholas' Church* Dating from the 17th century, it was rebuilt in the 19th century in Gothic style. Mildred Warner Gale, the grandmother of George

Key
MAIN ROUTES
ONE WAY STREETS
PARKING
PARKS ETC.
TOURIST INFORMATION CENTRE
TOILETS
CHURCHES
0    200 METRES

WHITEHAVEN

Washington, was buried here in 1700.

*The Harbour* This dates back to the 17th century and is surrounded by interesting old buildings. The last coal-fired dredger in Great Britain is still working here.

*South Beach Recreation Area* By the Old Quay on the site of Wellington Pit, this has the remains of three early pit structures. The beach is nearby.

*Civic Hall* Films, opera, brass band concerts, plays, wrestling and other entertainments are held here.

*Whitehaven Sports Centre* Indoor sports, including squash, badminton, trampolining, climbing tower. Sauna and solarium. *Sports* Swimming; bowling; fishing; sailing.

## St Bees

Once a quiet village, St Bees has now become a flourishing resort, with caravan sites.

St Bees School, the local public school, was founded in 1587 by Edmund Grindal, Archbishop of Canterbury.

The 12th-century sandstone *Church of St Mary and St Bega* was built on the site of a Benedictine nunnery.

The red sandstone cliffs are a haven for seabirds, and there is a nature reserve on the 323-ft *St Bees Head*.

## Egremont

A few miles inland from St Bees is Egremont.

*Egremont Castle* dates from 1130, and is now in ruins.

Paintings by local artists are exhibited at *Lowes Court Art Gallery* where there is also a craft centre.

Open Monday to Saturday 10.00am to 1.00pm, 2.00pm to 5.00pm, closed Wednesday afternoon.

Every September the *Egremont Crab Fair* is held, when people parade through the streets carrying crab apples, and there is a fun fair. The *World*

*Gurning Championship* is held at the same time, when there are competitions to see who can pull the most terrible face.

South-east is *Calder Bridge*, from which tracks cross the moorland wastes of Cold Fell. By the river Calder are the ruins of the 12th-century *Calder Abbey* built by the Savignac monks from Furness Abbey.

## Wasdale Head

The birthplace of British rock climbing, when Great Gable and Scafell were climbed in the 1880's. It is the centre for climbing Scafell Pike, which is 3,210 ft high.

The church is one of the smallest in England.

## Seascale

This coastal town offers sanddunes, good sands and coastline walks. The breakers are ideal for surfing. There is an 18-hole golf course.

## Eskdale Green

A pretty village on the banks of the river Esk, with pine trees and rhododendrons lining the road.

## Hard Knott Pass

The most difficult road in the entire Lake District, with very sharp bends and 1-in-3 gradients. The pass is 1,291 ft high and gives spectacular views. views.

The ruins of *Hardknott Castle*, a Roman fort, lie to the west.

Eastwards is *Wrynose Pass*, which climbs 1,281 ft. The summit overlooks the Three Shire Stone, the point at which the old counties of Lancashire, Cumberland and Westmorland met.

## Ravenglass

A picturesque village associated with Middle Ages smuggling. It is on the estuary of the rivers Esk, Mite and Irk.

At *Walls Castle* is a Roman bath house and a Villa.

The *Ravenglass and Eskdale Railway* is a narrow gauge railway with a steam train service operating between Ravenglass and Dalegarth. Open March to October.

The Ravenglass and Drigg Dunes is the largest British breeding colony of black headed gulls. The *Ravenglass Nature Reserve* is at Drigg Point, but a permit to visit must be obtained from Cumbria County Council.

## Bootle

The village of Bootle is two miles inland from the sea, where there are good sandy beaches.

Motorbike scrambles are held here.

## Millom

The *Folk Museum* has a unique full-scale model of a drift of the former Hodbarrow Iron Ore Mine. Steel was once smelted in the town. Open Easter to September daily 9.00am to 5.00pm.

There is a recreation ground in the town, and there is also tennis and miniature golf.

Ravenglass . . . steaming ahead

123

# Southern Lakes

The best-known lakes, with all their evocative names, lie to the south-east of the Cumbrian Mountains: Coniston, Windermere, and arguably Ullswater belong to this southern group.

Lake Windermere is ten miles long, and Ullswater stretches for seven miles. Helvellyn is the most frequently climbed peak.

This area is the most popular in the Lakes, but the wide-open spaces of the fells and hills, and the vast, glaciated valleys can still provide peace and solitude for the walker and climber.

William Wordsworth and Samuel Taylor Coleridge spent walking holidays in the Lakes. Wordsworth and his sister Dorothy later came to live here. The countryside has inspired many other writers, among them Arthur Ransome, Charles Lamb and Beatrix Potter.

The town of Kendal has many hotels and is a favourite centre from which to explore the lakes and hills to the north.

## Tourist Information Centres

Civic Hall, Duke Street, Barrow-in-Furness, Cumbria. (0229) 25795

The Glebe, Bowness-on-Windermere, Cumbria. (Summer only) (096 62) 2244 Ext 43

Main Car Park, Coniston, Cumbria. (Summer only) (096 64) 533

Victoria Hall, Grange-over-Sands, Cumbria. (044 84) 4331

Broadgate Newsagency, Grasmere, Cumbria. (096 65) 245

Town Hall, Kendal, Cumbria. (0539) 23649 Ext 253

The Art Stone (Kirkby Lonsdale) Ltd, 18 Main Street, Kirkby Lonsdale, Cumbria. (0468) 71603

The Centre, 17 Fountain Street, Ulverston, Cumbria. (0229) 52299

Victoria Street, Windermere, Cumbria. (096 62) 4561

## Patterdale

A popular and bustling Ullswater village, packed by visitors in the summer season. Many centuries ago, before the holidaymakers came, St Patrick is said to have preached here and won many converts. His holy well stands by the roadside a mile north of the village.

Patterdale offers many Lakeland pleasures, such as steamer cruises and strolls through the woodland and hills lining the shore.

From here, climbers set out to attack Helvellyn's 3,118-ft summit. The experienced climber makes for Striding Edge above Red Tarn, but an easier assent is from Thirlspot. Both routes to the summit are about three miles long.

The view from the top is unforgettable. Almost every fell in Lakeland, the Pennines in the east and the Scottish mountains, 60 miles to the north-west, can be seen in one sweeping vista.

## Grasmere

*Dove Cottage* in Grasmere was the home of William and Dorothy Wordsworth from 1799 to 1808. It is now open to a numerous and eager public along with the nearby *Wordsworth Museum* which has manuscripts and other items of interest from Wordsworth's life. *Rydal Mount*, at Rydal, nearby, was Wordsworth's home for 33 years. All three are open to the public. Telephone Grasmere Tourist Information Centre for details.

A simple stone marks Wordsworth's grave in St Oswald's Churchyard, Grasmere.

A major attraction to this village are the annual *Grasmere Sports* which are held on the Thursday nearest to August 20. The sports compare with the Scottish Highland Games, and include such contests as Cumberland and Westmorland wrestling, fell-racing to the top of Butter Crag and back, and training fox hounds.

Among the many traditional, sweet-tooth recipes from this region is one for Grasmere gingerbread. Sarah Nelson started her Gingerbread Shop at Church Cottage 123 years ago, and children in the Lake District were taught their alphabet with gingerbread letters when books were scarce.

## Ambleside

This hugely popular resort, at the centre of the Lake District, is always packed with visitors. Climbers can hire ropes, tackle and guides for rock-climbing trips, while the less energetic can board a boat at Waterhead for a scenic cruise the length of Lake Windermere.

The charming ceremony of rush-bearing takes place each July when local children parade through the streets carrying rushes and flowers. This tradition dates back to the Middle Ages when rushes were used to carpet the floors of the churches.

Ambleside, Bowness and Newby Bridge are the main centres for the water sports for which Windermere is famous.

Stockghyll Force, an impressive waterfall to the east of Ambleside, is worth the one-mile walk.

## Windermere

The town of Windermere, on the shore of the lake and at the foot of some fine hills, is an extremely popular holiday resort. Out of season, the more contemplative visitor can enjoy magnificent views and gentle strolls.

There are 14 islands on the lake, one of which is the privately owned Bell Island, covering 30 acres. Other islands where the pleasure steamers do not call may be visited by private boat.

The lakeside village of *Bow-*

*ness* has a 15th-century church which has some fine stained-glass windows. The village is the headquarters of the *Royal Windermere Yacht Club*.

From the water of the lake comes Windermere char, a fish that tastes like salmon, which cannot be fished commercially, but is sometimes available in local restaurants.

**Sawrey**
This superb village on the western edge of Windermere is divided into Far Sawrey and Near Sawrey.

*Hill Top Farm*, the home of Beatrix Potter, is at Near Sawrey just behind the Town Bank Arms. The famous writer and illustrator was born in London but moved to Lakeland before her first book, *The Tale of Peter Rabbit*, was published.

When she died in 1943, Beatrix Potter left her house and its land to the National Trust. Open to the public Easter Sunday to 31 October, weekdays 10.00am to 5.30pm, Sunday 2.00pm to 5.30pm.

**Kendal**
Kendal is the most popular centre from which to explore the Southern Lakes.

Just as Grasmere has its gingerbread so Kendal has its mint cake. This energy-giving sweet can be either white or brown, or it can be chocolate-covered. Snuff is also made locally.

The 12th-century *castle* where Catharine Parr, the sixth and last wife of Henry VIII, was born now stands a ruin, surrounded by its overgrown moat. It makes an impressive sight as it stands aloft, its crumbling Norman remains crowning a grassy hill.

In the 13th century the largest church in England, *Holy Trinity Church*, was built here. It was restored during the 19th century.

*George Romney* died in Kendal in 1802 but a number of his paintings remain in the town hall.

**Haverthwaite**
Half way between Ulverston and Windermere, near Newby Bridge, is Haverthwaite.

The *Lakeside and Haverthwaite Railway* begins its scenic journey here. The majority of the trains are steam hauled and they connect with steamers to Bowness on Lake Windermere. Tel (044 83) 594 for timetable.

**Coniston**
This tourist village is half a mile from the head of Coniston Water. It is the obvious centre for those intending to scale the Old Man of Coniston, a 2,635-ft peak.

John Ruskin, the art historian and painter, lived and died at Brantwood on the lake's eastern shore. He is buried at Coniston Church. Some of his drawings are in *Brantwood Museum*.

On the shores of Coniston Water, which is 5½ miles long, is a memorial to Donald Campbell. He was killed on the lake in 1967 when trying to break the world water-speed record.

Two miles to the north-east is the Tarns. This stretch of water, which many believe to be the prettiest in Lakeland, was once three smaller lakes. A dam, built about 50 years ago, joined all three together.

**Hawkshead**
As well as being in an area of great natural beauty, Hawkshead has historical and literary interest.

A Norman church overlooks the village which is near Esthwaite Water. *Esthwaite Hall* is where Edwin Sandys, onetime Archbishop of York, was born in 1516. Edwin Sandys founded the local grammar school where William Wordsworth was a pupil.

Both the school and the cottage of Ann Tyson, where Wordsworth lodged, are open to the public. Telephone Windermere Tourist Information Centre for opening times.

A *museum of Lakeland industry* is now housed in the Court House.

**The Furness Peninsula**
The Cumbrian Mountains slope down to the south-west through the Furness Fells to the Furness Peninsula.

At the tip of the Peninsula are three islands, the Isle of Walney, Roa Island and Peil Island. Peil Island has only two buildings. One of these is a superb castle ruin, the other, an inn.

**Broughton in Furness**
This attractive market town is a centre for the slate industry. Some of Britain's largest quarries are nearby.

The town overlooks the Duddon Estuary and is the starting point for walks to Ulpha Fell and Birker Fell. Further north is the highest peak in Lakeland, Scafell Pike.

**Barrow-in-Furness**
Barrow is an industrial town where ships and submarines are built. This industry attracted heavy bombing during WWII and the town suffered accordingly. The ruined Furness Abbey stands north of the town.

**Ulverston**
This is one of the most northerly towns on the Peninsula. It is renowned for being the birthplace in 1764 of *Sir John Barrow*, the founder of the Royal Geographical Society. A huge stone replica of the Eddystone Lighthouse stands on Hoad Hill as a memorial to him.

**Grange-over-Sands**
This town is on a peninsula and overlooks Morecambe Bay. It is a popular holiday resort and warm temperatures have earned it the reputation of 'the Torquay of the north'.

# Lancashire

High in the hills between the Cumbrian Mountains and the Pennines, by the pretty town of Sedbergh and the beautiful town of Kirkby Lonsdale, the river Lune begins to seek its way to the sea.

These hills lie at the most remote corners of several counties, but eventually the Vale of Lune determines its path and proceeds prettily to Lancaster.

Here, north of the river Wyre, with the Forest of Bowland spreading itself, is a rural and often wild Lancashire, with not an industrial town in sight.

Much of the forest is today rugged moorland countryside, with bracken, heather and limestone, and pretty villages like Slaidburn, Newton in Bowland and Bolton by Bowland to offer the traveller a bed.

South of the Wyre, the county remains rural as far south as the river Ribble, with the flat Fylde peninsula reaching out into the Irish to make room for the fishing port of Fleetwood, the great northern holiday resort of Blackpool and the more dignified charms of Royal Lytham St Anne's.

## Tourist Information Centres
Tower Block, Town Hall, Blackburn, Lancashire. (0254) 55201/53277

Central Promenade, Blackpool, Lancashire. (0253) 21623

Marine Hall, Esplanade, Fleetwood, Lancashire. (039 17) 71141

7 Dalton Square, Lancaster, Lancashire. (0524) 2878

The Square, Lytham St Annes, Lancashire. (0253) 725610

Marine Road Central, Morecambe, Lancashire. (0524) 414110/417120

Town Hall, Lancaster Road, Preston, Lancashire. (0772) 53731

## Morecambe
Morecambe and neighbouring Heysham are two ancient villages which over the centuries have merged into one resort.

Holiday attractions include an enormous swimming pool, performing dolphins starring at Marineland, and illuminations from August to October.

This is in addition to the miles of magnificent sands and the superb views across Morecambe Bay to the Lake District.

The remains of a church dating from before the Conquest, with graves carved out of rock, can be seen on a hill overlooking Heysham.

At low tide walkers can make the trip across Morecambe Bay from Hest Bank to Grange-over-Sands, which is an interesting expedition.

There are three tidal rivers which have to be forded and all walkers must be accompanied by an official guide.

## Carnforth
The *Steamtown Railway Museum* has 32 trains and is open daily. The trains operate every Sunday from March to October, Saturdays from May to September and daily from July 17 to August 30.

## Lancaster (*map p 128*)
The city of Lancaster is a combination of historic interest and modern charm, lined with Georgian houses and alleyways bearing such intriguing names as Bashful Alley, Old Sir Simon's Arcade, or Chancery Lane.

It was once a major port, trading with America, the West Indies and the Baltic.

The Gillow family gained distinction when they developed Lancaster's famous cabinet making and furniture tradition, evidence of which can be studied in the museum.

The quiet, tree-lined quay

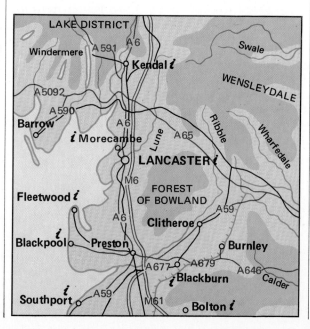

An imposing landmark . . . Ashton Memorial

houses the *King's Own Regiment Museum*. Open daily 9.00am to 5.00pm.
*Hornsea Pottery* Guided tours are readily arranged and visitors are welcome throughout the year.

**Fleetwood**
Standing at the mouth of the Wyre Estuary, this is one of the leading fishing ports in Britain.

In fact, watching the trawlers return from the fishing grounds as far away as Iceland is one of the attractions for visitors, along with the extensive sands, gardens and model yacht pool.

**Blackpool**
Social change has hardly made a dent in the popularity of this archetypal British seaside resort.

The town began its rise in the mid-18th century, and its resident population is now in excess of 150,000, while in the summer it attracts millions.

Dominating the six-mile long promenade is the *Blackpool Tower*. Built in 1894 it is 518 ft high, and houses such attractions as a tropical garden, an aquarium, a monkey jungle, a butterfly garden and children's playgrounds. There is also the famous ballroom.

The stretch of the promenade known as the *Golden Mile* has a massive funfair, numerous bingo halls and cafes.

Since their humble beginnings in 1912, the *Blackpool Illuminations* have progressed into a magnificent example of skill and imagination. Every September and October they transform the promenade at night in what is known locally as the Greatest Free Show on Earth. More than 375,000 different bulbs are used in the Illuminations and if the cables and wires were laid end to end they would stretch for 75 miles.

**Lytham St Annes**
This is an opportunity for the humblest club golfer to tread

conjures up visions of those exciting seafaring times, with the stone warehouses and the elegant 18th-century *Custom House*.
*Castle* A medieval building, with a Norman keep. John of Gaunt, Duke of Lancaster, and the father of Henry IV enlarged the castle, which was later further fortified by Elizabeth I as a defence against the Spanish Armada.

During the Civil War it was a Parliamentary stronghold and continues to house the court and the local jail, as it has done since the 18th century.

Open Easter to September daily 10.30am to 5.00pm.

*Market Cross* The spot where Charles II was proclaimed king.
*Cathedral* Built in 1859 and notable for its gilded chancel roof, frescoes and a carving of The Last Supper on the marble altar. Every chapel has an exquisitely decorated altar.
*Priory Church of St Mary* This site covers 12 centuries of Christian history. The church has magnificent oak-canopied stalls.
*Ashton Memorial* An imposing landmark, it was built as a memorial by Lord Ashton.
*Lancaster Museum* Prehistoric, Roman and medieval exhibits are on show, in addition to Gillow furniture. The building also

127

the fairways in the footsteps of such greats as Palmer, Nicklaus, Player and many others.

Royal Lytham St Annes golf course is one of the homes of the British Open golf championship, and of Ryder Cup matches.

For those not interested in golf, there are glorious sands, a village green and an old windmill by the charming promenade. There is sand yachting every weekend at Clifton Drive North.

The town is also the headquarters of the Football League, England's leading professional soccer competition.

### Ribchester
The history of this pleasant village on the river Ribble dates back to the first century when it was Bremetennacvm, a large Roman fort. Open December and January Saturday only 2.00pm to 5.00pm, May to August daily except Thursday 2.30pm to 5.30pm, other months daily except Thursday 2.00pm to 5.30pm.

There is a museum next to the village church which contains many objects discovered during excavations in the 19th century. Open December and January Saturday only 2.00pm to 5.00pm, February to November daily except Friday 10.00am to 5.00pm.

### Preston
The birthplace of Richard Arkwright, whose pioneering work in the development of spinning machines helped build the Lancashire cotton industry.

Although Preston is very much an industrial town, it stands right on the fringes of the Lancashire conurbation, with the attractive countryside of the Ribble Valley and the Forest of Bowland near at hand.

The town itself has some interesting Victoriana, but has been extensively redeveloped because of its growth as a container port.

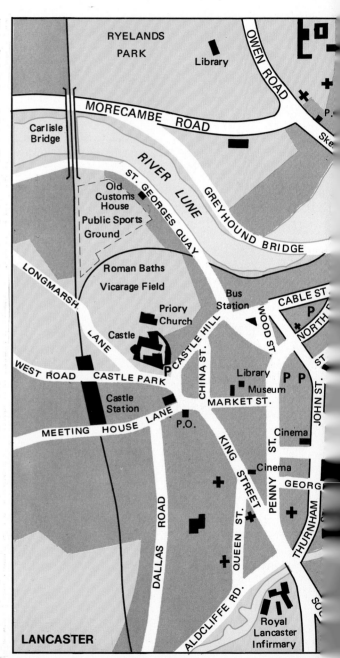

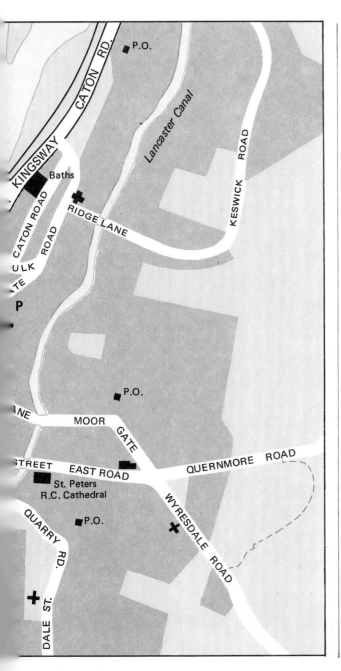

## Blackburn

In the *Lewis Textile Museum* are full-scale working models of Hargreaves' 'spinning jenny' and Crompton's 'spinning mule'.

Open Monday, Tuesday, Thursday and Saturday 10.00am to 5.00pm, Wednesday and Friday 10.00am to 7.30pm.

Four miles south-west is *Hoghton Tower*. This 16th-century house has some fine 17th-century panelling.

Open Easter to October Sunday.

Nearby on the river Calder is *Whalley*, an important centre in Anglo Saxon times. The remains of a 13th-century Cistercian abbey can be seen, the stones of which have been used to build several churches, farms and houses in the area.

The *Church of St Mary* is mainly 13th-century, and its fine canopied choir stalls with misericord seats were taken from the abbey.

Four miles to the east is the 1,831-ft high *Pendle Hill*, which gives spectacular views of the Forest of Bowland, Fylde Plain and the Irish Sea.

George Fox had a vision on the summit in 1652, leading him to preach and form the Society of Friends.

Pendle Hill is also associated with witchcraft – 19 of the witches tried at Lancaster Castle in 1612 were from this area.

## Burnley

Half a mile south-east is *Towneley Hall*, the fortified home of the Towneley family from the 13th century to 1902. The present house was built in the 14th and 16th centuries, with dungeons and battlements. There is a museum and art gallery.

Open Easter to September weekdays 10.00am to 5.30pm, Sunday 1.00pm to 5.00pm, October to Easter weekdays 10.00am to 5.00pm, Sunday 2.00pm to 5.00pm.

# Greater Manchester

Whatever may be said on the other side of the Pennines, or further north, Manchester is England's second capital.

Not only is it the greatest city of a Greater North, it is also a county in its own right, with a population of 2.7 million and a hinterland which reaches through Cheshire to the Peak District.

The opening in 1894 of the Manchester Ship Canal turned the city into a major inland port, and so it remains today.

The canal and the river Irwell separate the adjoining centres of Manchester and Salford, twin cities which are physically as one.

Just as Manchester is the trading centre of the British cotton industry, so the surrounding towns are the places of production, their towering, brick-built mills standing proudly in the Pennine valleys.

## Tourist Information Centres
Town Hall, Bolton, Greater Manchester. (0204) 22311
Council Offices, Toft Road, Knutsford, Cheshire. (0565) 2611
Town Hall, Macclesfield, Cheshire. (0625) 21955
Town Hall, Manchester, Greater Manchester. (061) 236 3377
County Hall Extension, Piccadilly Gardens, Manchester, Greater Manchester. (061) 247 3694
Manchester International Airport, Manchester, Greater Manchester. (061) 437 5233
Recorded Information Service (061) 832 5288
Crewe and Nantwich Borough Council, Beam Street, Nantwich, Cheshire. (0270) 63914
Greaves Street, Oldham, Greater Manchester. (061) 620 8930
9 Princes Street, Stockport, Greater Manchester. (061) 480 0315

## Manchester

The city is not only the commercial and industrial heart of the region, it is also the centre for culture, entertainment and sport.

*Cathedral* One of Manchester's showpieces now that its sandstone façade has been scrubbed clean. It is largely 15th-century, and built in the Perpendicular style, although the tower was added as recently as 1868. The site itself has been consecrated since the 10th century.

It has beautiful woodwork, and the choir stalls have intricate canopies and misericords. It is thought to be the widest church in England.

*Town Hall* This Gothic Revival building was designed by Alfred Waterhouse and was completed in 1877. Its main features are a tall clock-tower and flying buttresses.

*Platt Hall* A Georgian country house museum, now housing the *Gallery of English Costume*, which has a collection of English costume from the 17th century to the present day. Open May to August weekdays 10.00am to 6.00pm Sunday 12.00pm to 6.00pm, November to February weekdays 10.00am to 4.00pm Sunday 2.00pm to 4.00pm, other months weekdays 10.00am to 6.00pm Sunday 2.00pm to 6.00pm.

*Manchester Museum* Exhibits include the Cannon Aquarium and Vivarium. Open weekdays 10.00am to 6.00pm, Sunday 2.00pm to 5.00pm.

*Fletcher Moss Museum* This has a fine collection of English watercolours, including some by Turner. Open May to August weekdays 10.00am to 6.00pm Sunday 12pm to 6.00pm, closed November to February, other months weekdays 10.00am to 6.00pm, Sunday 2.00pm to 6.00pm.

*City Art Gallery* This Classical building was designed by Sir Charles Barry, who designed the Houses of Parliament. It has

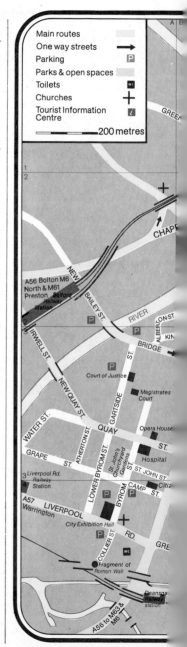

Main routes
One way streets
Parking
Parks & open spaces
Toilets
Churches
Tourist Information Centre
200 metres

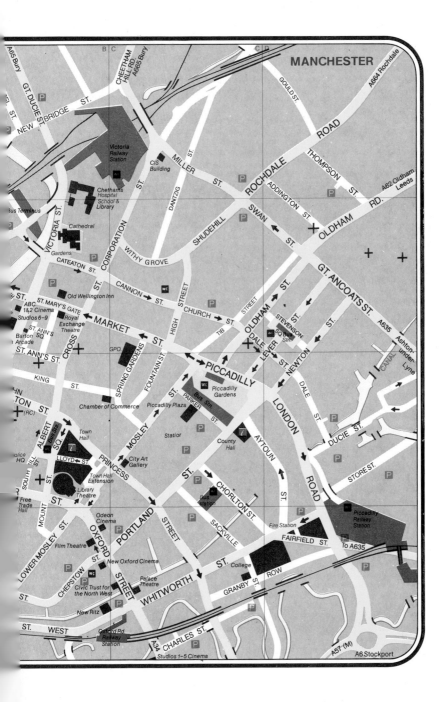

paintings by most well-known British artists, the Assheton-Bennett collection of English silver and the Thomas Tylston Greg collection of pottery.

The adjoining annexe *The Athenaeum* is a museum of ceramics.

Open weekdays 10.00am to 6.00pm, Sunday 2.30pm to 5.30pm.

*Queens Park Museum* Victorian and early 20th-century paintings and sculptures. It is also the regimental museum of the 14th and 20th King's Hussars.

The park in which the museum is housed has lawns, bowling greens and tennis courts.

Open May to August weekdays 10.00am to 6.00pm, Sunday 12.00pm to 6.00pm, November to February weekdays 10.00am to 4.00pm, Sunday 2.00pm to 4.00pm, other months weekdays 10.00am to 6.00pm, Sunday 2.00pm to 6.00pm.

*Whitworth Art Gallery* British drawings and watercolours from the 18th to 20th century, including some by Turner, and continental drawings by Cézanne, Gaugin, Van Gogh, Klee, Picasso.

Open Monday to Saturday 10.00am to 5.00pm.

*John Rylands Library* Early Bible fragments, European and Oriental manuscripts in over 50 languages. First editions in Greek, Latin and English classics.

Open Monday to Friday 9.30am to 5.30pm, Saturday 9.30am to 1.00pm.

*Wythenshawe Hall* A 17th-century half-timbered Cheshire manor house, furnished with articles and Dutch pictures of the period. The Hall is in *Wythenshawe Park*, one of the most beautiful in the country. Open May to August weekdays 10.00am to 6.00pm, Sunday 12.00pm to 6.00pm, November to February weekdays 10.00am to 4.00pm, Sunday 2.00pm to

The Town Hall . . . Gothic Revival

4.00pm, other months weekdays 10.00am to 6.00pm, Sunday 2.00pm to 6.00pm.

*Heaton Hall* Housing a collection of 17th- and 18th-century English pictures, furniture, ceramics, silver and glass.

*Heaton Park* has an 18-hole golf course, a boating lake and the only flat bowling green in the county. Open May to August weekdays 10.00am to 6.00pm, Sunday 12.00pm to 6.00pm,

November to February weekdays 10.00am to 4.00pm, Sunday 2.00pm to 4.00pm, other months weekdays 10.00am to 6.00pm, Sunday 2.00pm to 6.00pm.

*Free Trade Hall* Bombed and rebuilt in the Palladian style, this is the home of the famous *Hallé Orchestra*, founded in 1858 by Sir Charles Hallé.

*Royal Exchange Theatre* The latest and most exciting addition to the city's dramatic life. The 700-seat theatre, which opened in 1976, is a modular shape suspended within the walls of the historic Cotton Exchange in St Ann's Square.

*Belle Vue* As well as a small children's zoo, there is an amusement park, concert and exhibition halls and a dance hall.

*Port of Manchester* This port links the Mersey Estuary with the docks at Manchester, Runcorn and Ellesmere Port. The Ship Canal, 35 miles long, was opened in 1894, and tours of its upper reaches and the Manchester docks can be arranged.

Ring (061) 832 2244 for details.

*Theatres* Opera House; Palace Theatre; Library Theatre; Northern Dance Theatre.

*Food and drink* Manchester's small Chinese quarter has some excellent restaurants charging modest prices. The city was a pioneer of Armenian cuisine in Britain, and the Midland Hotel has a famous French restaurant. Greater Manchester has ten breweries.

*Shopping* The biggest shopping centre in the north, with fashion shops and boutiques in St Ann's Street and King Street. There are galleries of shops in the superbly Victorian Barton's Arcade, with its wrought-iron roof and great glass domes.

*Sport* Manchester United is arguably the world's most famous soccer team, though its deadly rival Manchester City is also a powerful force in English and European football.

There are Rugby League clubs dotted all around the city, among which Wigan is undoubtedly the most famous.

Old Trafford is a venue for Test cricket.

Swimming pool; tennis courts; bowling green; greyhound racing; football; cricket.

*Events* Manchester University Rag Procession, Shrove Tuesday; Manchester and Salford Boat Race, in February; Manchester Whit Walks, Spring Bank Holiday weekend; Manchester-Blackpool Vintage and Veteran Car Run, in June; Halle Proms, in June; Manchester Show, in July.

### Wigan
One of the oldest boroughs in Lancashire and now an industrial town. It was Royalist in the Civil War and a monument in Wigan Lane commemorates the site of a battle in 1651.

Wigan Pier, subject of a famous journey by George Orwell, is in fact a key loading point on the canal to Liverpool.

2½ miles north-east is *Haigh Hall*, a mid-19th-century mansion set in a 200-acre park. It was once the home of the Earls of Crawford. The Hall is not open but the park has many attractions, including hot houses, a zoo, a golf course and a play area.

### Bolton
*Hall i' th' Wood* is a fine 1483 half-timbered manor house, once the home of Samuel Crompton, inventor of the 'spinning mule', which revolutionized the textile industry.

Open April to September weekdays, closed Thursday, 10.00am to 6.00pm, Sunday 2.00pm to 6.00pm, October to March weekdays 10.00am to 5.00pm, closed Thursday and Sunday.

*The Old Man and Scythe* is a 13th-century inn standing in Church Gate. Lord Derby spent his final hours there before being executed by Cromwell in retribution for a Royalist massacre in the town.

Two miles north-west is *Smithill's Hall*, one of the oldest half-timbered houses in Lancashire. It was built in the 14th century with additions in Tudor times.

Open April to September weekdays, closed Thursday, 10.00am to 6.00pm, Sunday 2.00pm to 6.00pm, October to March weekdays 10.00am to 5.00pm, closed Thursday and Sunday.

Authentic *black puddings* are made in Farnworth, south-east of Bolton. At Morris' 'Gold Medal' Black Puddings Ltd in Gower Street, the pudding making takes place from 6.00am to 10.00am, and visitors can watch the process by appointment. Ring Mr J Morris, (0204) 73279, for details.

### Bury
Steam train aficionados can indulge their interest at *Bury Transport Museum*, where the six trains operate on the last Sunday of each month from March to September. The museum is open throughout the year at weekends.

Ring (061) 764 7790 for more details.

### Rochdale
For students of the historical and sociological, it is possible to visit the small museum where the Co-operative Movement was founded in 1844, by a handful of local men. Ring (0706) 47474 for details.

Apart from this, the other attraction of this Victorian country town is its proximity to the Moorlands and *Blackstone Edge*, where there is one of the best-preserved Roman roads in the country, running across the Pennines into York.

Rochdale's famous sons and daughters represent a diverse range of interests. Among them are John Bright, the 19th-

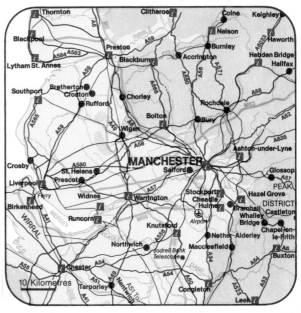

century opponent of the Corn Laws, and Gracie Fields, the 20th-century singer.

## Oldham

The *Local Interest Museum* has displays of clogs, toys, birds, and a 'spinning mule'. The Cobbett Gallery is for local artists to exhibit their work.

Open Monday, Wednesday, Thursday and Friday 10.00am to 7.00pm, Tuesday 10.00am to 1.00pm, Saturday 10.00am to 4.00pm.

The *Art Gallery* has collections of early English watercolours, paintings by Walter Sickert and L. S. Lowry and a bust of Sir Winston Churchill by Jacob Epstein. Open Monday, Wednesday, Thursday and Friday 10.00am to 7.00pm, Tuesday 10.00am to 1.00pm, Saturday 10.00am to 4.00pm.

There are displays of weaving and costumes at the *Saddleworth Museum*. Open Wednesday, Saturday and Sunday 2.30pm to 5.00pm. A general market is held at Tommyfield every Monday, Friday and Saturday, and on Wednesdays there is a flea market.

## Stockport

A market which is said to be 700 years old survives every Friday and Saturday, but Stockport's modern shopping precinct towers over all.

At *Vernon Park*, the museum has a window made of over 200 pieces of Blue John fluor spar, a display of ceramics, a natural history and a geology collection. Open Monday to Saturday 10.00am to 6.00pm.

Among the exhibits at the *War Memorial Art Gallery* are paintings by L. S. Lowry and a bust of Yehudi Menuhin by Jacob Epstein. Open Monday to Friday 12.00pm to 5.30pm, Saturday 10.00am to 4.00pm.

The viaduct which carries the railway line across the river Mersey at Stockport was completed in 1840, and then extended so that it was finally opened in 1842.

It consists of 27 arches, was built by G. W. Buck at a cost of £70,000 and is said to contain 11,000,000 bricks.

## Alderley Edge

Just across the Cheshire border, 600 ft above sea level, stands Alderley Edge. The town is a well-known picturesque spot, and there is a copper mine which dates back to pre-Roman times.

More than 200 acres of woodland is owned by the National Trust, including *Wizard's Wood* and *Wizard's Well*. Local legend has it that a wizard used to keep sleeping warriors and their horses in a cave under the wood.

## Knutsford

Mrs Gaskell's *Cranford*. The novelist lived in the town and was married in 1832 in the 18th-century parish church. Her grave can be found behind the Unitarian chapel.

Knutsford is a charming town with narrow streets of fine black-and-white houses.

Two miles north is *Tatton Hall*, one of the National Trust's most popular properties. It dates from 1800 and was once the home of the Egerton family, and is surrounded by 54 acres of beautiful gardens and woodland. Open mid-March to September daily 2.00pm to 5.00pm, Sunday 1.00pm to 5.00pm, October to mid-March closed.

Six miles south of the town is the *Jodrell Bank* radio telescope. The dish aerial is 250-ft in diameter and weighs more than 2,000 tons.

There is an exhibition of radio astronomy and a model radio telescope in the Concourse Building which can be visited.

Open March 18 to October 31 2.00pm to 6.00pm, November 1 to March 19 weekends only 2.00pm to 5.00pm.

## Northwich

This is salt mine country and some of the old houses lean over because of subsidence.

Just north of the town is Anderton where a unique canal lift hoists the boats from the River Weaver Navigation to the Trent and Mersey Canal.

## Macclesfield

Once a major silk-producing centre, Macclesfield is now a pleasant market town, dominated by the 18th- and 19th-century mill buildings.

The oldest church in town is St Michael's which still retains the look of its medieval origins, although it was substantially rebuilt in the 18th and 19th centuries. The church is reached on one side by climbing 108 steps.

Mary Fitton, Maid of Honour to Good Queen Bess, and believed to be Shakespeare's 'Dark Lady' of the sonnets, lived at *Gawsworth Hall*, three miles south of the town.

The half-timbered house was largely built in the 15th century and its estate includes a jousting ground, orangery and walled park. Open March 18 to October 29 daily 2.00pm to 6.00pm.

Four miles east of town is *Macclesfield Forest*, a small village which sits on the edge of a vast wild moorland, once the haunt of highwaymen.

More than 1,600 ft up in the midst of this desolate land is the *Cat and Fiddle Inn*, England's highest pub.

## Nantwich

Another old salt-mining town on the river Weaver. A wealth of attractive black and white Tudor houses crowds the narrow streets. The finest of these form Welsh Row, almshouses built in 1638 by Sir Edmund Wright and adorned with tiny carved figures.

# Merseyside

Liverpool was first famous as a great Atlantic port, and it remains an important maritime city. Its famous skyline can best be seen on the short ferry trip across the Mersey.

In the 1960s, Liverpool was the birthplace of British rock music, with the Beatles as its most famous sons.

Perennially, Liverpool has been one of England's greatest sporting towns, and the soccer team which bears the city's name has more than once been champion of all Europe. Liverpool also stages the famous Grand National steeplechase at the Aintree racecourse each March.

The nearby seaside resort of Southport has six golf courses, including Royal Birkdale, occasional home of the British Open.

Although Liverpool is in England, its geographical locale has made it culturally both a Welsh and an Irish city. It is a big-city base from which the coast and mountains of North Wales can be explored, and there are ferries and flights to the Isle of Man.

## Tourist Information Centres

Birkenhead Library, Borough Road, Birkenhead, Merseyside. (051) 652 6106
187 St Johns Centre, Elliot Street, Liverpool, Merseyside. (051) 709 3631/8681
Municipal Buildings, Sir Thomas Street, Liverpool, Merseyside. (051) 227 3911
The Pier, New Brighton, Merseyside. (051) 639 3929
Cambridge Arcade, Southport, Lancashire. (0704) 33133/40404
Town Hall, Wallasey, Merseyside. (051) 639 6106 ext 333

## Liverpool

The original dock in Liverpool was opened in 1715, and it now has seven miles of dockland and is the largest exporting port in the British Commonwealth.

The waterfront is dominated by the Cunard and Dock Board buildings, and the Royal Liver Building, its towers crowned by the famous Liver Birds, which is a view of the city known throughout the world.

There are more than 3,000 acres of public parks and gardens within the city limits, ranging from the botanic gardens at Harthill to the pleasant little garden by St George's Hall.

Liverpool has countless restaurants offering the national cuisine of many countries. Perhaps the most interesting area gastronomically is Chinatown.

The city boasts two fine modern cathedrals. The Anglican Liverpool Cathedral was begun in 1904 and is still unfinished, while the Roman Catholic Metropolitan Cathedral was consecrated in 1967.

The latter's conical roof, crowned by a stained glass lantern has led to it being affectionately dubbed 'Paddy's Wigwam' by the locals.

*City Museum* Diverse collections ranging from Oriental antiquities to space exploration; planetarium. Open weekdays 10.00am to 5.00pm, Sunday 2.00pm to 5.00pm.

*Walker Art Gallery* Wide range of paintings from early Flemish to 20th-century, including fine examples of Rembrandt, Stubbs and Cézanne. Experts regard this as the finest collection outside London. Open weekdays 10.00am to 5.00pm, Sunday 2.00pm to 5.00pm.

*Sudley Art Gallery* Mainly devoted to 18th- and 19th-century painters. Open weekdays 10.00am to 5.00pm, Sunday 2.00pm to 5.00pm.

The Liver Birds . . . perched on the Royal Liver Building

*Hornby Library* Prints, manuscripts and rare books, in addition to a large lending library. Open Monday to Friday 9.00am to 9.00pm, Saturday 9.00am to 5.00pm.

*Speke Hall* Richly half-timbered Elizabethan house set in beautifully wooded grounds.

Open weekdays 10.00am to 5.00pm, Sunday 2.00pm to 5.00pm.

*St George's Hall* A 19th-century building with a colonnaded front. It is used as the city's law courts, but regular organ recitals are held in the main hall.

*Bluecoat Chambers* Superb Queen Anne building, the oldest in Liverpool, now the headquarters of the Merseyside Arts Association. Various exhibitions and activities are held from time to time.

Open Tuesday to Saturday 10.30am to 5.00pm.

*Philharmonic Hall* Home of the Royal Liverpool Philharmonic Orchestra, it was bought for the orchestra by the city.

*Events* Lord Mayor's Parade, Liverpool Show, in June; Woolton Show, in August.

## New Brighton

A friendly resort with a seven-mile promenade from which the visitor can view ships entering and leaving Liverpool docks.

There is a large indoor amusement centre, cinemas and a theatre. Many of the country's top brass bands perform every Sunday when the town is at its busiest. The swimming pool is one of the largest in Europe.

Behind New Brighton is the extensive *Wirral Country Park* with views across the Dee to the Welsh hills. *Hilbre Island* bird sanctuary can be reached at low tide.

The Wirral peninsula has numerous golf courses including challenging links such as Hoylake's world famous championship course.

## Formby

Old Formby is gone, buried by 1910 under the shifting sands which are still building up as the sea recedes. Today there is a two-mile stretch of attractive dunes flanked by pine trees to prevent further movement.

The sandhills along Formby foreshore stretch for seven miles up the coast to Southport. Large sections of this coastline were bought for the National Trust by public subscription in 1967.

## Southport

For more than a century the sea has been retreating, leaving this dignified resort with a vast expanse of magnificent sand which is now the biggest beach in Britain.

The problem of providing convenient sea bathing was tackled by the resourceful Victorians. At the end of the last century, they built an 86-acre *Marine Lake*, with facilities for swimming and boating. The long pier has its own railway.

Southport has a good sunshine record, with an average of 5½ hours a day in the summer.

A major event in the town's calendar is in August, when the well-known flower show is held, displaying the widest possible selection of blooms.

Of international fame is Southport's Royal Birkdale golf course, where the Ryder Cup and the British Open are periodically staged.

## Rufford

Worth visiting is the *Old Hall*, a magnificent 15th-century manor house with a finely carved screen. Part of the building houses a museum.

Open daily except Monday 12.00pm to dusk.

The nearby river Douglas offers pleasant strolls along its banks. Overlooking the river is *Parbold Beacon*, with views right over the Lancashire Plain.

## Knowsley

Home of a safari park which has free-roaming big game animals and a dolphinarium.

Open March 31 to October 31 daily 10.00am to 5.00pm, April 1 to November 1 daily 10.00am to 3.30pm.

# Chester

The exquisite city of Chester is best known for its galleried, timbered, medieval shops which are called The Rows, but the town as a whole spans three major periods of building.

It is a walled Roman city, a Tudor city, and it has a considerable amount of Victorian reproduction timbering, freer in style and grander in scale than the original.

If Chester is lavishly decorated with half-timbering, so is the whole county. Cheshire is the heartland of a black-and-white townscape which dots itself through the western side of central England, from the Manchester suburbs to Shropshire and Herefordshire.

Once having escaped the grimy clutches of Manchester and Liverpool, the county has frequent stretches of suburbanism; it is barely Northern, owing much more to the style of the Home Counties.

The Cheshire Cat was a creature which could disappear, leaving behind only its smile. Its creator was, of course, Lewis Carroll, born Charles Dodgson in the Cheshire village of Daresbury.

Cheshire cheese is still made in the county, and visits to a farm can be arranged by the Tourist Information Centre in Cheshire.

**Tourist Information Centres**
Town Hall, Chester, Cheshire. (0244) 40144
Market Square, Congleton, Cheshire. (026 02) 71095
57 Church Street, Runcorn, Cheshire. (092 85) 76776/69656
80 Sankey Street, Warrington, Cheshire. (0925) 36501
Municipal Buildings, Kingsway, Widnes, Cheshire. (051) 424 2061

**Daresbury**

The fine old village church here, which sits prettily among meadows and flowers, has a charming memorial to Daresbury's most famous son – a stained glass window depicting many characters from Wonderland, and the author himself, Lewis Carroll.

**Helsby**

This charming village is noted for *Helsby Hill*, a 462-ft viewpoint where traces of Iron Age man have been discovered. This hill is used to train climbers.

**Chester**

One of the most beautiful cities in Britain. It has been an important centre on the river Dee for more than 2,000 years.

The Romans established the camp of Deva here in AD 79 and Chester is richly endowed with Roman remains, including a Roman amphitheatre.

Substantial sections of the original Roman wall remain, along with the towers and gates which were added in the Middle Ages. This combines to give Chester the best-preserved ancient city ramparts in Britain.

Visitors can walk a two-mile stretch along the crest of the red sandstone battlements.

Perhaps the pride and joy, and the feature most remembered by visitors, are the 13th-century galleried streets known as The Rows, which could well be the world's first pedestrian shopping precinct.

*Cathedral* Founded in the 10th century, but most of the building took place in the 14th century. It was once the Abbey of St Werburgh, a Mercian princess, and was used as a Benedictine monastery until the 16th century.

It became the cathedral for the new diocese of Chester in 1541, following the Dissolution.

The choir is the highlight of

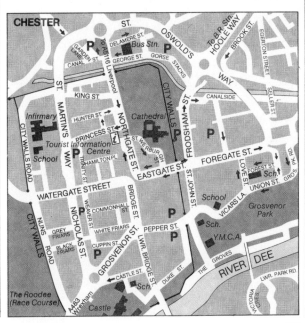

137

Verdant pastures . . . looking towards Beeston Castle in the Peckforton Hills

**Roman Gardens** Many Roman remains. Until recently this was the site of Chester High Cross, but this has now returned to its position outside St Peter's Church.

**Grosvenor Museum** A fine collection of Roman and Anglo-Saxon coins.

Open weekdays 10.00am to 5.00pm, Sunday 2.00pm to 5.30pm.

**Cheshire Regiment Museum** Exhibits associated with the Regiment include standards captured by General Sir Charles Napier in India in the 1840s.

Open March to September weekdays 9.00am to 6.00pm, Sunday 2.00pm to 5.30pm.

**Chester Zoo** These world-famous zoological gardens are two miles from the city centre. Animals, birds, reptiles and fish are all displayed in conditions similar to their natural environment.

Open daily 9.00am to dusk.

### Tarporley

An elegant town standing on the fringe of the Delamere Forest. Rich and serene woodland is broken by the waters of Hatch Mere and Oak Mere.

### Beeston Castle

In the Peckforton Hills, south-east of Chester, stand the ruins of a 13th-century castle overlooking a modern mock-medieval castle.

### Malpas

Overhanging houses, half-timbered cottages and steep streets fill this interesting small town.

*St Oswald's Church* dates from the 14th century and has medieval stone carving, stained glass and a 13th-century parish chest.

North-east of the town is *No Man's Heath*, with a splendid view across the park to *Cholmondeley Castle*, an 18th-century mansion owing much to the Gothic style.

the interior. It was largely built in 1300, but the magnificently-carved stalls were added 80 years later. Each has a misericord depicting fables.

*The Rows* Unique and beautiful, originating in the 13th century. These two-tiered shopping arcades open on to balustraded walks and radiate from *The Cross*, along Eastgate, Watergate, Bridgegate and Northgate. Many of Chester's historic buildings are on these four streets which still follow the lines laid down by the Romans.

*Watergate Street* This was known as Via Principalis in Roman times. Today it has fine examples of Tudor architecture, including *Bishop Lloyd's House*, which is the richest example of carved timberwork

in the city. It can be viewed only from the outside. Also in this street is *God's Providence House*, a 17th-century building with a Puritan text inscribed on the front beam. It now houses a kitchen shop.

*Bridge Street* The Romans knew it as Via Praetoria. Lower Bridge Street lies along the old Roman route to London. There are several splendid façades, notably of 17th-century 'Dutch' houses.

*Bridge of Sighs* Immediately beyond Northgate, the bridge crosses the canal and once joined Northgate Jail to the Chapel of Little St John, where the condemned prisoners were taken to hear their last service before death. It is no longer open.

# Shropshire

Twentieth-century souls have restored to the county its Anglo-Norman name 'Salop', but it remains the land of Housman's *Shropshire Lad*.

The only valid objection to the name Shropshire is that its soft syllables are just too mellow for a county of rocky ridges and dramatic skies.

Legend has it that, on a group of rocks called The Stiperstones, devils gather on Midwinter Night to choose their leader.

The Long Mynd and Wenlock Edge are rocky ridges stretching for many miles near the town of Church Stretton; the Wrekin is a sudden, mound-shaped hill near Shrewsbury; the Clee Hills rise near Ludlow.

Once, these hills echoed to the clamour of conflict; today they represent a slumbering border between England and Wales, though the cultures of both countries are evident in the towns of Shropshire.

### Shrewsbury

Although Shrewsbury was first settled by the Romans, the prevailing impression is of medieval architecture, particularly the timbered style of the Elizabethan period. Fine examples are to be found on Bear Steps.

A maze of tiny alleys with quaint names such as Gullet Passage, Pig Trough and Grope Lane lead away from the main streets and have remained unchanged for centuries.

Markets are held every Wednesday, Friday and Saturday in the Market Hall, and on Tuesdays a cattle market is held at Harlescott.

There are more than 260 acres of parks and open spaces in the borough. Superb floral displays are to be seen in The Dingle in Quarry Park and there is a nature trail which incorporates a horseshoe loop of the river Severn.

Charles Darwin was born in the town and educated at the famous public school.

Clive of India, protagonist of British rule in the sub-continent lived in Shrewsbury. He was mayor in 1762 and M.P. from 1761 to his death. His home *Clive House* is now used as the Shropshire Pottery and Regimental Museums. Open Tuesday to Saturday 10.00am to 1.00pm, 2.00pm to 6.00pm.

The 15th-century *Abbot's House* is now private, but *Rowley's House*, dating from the 16th century, containing collections of Roman, prehistoric and medieval material, can be visited. Open Monday to Saturday 10.00am to 1.00pm, 2.00pm to 5.00pm.

Shrewsbury Castle is a well-preserved partly-Norman building. Its interior was reconstructed in 1790 by Thomas Telford. Open Easter to September daily 10.00am to 5.00pm, October to Easter Monday to Saturday 10.00am to 4.00pm.

*Events* Shropshire and West Midland Agricultural Show, in May; Shrewsbury Regatta and

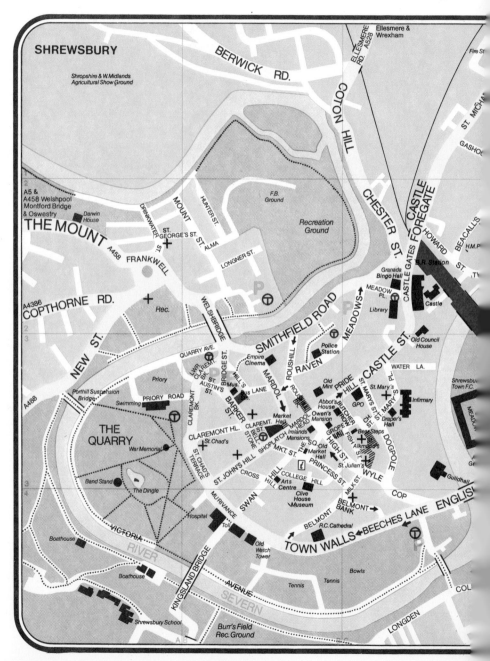

# SHREWSBURY

Shropshire & W. Midlands
Agricultural Show Ground

BERWICK RD.

ELLESMERE RD. A528
Ellesmere &
Wrexham

Fire St

ST. MICHA

COTON HILL

CHESTER ST.

CASTLE FOREGATE

CASTLE GATES

HOWARD ST.

GASHO

BEACALL'S

H.M.P

A5 &
A458 Welshpool
Montford Bridge
& Oswestry

THE MOUNT

Darwin
House

DRINKWATER

MOUNT

HUNTER ST.

F.B.
Ground

Recreation
Ground

B.R. Station

Granada
Bingo Hall

Castle

ST. GEORGE'S ST.

ALMA ST.

ST.

FRANKWELL

A458

LONGNER ST.

MEADOW
PL.

Library

Old Council
House

A4386 COPTHORNE RD.

Rec.

WELSHBRIDGE

SMITHFIELD ROAD

MEADOWS

Shrewsbu
Town F.C.

NEW ST.

QUARRY AVE.

LWR.
CLAREM.
ST.

BRIDGE ST.

HILL'S

ROUSHILL

RAVEN

Police
Station

CASTLE ST.

WATER LA.

A498

Priory

PRIORY ROAD

AUSTIN'S
ST.

B.Mus

Bus Lane

Empire
Cinema

MARDOL

ROUSHILL

Old
Mint

PRIDE HILL

St. Mary's

BUTCHER

ST. MARY'S ST.

Infirmary

Porthill Suspension
Bridge

Swimming

CLAREMONT BK.

BARKER ST.

ISP

Ho.

Market
Hall

Abbot's
House

Owen's
Mansion

GPO

MARY'S

Draper's
Hall

THE
QUARRY

War Memorial

CLAREMONT HL.

St. Chad's

CLAREMT
ST.

ST. CHAD'S
TERRACE

STONE

Irelands
Mansions

SHOPLATCH

MARDOL
HEAD

GROPE

Bear
Steps

St.
Alkmond's

DOGPOLE

Guildhall

Band Stand

The Dingle

ST. JOHN'S CROSS

SWAN HILL

MKT. ST.

COLLEGE HILL

Arts
Centre

SQ.Old
Market
Hall

PRINCESS ST.

HIGH ST.

St. Julian's

WYLE

COP

VICTORIA

Boathouse

MURIVANCE

Hospital

Toll

Clive
House
Museum

MILK ST.

BELMONT
BANK

BELMONT

R.C. Cathedral

TOWN WALLS

BEECHES LANE

ENGLIS

MEADO

Ge

RIVER

Boathouse

KINGSLAND BRIDGE

AVENUE

SEVERN

Old
Watch
Tower

Bowls

Tennis

Tennis

LONGDEN

COL

Shrewsbury School

Burr's Field
Rec. Ground

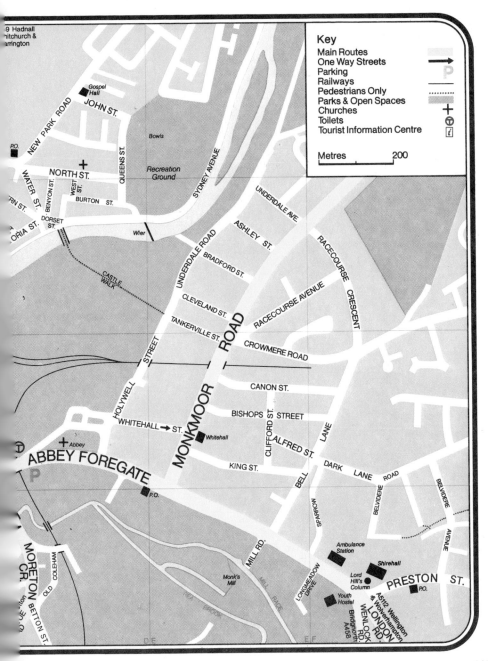

**Key**

Main Routes
One Way Streets
Parking
Railways
Pedestrians Only
Parks & Open Spaces
Churches
Toilets
Tourist Information Centre

Metres          200

Hunter Trials, in June; Shrewsbury Flower Show, in August; National Horse and Tractor Ploughing Championships, in October.

Shrewsbury has a League soccer team.

## Alrewas

A superb village, with magnificent black-and-white thatched cottages, dating from the 15th century.

## Tamworth

Once the capital of the Anglo-Saxon kingdom of Mercia, and much more recently a cradle of trade-unionism. Tamworth is now a pleasant market town with some light industry.

*Tamworth Castle* stands on a mound above the river Anker on the edge of the town. It has been added to since it was built and is now part Norman, part Tudor, part Jacobean and the last modifications were made in the early 19th century.

The castle is well preserved, and was lived in until quite recently. It now houses a *museum* of local history. Open April to September, weekdays 10.00am to 6.00pm, Sundays 2.00pm to 5.00pm, October to March, weekdays 10.00am to 5.00pm, Sundays 2.00pm to 5.00pm. Closed on Friday in winter.

Another interesting building is the *Moat House*, an Elizabethan town mansion owned by the Cumberford family who entertained Charles I there. It is now a restaurant, but has been preserved and has a magnificent staircase and heraldic ceiling.

## Uttoxeter

The town's main source of prosperity is its weekly *cattle market*.

However it is best known for its charming *racecourse*, and for the arrogance of the young Samuel Johnson.

His father, a Lichfield book-

A famous son of Shrewsbury . . . Charles Darwin

seller, asked him to look after a bookstall in Uttoxeter market place, but was steadfastly refused.

In his old age, Johnson was attacked by a guilty conscience and did belated penance by standing in the market place for several hours in drenching rain. A plaque near the spot reminds visitors of the incident.

## Burton on Trent

One of the world's great brewing centres and the home of a beer style as distinctive as those of Pilsen, Munich, Dortmund or Dublin.

In the 1700s, Pale Ale from Burton was shipped by canal to the river Trent and eventually the Humber ports for export to many European countries, Russia and later India. The town's unique brewing system is still used by Marston's and Bass.

Burton itself is an old industrial town straggling around its four breweries. The principal attraction for the visitor is the excellent *brewery museum* at the premises of Bass, most famous producers of Pale Ale. The museum has an exhibition on pub games, a steam engine, and a locomotive which once ferried the directors around the town.

Open Monday to Friday 10.30am to 4.30pm, Saturday, Sunday and Bank Holidays 11.00am to 5.00pm.

## Ruyton-XI-Towns

The village received its unusual name in 1301 when 11 local hamlets united.

## Oswestry

This attractive market town, close to the border, between farmland and the wild hills, saw centuries of warfare between England and Wales.

Most of it was rebuilt in the 19th century, although parts of the Norman church have survived along with the 15th-century grammar school which is now split into three cottages.

In Morda Street stands the *Weeping Stone*, the pedestal of a cross placed there in 1559 during the plague which killed one in seven of the population.

## Wem

A small market town, known for its brewery and infamous for its connections with the Hanging Judge Jeffreys. He took the title Baron of Wem and was imprisoned in the Tower of London after his Bloody Assizes.

## Whitchurch

A useful base from which to explore, close to the Welsh border, and to the English county of Cheshire.

It was the birthplace of Sir Edward German, composer of *Tom Jones* and *Merrie England*.

The *Church of St Alkamund*, built in 1712–13, has a 17th-century font.

## Market Drayton

True to its name, the town has had a market every Wednesday for 700 years.

Market Drayton was the birthplace in 1725 of Robert Clive. His initials are carved on a desk at the local grammar school.

## Telford

The great engineer *Thomas Telford* carried out his first major works in Shropshire, in the late 1700s, and was for a time County Surveyor. He became as much a son of Shropshire as he was of his native Scotland.

In his honour, a group of several adjoining towns around Wellington have collectively been given the name of Telford. Within the district of Telford is a three-mile stretch of the river Severn which has been turned into a remarkable open-air museum of industrial archaeology.

River transport, local coal and local clay all helped, but the Industrial Revolution here in the 1700s was made possible by the inventive fervour of a Quaker family called Darby.

In 1709, Abraham Darby pioneered the smelting of iron-ore; in 1779, his grandson, who had the same name, built the world's first iron bridge, which still spans the river; another member of the family built Coalport, where the famous china of the same name was originally made.

*The Ironbridge Gorge Museum* embraces all of these sites, and more. It is open daily from 10.00am to 5.00pm, and for an hour longer from April to October.

A fine example of Telford's own work, near the district which bears his name, is the world's first cast-iron aqueduct, at Longdon upon Tern.

## Bridgnorth

An interesting cliff railway links High and Low Bridgnorth. The track has a 1 in 1½ gradient.

High Town, perched on the cliff top has stepped streets. The tower of the ruined Norman *castle* keep leans 17 degrees from perpendicular – three times as much as the Leaning Tower of Pisa.

Low Town, on the banks of the Severn, boasts many fine buildings.

The town is a more than adequate place on which to base further exploration.

The *Severn Valley Railway* runs from Bridgnorth to Bewdley, and there are 31 steam trains.

Open weekends from March 4 to October 29, daily in June and July and other selected days. Ring (0299) 403816 for details.

## Church Stretton

A small resort and market town.

The parish church was built partly in the 12th century and partly in the 17th, with a 14th-century nave roof. A Saxon fertility figure stands over the bricked-up Norman north door.

*Acton Scott Working Farm Museum* is a small farm run as it would have been before mechanisation, and has cattle, pigs, sheep and poultry. Camping volunteers are accepted every year to help.

Ring Marshbrook (069 46) 322 days or Church Stretton (069 42) 2954 evenings.

There is a charming 17th-century manor house one mile north at Little Stretton.

Beautiful scenery surrounds the town, and a splendid walk to The Long Mynd starts at Cardingmill Valley. Another walk leads to the summit of Caer Caradoc.

## Cleobury Mortimer

Named after the famous Norman family who established themselves here in 1086.

The ancient market cross marks the spot where the body of Arthur, brother of Henry VIII, was laid during its journey from Ludlow to Worcester where he is buried.

There is a prehistoric camp on top of the nearby 1,750-ft Titterstone Clee Hill.

## Ludlow

A town of much architectural and historical interest with the ruins of a massive red sandstone *castle* built in 1085 by Roger Montgomery, Earl of Shrewsbury. It is now the backdrop for the annual festival of Shakespeare plays, held in June and July.

It was here in 1509 that Arthur, eldest son of Henry VII, brought his wife Catherine of Aragon. His death a few months later changed the course of English history for his brother became Henry VIII and married Catherine.

The *Church of St Lawrence* has a majesty usually found only in cathedrals. Its magnificent interior dates from the 15th century and the misericords are believed to be the finest in England. The ashes of A. E. Housman are in the churchyard.

Lord Nelson once stayed at the *Angel Inn*, which is 300 years old. Another old inn is the 17th-century *Feathers Hotel* in the Bull Ring.

## Bishop's Castle

A tiny town right on the border, near the Clun Forest. The *Three Tuns* pub has its own adjoining brewery, built on the traditional tower principle.

# Staffordshire

Neighbouring counties to the north are better known for their Peak District scenery, but Staffordshire has a surprisingly large share of this dramatic National Park, with the town of Leek as a centre from which to explore.

At the opposite end of the county is another large stretch of open country, Cannock Chase, named for its hunting history. There, the obvious centre from which to explore is Lichfield, a pleasant town which was the birthplace of Dr Johnson.

Between these two stretches of open country are two particularly distinctive industrial towns. Stoke is the centre of The Potteries, and the setting for the stories of Arnold Bennett; the smaller town of Burton is a famous brewing centre.

**Tourist Information Centres**
Town Hall, Burton-upon-Trent, Staffordshire. (0283) 45369
18 Edward Street, Leek, Staffordshire. (0538) 385509/385181
9 Breadmarket Street, Lichfield, Staffordshire. (054 32) 52109
Borough Hall, Eastgate Street, Stafford, Staffordshire. (0785) 3181
Central Library, Bethesda Street, Hanley, Stoke-on-Trent, Staffordshire. (0782) 21242/25108/23122
Municipal Offices, Church Street, Tamworth, Staffordshire. (0827) 3561

144

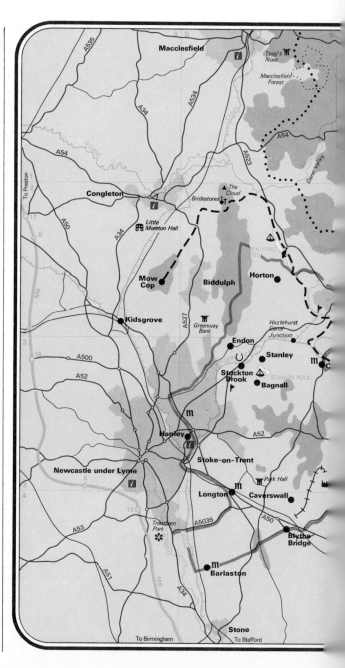

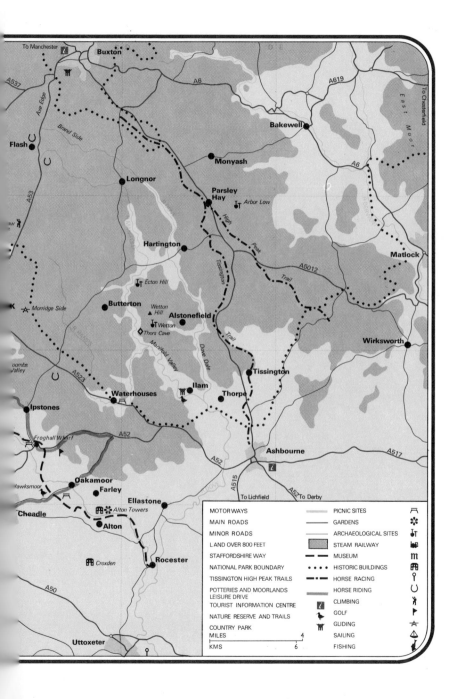

To Manchester · Buxton

A537

Axe Edge

A6

A619

To Chesterfield

East Moor

Brand Side

Bakewell

Flash

Monyash

A6

Longnor

Parsley Hay · Arbor Low

High

Peak

Hartington

Matlock

Tissington

A5012

Ecton Hill

Butterton

Wetton Hill

Alstonefield

Morridge Side

Wetton

Thors Cave

Dove Dale

Manifold Valley

Trail

Wirksworth

coombs Valley

A523

Ilam

Thorpe

Tissington

Waterhouses

Ipstones

Froghall Wharf

A52

Ashbourne

A517

A52

A515

To Lichfield

A52 To Derby

Oakamoor

Farley

Hawksmoor

Ellastone · Alton Towers

Cheadle

Alton

Croxden

Rocester

A50

Uttoxeter

| | |
|---|---|
| MOTORWAYS | PICNIC SITES |
| MAIN ROADS | GARDENS |
| MINOR ROADS | ARCHAEOLOGICAL SITES |
| LAND OVER 800 FEET | STEAM RAILWAY |
| STAFFORDSHIRE WAY | MUSEUM |
| NATIONAL PARK BOUNDARY | HISTORIC BUILDINGS |
| TISSINGTON HIGH PEAK TRAILS | HORSE RACING |
| POTTERIES AND MOORLANDS LEISURE DRIVE | HORSE RIDING |
| TOURIST INFORMATION CENTRE | CLIMBING |
| NATURE RESERVE AND TRAILS | GOLF |
| COUNTRY PARK | GLIDING |
| MILES 4 | SAILING |
| KMS 6 | FISHING |

145

## Leek

Close to the south-west edge of the Peak National Park is Leek, which is regally personified as the Queen of the Moorlands. The soubriquet reflects not only the splendid position of the town, but also its importance to the agricultural community in the surrounding rural area. Farmers bring their livestock and produce to the open-air and cattle markets which are held every Wednesday. There is a small covered market on Fridays and Saturdays.

Leek is also an industrial town, albeit a small one. During the 19th century, dyes and silk products were manufactured. The old mills are still used but they now produce synthetic fibres.

The shopping centre has a good number of antique dealers, and some buildings of antiquity. The oldest is the parish church of Edward the Confessor, built in 1297. *The Roebuck Inn*, in Derby Street, was built in 1627. Many of the attractive 19th-century buildings were designed by the Sugden brothers, two local architects. From the centre of the town, there are vistas of the countryside beyond.

### The Peak National Park

A quaintly-named place called Flash, to the north of Leek and in the heart of the park, is said to be the highest village in England, at 1,518 ft.

Its name derives from its past role as a centre for the counterfeiting of money. The counties of Staffordshire, Cheshire and Derbyshire meet at Three Shires Heads, and it was easy for the counterfeiters to escape the Sheriff by crossing into another county with their 'flash' money.

*The Roaches*, between Leek and Flash, are tor-like formations of Millstone grit. A favourite haunt of climbers are the nearby *Ramshaw Rocks*.

To the east of Leek are the *Ecton Upper Mines*, at Wetton. There are remains of extensive 18th-century workings, and many of the shafts and other features are still visible.

Thors Head is in the north of the Manifold Valley, one of the most splendid limestone valleys in the Pennines. The river Manifold disappears underground near Thors Cave (occupied from Paleolithic to Roman times) and reappears at Ilam, where there is a country park and a nature reserve.

To the west of Leek runs the 32-mile Staffordshire Way. This is a long-distance footpath, created from former railway lines, which runs from Mow Cop to Rocester. It is possible to walk, cycle or ride a horse along the route.

### Ilam

This village is set in the heart of the lovely Manifold Valley. The church has a carved Norman font, and there are two Anglo-Saxon crosses in the churchyard. In the nearby valley caves there are traces of much earlier life. The teeth of ancient lions and hyenas have been found there.

### The Potteries

From the moorlands by the 18th-century folly of Mow Cop, the salutations of Primitive Methodism first echoed across northern valleys; in the Five Towns below, Arnold Bennett's Wesleyans lived the industrious provincial life of The Potteries.

In their very titles, Bennett novels like *Clayhanger* and *Anna of the Five Towns* cast a permanent memory of the region. The Five Towns – Stoke, Longton, Tunstall, Burslem and Fenton – merged with Hanley in 1910. Today, they are collectively known as Stoke on Trent.

Arnold Bennett's home in Waterloo Road, Hanley, is now

a museum. The *Bennett Museum* is open Monday, Wednesday, Thursday and Saturday, 2.00pm to 5.00pm.

Another of Stoke's father-figures, and its most famous potter, was Josiah Wedgwood, who was born in Burslem in 1759, and who set up his company at the age of 29. Wedgwood's vision also gave Stoke a canal which linked the city by way of the Trent and Mersey to the sea. Today, the canal has been cleaned, and has become a popular place for boating.

There is a memorial to Wedgwood in Stoke's Regency church. In the 19th century, a memorial building was erected on the site of his first factory at Burslem. This is now a branch public library (closed Thursdays). There is a museum at the visitors' centre in the Wedgwood pottery.

### Pottery Visits
*John Beswick (Royal Doulton Group)* Visits by appointment only on Tuesday and Thursday. Parties of 12–24, minimum age 16. (0782) 313041
*Crown Staffordshire (Division of Josiah Wedgwood)* Visits by appointment only from Monday to Thursday. Parties of 10–35, minimum age 14. Factory souvenir shop. (0782) 45274
*Doulton Fine China* Visits by appointment only. Monday to Friday. Parties of 10, minimum age 14. Small gift shop. (0782) 84271
*Elijah Cotton* Visits by appointment only. Monday to Friday. Parties of 12–15, all ages. (0782) 21741
*Minton (Royal Doulton Group)* Visits by appointment. Tuesday to Thursday. Parties of 10, all ages. Museum. (0782) 49171
*Spode* Visits by appointment only from Monday to Thursday. Parties of 40 maximum, minimum age 12. Admission 50p. (0782) 46011
*Josiah Wedgwood* Wedgwood

Visitors' Centre. Open Monday to Friday, 9.00am to 4.45pm. Admission 50p adults, children 25p. Films are shown at various times. (078 139) 2141

### Rudyard
The reservoir at Rudyard was built to supply the Trent and Mersey Canal with water, and it is possible to fish there and go boating. There are delightful walks along the banks and through the woods to the village of Rudyard. It was here that Rudyard Kipling's parents became engaged, hence their son's name.

The village itself is a delightful collection of houses and gardens.

To the north-east are the Bridestones, a burial chamber in which a Viking king and his Anglo-Saxon wife are said to be laid to rest.

### Shallowford
South-west of Stone, between the Trent and Sow, is Shallowford, once the home of Izaak

Walton who wrote *The Compleat Angler*. He gave his cottage to Stafford and it is kept as a *memorial*. Open Thursday to Sunday, 10.00am to 1.00pm and 2.00pm to 5.00pm.

### Stafford
This attractive county town was listed in the Domesday Book of 1086, although its history goes back before the Conquest.

*St Mary's Church* has a central tower dating from the 13th century, and a Norman font, where Izaak Walton was baptised. A bust in the North Aisle is inscribed, 'Izaak Walton, Piscator'.

The town has many fine old houses from the 17th and 18th centuries, the oldest being High House, in Greengate Street, where Charles I and Prince Rupert sheltered for three nights in 1642.

The ruins of *Stafford Castle*, dating from the 14th century but rebuilt in the 19th century, are south-west of the town.

Cheddleton Flint Mill near Leek . . . from the Industrial Revolution

### Abbots Bromley

This beautiful old town is best known for the medieval Horn Dance which takes place each year on the Monday following September 4.

The dancing is at various venues and times throughout the day until dusk. It commemorates the granting of Needwood Forest hunting rights to the villagers. Dancers and musicians all wear Tudor dress and reindeer horns dating from Anglo-Saxon times.

### Shugborough

The white colonnaded mansion in Shugborough is the ancestral home of the Earls of Lichfield. It is now owned by the National Trust, although the present earl, a noted society photographer, still lives in part of it.

The house was built in 1693 and enlarged in the following century. It contains magnificent collections of paintings and furniture which are on show to the public. There are beautiful gardens, with a bridge spanning the landscaped lake.

Open March to October, Tuesday to Friday, 10.30am to 5.30pm, Saturday, Sunday and Bank Holidays 2.00pm to 6.00pm.

The Staffordshire County *Museum* in Shugborough houses items of agricultural and industrial interest. Open weekdays except Monday.

### Cannock Chase

This is 26 square miles of forest and heath standing on the fringe of the Black Country. The Chase is all that remains of the hunting ground that once covered most of the county.

It is a haven for wildlife, including foxes, badgers, lizards and a large herd of fallow deer – descendants of the animals which managed to escape the arrow of medieval hunters.

There are many magnificent viewpoints, such as Coppice Hill which is 600 ft high.

Cannock itself is a small industrial town.

### Lichfield

The birthplace on September 18, 1709, of Samuel Johnson. The house on the corner of Breadmarket Street is now the *Johnsonian Museum*.

The house can be visited Tuesday to Saturday, 10.00am to 5.00pm, Sunday 2.30pm to 5.00pm. Not open on Sundays in winter. Other winter opening times, Tuesday to Saturday, 10.00am to 4.00pm.

A statue of Dr Johnson and one of his famous biographer James Boswell, stand in the cobbled square. Each year on the Saturday nearest Johnson's birthday, townspeople gather to honour his memory.

Another famous son of Lichfield was David Garrick, the actor. In 1736 Dr Johnson, then a schoolmaster at the grammar school, taught him Latin and Greek.

The city is still dominated by its beautiful *cathedral* and its three spires, known as 'The Ladies of the Vale'. The largest was destroyed by Cromwell's men during the Civil War, but was later rebuilt.

Lichfield's first cathedral was consecrated in AD 700, but the present building dates from 1195. The stained glass windows in the Lady Chapel are 16th-century and are considered to be among the finest in England.

The cathedral library has some of the finest illuminated manuscripts to be found in Europe, including the Gospels of St Matthew and St Mark.

Three miles to the south-west of the city can be found an excavated bath house of the Letocetum, a Roman posting station on Watling Street.

It is closed Mondays and alternate Tuesdays. Open Tuesday to Saturday 9.30am to 7.00pm. Sundays 2.00pm to 7.00pm.

LICHFIELD

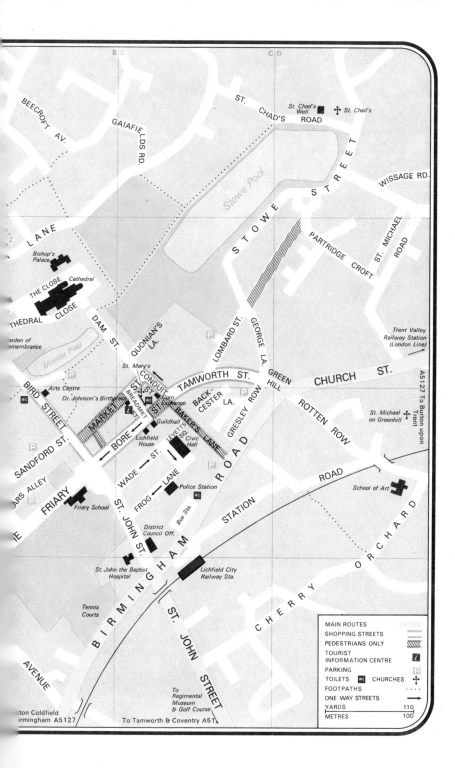

BEECROFT AV.

GAIAFIELDS RD.

ST. CHAD'S ROAD

St. Chad's Well ■ ✝ St. Chad's

WISSAGE RD.

Stowe Pool

S T O W E   S T R E E T

ST. MICHAEL ROAD

LANE

PARTRIDGE CROFT

Bishop's Palace

THE CLOSE   Cathedral

THEDRAL   CLOSE

DAM ST.

Trent Valley Railway Station (London Line)

arden of emembrance

Minster Pool

QUONIAN'S LA.

LOMBARD ST.

GEORGE LA.

GREEN HILL

A5127 To Burton upon Trent

St. Mary's

CONDUIT ST.

TAMWORTH ST.

BACK-CESTER LA.

CHURCH ST.

ROTTEN ROW

BIRD STREET

Arts Centre

MARKET ST.

BREADMKT

Corn Exchange

GRESLEY ROW

St. Michael on Greenhill

Dr. Johnson's Birthplace

WC

BORE ST.

Guildhall

LEVETT'S SQ.

ROAD

SANDFORD ST.

Lichfield House

Civic Hall

STATION

School of Art

FRIARY

WADE ST.

FROG LANE

Police Station

ROAD

ARS ALLEY

Friary School

ST. JOHN ST.

Bus Sta.

WC

C H E R R Y   O R C H A R D

District Council Off.

St. John the Baptist Hospital

B I R M I N G H A M

Lichfield City Railway Sta.

Tennis Courts

 S T.   J O H N   S T R E E T

AVENUE

ton Coldfield
irmingham A5127

To Regimental Museum & Golf Course

To Tamworth & Coventry A51

| | |
|---|---|
| MAIN ROUTES | |
| SHOPPING STREETS | |
| PEDESTRIANS ONLY | |
| TOURIST INFORMATION CENTRE | 🄹 |
| PARKING | P |
| TOILETS | WC   CHURCHES ✝ |
| FOOTPATHS | .... |
| ONE WAY STREETS | → |
| YARDS | 110 |
| METRES | 100 |

# West Midlands

The whole of England between the Peaks and the Severn estuary is regarded as the West Midlands, but the same term has since the early 1970s described a single county based on Birmingham, Britain's second largest city.

Apart from being an international business city, Birmingham is notable for its canals (it has more than Venice), and as a centre from which to explore Shakespeare country.

Within a few miles of Birmingham are the cathedral city of Coventry, the phoenix which rose from wartime destruction, and the old foundry towns of the industrial 'Black Country'.

Among these, the largest are Wolverhampton and Dudley, the latter noted for its crystal glass.

## Dudley

The town was named after a 13th-century Duke who built a *castle* there. The castle ruins can be visited daily, 9.00am to dusk, and there are the ruins of a 12th-century Clunaic *priory* nearby.

The hillsides around the castle provide the setting for *Dudley Zoo*, one of England's largest, noted for its apes, reptiles and sea-lions.

Open daily 9.00am to dusk.

Britain's only *geological nature reserve* can be found at Wren's Nest Hill. Visitors can follow a signposted geological trail. The outcrop of Silurian limestone is famous for its fossils, which are 300 million years old.

There are two labyrinthine *canal tunnels* under the limestone hills. Boat trips from Parkhead, Tipton, or Birmingham New Road Bridge go through the Dudley Canal Tunnel, which is 3,154 yards long. It was built around 1790 and reopened in 1973 after years of disuse.

The *Netherton Canal Tunnel* was built relatively recently, in 1859. At the southern end is Bumble Hole, a canal junction complete with ruined engine house.

*Industrial Archaeology* is further represented by a reconstructed chain shop – with working demonstrations – open the first Sunday of the month. Chain-making was once a cottage industry in the Cradley, Old Hill and Netherton areas.

Anchor-making and nail-making were also local craft industries, and there is a preserved *forge*, which is occasionally operated, at the *Central Museum and Art Gallery*.

Open Monday to Saturday 9.00am to 5.00pm.

An embryonic *Black Country Museum*, in Tipton Museum, will eventually have canal boats, a steam locomotive and trolley-buses.

*Visits to glass factories* are arranged on weekday mornings by Stuart, Webb and Corbett and Royal Brierley Crystal Works.

*Brewing* is another remarkable local industry. No town in England has as many tiny breweries, among which the best known serves only one pub, the Old Swan, in Netherton High Street.

The canal . . . Stourbridge

Such 'home brew' establishments aside, two breweries in the district of Brierley Hill are among the smallest in England. These are Daniel Batham and J. P. Simpkiss, each serving only a handful of pubs. Holden's is another tiny brewery, and Hanson's is associated with the Banks brewery of Wolverhampton.

## Wolverhampton

Many an Englishman would be unable to say 'Wolverhampton' without adding the word 'Wanderers'. This alliterative soccer team has a proud history which matches that of the town.

Wolverhampton's past prosperity was based on iron and brass foundries, and the town looked its part as 'capital' of the Black Country. In recent years, the demolition men have been busy, and impressive new shopping precincts have risen, though the end product is a distinctly uneven townscape.

Three miles to the west, Wightwick Manor has *William* *Morris* wallpapers and fabrics, and pre-Raphaelite works of art, Kempe glass, and gardens with yew topiary.

Closed in February. Open on Thursdays, Saturdays, and Bank Holiday Sunday and Monday. Also Wednesdays during the summer, 2.30pm to 5.30pm.

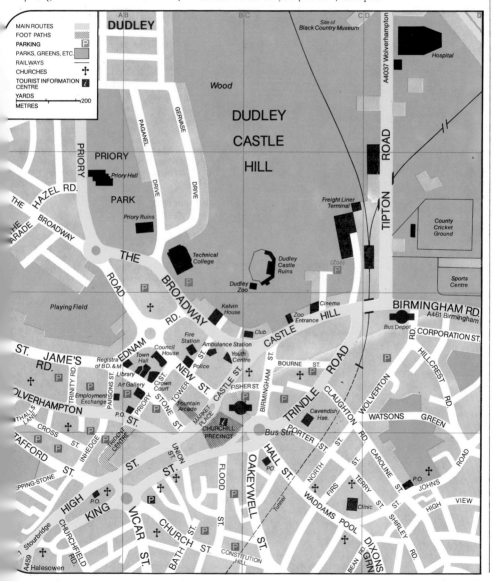

**Birmingham** (*map p 154*)
Its nearness to London has robbed Birmingham of the regional status proclaimed by some of England's other great cities. Nor, for all that it has a fair share of surviving Victorian architecture, does Birmingham show quite such a powerful awareness of a golden age.

The city's greatest growth was powered by the automotive industry; its endless network of motorways has drawn it even closer to the South; its multi-level Bull Ring shopping centre represents one post-war burst of civic pride; and another was manifested in the opening of the National Exhibition Centre, with Britain's annual Motor Show in October as its prize exhibit.

All of this excitement has left Birmingham a bewildering city for the visitor, but exploration can be revealing.
*Canals* The Birmingham Navigation System, which stretches throughout the conurbation of the West Midlands, has more canals than Venice.

There are towpath walks along all the canals in the city, passing old buildings and crossing the turnover bridges on the way.

Gas Street Basin is a restored canal basin, which now has pubs and even a nightclub, called Opposite Lock. Another restored basin, at Cambrian Wharf has pubs and restored buildings.

Leisure Line Canal Cruises operate *public trips* to Selly Oak and back during the summer from the Canal Shop at Cambrian Wharf. They also organise charter trips.

Ring (021) 236 2645 for details of these and for more information on canals in Birmingham.
*Shakespeare* Housed in the City and Museum Art Gallery is the *Shakespeare Memorial Library*, which has 40,000 books in 90 languages.

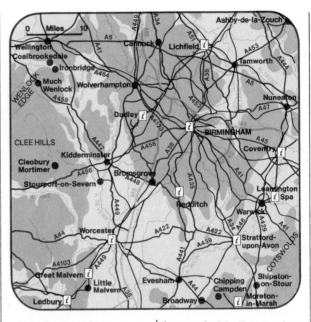

For those wishing to see the city more traditionally associated with The Bard, buses X20 and X50 run hourly from the bus station at The Bull Ring to Stratford. Ring (021) 622 6991 for details.

L. S. Bowen Ltd organise coach trips to Stratford and also to 'Shakespeare Country'. Ring (021) 373 7415 for details.
*Birmingham Repertory Theatre* was built in 1971 and has won awards for its design. It is renowned for the quality of its drama and actors.

Other theatres are the Alexandra Theatre and the Birmingham Hippodrome, and there are seven studio theatres.
*Birmingham City Museum and Art Gallery* Fine collection of Old Masters, Italian 17th-century paintings, English watercolours and Pre-Raphaelite paintings. Archaeology, local history, natural history, modern sculpture, costumes. The ultra-modern library is one of the largest and

best-stocked in Europe. Open weekdays 10.00am to 6.00pm, Sunday 2.00pm to 5.30pm.
*Museum of Science and Industry* Excellent collection, including the City of Birmingham locomotive and early cars.

Open Monday to Friday 10.00am to 5.00pm, Saturday 10.00am to 5.30pm, Sunday 2.00pm to 5.30pm.
*Cannon Hill Natural History Museum* Natural history illustrating bird watching, bee keeping, fishing and pets.

Open summer weekdays 10.00am to 8.00pm, winter weekdays 10.00am to 5.00pm, Sunday 2.00pm to 5.00pm.
*Birmingham Railway Museum* A live steam depot with locomotives, reproductions of historic coaches and machinery. Open Sunday 2.00pm to 7.00pm.
*Barber Institute of Fine Arts* University of Birmingham's collection of masterpieces by Botticelli, Rembrandt and Goya. Open Monday to Friday 10.00am to 5.00pm, Saturday

10.00am to 1.00pm. Open only during term time.

*St Philip's Cathedral* An 18th-century church in the Baroque style, which became a cathedral in 1905. It was designed by Thomas Archer, a contemporary of Wren.

It has a wrought iron screen, a 1715 organ case, and four stained glass windows designed by Edward Burne-Jones and constructed by William Morris.

*Metropolitan Cathedral Church of St Chad* The first Roman Catholic cathedral to be built in England after the Reformation. Dates from 1839.

*St Martin's Parish Church* In the original Bull Ring. It was rebuilt in gothic style in 1873, and has a Burne-Jones stained glass window.

*The Town Hall* Opened in 1834. It was designed by Joseph Hansom, inventor of the Hansom Cab, and modelled on the Temple of Castor and Pollux in Rome. It is also the home of the *Birmingham Symphony Orchestra*.

*The Council House* Designed by H. R. Yeoville Thomason in the Renaissance style, it was completed in 1879, and now houses the council offices. Above it is the 160-ft clock tower called *Big Brum*.

*Hall of Memory* Commemorates citizens of Birmingham who fell in the 1914–18 and 1939–45 wars. Contains illuminated Roll of Honour, one page of each book being turned every other day.

Open daily.

*Aston Hall* Magnificent Jacobean house with fine examples of English furniture. Open summer weekdays 10.00am to 5.00pm, Sunday 2.00pm to 5.00pm. Winter weekdays 10.00am to dusk.

*Blakesley Hall* A yeoman's 16th-century timber-framed house, now a museum with displays of rural crafts, toys, kitchen and domestic utensils. Open weekdays 9.30am to

6.00pm, Sunday 2.00pm to 5.00pm.

*Sarehole Mill* An 18th-century water-powered corn mill, now restored.

Open March to November Monday to Friday and Sunday 2.00pm to 7.00pm, Saturday 11.00am to 7.00pm.

*Weoley Castle* Former fortified dwelling, surrounded by a moat which is still full of water. It was built between 1100 and 1320.

Open Wednesday 2.00pm to 5.00pm, Saturday 10.00am to 5.00pm.

*Cannon Hill Park* Nature centre showing animals, birds, freshwater fish and insects in their natural surroundings.

Open summer Monday, Wednesday, Thursday, Friday and Sunday 1.00pm to 8.00pm, Saturday 10.00am to 8.00pm. Winter Monday, Wednesday, Thursday, Friday and Sunday 1.00pm to 4.00pm, Saturday 10.00am to 4.00pm.

*Sports* Swimming pools; golf; tennis; bowls; Warwickshire County Cricket Club; Aston Villa, Birmingham City, West Bromwich Albion Football Clubs; Moseley Rugby Union Club; ten-pin bowling; squash; speedway; cycle racing;

greyhound racing; ice skating.

*Events* Boat Show, in February; Lord Mayor's Procession, and Tulip Festival, in May; Highland Gathering, in June; Birmingham Symphony Orchestra Promenade Concerts in July; Birmingham Show, in August; Ideal Home Exhibition, in October.

## Edgbaston

The home of Birmingham University and Warwickshire County Cricket Club. This suburb also has fine *botanical gardens* with a large collection of shrubs, trees, an alpine garden, a palm house and a small zoo.

Open daily 9.00am to dusk.

*Edgbaston Reservoir* is a 60-acre lake with sailing, rowing and fishing.

The clock tower of the university can be seen for many miles.

## Sutton Coldfield

Well worth visiting for the 2,400 acres of natural parkland, with woods, valleys and moors; lakes for boating, bathing and fishing; bird sanctuaries and a championship golf course.

The park is crossed by the old Roman Ryknild Street.

Fine furniture . . . Aston Hall

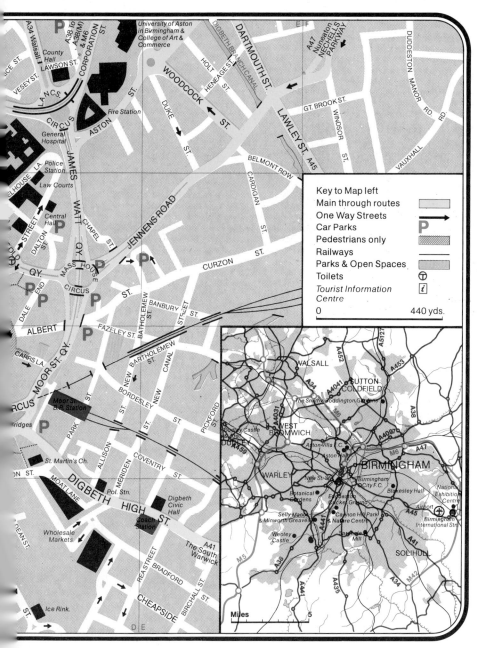

Key to Map left
Main through routes
One Way Streets
Car Parks
Pedestrians only
Railways
Parks & Open Spaces
Toilets
Tourist Information Centre

0                    440 yds.

## Coventry

A naked lady made Coventry famous. Every Englishman knows the legend of Lady Godiva, who rode nude through the streets protesting on behalf of the people against the taxes imposed by her husband Leofric, Earl of Mercia, in the 11th century.

A statue of her stands in Broadgate.

On November 14 1940 more than 40 acres of Coventry were destroyed by German bombs. The city was rebuilt, complete with a new cathedral that has become one of the great sights as it stands alongside the ruins of the old.

A wooden cross, created out of the charred timbers stands on the original altar bearing the inscription 'Father Forgive'.

*Cathedral* Consecrated on May 25, 1962, it stands by the ruins of the bombed St Michael's to symbolize death and regeneration.

It was designed by Sir Basil Spence and is a magnificent example of contemporary architecture.

John Piper's Baptistry Window, John Hutton's engraved glass screen and Epstein's statue of St Michael and the Devil, all complement Graham Sutherland's avant-garde tapestry which is thought to be the largest in the world.

*Church of St John* Stands in fascinating Spon Street. It has an interesting nave and was once a prison for the Royalists captured by Cromwell, thus becoming the first unfortunates to be 'sent to Coventry'.

*Whitefriar's* A renovated Carmelite friary of the 14th-century Coventry Whitefriars. The exterior is always viewable and there is limited opening. Enquire at the Tourist Information Centre.

*Golden Cross Inn* According to local tradition, this 17th-century inn was built on the site of Coventry mint.

Avant-garde . . . Sutherland's tapestry

### Medieval Coventry

The medieval Guildhall is a splendour of old glass and carved wood. Bonds Hospital and Ford Hospital are delightful half-timbered Tudor almshouses, while Bayley Lane and Hay Lane are quiet reminders of an illustrious past.

A medieval cul-de-sac has been created in *Spon Street*, some of the buildings having been moved here from other parts of the city. The Windmill Inn is an Elizabethan hostelry, still serving the drinkers of today.

*Coventry Zoo* Many animals and a dolphinarium. Open daily 10.00am to sunset.

*Coombe Park* There are 300 acres of formal gardens and woodland nature trails. There is also angling, and paddle-boating.

*Lunt Roman Fort* A replica standing on its original site at Baginton. Ask at the Tourist Information Centre for times.

*Events* Coventry Carnival and International Week, in June; Crock Fair, on Spring Bank Holiday; Coventry Angling Open Championship, in June and July; Air Display, in August.

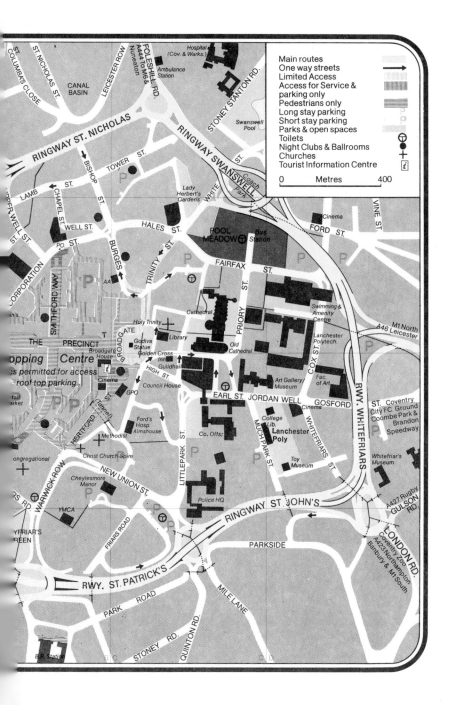

## Coleshill

A pretty village standing, as its name would suggest, on a hill above the river Cole.

The church has a 14th-century tower, and nearby are such Christian appliances as pillory stocks and a whipping-post.

*Maxstoke Castle* is only two miles to the east and is a red sandstone building dating back to the 14th century.

## Meriden

The very centre of England is said to be the medieval cross on the village green at Meriden.

The 18th-century Forest Hall is the headquarters of the famous Woodmen of Arden, one of England's oldest archery societies.

## Henley-in-Arden

The heart of what used to be the Forest of Arden. A magnificent small market town with a wealth of oak-timbered houses, from the 15th, 16th and 17th centuries gracing its streets. Like all good towns of the period it boasts fine inns – the 15th-century Blue Bell and the 16th-century White Swan.

All that remains of *Beaudesert Castle* are some earthworks, but nearby there is a 12th-century church with a Norman chancel arch and Perpendicular tower.

## Packwood House

Standing just outside Hockley Heath, this timber-framed Tudor house has a truly remarkable garden, laid out in the 17th century. Its main feature is a configuration of shaped yew trees which depict the Sermon on the Mount.

Trees representing Christ, the four evangelists and 12 apostles are arranged on the lawn, above another collection of trees which represent the multitude. Open April to September daily except Monday and Tuesday 2.00pm to 7.00pm.

Ford's Hospital . . . Coventry

## Alcester

This old market town stands where two Roman roads and two rivers, the Alne and the Arrow meet.

There is very little left of the Roman Ryknild Street camp, but there are many timber-fronted houses of the 17th century, notably the timber-topped town hall.

Only 1½ miles south-west is *Ragley Hall*, which has records going back to AD 710. This is the home of Marquis of Hereford, whose family have been here since 1591.

The present house is 17th-century and has a fine interior with many paintings and much china and furniture. 8,000 acres of agricultural land surround it and the 500-acre park was landscaped by Capability Brown.

House open March to October daily except Monday and Friday 1.30pm to 5.30pm; Park open May to September daily 11.00am to 7.00pm.

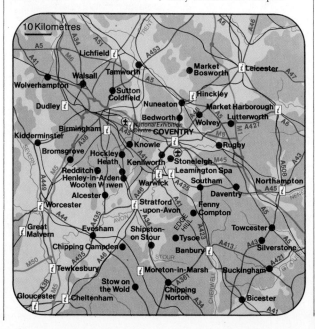

# Warwickshire

With its tall church tower visible for miles around, its castle, its Georgian and Tudor buildings and its racecourse, Warwick is the definitive English country town. It is compact, easy to walk around, the small county town of a somewhat abbreviated county.

Warwick nudges the spa town of Leamington, with Kenilworth just across the river Avon. Kenilworth was the setting for Sir Walter Scott's book of the same name. Leamington was accorded the prefix 'Royal' by Queen Victoria. It is thus properly known as Royal Leamington Spa.

All three towns are useful centres from which to explore Shakespeare country and the northern part of the Cotswolds.

**Tourist Information Centres**
The Library, 11 Smalley Place, Kenilworth, Warwickshire. (0926) 52595
Southgate Lodge, Jephson Gardens, Leamington Spa, Warwickshire. (0926) 311470/27072 Ext 216
Nuneaton Library, Church Street, Nuneaton, Warwickshire. (0682) 384027/8
Rugby Divisional Library, St Matthews Street, Rugby, Warwickshire. (0788) 2687/71813
Court House, Jury Street, Warwick, Warwickshire. (0926) 42212

## Nuneaton

An industrial town which claims attention only as the birthplace of George Eliot whose real name was Mary Ann Evans. She was born in the farmhouse at *Arbury Hall* which is not open to the public.

This 18th-century building in the Gothic revival style was the home of the Newdigate family.

It was Cheverel Manor in George Eliot's *Scenes From Clerical Life*.

Open Easter to October Sunday and Bank Holidays 2.30pm to 6.00pm.

The *Museum and Art Gallery* has some of her personal possessions, and also collections of glass, silver and pottery.

Open Monday to Friday 12.00pm to 7.00pm, weekends 10.00am to 5.00pm.

## Rugby

Most often associated with *Tom Brown's Schooldays* and the public school, founded in 1567. Rugby football originated here, and a tablet on the school wall commemorates this.

Dr Thomas Arnold, onetime headmaster, was described in *Tom Brown's Schooldays*, and his son was Matthew Arnold. Another poet connected with Rugby is Rupert Brooke, who was born here.

An art gallery in the local library displays the work of local artists and local society exhibits. The collection of original paintings includes those by Graham Sutherland, L. S. Lowry and Stanley Spencer.

Open Monday to Friday 10.00am to 8.00pm, Saturday 9.30am to 4.00pm.

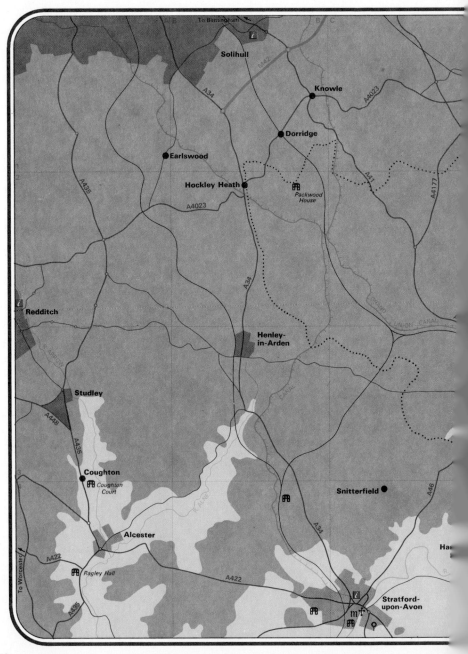

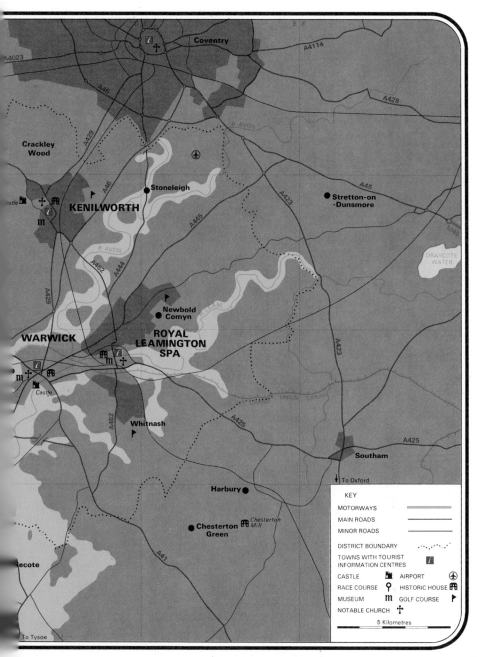

Coventry

A4023

A4114

A428

Crackley
Wood

A429

A46

Stoneleigh

A45

Stretton-on
-Dunsmore

A423

KENILWORTH

A45

R. AVON

DRAYCOTE
WATER

A46

Castle

A452  A444

R. AVON

A429

Newbold
Comyn

ROYAL
LEAMINGTON
SPA

WARWICK

A423

Castle

UNION CANAL

A452

Whitnash

A425

A425

Southam

To Oxford

Harbury

Chesterton
Mill

Chesterton
Green

A41

ecote

To Tysoe

| KEY | | |
|---|---|---|
| MOTORWAYS | | |
| MAIN ROADS | | |
| MINOR ROADS | | |
| DISTRICT BOUNDARY | | |
| TOWNS WITH TOURIST INFORMATION CENTRES | | |
| CASTLE | AIRPORT | |
| RACE COURSE | HISTORIC HOUSE | |
| MUSEUM | GOLF COURSE | |
| NOTABLE CHURCH | | |

5 Kilometres

A market is held every Monday, Friday and Saturday, but Rugby is otherwise an industrial town.

North-east of the town is *Stanford Hall* at Lutterworth. This William-and-Mary house built in 1690 has an 1898 Flying Machine, motor cycle and car museum, a working crafts centre, a walled rose garden and a nature trail.

Open March to September Thursday and weekends 2.30pm to 6.00pm.

## Stoneleigh

Duchess Dudley, the first woman ever to be created a duchess in her own right, is buried in the village churchyard. She died in 1669, aged 98.

Part of the grounds of the former Stoneleigh Abbey are now the permanent site of the *National Agriculture Centre*, where the Royal Show is held every year. It is also the headquarters of the *British Show Jumping Association*.

## Kenilworth

The *castle*, which is a short distance from the town, was a stronghold from the 11th century to the Civil War.

It was remodelled as a palace in the 14th century by John of Gaunt, fourth son of Edward III. Robert Dudley, Earl of Leicester entertained Elizabeth I there in July 1575. The castle was partially demolished by Cromwell in 1649.

The keep, the northern gatehouse and most of John of Gaunt's banqueting hall have survived, and the outlines of Dudley's gardens can still be seen.

The castle is the setting for much of Sir Walter Scott's book *Kenilworth*. Open summer daily 9.30am to 7.00pm, winter 9.30am to 5.30pm, Sunday 2.00pm to 5.30pm.

*Abbey Barn* is the remains of a ruined abbey on Castle Hill.

*Little Virginia* A group of thatched cottages near the castle where Sir Walter Raleigh is reputed to have planted some of the potatoes he brought back from his travels in America.

## Warwick (*map p 159*)

The county town, founded by the daughter of Alfred the Great, and moulded by the Beauchamps, who were then the Earls of Warwick, and later by the Dudleys who succeeded them.

Much of medieval Warwick was destroyed in a fire in 1644 . However, parts of the old church survive within the rebuilt building including the Beauchamp Chapel, paid for by ransoms collected by Thomas Beauchamp after the Battle of Poitiers.

The chapel contains the tomb of Richard Beauchamp, Earl of Warwick, who died in Rouen in 1439. He was largely responsible for the execution of Joan of Arc.

Elizabeth I's friend, Robert Dudley, Earl of Leicester, is also buried there.

Like his ancestors before him, the Earl of Warwick lives in *Warwick Castle* which stands above the river.

This is one of the very few medieval castles which is still habitable and it is a day's outing in itself.

*Warwick Castle* The earlier parts of this magnificent building date from the 13th century. Many rooms including the Great Hall, State Dining Room and Queen Anne's Bedroom, are open to the public.

Also open are the armoury, dungeons, torture chamber, ghost tower, peacock gardens, Guy's Tower (from 1394) and Caesar's Tower (1356).

Open daily 10.00am to 5.30pm.

*Lord Leycester's Hospital* A 14th-century half-timbered building, now almshouses.

Open summer weekdays 10.00am to 5.30pm, winter weekdays 10.00am to 4.00pm.

*Westgate* Dates from the 12th century, with St James's Chapel over the gate.

*Eastgate* 15th-century up to the battlements. St Peter's Chapel above was pulled down and rebuilt by Henry VI.

*Oken's House* The home of

Sir Walter Scott's inspiration . . . Kenilworth Castle

Thomas Oken, one of the principal citizens of Warwick in the 16th century. It survived a fire in 1694 and is now the home of Joy Robinson's *Doll Museum*.

Open daily 10.30am to 4.30pm.

*St Nicholas Park* Yachting and boating on the river, open-air swimming pool, children's play area, recreation ground, miniature railway, pitch and putt golf, picnic area.

## Leamington Spa

This popular conference and touring area on the river Leam is quite modern as English watering places go. Its saline springs were first noted in 1586, but their potential was not realized until 1814 when the Pump Room was built.

The next 30 years brought prosperity to Leamington and in 1838 it was granted its 'Royal' prefix by Queen Victoria after her visit there.

Leamington's spa waters are still in medicinal use and they provide a focus for about 60,000 physiotherapy and hydrotherapy treatments each year in a modern treatment centre.

The waters can be drunk

Now almshouses . . . Lord Leycester's Hospital, Warwick

from the fountain in the patients' lounge. To make an appointment for treatment, ring (0926) 27072.

The ancient game of *real tennis* is played at a private tennis club, The Tennis Court Club.

Interesting typical Regency and early Victorian houses can be seen in Waterloo Place, Lansdowne Crescent, Clarendon Square, Lansdowne Circus and Newbold Terrace.

*Royal Pump Rooms* Built in 1814, although Campden discovered the natural saline water in 1586. Various treatments are available.

*Jephson Gardens* Named after Dr Henry Jephson, whose exploitation of the spa promoted the prosperity of the town. There is an aviary, lake and fountains, and a floral clock. The gardens are noted for the particularly fine displays of dahlias and rare trees.

*Newbold Comyn* 309 acres of recreational and pleasure grounds. 18-hole golf course, nature trail, sports.

## Southam

A pleasant old market town on the river Itchen. Like so many towns in this area, it has associations with the Civil War. The doomed Charles I once stayed at the Manor House on Market Hill. The house is now a chemist's shop.

There is also a fine inn, *The Old Mint*, which recalls the medieval days when Southam had its own currency, called 'tokens'.

These small denomination coins were used because the local people had little use for normal money as its value was too high for their everyday purposes.

Sample the waters . . . Royal Pump Rooms

163

# Stratford upon Avon

In Shakespeare's day, Stratford was an important regional centre, with a substantial trade in corn, malt and livestock. It remained a country town when other parts of the West Midlands were being industrialized, and today Stratford earns its living from tourism.

The layout of the town has changed little over the centuries, but from spring to autumn the streets now ache under the feet of the visitors.

To walk is the best way in which to see Stratford, though the eyes are best averted from much that is plastic and phoney. There remains much that is worth seeing, not least such simple delights as the swans on the river, and an interesting exploration can be carried out in two hours.

**Tourist Information Centre**
Judith Shakespeare's House, 1 High Street, Stratford upon Avon, Warwickshire. (0789) 3127/ 66175/66185

## Stratford upon Avon

The obvious starting point is *Shakespeare's birthplace*, a half-timbered, 16th-century house in Henley Street. Inside there are numerous Shakespeare relics and outside in the garden is a statue of the man.

Open daily 9.00am to 7.00pm.

A walk down Bridge Street leads to the river, crossed by Clopton Bridge. This was built in the 15th century by Hugh Clopton. Like Shakespeare, he too found success in London, for he became its Lord Mayor.

He also built New Place in Chapel Street. This was one of the largest and most elegant houses in Stratford. In 1610, Shakespeare retired here and died six years later. The house was demolished around 1702.

From Clopton Bridge there is a road along the west bank which passes the *Royal Shakespeare Theatre*. This is an unlikely, red-brick building dating from 1932. It is here that the Royal Shakespeare Company performs during its long summer season.

Box office tel. (0789) 2271.

Advance booking is almost essential. There are long queues of hopeful tourists waiting outside hoping for returned tickets or vacant seats for performances. The Company has a smaller theatre, *The Other Place*, in Stratford where plays by other writers as well as Shakespeare are performed.

The theatre also has a brass rubbing centre which is open daily.

The theatre's pleasant gardens sweep down to the river bank with its peaceful views of swans gliding on tranquil waters overhung by the branches of willow trees.

To the south of the theatre is a gate leading to Southern Lane and then on through the trees to *Holy Trinity Church*.

This is the burial place of Shakespeare and his family. Their tombs are marked by simple stones by the altar.

Nearby is *Hall's Croft*. This was the home of Shakespeare's daughter Susanna, who was married to Dr John Hall. This magnificent, Tudor-gabled house stands in a walled garden. Open daily, 9.00am to 5.45pm.

The bard's old school, the King's New Grammar School, is one of England's finest grammar schools. It is not open to the public, but the building can be seen from outside. When Shakespeare was a student here, the school occupied the upper floor.

On the lower floor was the Guildhall where touring players gave performances to the Town

Council. Their visits were so much appreciated that the council gave the company a licence to play in Stratford. These performances were probably of greater interest to the young Will than the academic regime on the floor above.

The mass of pilgrims from all over the world who visit Stratford annually owe a great debt to the Shakespeare Birthplace Trust, which is responsible for the preservation of so much of the old town.

Stratford is not only the birthplace of Shakespeare. At 60 Ely Street there is the *Tibor Reich Collection* of miniature and model cars, textiles and ceramics. This permanent display is well worth a visit.

### Shottery
The attraction in this village a mile from Stratford centre is *Anne Hathaway's cottage*.

Any notion that the ill-used future Mrs Shakespeare lived in a cramped rural backwater disappears at first sight of the 'cottage', for it is in fact a rambling 12-roomed house with a magnificent thatched roof.

The narrow bench where Shakespeare suffered discomfort while he courted Anne can be seen in the parlour.

Part of the house was seriously damaged by a fire in 1969, but it has now been fully restored.

Open 9.00am to 7.00pm daily.

### Charlecote
Legend has it that *Charlecote Park*, a huge Tudor mansion, played a decisive part in young Will Shakespeare's career. He is said to have been caught poaching deer by the angry landlord, Sir Thomas Lucy. Shakespeare was birched but got his revenge by penning some savage lampoons about his tormentor.

Sir Thomas discovered the name of the author of these scurrilous writings and Shakespeare was obliged to flee his home and make for London and a new career.

The National Trust now owns Charlecote, which is open every day except Friday, from April to September, 11.45am to 5.30pm.

The nearby farm buildings now house a collection of historic carriages, one of which is a phaeton once owned by Alphonso XII of Spain. There is also a walled garden with waterfowl and other birds.

### Wilmcote
Shakespeare's mother *Mary Arden* was born here and her well-preserved Tudor farmhouse home is open for visitors every day from April to October, 9.00am to 5.45pm.

### Edge Hill
The site in 1642 of the first major battle of the Civil War.

Edge Hill Tower offers fine views over this breathtaking stretch of countryside. The Tower was built in the 18th century by the eccentric Sanderson Miller, a local squire and architect. It is now part of a pub, *The Castle*.

On the other side of the valley is *Farnborough Hall*, a fine Italianate building now owned by the National Trust. It contains many Italian paintings and sculptures. Open Wednesday and Saturday 2.00pm to 6.00pm.

### Upton House
The National Trust own this William-and-Mary mansion which is situated in gently sloping grounds. It has an impressive collection of paintings including works by Peter Breughel and George Stubbs and some Sèvres porcelain.

Open daily except Friday 11.00am to 5.00pm.

### Compton Wynyates
This is frequently described as the most beautiful house in England and it is hard to argue with this claim.

The magnificent Tudor architecture has remained virtually unaltered, its crowning glory being some superb corkscrew-shaped chimneys.

Compton was the name of the family who built the house between 1480 and 1528, and Wynyates is the Old English way of saying 'valley through which the wind blows'.

The building material came from the ruins of Fulbrook Castle, near Warwick, and the finished house came complete with a minstrels' gallery and a deviously hidden priesthole.

The Comptons were ardent Royalists and their house was captured by Cromwell's troops. It was returned on the strict condition that the escape route, which led out to the moat, was to be sealed up for all time. Open daily except Friday, 11.00am to 5.00pm.

The Avon . . . passing through Stratford

165

# Worcester

After only a brief encounter with the Black Country (needle-making at Redditch, heavy engineering at Bromsgrove, and carpets at Kidderminster), Worcestershire flirts with spa-town style at Droitwich and Tenbury, then settles down to rural calm . . . nature-trails in the Wyre Forest, hop-yards between Tenbury and Worcester, walking country in the Malvern Hills, orchards at Pershore, asparagus at Evesham, and the beginnings of the Cotswolds at Broadway.

In April, a journey through the southern part of the county will be made through a haze of blooms. From June to October, visitors can pick their own fruit at the farms.

## Tourist Information Centres

47/49 Worcester Road, Bromsgrove, Worcestershire. (0527) 31809

Norbury House, Friar Street, Droitwich, Worcestershire. (090 57) 2352

37 High Street, Pershore, Worcestershire. (038 65) 2442

Leominster District Council, Teme Street, Tenbury Wells, Worcestershire. (0584) 810465

Guildhall, Worcester, Worcestershire. (0905) 23471

## Worcester

A bustling county town and cathedral city on the river Severn.

It is best known for its porcelain, gloves and, of course, its spicy sauce. It also boasts England's oldest newspaper, Berrow's Worcester Journal, and one of the loveliest cricket grounds in the world.

The architecture of the city spans five centuries. Friar Street, with its overhanging timber houses, has survived well from the 16th century.

Cornmarket and Foregate Street also contain many memories of medieval Worcester. New Street boasts King Charles' House and Nash House.

Worcester flourished during the 18th century, and witnessed the growth of buildings such as Berkeley's Hospital, also in The Foregate. Edgar Street, College Precincts, The Tything, The Guildhall and the Royal Porcelain works are also 18th-century.

There are several interesting pubs, with traditional skittle alleys as a diversion for drinkers.

The Avon was the first English river to be adapted for artificial navigation and it offers a pleasant walk from Comberton to Birlingham to look at the locks.

*Worcester Cathedral* The present cathedral was begun in 1062, but fared badly in the Civil War. Restoration was carried out in the last century by Sir Gilbert Scott.

There is still some Norman work in evidence, principally in the aisles and transepts. The cathedral also has an early English choir, a fine Norman crypt and the tomb of King John.

*The Commandery* A pre-Reformation hospital founded in 1085, and re-opened only in 1977 after restorations.

It was the Royalist headquar-

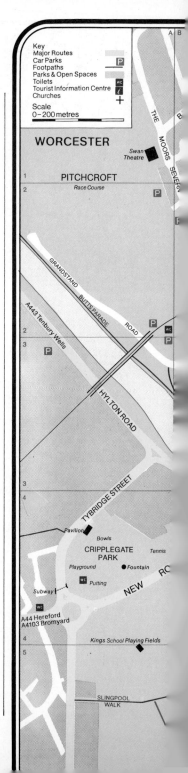

**Key**
Major Routes
Car Parks
Footpaths
Parks & Open Spaces
Toilets
Tourist Information Centre
Churches

Scale
0 – 200 metres

WORCESTER

Swan Theatre

PITCHCROFT
Race Course

GRANDSTAND
A443 Tenbury Wells
BUTTS PARADE
ROAD

HYLTON ROAD

TYBRIDGE STREET

Pavilion
Bowls
CRIPPLEGATE PARK
Tennis
Playground
Fountain
Subway
Putting
NEW RO
A44 Hereford
A4103 Bromyard

Kings School Playing Fields

SLINGPOOL WALK

THE MOORS
SEVERN

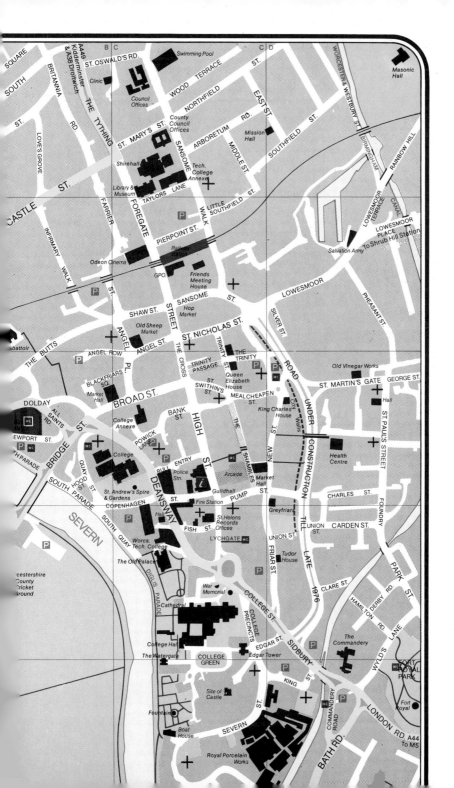

SQUARE

SOUTH ST.

BRITANNIA

LOVE'S GROVE

CASTLE ST.

A449 Kidderminster & A38 Droitwich

THE TYTHING

RD.

FARRIER

INFIRMARY WALK

THE BUTTS

abattoir

DOLDAY

EWPORT ST.

H PARADE

BRIDGE ST.

SOUTH PARADE

SOUTH QUAY

SEVERN

Worcestershire County Cricket Ground

B

ST. OSWALD'S RD.

Clinic

Council Offices

ST. MARY'S ST.

Shirehall

Library & Museum

TAYLORS LANE

FOREGATE

PIERPOINT ST.

Odeon Cinema

GPO.

SHAW ST.

Old Sheep Market

ANGEL ST.

ANGEL ROW

BLACKFRIARS SQ.

Market Hall

College Annexe

College

St. Andrew's Spire & Gardens

COPENHAGEN

Hall

QUAY ST.

HOOD ST.

DEANSWAY

The Old Palace

Worcs. Tech. College

C

Swimming Pool

WOOD TERRACE

NORTHFIELD

County Council Offices

SANSOME ST.

ARBORETUM RD.

Tech. College Annexe

LITTLE SOUTHFIELD

WALK

Railway Station

Friends Meeting House

SANSOME ST.

Hop Market

ST. NICHOLAS ST.

THE CROSS

TRINITY PASSAGE

ST. SWITHIN'S ST.

ANGEL

THE TRINITY

Queen Elizabeth House

BROAD ST.

BANK ST.

HIGH ST.

MEALCHEAPEN ST.

THE SHAMBLES

King Charles House

NEW ST.

BULL ENTRY

Police Stn.

Arcade

Guildhall

Fire Station

FISH ST.

St Helens Records Offices

LYCHGATE

PUMP ST.

Market Hall

Greyfriars

UNION ST.

DIGLIS PARADE

Cathedral

College Hall

The Watergate

COLLEGE GREEN

War Memorial

COLLEGE PRECINCTS

COLLEGE ST.

EDGAR ST.

Edgar Tower

Site of Castle

Fountain

Boat House

SEVERN

Royal Porcelain Works

C D

ST.

EAST ST.

Mission Hall

MIDDLE ST.

SOUTHFIELD

ST.

WORCESTER & WESTBURY ST.

BIRMINGHAM

LOWESMOOR TERRACE

Salvation Army

LOWESMOOR

SILVER ST.

ROAD

UNDER CONSTRUCTION

CITY WALLS

Old Vinegar Works

ST. MARTIN'S GATE

Hall

Health Centre

CHARLES ST.

TITH LATE

UNION ST.

CARDEN ST.

Tudor House

FRIAR ST.

1976

CLARE ST.

SIDBURY

KING ST.

COMMANDERY ROAD

BATH RD.

Masonic Hall

RAINBOW HILL

CANAL

LOWESMOOR PLACE

To Shrub Hill Station

PHEASANT ST.

GEORGE ST.

ST. PAUL'S STREET

FOUNDRY ST.

PARK ST.

HAMILTON RD.

DERBY RD.

WYLD'S LANE

The Commandery

FORT ROYAL PARK

Fort Royal

LONDON RD. A44 To M5

167

ters during the Civil War, during which Worcester earned the soubriquet 'the faithful city', for it was the only town of any importance which remained true to the king. Open weekdays 10.00am to 5.30pm, Sunday and Bank Holiday Monday 2.00pm to 5.00pm.

It has a magnificent Great Hall and interesting wall paintings.

*King Charles' House* A 16th-century building where Charles II took refuge after the Battle of Worcester in 1651. It is now a restaurant.

*The Greyfriars* A 15th-century timber-framed house built for a Franciscan friary which once adjoined it.

Open 1st Wednesday of each month 2.00pm to 6.00pm.

*The Guildhall* One of the finest 18th-century guildhalls in England, with a superb collection of armour. Open Monday to Friday 9.30am to 5.00pm.

*Fort Royal Park* The site of one of the battles of Worcester.

*Radley Hall* Unique collection of replica crown jewels of the world.

Open March to October daily except Monday and Friday 1.30pm to 5.30pm. Park open daily 11.00am to 7.00pm.

*City Museum and Art Gallery* Local history, including the Museum of the Worcestershire Regiment and the Worcestershire Yeomanry Cavalry.

Open Monday to Saturday 9.30am to 5.00pm.

*The Royal Worcester Porcelain Works* (Dyson Perrins) Porcelain has been made in Worcester since 1751.

Visits to the pottery can be made by previous appointment. Parties of up to 40 people may visit between 10.00am and 11.45am and 2.00pm and 3.45pm.

There is a *museum* which houses the largest collection of porcelain in the world, with items dating from 1751 to the present day.

Open Monday to Saturday, April to September, 10.00am to 1.00pm, 2.00pm to 5.00pm. Closed Saturdays in winter. There is also a shop which is open from Monday to Friday 9.00am to 5.00pm.

*Tudor House Museum* Displays illustrating the domestic and working life of the city. Open daily except Thursday and Sunday 10.00am to 5.00pm.

*Worcester Sauce* A local nobleman who had been the Governor of Bengal asked two chemists from the city, Mr Lea and Mr Perrins, in 1823 to make up a sauce from a recipe which he had brought from India.

The chemists produced more of the mixture than had been ordered and, because they did not much like the taste of it themselves, they put it in the cellar of their shop in Broad Street. After the mixture had matured, they pronounced it delicious and marketed it. It was an instant success, and the formula has to this day remained a secret.

The Lea and Perrins Worcester Sauce factory is one of several architecturally-interesting industrial sites in the town.

*Industrial architecture* Other sites include the Hill Evans vinegar works; Shrub Hill railway station; Worcester and Birmingham Canal and Diglis Basin; Worcester Bridge; Old Power Station.

*Events* City Show, on Spring Bank Holiday; Regatta, on Whit Saturday; Three Choirs Music Festival, held every third year, next 1981.

**Tenbury Wells**
A saline spring was discovered here in 1839, but by the time the pump room was built, spa resorts were going rapidly out of fashion. The water is no longer available.

The town is a most attractive mixture of Tudor and Georgian, surrounded by apple orchards and hop fields.

**Abberley**
This village should not be missed on a walking or motoring tour of the Teme Valley. There are ancient earthworks covering 20 acres at Woodbury Hill.

**Stourport-on-Severn**
The centre for canal boat enthusiasts. When the canals were opened in the 18th century, the village immediately lost its sleepy air and became a business community. After Birmingham, it was the most important inland port in the Midlands.

Those days are now gone and some of the tranquillity of the past has returned.

**Bewdley**
Among the finest old towns in England, it has much to offer the visitor, including a Georgian church and many 18th-century houses.

The *Severn Valley Railway* runs from Bewdley to Bridgnorth, with 31 steam trains. It operates March 4 to October 29 weekends, May 2 to May 31 Tuesday, Wednesday and Thursday, June 6 to July 13 daily.

The nearby *Wyre Forest* has a nature trail covering 3½ miles, with a starting point at the Duke William Inn.

**Chaddesley Corbett**
One of a series of picturesque villages in this area.

It has a wealth of charming half-timbered buildings, an inn and a church dating from the 14th century. The latter is dedicated to St Cassian who, in less sleepy days, was murdered in the village.

*Harvington Hall*, with moat and secret passages, is north-west of the village. Open February to November daily except Monday and Friday 2.00pm to 6.30pm.

**Hartlebury Castle**
The home of the Bishop of

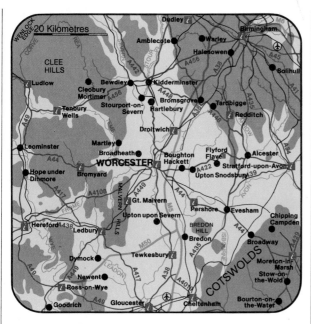

houses in the High Street.

The *Avoncroft Open-Air Museum* contains many restored old buildings on a 10-acre site.

Open March to November daily 10.30am to 5.30pm

### Pershore

This attractive market town has many fine Georgian buildings and is set among woodlands and the fruit farms which produce the famous Pershore plums.

It is best approached across the six-arched bridge over the Avon.

### Evesham

The centre of the Vale of Evesham fruit-growing industry. It is perhaps best visited in spring when the trees are in blossom. In spite of its growth, the town has retained its elegant character.

Ruins of the 14th-century abbey sit by the river. All that remains is a half-timbered gateway in Norman stone and the Bell Tower.

There are many fine old buildings in the town and one of the best, *Booth Hall*, has been lovingly restored to house the branch of a bank.

All Saints' and St Lawrence's churches date back to the 12th century.

However, among the town's major attractions for visitors are the water sports on the Avon. Pleasure craft can be hired and the annual regatta takes place on Spring Bank Holiday.

Only two miles north-east is the riverside village of *Offenham* which is worth visiting to see the maypole, one of the few left in England.

### Broadway

Because its rows of Cotswold-stone cottages so well represent the style of the area, Broadway has become a magnet for tourists. Its magnetic field stretches across the Atlantic, as is evidenced by the trade in its busy antique shops.

Worcester. All that remains of the original castle is the moat. However the present house was built on the site in 1675, and was completely restored in 1964.

The *State Rooms* are open from April to September on the first Sunday of the month, and Bank Holiday Sunday, Monday and Tuesday 2.30pm to 5.30pm.

The house also houses the *Hereford and Worcester County Museum*, open Monday to Thursday 10.00am to 6.00pm, weekends 2.00pm to 6.00pm.

### Ombersley

A very pretty village with half-timbered houses and inns.

*Ombersley Court* dates from the 18th century, with refacing done in the last century.

### Droitwich Spa

The water here is made very briny by salt deposits under the town. It was used for baths by the Romans, but its beneficial properties were not discovered until 1830, during a cholera epidemic.

Treatment is now by prescription only. The open-air lido just outside the town is filled with the salt water, which is very invigorating.

St Richard of Chester was born at Droitwich in 1197, and the *Raven Hotel* stands on the reputed site of his birth. Another famous son of the town was Edward Winslow, one of the Pilgrim Fathers.

### Feckenham

This village standing on the line of a Roman road was once a major centre for fish-hooks and needles. These articles are now manufactured at Redditch, four miles away.

### Bromsgrove

There are several interesting buildings, including a partly 16th-century grammar school and some attractive Georgian

# The Malverns

The Malvern Hills stretch for nine miles, with six townships along their line. The largest of these is Great Malvern, a holiday spa and splendid walking centre.

The area offers a variety of gentle and strenuous climbs, with soft views westwards across Herefordshire towards Wales and eastwards over the Severn Valley.

The hills are criss-crossed by a network of footpaths, some leading up to Worcester Beacon, at 1,394 ft the highest point.

Composers Edward Elgar, Vaughan Williams and Gustav Holst were inspired by the Malverns.

Elgar was born at Broadheath, within sight of the hills, in 1857. Apart from a few years spent in London between 1912 and 1920, he always lived in the area.

He, his wife and daughter are buried in the churchyard of St Wulstan's at Little Malvern.

Elgar's great friend George Bernard Shaw was a frequent visitor and his plays were performed each year at the Shaw Festival.

**Tourist Information Centre**
Winter Gardens, Grange Road, Malvern, Worcestershire. (068 45) 4700

## Great Malvern

The town began in the 11th century with the foundation of a Benedictine priory.

The fine Priory Church of SS Mary and Michael still stands, although it was rebuilt by medieval craftsmen in 1460. The most dominant features are the magnificent stained-glass windows, the choir stalls, and the tiles on the floor, walls and apse. The discovery of a kiln suggests that the tiles were made *in situ*.

In *Priory Park* is a fishpond which was used by the monks 400 years ago.

Great Malvern grew in importance as a spa resort in the last century. Malvern Water was first used medicinally 200 years ago by Dr John Wall.

His analysis is recalled in an 18th-century couplet:

*The Malvern Water, says Dr John Wall*
*Is famous for containing nothing at all.*

A Pump Room and baths were built and hotels appeared on the grounds around the priory.

Traces of the original spa can still be found in such establishments as the Georgian Mount Pleasant Hotel and the Regency Foley Arms Hotel.

In the 19th century Malvern became a national spa attraction when Dr Wilson and Dr Gully introduced hydrotherapy – the Water Cure – from Austria.

Large water cure establishments and boarding houses in many styles sprung up.

Malvern Water can still be obtained from several wells, including two of the oldest – Holy Well, so called because its waters are said to have performed miraculous cures and St Ann's Wells, above the priory church.

The opera singer Jenny Lind, the 'Swedish Nightingale', who settled in England, is buried at Great Malvern Cemetery.

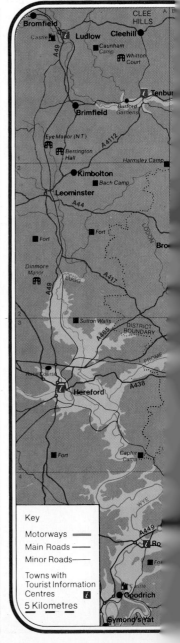

Key

Motorways ▬▬

Main Roads ▬▬

Minor Roads ▬▬

Towns with Tourist Information Centres

5 Kilometres

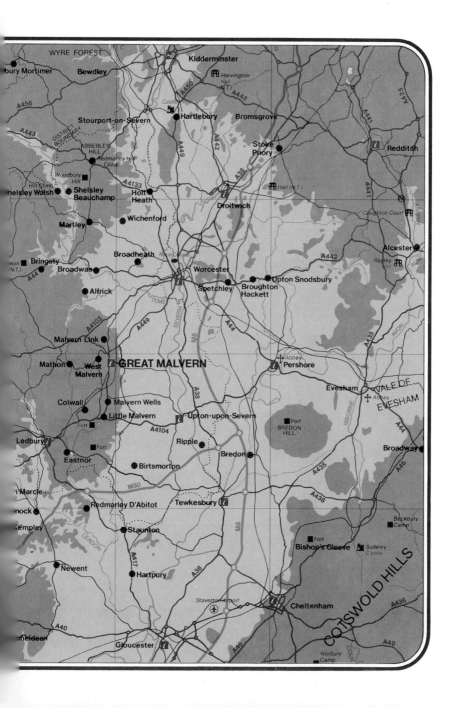

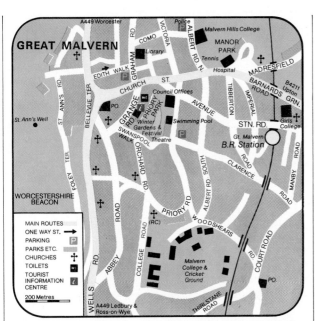

GREAT MALVERN

MAIN ROUTES
ONE WAY ST.
PARKING
PARKS ETC.
CHURCHES
TOILETS
TOURIST
INFORMATION
CENTRE
200 Metres

Malvern is the perfect centre for a walking holiday and leaflets giving details of suggested routes can be obtained from the Tourist Information Centre.
*British Camp* The remains of an Iron Age hill fort built about 350 BC and occupied for about 400 years.
*Great Malvern Railway Station* Magnificent Victorian building with fine wrought ironwork.
*The Priory Church* A 15th-century building with fine stained glass windows and monks stalls featuring superb misericords. Medieval tiles line the apse.
*Wells* Holy Well, at Malvern Wells; St Ann's Well, above the Priory Church. The Pump Room and Baths were built between 1815 and 1819.
*Events* West Midlands Stallion Show, in April; Malvern Gala and Three Counties Show, in June; National Pony Show, in August.
*Malvern Hills* A nine-mile range, with a 1,394-ft summit at Worcester Beacon. Three trail guides for all paths on the hills are available from the Tourist Information Centre: *British Camp to Gullet Quarry; North Hill; Around Worcester Beacon.*

**Little Malvern**
By far the smallest of the Malverns, it boasts the remains of the 12th-century Benedictine Little Malvern Priory of St Giles. It now forms part of Little Malvern Court.
The other Malvern villages are Malvern Wells, Malvern Links, North Malvern and West Malvern.

**Ripple**
A noted spot for salmon and coarse fishing. In addition to this attraction the village itself is an enticing place with its houses grouped around the green.
It has a half-timbered manor house from the 16th century, village stocks and some 18th-century almshouses.

The church has 15th-century misericords depicting agricultural scenes.

**Bredon**
This large village on the Avon has a 14th-century tithe barn, which is among the best-preserved in the country. It once stored the grain paid in taxes to the church.
The area is best-known for *Bell Castle*, a Gothic folly which sits on top of the 961-ft Bredon Hill. From its tower there are magnificent views over the plain of Malvern.
Opinions differ on exactly how many counties can be seen from this vantage point. At least eight are usually visible, while on a clear day the total has been said to rise to 14.
The beautiful villages of Bredon's Norton, Kemerton and Beckford make an attractive small tour by car or by foot.

**Elmley Castle**
The castle has long since vanished, but the village at the foot of Bredon Hill is still there with lovely half-timbered cottages to be admired. The Church of St Mary dates from the 12th century and has some fine sculpture.

**Ledbury**
This charming town inspired such poets as the Brownings and Wordsworth. It was the birthplace of John Masefield who always insisted that his work was influenced by the county.
The 16th-century *Feathers Inn* is among the most attractive buildings in the area.
The arcaded market hall, which dates from the 17th century, is supported on chestnut pillars.
*Eastnor Castle* is nearby, with art treasures and a magnificent park. Open Sunday 2.00pm to 6.00pm, July and August Wednesday and Thursday 2.00pm to 6.00pm.

# Hereford

Like neighbouring Shropshire, the county of Herefordshire is very much border country, with a Welsh influence in places. Across the Welsh border from Kington lies the interesting countryside of the Radnor Forest; to the west and south of Hereford itself are the Brecon Beacons and the Black Mountains.

Arguably England's most thoroughly rural county, Hereford is famous throughout the country for its beef and its cider, though the latter distinction might grudgingly be shared with places further west. There are also hop-yards in the area of Bishops Frome, Bosbury and Ledbury.

The charming market-town of Ross-on-Wye, surrounded by some of England's most attractive countryside, is a very popular base from which to explore.

**Tourist Information Centres**
Trinity Almshouses Car Park, Hereford, Herefordshire. (0432) 68430
Council Offices, 1 Rowberry Street, Bromyard, Herefordshire. (088 52) 2341
Council Offices, 2 Mill Street, Kington, Herefordshire. (054 43) 202
The Library, South Street, Leominster, Herefordshire. (0531) 2461/3429
20 Broad Street, Ross-on-Wye, Herefordshire. (0989) 2768

## Hereford

The city was first settled as a base for the English advance on Wales in AD 760. With its strategic position on the river Wye, it had for many years a turbulent history of sieges, raids and battles.

The cathedral was burned, the castle bombarded and the streets pillaged in a series of grisly encounters covering a period of 600 years. The city was finally captured by the English in 1645 during the Civil War.

Modern, peaceful Hereford stands in one of England's most unspoilt rural areas. It is famous for Wye salmon, hops, cider and white-faced cattle.

A *cattle market* is held in the town every Wednesday.

Cider produced from locally grown apples is made in large quantities by the Bulmer company.

On the premises of the cider factory is one of the two local exhibits of items from the Age of Steam. The Great Western Railway *locomotive* King George V is on display on Saturdays and Sundays from March 25 to September 30, and the engine can be seen under steam on the last Sunday in each month.

*Bulmer's Cider Works* Conducted tours are given from April through until September, Monday to Thursday, 10.30am to 2.15pm. Maximum number of visitors on each tour is 40, and it is necessary to book 12 months in advance for tours.

There are two fine steam *pumping engines* at Broomy Hill, where there is a unique *museum* based on the old Victorian *waterworks*.

The museum can be visited on the first Sunday of the month, April to September, and Saturdays and Sundays in July and August. Opening hours are between 11.00am and 5.00pm.

Probably the item of greatest interest in the city is the *cathed-*

173

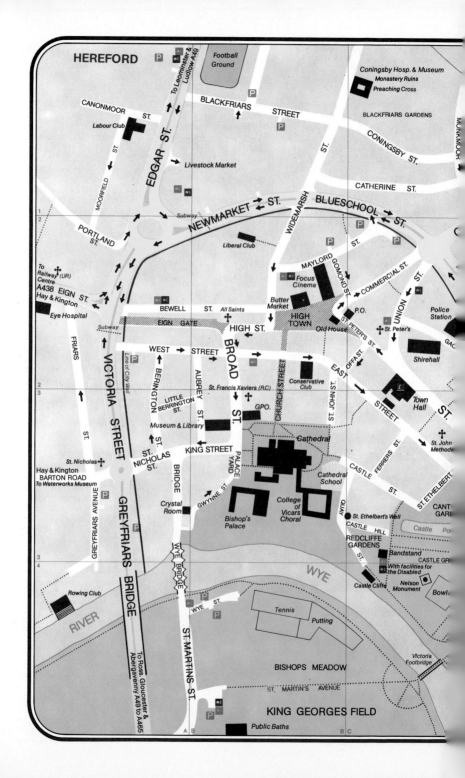

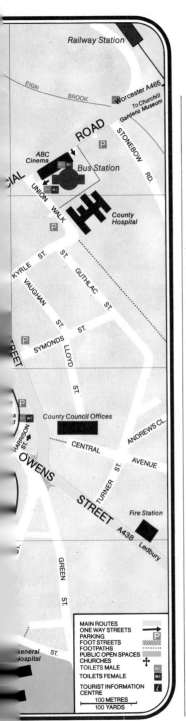

Church Street, Hereford . . . almost hiding the cathedral

ral. It contains one of the two *chained libraries* in Hereford. The other is in All Saints church. The antiquarian books of great value are chained to the shelves. The cathedral collection contains 1,500 books, some dating back to the 9th century.

The most prized of the cathedral's treasures is the *Mappa Mundi*, a unique map of the world drawn about 1300.

The building itself is dedicated to the Saints Mary the Virgin and Ethelbert the King. It is a mixture of architectural styles, the earliest work dating from the 11th century. The Norman nave has massive circular piers which are an outstanding feature. Beyond the 14th-century choir stalls is an early English Lady Chapel.

The chair that King Stephen used when in the cathedral is still there. It dates back to the 13th century, and the Bishop uses it now when he ordains priests.

*All Saints Church* Dates from the 13th century with 14th-century canopied stalls, misericords and a chained library of 300 books. The library is open by appointment only.

*The Old House* Built in 1621, this is a fine example of Jacobean domestic architecture. It was originally part of Butcher's Row.

Open Monday to Friday 10.00am to 1.00pm, 2.00pm to 5.30pm; Saturday April to September 10.00am to 1.00pm, 2.00pm to 5.30pm, October to March 10.00am to 1.00pm. Sunday, April to September 2.00pm to 5.00pm.

*City Walls* The 13th-century walls still remain in Victoria Street and West Street.

*Wye Bridge* A stone bridge with six arches, dating from 1490.

## Weobley

A perfectly preserved village, with timber-framed houses, to the north-west of Hereford.

175

Noble and impressive . . . Goodrich Castle

## Kington
A border town where visitors can still examine the *Offa's Dyke* *earthworks*. Offa was the King of Mercia and his dyke was the defence wall which he built to keep out the Welsh. The footpath along the dyke stretches for 168 miles from Prestatyn to Chepstow.

*Hergest Croft Gardens*, near Kington, offer 50 acres of trees, shrubs, rhododendrons and azaleas.

Open daily, May 1 to August 29.

## Pembridge
The village church in Pembridge is 600 years old, and was once a refuge for local people when the Welsh stormed over the border. The detached tower is one of seven in the country.

## Leominster
The traditional industry of this town is the manufacture of wool. The fine-textured wool produced here since the 13th century is known as Lemster Ore.

The Ryelands sheep, from which the wool is produced, were bred by the monks of ancient times, and have since been exported to Australia, New Zealand, and South America.

Priory Church, just off Broad Street, dates from the 11th century. The church is notable for its three naves. Broad Street itself has some fine 18th-century buildings, and there is a ducking stool here, which was used until 1809 to silence nagging wives.

Eye Manor, a 17th-century Carolean manor house which has fine plaster ceilings and lovely grounds, is open to the public daily July to September, Wednesday, Thursday and weekends April to June.

Five miles to the north-west of Leominster is *Croft Castle*, a restored building dating from the 14th century. It is approached along avenues of 350-year-old chestnut trees.

Open Easter to September, Wednesday, Thursday, Saturday, Sunday and Bank Holidays.

## Bromyard
A market town with half-timbered houses. Nearby is Lower Brockhampton, a 15th-century, moated, half-timbered manor house.

Open February to December weekdays, except Tuesdays and Thursdays.

## Much Marcle
This small village's main claims

to fame are its fine herd of beef cattle and its cider factory, Weston and Sons Ltd. It has two mansions.

*Hellens* dates from the 13th century and can be visited every Sunday and Bank Holiday from 2.00pm to 6.00pm.

## Ross-on-Wye
This steep town is crowded in summer when it is the centre for the Wye Valley tourist trade. In winter, it reverts to its old role of quiet market community with a 17th-century arcaded market hall.

The town owes much to the philanthropist John Kyrle, who was born in 1637 and spent most of his 87 years in Ross.

He laid out The Prospect public gardens which have magnificent views of river and hills.

More important, he gave the town its first public water supply. He built the causeway to Wilton Bridge, and the church spire pinnacles.

Kyrle's house in the High Street has now been converted into shops. It is marked by a plaque commemorating 'The Man of Ross'.

## Goodrich Castle
A noble and impressive ruin on a hill overlooking the Wye. The square castle has a tower in each corner and a moat hacked out of solid rock.

It was started in the late 12th century and became the home of the Earls of Shrewsbury until Cromwell's men destroyed it during the Civil War.

The instrument of destruction was a mortar called Roaring Meg, which is preserved on view at Castle Green, near Hereford Cathedral.

Southwards is Symonds Yat, one of the most superb views of the Wye. Yat is Old English for gate. It describes the point where the river rolls its way through a narrow gorge and swings round in a five-mile loop.

# Gloucestershire

Not only does Cheltenham have the characteristic attractions of a spa town, it is also the main centre for exploration in the northern part of Gloucestershire.

The borders of Gloucestershire make three ambitious sorties northwards: nudging the Malverns near Ledbury; watching over the meeting of the rivers Severn and Avon at Tewkesbury; and following the Cotswolds to Moreton-in-Marsh and Chipping Campden.

Though four or five counties have stretches of Cotswold country, Gloucestershire can lay claim to the greatest share of these much-appreciated hills. Indeed, the Cotswolds run the length of the county, separating the cities of Gloucester and Cirencester.

The county town is also a centre from which to explore Severn country as the river begins to broaden, the Forest of Dean, and the Vale of Berkeley.

Cirencester is an agreeable centre from which to explore some of the less tourist-trampled parts of the Cotswolds, close to the Wiltshire border.

## Cheltenham (map p 178)

A visit by George III in 1788 led to the growth of this elegant inland spa town. It was laid out in an imposing manner with wide tree-lined streets and promenades, and the best of Regency architecture.

Some visitors came to take the waters at the Pittville Pump Room which, with its colonnade and dome, is regarded by many as the town's most beautiful building.

However, many more came simply for a fashionable holiday among their peers in polite society.

It is now a town with a lively interest in art, music and sport. Cheltenham Music Festival began in 1944 to encourage contemporary British music and it has been the setting for first performances of work by Sir Arthur Bliss, Sir Benjamin Britten, Sir Arnold Bax and Malcolm Arnold.

Cheltenham's County Cricket Festival is also a major attraction for lovers of this noble old game.

Racegoers the world over will know the town as the only place to be when the National Hunt Festival is held at the Prestbury Park racecourse.

*Pittville Pump Rooms* The waters can still be taken here, and the park has a lake and floral display.

Open May to September weekdays 10.00am to 4.00pm, Sunday 2.00pm to 5.00pm.

*Montpellier Rotunda* and *Montpellier Walk* Superb Regency buildings line this 'street of statues' which is noted for its fascinating shops.

*Landsdowne Terrace* and *Suffolk Square* Interesting and elaborately-modelled façades.

*Promenade* An elegant long terrace, which houses the Tourist Information Centre, and has many fine ironwork balconies.

*Clarence Street Library Museum* The local historical archives are stored here. The art gallery has Dutch and Flemish paintings, Chinese Porcelain.

Open Monday to Saturday 10.00am to 5.30pm.

*Holst Birthplace Museum* Mementoes of the famous composer of Swedish descent.

Open Tuesday to Saturday 11.00am to 5.30pm.

*Imperial Gardens* Pleasant displays of sub-tropical plants; open-air art show in the summer.

*Sports* Swimming; tennis; bowling; horse racing; cricket; golf; hunting.

*Events* International Festival of Music, Cheltenham Horse Show, in July; County Cricket, in August; Antiques Fair, Festival of Literature, in September; steeplechase racing from September to April, the season ending with the National Hunt Festival.

## Tewkesbury

The meeting place of the Severn and the Avon. In 1471 it was also the bloody meeting place of the Roses Warriors, with victory going to the Yorkists.

King John's Bridge, crossing the Avon, includes parts of the original 13th-century bridge.

This pleasant old town has its fair share of black and white timbered buildings, and more than its share of good inns. Notable is the Royal Hop Pole, which was mentioned in *The Pickwick Papers*. The inn dates from the 13th century.

However, the architectural pride of Tewkesbury is the 12th-century abbey with its impressive Norman tower, standing 132 ft high.

The climb to the top is worthwhile for there are unmatched views across the surrounding valleys.

## Chipping Campden

A picturesque old village in Cotswold stone, and a popular base from which to explore the hills.

Parts of the church date back

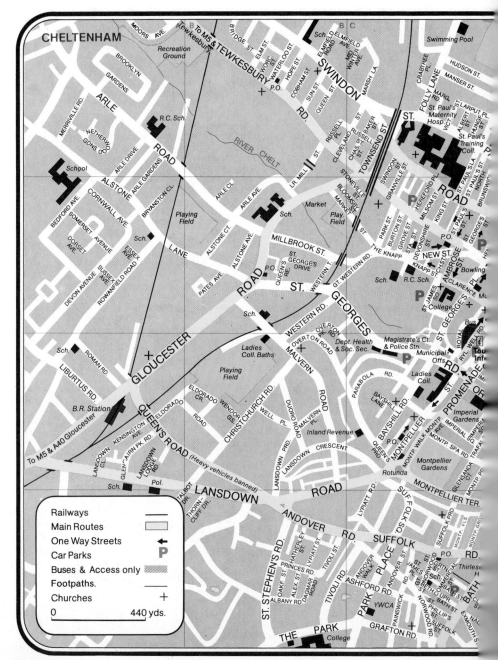

CHELTENHAM

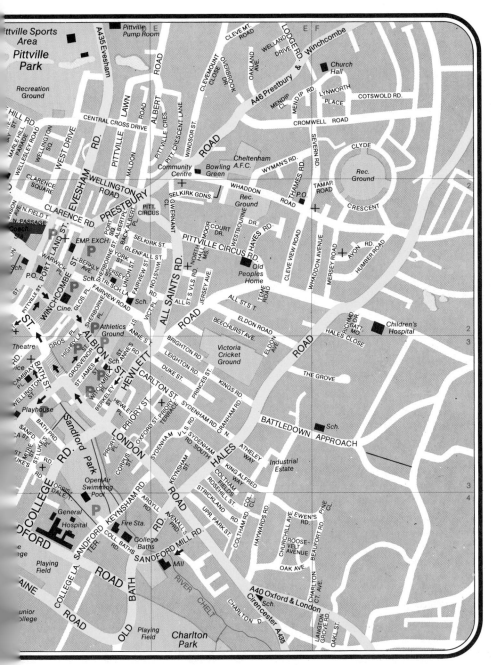

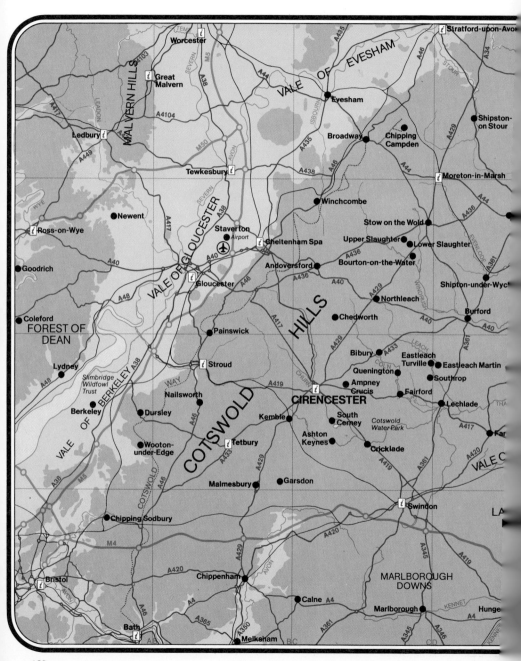

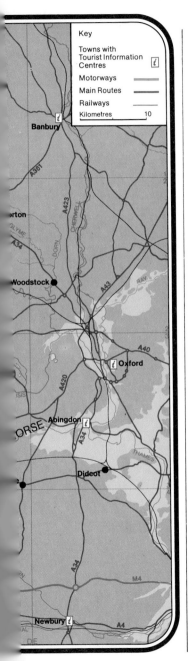

to the 14th century, but the Jacobean *market hall* is probably the finest piece of architecture.

## Stow-on-the-Wold

For many centuries the town was the home of one of the biggest livestock markets in Britain. The event is still held in May and October, although it is now mainly a show.

Like many other towns in the immediate area, it was once a centre of the wool industry. Now it is just a quiet cluster of old houses and pubs.

Stow-on-the-Wold has England's prettiest brewery, a Cotswold stone building with a mill-pond, exotic waterfowl and a trout stream. Its products, Donnington Ales, are available in several Cotswold towns and villages.

## Bourton-on-the-Water

The river Windrush flows down the main street of this famous and delightful village. It is a noted beauty spot and is very busy during the summer and at weekends.

At *Birdland* is a 3½-acre garden with over 600 species of exotic birds. There is also an art gallery.

Open March to November daily 10.00am to 6.00pm, November to February daily 10.30am to 4.00pm.

The *model village* is a miniature version of Bourton-on-the-Water itself, and it has a model railway. Open daily 10.00am to 6.00pm.

*Hertford House* is an art gallery, featuring the work of local artists.

Open March to October daily 9.30am to 5.30pm.

A perfume laboratory and shop can be visited at the *Cotswold Perfumery*. Open daily.

Old cars are on show at the *Bourton-on-the-Water Motor Museum*. Open daily 10.00am to 6.00pm.

For those interested in entymology, the *Butterfly*

*Exhibition and Insect Zoo* is well worth a visit.

Open daily 10.00am to 6.00pm.

## Northleach

A feature of this unchanging village is the *Blind House*, a building which has no windows and was once used as the local prison.

The fine old 15th-century church recalls the days when Northleach was a busy wool centre with prosperous merchants among its parishioners.

## Gloucester

Once the Roman fortified town of Glevum.

Medieval architects added several fine buildings, but the city did not really achieve any importance until the Gloucester and Sharpness canal was opened in 1827.

The Gloucester of today is a major inland port handling not only local products, but also timber shipments from Finland, Norway, Canada and Russia.

The pinnacled tower of the cathedral dominates the city. Its medieval stained glass east window is second in size only to that of the mighty York Minster.

The cathedral is a splendid example of Norman architecture, later partially transformed by King Edward III into the style which became known as Perpendicular. There is a fine Norman crypt and the tomb of the murdered Edward II.

Replica brass rubbings may be taken. The 14th-century choir stalls and the 16th-century painted organ case are also worth attention.

Gloucestershire also has a fine tradition of pub sports, especially skittles. There are no less than 8,000 skittle players registered in the city of Gloucester alone.

*Prinknash Abbey and Pottery* A Benedictine monastery with a house dating back to the 14th century. The monks also run their own pottery. There is a pottery shop, a farm shop and refreshments are available. Open daily 10.00am to 6.00pm. *Prinknash Bird Park* This wildlife centre covers seven acres of the abbey grounds. There are more than 60 species of birds, an otter pen, pets corner and 'secret garden'. Open daily 10.00am to 6.00pm.

## Paradise

This hamlet was so named by Charles I who stayed there while his forces attacked Gloucester. The king described the village as the most beautiful place he had ever been.

The village inn was then called the Plough. Now the name has been changed to the more apt Adam and Eve.

## Painswick

An old wool town with many legends and traditions.

On the first Sunday after September 19, the children take part in the medieval *Clipping ceremony* in which they all join hands around the 15th-century St Mary's Church while a hymn is sung.

This charming ceremony was once an ale-swilling dance, and has nothing to do with sheep shearing.

There is an interesting legend attached to the clipped yew trees in the churchyard, some of which have been there since 1714.

Traditionally there were only 99 trees, for every time the 100th was planted, the Devil was said to come and rip it out.

Clearly the Devil has found other tasks these days, for there are now more than 100 trees.

## Stroud

*Minchinhampton Common,* above the town, is 600 acres of National Trust land giving magnificent views over the Golden Valley and the Stroudwater Hills.

## Slimbridge

The home of Peter Scott's famous *Wildfowl Trust,* with the world's largest collection of 2,500 swans, geese and 160 species of ducks. There are also six flocks of flamingoes.

However, the most spectacular sight of the year takes place in winter when thousands of wild geese take flight to find sanctuary in the Severn Estuary.

## Berkeley

Home of a castle and a famous Hunt. It is an old tradition of the Berkeley family that yellow is worn during the Hunt, instead of the customary pink.

Edward II was murdered in the dungeons in 1327. The Elizabethan terraced gardens include a bowling alley, and there is an extensive deer park nearby.

The castle is open Easter to September daily except Monday 2.00pm to 5.00pm, and the grounds are open Easter to October daily 11.00am to 5.00pm.

The local parish church contains the grave of Edward Jenner, who discovered vaccination.

His memorial is the church's east window with pictures of Christ healing the sick.

## Badminton

The *Badminton Horse Trials* are held here every April, attracting riders from all over the world and equally cosmopolitan spectators.

Badminton and its Palladian mansion has been the home of the Dukes of Beaufort for more than 300 years and the estate covers 15,000 acres.

The house and the kennels of the famous Beaufort Hunt are open to visitors every Wednesday from June to September, 2.00pm to 5.00pm.

The Beaufort hunters always wear green, which is another old family tradition.

## Westonbirt Arboretum

This Forestry Commission area covers 117 acres with unusual and beautiful trees.

The collection was started 150 years ago by the local squire, Robert Stainer Holford, and it is now among England's finest. From spring to October the rhododendrons are a riot of colour.

The arboretum is open daily 10.00am to sunset.

## Wotton-under-Edge

The 14th-century church boasts an organ built in the 18th-century for St Martin-in-the-Fields which was played by Handel himself when George I attended services at the London church.

The local vicar bought it when St Martin's decided to buy another.

Shorthand writers everywhere should feel a spiritual link with this market town, for in Orchard Street is the house in which local schoolmaster Isaac Pitman devised his shorthand system.

## Bisley

Few Cotswold villages can have so much of interest to offer the visitor. It is known as Bisley-God-Help-Us because of the winter winds.

The village has a spring-fed fountain, a 19th-century lock-up, a Saxon cross. A fascinating pub, the *Bear Inn,* has two secret passages and a priesthole.

## Nailsworth

A town for all motor enthusiasts, for it has a chalky hill, the Nailsworth Ladder, with a 1-in-3 gradient used in motor trials.

## Tetbury

A fine Elizabethan market town with a 17th-century town hall built on pillars. The market is held on alternate Wednesdays.

Two miles west are the ruins of *Beverstone Castle* where King Harold stayed in 1051. It was

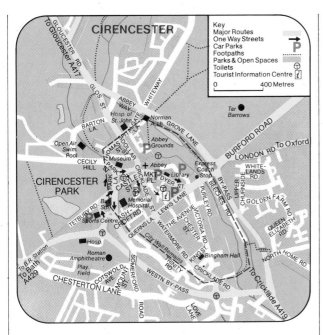

*Barnsley Park* A Georgian Baroque building of local quarry stone. Open by appointment with the National Trust.

*Corn Hall* An interestingly-decorated Victorian building.

*Bowly's Almshouses* A row of 19th-century almshouses.

*Sports* Bowls; rugby; cricket; football; golf; squash; tennis; swimming; badminton; basketball; volley ball; table tennis.

*Events* Polo weeks, in May, June and August; Sheep Fair, in September.

## North Cerney
A delightful village by the river Churn, with an unusual 12th-century church with a saddle-back tower and gabled roof.

## Lechlade
This attractive little town takes its name from the river Leach, but is best known to watermen as the highest navigable point of the Thames, into which the Leach runs.

All Thames boats stop at Halfpenny Bridge – so named because it once charged a halfpenny toll.

The point where the two rivers join, beside the Trout Inn, is also the meeting place of the counties of Gloucestershire, Berkshire and Wiltshire.

Although boats can go no further than Lechlade, the great river rises at Thames Bridge, eastwards towards Cirencester. A statue of Father Thames marks the spot.

*Parish Church of St John the Baptist* One of the great 'wool' churches of the Cotswolds with a 15th-century pulpit, superb tower, a magnificent three-storied fan-vaulted porch and many brasses.

*Watermoor Church* A 19th-century church designed by Sir Gilbert Scott in the Victorian Gothic style.

*Historic Inns* King's Head, Market Place; Bear Inn, Dyer Street; The Crown, West Market Place.

---

besieged in 1145 by King Stephen and was then held by the Berkeleys.

## Cirencester
A thriving market town with a spacious market place presenting a colourful and lively scene.

The most striking feature is the magnificent 15th-century parish church of St John Baptist. Like many churches in the Midlands, this was built on the earnings of the local wool trade.

The church possesses a collection of communion plate which is said to be the best in England, including the Anne Boleyn Cup, which is on permanent display.

*Corinium Museum* is a worthy setting for one of the most important collections of Roman antiquities in Britain.

Open May to September weekdays 10.00am to 6.00pm, Sunday 2.00pm to 6.00pm, October to April weekdays 10.00am to 5.00pm, Sunday 2.00pm to 6.00pm.

*Cirencester Park*, Earl Bathurst's 3,000-acre estate is open to the public for riding and walking.

*Cirencester Park, Polo and Leisure Centre* A 3,000-acre park with nature walks, model farm and children's playground. Occasional events include international hot air balloon meetings, horse trials, shows and car rallies. Polo is played almost every Sunday from May to September. Open daily.

The *Abbey Grounds* park extends into the centre of town where the river Churn winds through well-kept lawns into a large lake populated by swans and wildfowl. The remains of the town's Roman walls can be seen here.

Only four miles away is the *Cotswold Marina*, with excellent facilities for swimming, fishing, sailing, water skiing or hydroplane racing.

# Wiltshire

Salisbury Plain, 20 miles wide and 12 miles from north to south, is a dominant feature of the Wiltshire landscape. At the heart of the Plain, the prehistoric mystery of Stonehenge looms large, almost as a motif for the whole county. No stretch of England casts quite as many shadows of Ancient Man and his inexplicable ways. Wiltshire has been elaborately furnished with stone-circles, man-made mounds and such like, and it is a county which can greatly excite the imagination.

Those who attribute such constructions to the activities of early visitors from Space, might also care to visit Warminster, a popular spot from which to sight UFOs. A more mundane explanation for things that go flash in the night may be the number of military establishments in this county.

As a base for exploration, Salisbury is conveniently poised at the meeting point of the West of England, the 'Wessex' region, and the South.

**Tourist Information Centres**
Redworth House, Amesbury, Wiltshire. (098 02) 3255
Endless Street, Salisbury, Wiltshire. (0722) 4956
Fisherton Street, Salisbury, Wiltshire. (0722) 27676/4432
32 The Arcade, David Murray John Building, Brunel Centre, Swindon, Wiltshire. (0793) 30328/26161 Ext 518

## Salisbury (*map p 186*)

The ancient town of Old Sarum has been in existence since the Iron Age. The Romans built a fort and the Saxons then developed it into an industrial town.

In the 13th century a bad water supply led the Bishop, Richard Poore, to leave his old Norman cathedral on top of the hill and move down to the valley.

He began to build the present cathedral there in 1220. The site became known as New Sarum, and eventually Salisbury.

The city has examples of various architectural styles.

The foyer of the cinema in New Canal was once the banqueting hall of the merchant John Halle, four times Mayor of the city. It is a splendid example of 15th-century black and white timbering.

Away from the town centre is the tranquillity of Cathedral Close where beautiful houses overlook the green.

*Old Sarum* Now an archaeological site. The huge earthworks occupy 56 acres.

Old Sarum has the dubious distinction of being one of the old 'rotten boroughs', a corrupt system whereby a town could still return Members of Parliament even though most of the inhabitants had gone.

*Cathedral* Except for parts of the tower and spire, this cathedral is all Early English Gothic. Most cathedrals demonstrate a far greater mixture of styles.

Salisbury's spire is the tallest in Europe, at 404 ft, and was added to the building in 1334, about 54 years after the rest was completed.

In the library over the East Walk is one of the four original copies of Magna Carta.

*Malmesbury House* Queen Anne with baroque and rococo plaster work. Open April to September Tuesday, Wednesday and Thursday 9.30am to 5.00pm.

*Mompesson House* Queen Anne town house. Open March to September Wednesday to Sunday 11.00am to 6.00pm.

*North Canonry* A 17th-century flint and stone house with remains of a 13th-century undercroft. Open daily in summer 9.30am to 5.30pm.

## Wilton

The town is world-famous for its carpets which have been made here since the 17th century. Visits can be made to the Wilton Carpet Factory by appointment.

Wilton was the capital of Wessex in Saxon times and, although it has never managed to live up to that early distinction since, it retains an air of dignified charm and peace.

*Wilton House* is the home of the Earls of Pembroke, and it stands on the site of an abbey which was founded by Alfred the Great.

Inigo Jones and his son-in-law John Webb reconstructed the house after it was wrecked by fire in 1647.

Visitors can see the fine collection of paintings and the extensive display of model soldiers from the 19th century.

Open Easter to October weekdays 11.00am to 6.00pm, Sunday 2.00pm to 6.00pm.

## Warminster

An attractive market town at the head of the Wylye Valley.

Nearby is *Longleat House*, home of the Marquis of Bath and Europe's first wildlife safari park.

The magnificent house was begun in 1568 and is the very epitome of the English stately home.

Open all the year round daily 10.00am to 6.00pm.

## Westbury

Wiltshire's most famous White Horse looks down on this small weaving town, which has Georgian houses gathered

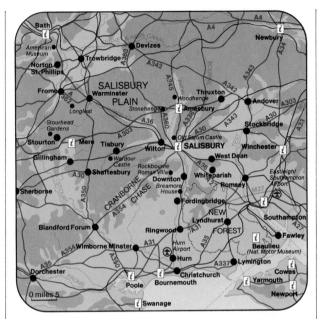

round an attractive market place.

The horse is cut into the chalk 1½ miles north-east at Bratton Down. The existing figure dates only from the 18th century, but it replaced another reputed to have commemorated the victory of King Alfred over the Danes at Ethandun in AD 878.

Above the horse visitors can see the extensive prehistoric earthworks of Bratton Castle.

The Palace Green takes its name from the home of the Kings of Wessex.

### Trowbridge
West of England broadcloth is still made in this town, as it has been since the Flemish weavers settled, bringing great prosperity with them.

### Devizes
An interesting market town with several fine 18th-century buildings. The 19th-century

castle stands on a Norman site. The *Devizes Museum* exhibits Neolithic, Bronze and Iron Age finds from Wiltshire. Open weekdays 10.00am to 5.00pm, Sunday 2.00pm to 5.00pm.

### Swindon
The town's prosperity grew with the arrival of the Great Western Railway in 1841, and railway engineering is still one of its principal industries.

*The Great Western Railway Museum* has several locomotives on display, as well as a room devoted to the engineer Isambard Kingdom Brunel. Open weekdays 10.00am to 5.00pm, Sunday 2.00pm to 5.00pm.

At the *Museum and Art Gallery* are works by Graham Sutherland, Henry Moore, John Nash and Ben Nicholson. The museum houses geological collections and natural history exhibits. Open weekdays 10.00am to 5.00pm, Sunday 2.00pm to 5.00pm.

### Marlborough
A market town noted for its very wide main street, with many Georgian buildings. The back streets are lined with half-timbered medieval cottages.

At the western end of the town an arched bridge leads to the public school, Marlborough College, which was built in 1843 on the site of an old castle.

### Avebury
An attractive village ringed by the *Avebury Stone Circle*, one of the most important prehistoric monuments in Britain.

100 sarcen stones of sandstone from Marlborough Downs remain.

### Pewsey
The white horse cut into the hills overlooking the Vale of Pewsey was created in 1937 by a local man, George Marples. It replaced the 18th-century horse which was no longer visible.

### Woodhenge
Some authorities believe that this Neolithic earthwork is even older than Stonehenge. In 1925, six concentric rings of holes were discovered here, apparently made for wooden posts indicating the position of sunrise on Midsummer Day.

### Amesbury
Queen Guinevere is supposed to have retired to the abbey of this Avon town after hearing of the death of King Arthur. A later abbey stands on the same spot.

### Stonehenge
Even though the dates are conjecture, but it is likely that this Bronze Age site was begun before 2150 BC. A double circle of bluestones was erected about 475 years later. These original stones came from Pembrokeshire and historians believe they were floated across the Bristol Channel on rafts and then dragged over logs to Salisbury Plain.

185

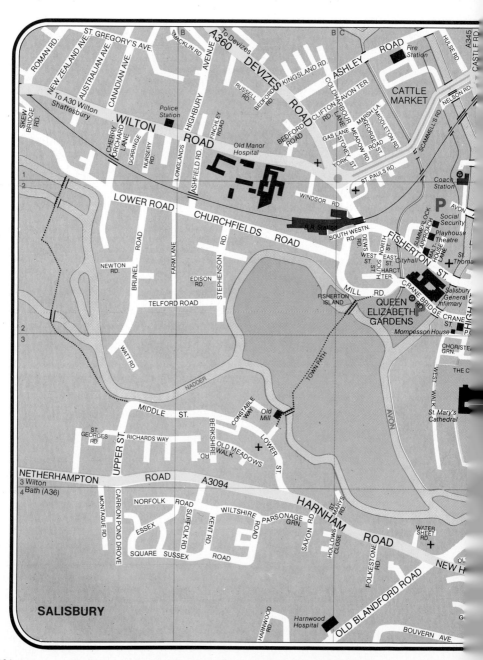

SALISBURY

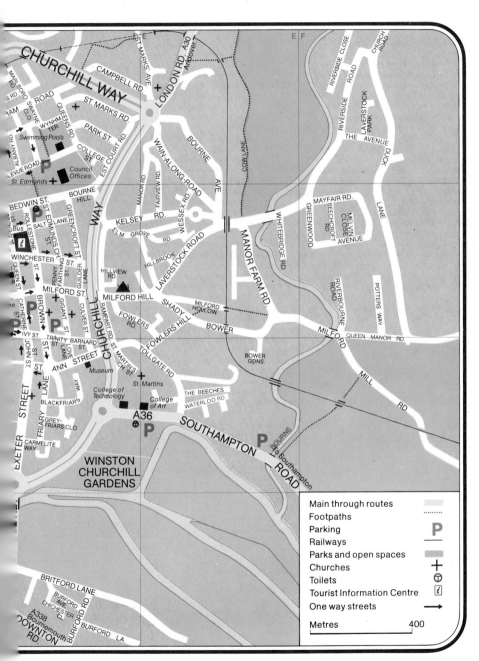

**Legend**

| | |
|---|---|
| Main through routes | |
| Footpaths | |
| Parking | **P** |
| Railways | |
| Parks and open spaces | |
| Churches | + |
| Toilets | ⊕ |
| Tourist Information Centre | 𝑖 |
| One way streets | → |
| Metres | 400 |

# 'Wessex'

At the border of Wiltshire and Dorset lies the little town of Shaftesbury, which was the inspiration for the fictitious 'Shaston' of Thomas Hardy's novels. Further into Dorset is the county town, Dorchester, which Hardy re-styled as 'Casterbridge'.

Hardy set his novels in an imaginary county called 'Wessex'. This name originally belonged to a Saxon kingdom, and survives today as an occasional description for an imprecise region comprising Dorset and those adjoining two or three counties which are less than wholly West Country.

Hardy's Wessex was particularly Dorset, and especially its inland area, agricultural still, where his characters lived their lives of the soil.

## Dorchester

The undoubted capital of Hardy Country. The town's *museum* has a collection of the novelist's manuscripts, in addition to an interesting reconstruction of the study at his former home, Max Gate. Open daily 10.00am to 1.00pm, 2.00pm to 5.00pm.

South of the town are *Maumbury Rings*, a Stone Age circle which the Romans made into an amphitheatre to seat 10,000. In the 1700s it was used for the Hanging Fairs – a cheerful title for what were public executions.

Thomas Hardy's Ale, originally produced by the local brewery of Eldridge Pope for a commemorative festival, is arguably the world's strongest beer.

It leaves the brewery with an alcoholic strength in excess of 12.5 per cent by volume, but continues slowly to ferment and therefore strengthens in the bottle. It is intended to be kept for

four or five years before being opened.

Nearby is *Maiden Castle*, among the largest earthworks in Europe and dating from 2000 BC. It was fortified in the Iron Age around 300 BC. The Romans captured it in AD 43

## Bockhampton

No true Hardy lover will miss the opportunity to visit the author's birthplace. A study of the visitor's book at the thatched cottage shows that many return again and again.

Hardy was born in 1840 and lived in the cottage for many years. Few authors can have had more inspirational views than the one over the heathland from the room in which he wrote.

The cottage is now owned by the National Trust and is open by appointment with the tenant. Ring (0305) 2366.

Hardy is buried in Westminster Abbey at Poets' Corner, but fittingly his heart was returned

**Tourist Information Centre**
District Council, 60 High West Street, Dorchester, Dorset. (0305) 66969

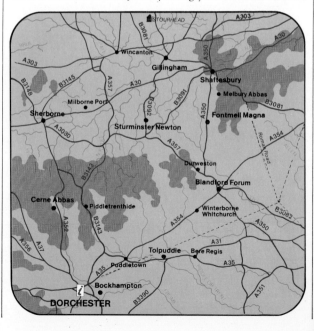

to the land he loved and lies in a grave at nearby Stinsford.

## Cerne Abbas

Another stopping point for Hardy devotees. *Cross and Hand*, a weird rugged prehistoric stone is the spot where Tess of the D'Urbervilles was made to swear an oath of fidelity.

North-east of the village is the *Cerne Abbas Giant*, the 180-foot upright figure of a naked chalk man. The figure is about 1,500 years old and is believed to have been part of a fertility rite. Legend had it that local women could cure barrenness by sleeping on the hillside.

## Tolpuddle

This village is famous for the six Tolpuddle Martyrs who formed a trade union in 1834 but were arrested. They were sentenced to seven years' transportation to Australia but were pardoned after two years and sent home.

There are several memorials to the men in the village, including the *Martyr's Tree* on the village green and a *Methodist chapel*. At the *Memorial Hall*, next to six cottages named after each convict, is an exhibition devoted to the Martyrs. Open daily 9.00am to dusk.

A labour *rally* is held at Tolpuddle on the 3rd Sunday in July.

## Sherborne

Perhaps best known for its public school which incorporates many of the old buildings of Sherborne Abbey.

Sir Walter Raleigh lived at Sherborne Old Castle for 15 years, but it is now a ruin. The New Castle has many art treasures. Open Easter to September, Thursday and weekends 2.00pm to 6.00pm.

To the west at the Yeovilton Airbase is the *Museum of Fleet Airarm* featuring exhibits from both World Wars and also the Concorde 002 prototype. Open weekdays 10.00am to 5.30pm, Sunday 12.30pm to 5.30pm.

## Stourhead

This magnificent *stately home*, on the outskirts of the village of Mere, was built in 1722 and is now owned by the National Trust.

It contains a treasure house of artistry. There is carved woodwork by Angelica Kauffman, sculpture by Michael Rysbrack and furniture by Thomas Chippendale. Open March to September daily 8.00am to 7.00pm.

Stourhead is equally impressive outside, with some of the finest landscaped gardens of the 18th century, with lakes and temples, trees, shrubs and flowers.

Mere has two historic pubs – the Ship, dating from the 18th century, and the now modernized Talbot, where Charles II hid in disguise after the Battle of Worcester.

## Gillingham

Unlike its namesake in Kent, this town's initial letter is hard.

There is some excellent Georgian architecture, and John Constable pronounced the town a beauty spot. His painting of the old silk mill now hangs in the Tate Gallery in London.

## Shaftesbury

This is the town of Shaston which featured in Hardy's novels.

It is set on the edge of a 700-ft plateau, with awesome views of the Blackmoor Vale. The town is an excellent touring base.

## Fontmell Magna

As attractive as its name, taken from Fontmell Brook which flows from the downs above the village.

## Sturminster Newton

Hardy wrote *Return of the Native* at Riverside, a greystone mansion on the outskirts of this market centre for the farmlands of the Stour.

He is not the only 19th-century poet to have graced the town, for William Barnes, who wrote *Linden Lea*, was born at Pentridge Farm.

There is a superb 15th-century bridge with six arches crossing the river.

## Blandford Forum

A splendid Georgian town almost destroyed by a fire in 1731. It was rebuilt to conform with the classical leanings of builders of the early 18th century.

The overwhelming impression now is of rich red- or rust-coloured brickwork. The Corn Exchange and the pump, sheltered by a 200-year-old Doric porch, are outstanding.

## Wimbourne Minster

Few towns anywhere can match the magnificent approach to Wimbourne from Blandford Forum.

The road is flanked by a guard of honour comprising 365 noble old beech trees – one for each day of the year.

Five main roads radiate from Wimbourne. This excellent position at the heart of the hills and heaths of east Dorset makes it a useful touring base.

The Church of St Cuthberga is one of the most outstanding in all of Dorset. It has superb twin towers and was built in a mixture of styles, ranging from Norman to Gothic.

The west tower has an interesting clock with the figure of a grenadier marching out to strike the quarter hours with a hammer.

Antiques and the best collection in Britain of horse brasses are on show at the *Priest's House Museum*.

Open Easter to September Monday to Saturday 10.30am to 12.30pm, 2.30pm to 4.30pm.

# Bath

Doubly renowned as both a Roman and a Georgian town, Bath is also England's best-known spa.

It has been described as Britain's most distinguished small city. Small it is, and very crowded with tourists in the summer, being less than 100 miles from London.

In size, it is far overshadowed by the neighbouring city of Bristol, with which it shares the new county of Avon. Emotionally, Bath belongs to Somerset, while retaining a place in its heart for Wiltshire, with which it shares a boundary.

On the Somerset side of Bath are the Mendips and then the city of Wells; on the Wiltshire side the little town of Bradford-on-Avon and then the Salisbury Plain; to the north, the edge of Cotswold country; to the west, the resorts of Clevedon and Weston-super-Mare.

**Tourist Information Centre**
Abbey Churchyard, Bath, Avon.
(0225) 62831.

## Bath

King Lear's father, Prince Bladud, is said to have discovered the curative properties of Bath's warm springs. He had contracted leprosy, and had been banished to keep pigs. One day, he followed his pigs into the water, and he was subsequently restored to health and favour.

This legend may date back as far as 800 BC, but there can be no doubt that the Romans found the springs soon after arriving in Britain. They built a bath there, and a small city, which they named Aquae Sulis after the god of hot springs.

In 973, Edgar was crowned first king of all England in a Saxon abbey at Bath. This was replaced by a Norman cathedral, an arch and aisle of which remains, and later by the 15th-century abbey which is now the centre of the city.

In 1616, Queen Anne of Denmark, wife of James I, took the cure in a new bath. In 1702 and 1703, Queen Anne came, and began the city's greatest period of fashionability. Bath had long been a centre of social life, gossip and scandal, but the Georgian period was its heyday.

A Doctor Oliver, inventor of a healthful biscuit which still enjoys some reputation, founded the Royal Mineral Water Hospital, which is now closed.

Among his colleagues in this venture was Beau Nash, the Georgian playboy and arbiter of social graces who became the uncrowned 'Prince' of Bath.

Another associate was Ralph Allen, a pioneer of the British postal system, who commissioned another member of this social set, John Wood, to build a magnificent house in Prior Park. It is now a boy's public school, but the grounds and church are open daily.

Wood went on to expand the city in a grand Palladian style, following the tradition of Inigo Jones. His masterpiece, completed by his son, is a circle of houses called *The Circus*. The younger Wood went on to design the superb *Royal Crescent*.

The city has an embarrassment of Georgian riches, including Lansdowne Crescent, Pulteney Bridge, the Assembly Rooms and the Pump Room (built over the Roman baths).

*Pump Room* Every day 250,000 gallons of water at a constant temperature of 51° centigrade gushes out of the earth. The springs cannot be seen, but the

190

overflow is visible at the *Roman Baths Museum*.

The famous waters can still be taken in the *Pump Room* above and at the *fountain* in Stall Street outside.

Swimmers can also enjoy the waters, for they are piped to the city's public swimming pools.

During the Music Festival, in June, and the Folk Week and the Floral Week, both in July, it is possible to swim in the Roman Baths themselves.

The Pump Room and Roman Baths are both open daily 9.00am to 6.00pm.

*Health Treatment* Although National Health Service treatment is no longer available, the Bath Spa Trust has been formed to restore the 18th-century treatment centre at Old Royal Bath. Advanced physio and hydrotherapy techniques will be used.

*Assembly Rooms* A magnificent suite of rooms, completely restored after war damage and housing the Museum of Costume, with exhibits of fashion going back to the 17th century.

Open summer weekdays 9.30am to 6.00pm, Sunday 10.00am to 6.00pm, winter weekends 10.00am to 5.00pm, Sunday 2.00pm to 5.00pm.

*Banqueting Room* On the first floor of the Guildhall. This is one of the finest rooms in the entire West Country. Decorated in Adam style, with three magnificent chandeliers.

Open Monday to Friday 9.00am to 4.00pm, Sunday 2.30pm to 4.00pm.

*Royal Crescent* and *Lansdowne Crescent* Perfect examples of Georgian town planning. 1 Royal Crescent is open to visitors from March to October Tuesday to Saturday 11.00am to 5.00pm, Sunday 2.00pm to 5.00pm.

*Pulteney Bridge* Designed by Robert Adam in 1771, it is a charming carriageway over the Avon with shops on either side. Excellent views from Parade Gardens which are open from Easter to September.

*Bath Abbey* The present abbey was begun in the 15th century, standing on the site of a vast Norman cathedral which in turn replaced a Saxon abbey. Only the Norman arch and south aisle remains.

The moving spirit behind the present building was Oliver King, Bishop of Bath and Wells, and former chief secretary to Henry VII, who dreamt that he should rebuild the church.

It went into ruin again with the Dissolution, but in 1574 Elizabeth ordered the instigation of a restoration fund.

The Victorians added pinnacles and flying buttresses. Sir Gilbert Scott urged that the nave be given the stone fanvaulting which was intended for the original cathedral.

It is the last church of the Perpendicular English Gothic style. In the Second World War, German bombs nearly destroyed it, but the abbey has survived.

*Carriage Museum* A collection of 30 carriages, some of which occasionally clatter through the streets of Bath.

The museum was once the stables and coach house for the residents of the Circle in the 18th century.

Open Monday to Saturday 9.30am to 6.00pm, Sunday 10.00am to 6.00pm.

*Burrows Toy Museum* A social history in miniature, with dolls, dolls' houses, accessories and carriages, toys, books and games, all set in the 18th-century Octagon.

Open daily 10.00am to 5.30pm.

*Holburne of Menstrie Museum* Built in the Palladian style in 1796–7, as part of Sydney Gardens, this building was adapted into a museum in 1913–15, and now houses a unique collection of paintings by such English Masters as Gainsborough, Reynolds and Stubbs, furniture, silver, porcelain, miniatures, glass and silhouettes.

Open daily 9.30am to 5.00pm, closed Wednesday and Sunday in winter.

*Museum of Bookbinding* An extension of the firm of George Bayntum, the city booksellers

Bath . . . some of its Georgian riches

and binders. It shows the history and art of bookbinding, with a reconstruction of 19th-century craft. Open summer Monday to Saturday 9.00am to 5.30pm. By appointment in winter.

*The Kennet and Avon Canal Trust* A registered charity set up to preserve the canal and make it navigable.

Canal trips run every weekend to Bathampton and back and there are river trips to both Bathampton and Weston Lock.

The Dundas Aqueduct runs over the river Avon, and at Limpley Stoke it crosses the river, road and railway.

## Claverton

Ralph Clayton, one of the philanthropists whose money helped to pay for Bath's Georgian heritage, is buried here.

The 1820 manor house at Claverton Down is the setting for a unique museum of American life. Furniture and exhibits have all been brought from the US.

The *American Museum* is open March to September daily except Monday 2.00pm to 5.00pm.

In 1897, Claverton Manor was the scene of the young Winston Churchill's first political speech.

## Monkton Combe

This delightful hamlet of stone cottages is worth a visit to see *Midford Castle*. It is built in a clover-leaf shape to mark a gambling success of its owner Henry Roebuck, who liked to bank on the ace of clubs. It is not open to the public.

## Hinton Charterhouse

The 13th-century Carthusian priory, after which the village is named, is the second oldest in England.

*Hinton House* is an 18th-century mansion which incorporates part of the priory.

## Norton St Philip

The 15th-century George Inn is believed to be the country's oldest surviving pub.

An attempt was made to shoot the Duke of Monmouth at this village during the ill-fated rebellion of 1685.

## Frome

A charming market town which becomes very congested with traffic in the summer.

However, it is a good centre for touring the surrounding areas.

There are many fine buildings, the best of which are the 1726 almshouses and the Bluecoat School, now both converted into flats.

The gardens of Orchardleigh Park are open daily.

## Nunney

A pretty village on the eastern fringe of the Mendips. The 1373 castle is the finest in the county. It was damaged during the Civil War, but is still an impressive sight. Open weekdays 9.30am to 5.30pm, Sunday 2.00pm to 5.30pm.

## Witham Friary

The village reading room is the only surviving part of a monastery founded by Henry II as part of his atonement for the murder of Becket at Canterbury.

There are also traces of the Roman road to the Mendips.

## Mells

This beautiful village has thatched cottages and fine stone houses.

## Midsomer Norton

Although the river Somer flows through the town, this attractive name is taken from Midsummer Day, the festival day of the church's patron St John the Baptist.

## Wansdyke

These are the most extensive earthworks in Britain consisting of a single bank with a ditch, stretching from Hampshire across Wiltshire and into Somerset.

The name comes from the Saxon-Woden's Ditch. The sections can be seen near Corston village, west of Bath.

An impressive sight . . . Nunney Castle

192

# Bristol

Some ancient cities are now asleep amid their history; others lost much dignity in the scramble for the 20th century. By some sleight of hand, Bristol has chosen neither course.

It remains a city of maritime adventure, and Georgian and Victorian style, with its Clifton Suspension Bridge and its SS 'Great Britain', but it is also, in its 20th-century incarnation, the birthplace of Concorde, and a substantial regional capital for the West Country (the latter role to some extent shared with Plymouth, 100 miles to the south-west).

Apart from being a lively and fascinating city, Bristol is splendidly positioned between the Cotswolds, the Mendips and the coastal resorts of the Severn estuary, with the ancient city of Bath, and the Wiltshire countryside, close at hand.

**Tourist Information Centre**
Colston House, Colston Street,
Bristol, Avon. (0272) 293891

## Bristol

The earliest evidence of Bristol being a commercial centre is two silver coins minted in the city during the reign of Ethelred II in the 10th century.

Trade and exploration have been at the centre of Bristol life ever since.

In 1497 John Cabot and his son Sebastian set off from Bristol docks on their epic voyage of discovery to North America.

Bristol was also the place where the Society of Merchant Venturers was incorporated in 1552. The Society did much to build the prosperity of the British Empire.

William Penn of Bristol set off in 1681 to establish a Quaker colony in Pennsylvania, North America.

Many of the landmarks familiar to these early voyagers are still here today to excite the imagination of the 20th-century visitors.

For example, alongside the cobbled streets of the old city docks is the ancient Llandoger Trow Tavern. This was once a drinking den of pirates and it is said that Robert Louis Stevenson used it as the model for Spy Glass Inn which Long John Silver frequented in *Treasure Island*.

Less than a mile away is the church of St Mary Redcliffe esteemed by Good Queen Bess herself as 'the fairest, goodliest and most famous parish church in England'.

Across the floating harbour from St Mary Redcliffe is the Corn Exchange. Outside are the low, flat-topped pillars, called nails. It was on these pillars that the corn dealers would place their pieces of silver, hence the saying 'cash on the nail'.

'I never knew a city so mercantile that was so literary', said Robert Southey, who was born in Bristol in 1774, and became Poet Laureate in 1831.

The city has maintained its lively artistic tradition. The theatre was the first of the performing arts to find a home and an audience in Bristol. Edward Alleyn and Richard Burbage laid the foundations of an enduring theatrical tradition when they played in the city in 1593.

The foundation stone of the Theatre Royal was laid in 1764, and the first performance was on 30 May 1766. The star attraction on that night was none other than David Garrick, who pronounced the theatre, 'the most complete of its dimensions in Europe'.

The Theatre Royal is now the home of the Bristol Old Vic company. The Old Vic Centre was completed in May 1972 by the addition of the New Vic and The Little Theatre.

A Bristol bookseller, Joseph Cottle, was the first man to publish *The Lyrical Ballads* by William Wordsworth and Samuel Taylor Coleridge. He paid 30 guineas for them in 1798. The City Library contains a rare copy of Coleridge's *Poems on Various Subjects*.

The Arnolfini Arts Centre, a modern addition to Bristol's arts scene, makes it possible for the public to see some of the things that are happening now in the visual arts, music, cinema, dance and jewellery.

The centre occupies what was once one of the finest commercial buildings in Bristol. The building has attractive waterways and quays on two sides.

The exterior has been renovated and the interior reconstructed to provide two large galleries; an auditorium which seats at least 200 people for films, music, dance and multi-media events; a bookshop; and bars and a restaurant.

Bristol is replete with ancient churches. St Nicholas' was gutted during WWII but has been restored and is now a museum of local history and church art.

St Mary's on the Quay was built by the architect R. S. Pope.

All Saints is a Norman and late Gothic building with some fine monuments, including that of Bristol's famous merchant and philanthropist Edward Colston (died 1721).

Away from the bustle of the vigorous city centre is the 18th-century residential suburb of *Clifton*. Windsor Terrace and Cornwall Crescent were started in 1780 and Royal York Crescent and The Paragon were added during the 19th century.

The beauties of Bristol are not entirely man made. Clifton and Durdham Downs cover 442 acres of rolling land. To the south-west of Bristol is the Ashton Court Estate, which was acquired by the Bristol Corporation in January 1960. There is a nature trail in the grounds.

*Cathedral* Founded in the 1140s as the Church of St Augustine's Augustinian Abbey, it became a cathedral in 1542. It stands on the traditional site of the 7th-century meeting of St Augustine of Canterbury and the Celtic Christian leaders.

Features of interest include the finest Norman chapter house in England, the 14th-century Hall Church Choir, tombs and monuments of various dates, and the candlesticks of 1712, a thanksgiving from the privateers who rescued Alexander Selkirk, on whom Robinson Crusoe was based.

*Clifton Cathedral* The headquarters of the Roman Catholic diocese of Clifton. The Cathedral of Saints Peter and Paul was completed in 1973 and is a most important example of contemporary church architecture.

It contains many important works of modern art and the building itself won an architectural award in 1973.

*St Mary Redcliffe* This is an outstanding example of perpendicular Gothic architecture. Most of it was built in the 14th and 15th centuries, although some parts are much earlier.

The soaring nave and choir, the roof bosses, the north porch and the monuments are the most notable features. The church also possesses one of the finest organs in England.

*John Wesley's New Room* This chapel is the cradle of Methodism. It dates from 1739, with alterations and additions in 1748.

It was here that Wesley commissioned his first preachers and where, in 1771, Francis Asbury offered to serve in America and later became elected Bishop of the American Methodist Church.

There are statues of both John Wesley and his brother Charles, the hymnwriter.

Open daily except Wednesday and Sunday, 10.00am to 4.00pm.

*St Nicholas Church Museum* Open Monday to Saturday, 10.00am to 5.00pm.

*SS Great Britain* Isambard Kingdom Brunel's 3,443-ton ship was launched in Bristol by the Prince Consort in 1843. She was the first ocean-going, propeller-driven ship in history, and the largest iron ship of her time.

In 1886 she was damaged at sea and was beached in the Falkland Islands. Now she is home again in Bristol after being salvaged and brought back in 1970.

Preservation and restoration work has been going on since the ship arrived and the aim is to restore the exterior to its original appearance.

Enough of the interior will be restored to show visitors what life aboard this Victorian liner was like, and to demonstrate the technical features, such as the very large engine.

The ship is moored at Great Western Dock and is open daily during the summer 10.00am to 6.00pm and during the winter, 10.00am to 5.00pm.

*Industrial Museum* In M Shed, a 1950's transit shed in Prince

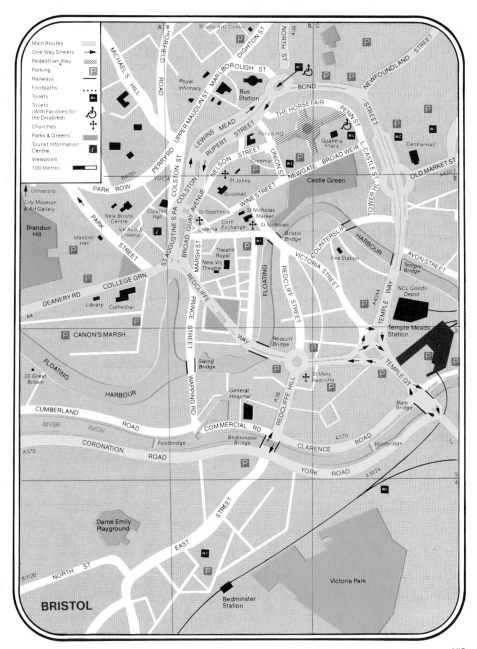

Street in the City Docks, are exhibits of Bristol's transport history, from horsedrawn carriages to Concorde. The Grenville Steam Carriage of 1897 is unique. The museum is linked by a railway line to *SS Great Britain*. Admission free.

Open Saturday to Wednesday 10.00am to 12.00pm, 1.00pm to 5.00pm.

*Clifton Suspension Bridge* 'The Ornament of Bristol and the Wonder of the Age' was how Sir Abraham Elton described Brunel's bridge at the foundation ceremony in 1831.

The bridge spans the Avon Gorge connecting Clifton with the south side of the river Avon. The gorge is a strikingly beautiful, steep-sided limestone valley, rich in rare trees and flowers. Rock climbing is popular but much of the rock is crumbly and inexperienced climbers should beware of taking unnecessary risks.

*Clifton Observatory* An observation point situated above the Avon Gorge.

It has a large camera obscura in the summit of the tower. A passage below the tower leads to Giants Cave.

*The Severn Bridge* The Severn Bridge spans the River Severn. It connects the M4 Motorway to South Wales. Another suspension bridge, its centre span is 3,240 ft long, and the two side spans are each 1,000 ft long.

There is a footpath and cycle track separated from the road by a fence which the public may use free of charge. There is a toll for motorists.

The bridge is sited between the Aust Cliff and the Beachley Peninsula where the river Severn is almost exactly one mile wide. There is an observation wall which overlooks the bridge and the river and a service area with restaurant facilities.

*The Avon Bridge* The motorways from Birmingham and the Midlands (M5), Newport and

South Wales (M4), London and the south-east of England (M4) converge on Bristol. There is a recently opened motorway (M5) to Exeter and the south-west and the Avon Bridge is the linchpin connecting the south-west to all of these areas. The bridge is 4,550 ft long, and spans the River Avon from Avonmouth to Easton in Gordano. There is a public footpath separated from the three-lane motorway traffic by a fence. There are no tolls or charges.

*The City Museum and Art Gallery* At one time the city's museum exhibits were housed in a Venetian Gothic building built in 1870 on the Queens Road. The building was gutted by fire in 1940 and all the remaining exhibits were moved to the art gallery next door. The shell of the old building was sold to the University.

Open daily except Sunday 10.00am to 5.00pm.

*The Georgian House*, with 18th-century decor, was where Coleridge met Wordsworth.

Open Monday to Saturday 10.00am to 5.00pm.

*Quakers Friars* was once the cloisters of the Dominican Friary. The building has a 14th-century roof. It was bought during the 17th century by the Society of Friends as a meeting house, and has been used for meetings of various societies ever since. It now houses the city's Permanent Planning Exhibition.

Open Monday to Friday 1.00pm to 4.30pm, Saturday 9.30am to 12.30pm.

*Colston Hall* is one of the finest concert halls in England. Visitors can listen to classical or pop music, watch wrestling or dance, as the front area of the auditorium can be converted into a dance floor.

*Bristol Arts Centre* was opened in 1964 as a meeting place for people interested in the arts. It has an auditorium seating 124 people, which can be used as a

theatre or cinema, and a studio theatre seating 50 people which is used for experimental drama, recitals and lectures. Open daily except Bank Holidays 10.00am to 11.00pm, Sundays 6.00pm to 11.00pm.

*New Bristol Centre*, between Park Street and Park Row, is one of the newest and largest entertainment centres in Europe, offering an ice-skating rink, a ballroom, discotheque, bingo hall and cinema.

*The Zoo* has many attractions. There is an extensive collection of birds and reptiles and a fine aquarium, which are set amongst lakes, lawns, flowers and trees. Open weekdays 9.30am to dusk and Sundays 10.00am to dusk.

*Blaise Castle Estate* is about 4 miles north-west of Bristol. Humphrey Repton, the 18th-century landscape gardener, designed the grounds in 1796.

The museum, a branch of the City Museum, houses an exhibition of West Country history since the 17th century.

The house itself was designed by the local architect William Paty for John S. Harford, a Bristol banker.

Blaise Castle is not a medieval castle, as it appears to be. It is a Gothic-style folly, built in 1766 by Thomas Farr, who in 1771 became Master of the Society of Merchant Venturers.

Blaise Castle House is open Monday to Saturday, 2.00pm to 5.00pm.

*Bristol Sherry* is a trade dating from the days when the Royal Navy was in the habit of sacking the Spanish ports. The firm of Harvey's has a wine museum at 12 Denmark Street, Bristol. Visits by appointment, telephone (0272) 298011.

*Shrub and Lovage* are two alcoholic cordials made by J. R. Phillips of Avonmouth. Lovage is made from the herb of the same name, and both of these drinks are said to have originated from the West Country.

# The Mendips

The West Country is notable for at least eight clusters of hill or moorland, varying from the gentle to the wild. The Mendips, with their well-known caves at Cheddar and Wookey, are among the most accessible of these hills, and the most gentle, offering excellent walking country.

The same is true of the Polden Hills, a few miles further south. Between the two ranges, cattle graze on the lowland levels known as the Plain of Sedgemoor, and Arthurian enthusiasts seek Avalon at the town of Glastonbury.

The whole of this peaceful stretch of countryside – the two ranges of hills, and the Plain – would probably defer to the tiny cathedral city of Wells as its main town, though its great dignity can be dented by traffic and tourism.

An alternative base for the visitor can be found at the foot of the hills, on the coast: the sizable seaside resort of Weston-super-Mare.

**Tourist Information Centres**
Berrow Road, Burham-on-Sea, Somerset. (0278) 782377 Ext 43/44
The Library, Union Street, Cheddar, Somerset. (0934) 742769
Town Hall, Market Place, Wells, Somerset. (0749) 72552
Beach Lawns, Weston-super-Mare, Avon. (0934) 26838

## Weston-super-Mare

Weston's resort days began in Victorian times and gradually the fishing village grew into a spacious seaside town boasting two *piers*, extensive amusements and the Italian-style Winter Gardens.

There are many features of the town's surrounding rural area which remain unchanged. The 363 acres of Weston Woods to the north of the town offer delightful walking. *Worlebury Hill* is the site of an ancient British camp.

There are miles of sandy beaches and to the south of the town, at Uphill and Brean Down, the loudest sounds to be heard are usually the cries of sea birds.

The safe, golden beaches of Weston are the focal point of the town. Children can build sandcastles or ride the donkeys which are bred locally and for which Weston is famous. There are car parks close to the beach.

The two piers are open to the public. Grand Pier is nearest to the centre of the town and to the Winter Gardens, which have romantic pools and pillars and thousands of rose bushes.

A short walk northwards from the gardens leads to the *Model Yacht Pond* and then to the enclosed *Marine Lake* which has its own beaches.

These are just a few of the attractions in Weston. There are Punch and Judy shows, a model village and railway, an aquarium and mini-zoo.

Weston is an excellent sporting centre, with cricket, golf, tennis, and a bowls tournament is held in August which attracts competitors from all over England.

*Aquarium and Mini-Zoo* Open one week before Easter and closes the first weekend in October. Opening hours are from 10.00am to 6.00pm or 10.00pm, depending on the weather.

*Little Britain Model Village* An interesting display set in half an acre of landscape gardens.

Open daily in summer, 9.00am to dusk, in winter 10.00am to dusk.

*Ashcombe Park* The parkland covers 34 acres and has splendid views.

## Burnham-on-Sea

This small seaside resort has marvellous views across Bridgwater Bay from its seven miles of sand. Visitors should not miss the 14th-century church of St Andrews with its 78-ft tower which leans three feet from the vertical.

The ornamental screen covering the wall at the back of the altar is quite outstanding. It was designed by Inigo Jones and made by Grinling Gibbons, originally for James II for the chapel at Whitehall Palace. In 1820 George IV gave it to the Vicar of Burnham.

## Glastonbury

The ruins of *Glastonbury Abbey* are an inspiring sight as well as being the source of many legends.

That there was a place of worship built here in the first place is due to the missionary zeal of Joseph of Arimathea. This saintly man leant on his staff on Wirrall Hill in prayer and the staff took root. Joseph took this as a sign that he should start a religious order here.

The thorn bush that grew from the staff was destroyed during the Civil War, but the thorn surviving in the grounds of the Abbey is said to be a cutting from it.

Arthurian scholars from all over the world visit the Abbey since it is here that King Arthur is said to be buried.

The Holy Grail, that Arthur's knights and many others have sought, is said to have been brought by Joseph to Glastonbury and to be beneath Chalice Spring on Glastonbury Tor.

There has probably been a

place of worship at Glastonbury since the 5th century. The present ruins are of a building begun early in the 13th century and finished shortly before Henry VIII dissolved the monasteries.

Hunting legends and climbing tors is thirsty work. It is here that the small town of Glastonbury itself can help for there are some fine pubs. None is more memorable than the George, which goes back to pre-Reformation times.

### Shepton Mallet
This pleasant country town, nestling in the foothills of the Mendips, belies the presence of a notorious military prison.

Once a medieval wool town of some importance, Shepton is now famous for the production of Cheddar cheese. One producer at nearby Ditcheat also makes Caerphilly, Wensleydale, Double Gloucester and Leicester cheeses.

### Wells
This busy city nestles at the foot of the Mendips and is a centre for tourism. There is an area of peace and quiet around the *cathedral* and its grounds, the Vicar's Close and the Bishop's Palace.

Wells may not have one of the largest of England's many cathedrals, but it is certainly one of the most beautiful. The west front is decorated with 400 statues. Unfortunately, many of these were damaged in the 17th century, but they are gradually being restored.

The cathedral building was begun in the 12th century and finished during the 14th. The latest addition, some impressive inverted arches supporting the main tower, dominate the interior at eye level.

Also inside the cathedral is a famous mechanical clock, constructed in 1380. It has figures which move when the hour is struck.

Vicar's Close is the oldest complete street in Europe. It is lined with 14th-century houses.

The Bishop's Palace is a haven of peace. Some majestic swans, which live on the moat, have learned to strike a bell to call for their supper.

### Wookey Hole
A famous group of caves and grottoes north of the village of Wookey. Three of the chambers are now floodlit and the river Axe flows through them to widen into an underground lake.

One of the features best known to visitors is the huge *stalagmite*, the Witch of Wookey.

Open April to September daily 10.00am to 6.00pm, October to March daily 10.00am to 4.30pm.

### Cheddar
Famous for at least two items of local interest, Cheddar attracts thousands of visitors annually.

The taste of *Cheddar cheese* is internationally known. Although imitations are produced in other countries, there is nothing to compare with the local product and the people of Cheddar are justly proud of it.

The breathtaking views of the *Cheddar Gorge* are the other major attraction of the area. The top of the Gorge is 450ft high and a road winds down through the towering rocks. There are caves in the rocks which are famous for beautifully shaped stalagmites and stalactites which glow in rich colours.

Open daily, 10.00am to dusk.

At the foot of the Gorge is the *Cheddar Motor Museum* which houses veteran cars and bicycles.

Open April to September daily, 10.00am to 6.00pm; October to March, Tuesday to Sunday, 10.00am to 4.00pm.

### Chewton Mendip
On the northern side of the Mendip Hills it is possible to see the traditional farmhouse Cheddar cheese being made at Priory Farm. Telephone to make an appointment, maximum size of party 20. Farm shop open 8.00am to 5.00pm.

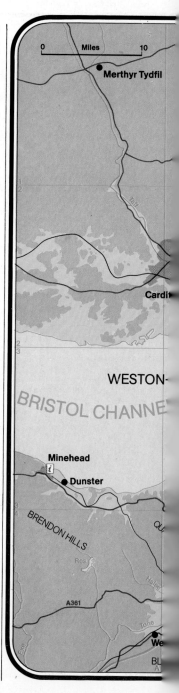

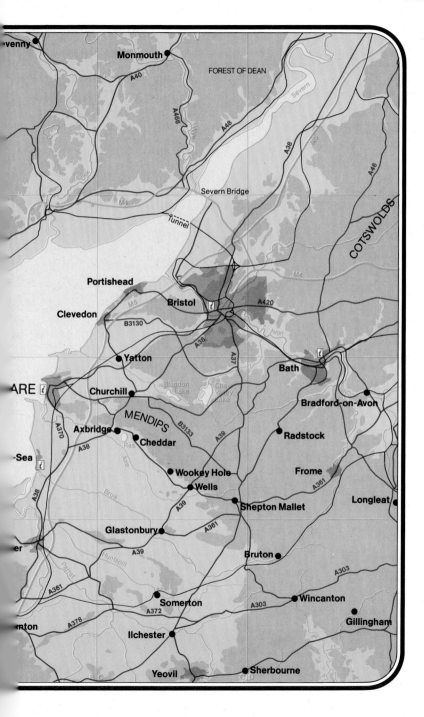

# Somerset

Away from the Avon and Severn area, Somerset becomes uncompromisingly West Country, with the county town of Taunton at its very heart.

Between Taunton and the coast are first the Quantock Hills, an area of rolling woodland regarded by many as the most beautiful part of Somerset, then the varied countryside of the Brendon Hills and the Exmoor Forest.

This stretch of countryside includes some pastoral moorland and some heathland – the country of 'Lorna Doone'. It is often rugged, but rarely bleak.

The hill country of Somerset has few towns and villages, and often just a smattering of hamlets and farms. The roads between Bridgwater, Taunton and Wellington become heavy with tourist traffic in the summer, but peace reigns a few miles to the south, in the Blackdown Hills.

South of the hills, Chard and Yeovil are close to the Dorset county boundary.

## Taunton

A rural county-town between the Quantocks and the Blackdown Hills, and a most agreeable centre from which to explore. Taunton grew around a Norman castle, the keep of which survives.

It was in the castle that Judge Jeffreys conducted his *Bloody Assize* in 1685. He sentenced more than 500 people to death and deported many more to the West Indies, following the defeat of the Duke of Monmouth's rebellion.

Taunton is known for two major activities – county cricket, for it is the home of the Somerset County Cricket Club, and cider.

Cider apples grow in abundance here and the end product is nationally acclaimed. The famous *Taunton Cider Company* operates from nearby Norton Fitzwarren, and some local farmhouses still produce their own.

There are several delightful villages nearby – Milverton has a fine Georgian main street; North Curry is gathered around its pretty church and stands on the edge of moorland; Athelney is where King Alfred burned the cakes.

*Castle* This building, founded in the 8th century, now houses the *Somerset County Museum and Military Museum*. There are interesting collections of archaeology and natural history. The Norman Keep and the Great Hall were the scene of the Bloody Assize in 1685.

Open Monday to Saturday 10.00am to 5.00pm.

*Post Office Telecommunications Museum* The only exhibition of its kind in the west. Open Saturday 1.30pm to 5.00pm.

*Municipal Buildings* Built about 1480, this fine building once housed the town's grammar school. It is open by arrangement.

*Tudor House* A wool merchant's

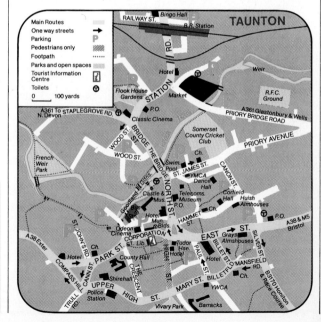

timber-framed house, built in 1578. Now a restaurant.

*Gray's Almshouses* Interesting example of a 1635 building.

*St Mary Magdalene Church* Early 16th-century, the tower is the finest example of Perpendicular architecture in the county. The church was designed by Bray, Henry VII's architect.

*Octagon Chapel* Opened by John Wesley in 1776, the building has an interesting and well-preserved interior.

*Vivary Park* Pleasant gardens with a stream, recreational facilities, model boating pond and golf course.

*Widcombe Bird Gardens*, Blagdon Hill. Many fine examples of tropical birds. Open daily 10.00am to 7.00pm.

*Markets* Cattle on Tuesday, general on Saturday.

*Cider-making* R. J. Sheppy and Sons at Bradford on Tone produce cider from their own orchards, which are open to the public. There is also a cider-making plant and a museum. Ring (082 346) 233 for details.

*Sports* Swimming; tennis; bowls; riding; fishing; golf; horse-racing; polo; cricket.

*Events* Taunton Flower Show, in July/August; Tone River Struggle, in September; Music and Drama Festival, in November.

## Wellington

The ancient wool industry is still going strong in this pleasant Georgian town. The cloth produced is on sale from the factory, Fox Brothers.

The town is overlooked by the monument to the Duke of Wellington, which stands on the highest point of the Blackdown Hills, south of Wellington. The Iron Duke took his title from the town.

There is an impressive parish church, an interesting high street, and a superbly-equipped sports centre, offering a wide range of activities for all ages and abilities.

## Combe Florey

This town's celebrated inhabitants have included novelist Evelyn Waugh and 'the wittiest man in England', Sydney Smith.

Two miles east is *Cothelstone Manor*. Judge Jeffreys hanged two of Monmouth's followers in the gateway after the duke's defeat at Sedgemoor in 1685. It is not open to the public.

## Crowcombe

A handsome village with a well-preserved 16th-century church house. The church has a Tudor carving symbolising fertility.

## Nether Stowey

*The Ancient Mariner* and the first part of *Christabel* were written by Samuel Taylor Coleridge in his cottage here. Owned by the National Trust, it is open March to September daily except Friday and Saturday 2.00pm to 5.00pm, winter visits by arrangement with the caretaker.

The prehistoric earthworks of *Danesborough Camp* are two miles south-west.

## Watchet

The tiny harbour is the point from which Coleridge's Ancient Mariner set forth on his fateful voyage.

At one time the port served Exmoor and the Quantocks, but it has now settled down to a peaceful 100 ships a year, mainly landing wood and wood pulp from the Baltic regions and wine from Portugal and Spain. The sandy beach makes it a quiet but popular seaside resort.

## Minehead

This coastal town on the edge of Exmoor has a sandy beach with safe bathing, children's pool on the sands, and a model village and miniature railway.

The oldest part of Minehead is Quay Town, where the harbour dates back to 1616. It is

now a regular port of call for the pleasure steamers.

## Culbone

Villages do not come much smaller than this. There is a small house, smaller cottage and the smallest church in England, only 12 ft wide.

Culbone cannot even be approached by car, and visitors must make their way along a two-mile footpath.

## Dunster

Said to be one of the finest villages in Exmoor, Dunster has a main street lined with old-world houses and the eight-sided Yarn Market.

The *castle* at the end of the street is still owned by the Luttrell family, who are the second of only two families to live there in a thousand years.

The village church, once a Benedictine priory, dates from the 15th century.

## Bridgwater

In 1685 the town was used by the *Duke of Monmouth* as his headquarters for the decisive and doomed Battle of Sedgmoor. The rebellious Duke was proclaimed king here as well as in Taunton.

## Yeovil

A very small industrial town which is a useful base from which to explore.

A stroll to the foot of *Hendford Hill* leads to the Nine Springs which flow into a delightful lake. On top of the hill there is a large Iron Age fort.

## Chard

The highest town in the county – there are memorable views from Snowdon Hill and the aptly-named Windwhistle Hill.

Nearby is the *Cricket St Thomas Wildlife Park*, in the grounds of Cricket House. Many wild animals and birds can be seen. Open daily 10.00am to 6.00pm.

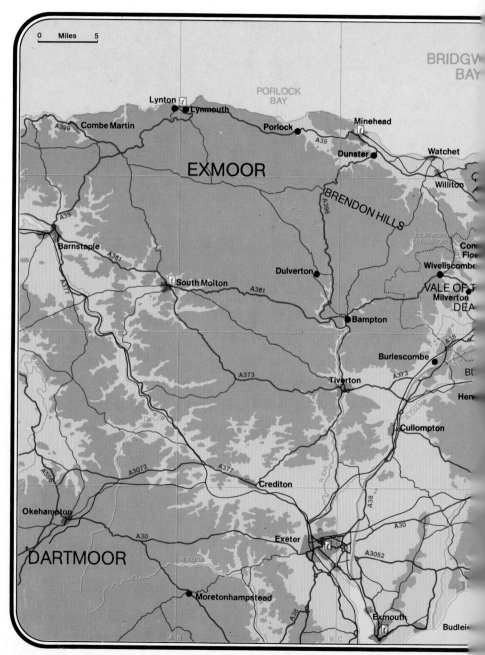

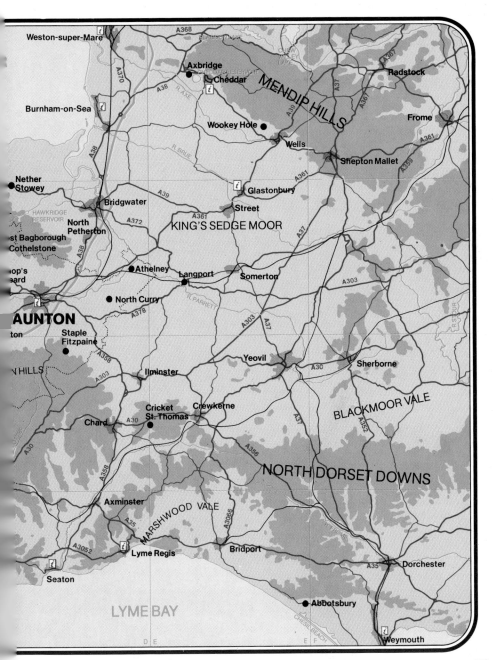

# North Devon

The widest part of the West Country peninsula is the county of Devon. One coast of the county, in the north, faces the Bristol Channel and the Atlantic; the other coast faces the English Channel and France. As if that were not difference enough between these two Devons, they are also forced apart by the great expanse of Dartmoor.

The coast of North Devon stretches from the edge of Exmoor, with the twin resorts of Lynton and Lynmouth, by way of Ilfracombe, to the large bay variously named after the towns of Barnstaple and Bideford, and then on to the rocky grandeur of Hartland Point.

**Tourist Information Centres**
The Quay, Bideford, Devon. (023 72) 77676
The Promenade, Ilfracombe, Devon. (0271) 63001
Lee Road, Lynton and Lynmouth, Devon. (059 85) 2225
Hall '70 Beach Road, Woolacombe and Morethoe, Devon. (027 187) 553

## Barnstaple
One of the oldest towns in Britain, Barnstaple became a borough in the 10th century, and even minted its own coins. It remains the administrative centre of North Devon, and is the logical base from which to explore.

The 16-arched bridge, dating from the 13th century, spans the river Tor, and some of the original stonework is still visible.

In the 18th-century Queen Anne's Walk is the Tome Stone, on which merchants used to place their money to bind a contract.

St Anne's chapel is partly 14th-century and once contained a grammar school, at which John Gay, who wrote *The Beggar's Opera* was educated.

The surfer's paradise . . . Woolacombe Bay

It now houses the local *museum* and is open Monday to Saturday 10.00am to 1.00pm, 2.00pm to 5.00pm.

A market is held every Tuesday and Friday at *Pannier Market*. The town was an important wool centre and was very prosperous in the 18th century. It has remained largely Georgian.

## Great Torrington
On top of a steep hill above the river Torridge, this town has one of the finest vantage points in Devon.

The town hall is Georgian, the market house is early Victorian and the Black Horse Inn dates from the 17th century.

## Holsworthy
Home of the *Devon Museum of Mechanical Music*. Among the exhibits are a fairground organ, player piano, phonograph, organette, barrel piano and calliope. Open daily 10.30am to 12.30pm, 2.30pm to 5.30pm.

## Welcombe
This attractive village is only a few steps from the Cornish border and is almost completely Cornish in character.

The local church is dedicated to St Nectan, the Celt, and there is a holy well close by.

This is excellent walking country and a five-mile coastal lane leads from Welcombe Mouth northwards through magnificent cliff scenery to Hartland Quay.

## Hartland
The parish church of St John in this village has one of the earliest pendulum clocks in Britain, made in the 17th century.

Rugged and spectacular coastal scenery can be found at *Hartland Point*, three miles from the village.

## Lundy
Twelve miles north-west of the Point is the island of Lundy, owned by the National Trust.

Its population is only around 20, but they issue their own postal stamps, although these are not valid when used on their own.

Lundy is an ancient Norse word for puffin, and these birds nest along the cliffs.

A steamer connects the island to the mainland at Ilfracombe.

## Clovelly

One of the best-known, and popular of Devon's coastal villages. The cobbled main street drops 400 ft in a series of steps, so cars cannot enter the village.

Colour washed cottages line the way to the small stone harbour where boats are moored.

Nearby is *Clovelly Dyke*, a prehistoric hill fort, believed to date from the Iron Age.

## Bideford

The town lies on the west bank of the river Torridge where it widens into an estuary. The famous bridge over the water is 677 ft long and has 24 arches. Part of the original stone bridge from the 15th century is still in use.

In the 16th century Bideford was North Devon's major port. Its importance as a shipping centre declined in the 18th century, leaving it a pleasant town and good centre for touring the region.

## Westward Ho!

Fairly unknown until in 1855 the town was named after Charles Kingsley's famous novel.

It has remained small, but has magnificent sandy beaches, a challenging golf course and the renowned *Pebble Ridge*, stretching for two miles.

## Appledore

The meeting place of the rivers Taw and Torridge as they flow to Bideford Bay two miles away.

A famous ship-building

centre, its importance has increased since the largest covered dock in Europe was opened here in 1970.

It is a very picturesque town, with narrow streets climbing steeply from the quay.

## Woolacombe and Mortehoe

The North Devon centre for surfing enthusiasts, with three miles of outstanding coastline between Morte Point and Baggy Point on the sweep of Morte Bay.

This is an area of outstanding natural beauty and much of it is safeguarded by the National Trust.

## Ilfracombe

Built around an old harbour, this is North Devon's largest seaside resort with a hilly landscape.

On a peninsular hill beside the harbour is the 14th-century St Nicholas Chapel, named after the patron saint of sailors. Since the Middle Ages a light has shone from the chapel to guide the boats into the safety of the harbour.

The local beaches are good, mainly of shingle, and some are reached through tunnels in the rocks.

Ilfracombe's town *museum* contains many interesting items of natural history, local folklore and Victoriana. Open daily 10.00am to 5.00pm.

Those fond of walking will find many bracing excursions to such noted viewpoints as Beacon Point.

*Chambercombe Manor* is about 1½ miles south-west of the harbour and is a small, mainly 16th- and 17th-century house, built around courtyards decked with flowers. Open Easter to September Monday to Friday 10.30am to 5.30pm, Sunday 2.00pm to 5.30pm.

## Arlington

This remote hamlet is best-known for *Arlington Court*, built

from 1820 to 1823 and now owned by the National Trust.

It was for many years the home of the Chichester family, whose most famous modern son was yachtsman Sir Francis Chichester. The Court stands in a richly-wooded estate.

There are collections of model ships, pewter, seashells and a water colour by William Blake. There are horse-drawn vehicles in the stable. Open April to October daily 11.00am to 6.00pm.

## Lynton

A Victorian town perched on a cliff above the Bristol Channel. Its small *museum* houses many Exmoor curiosities. Open Easter to September Monday to Friday 10.00am to 12.30pm, 2.00pm to 5.00pm, Sunday 2.00pm to 5.00pm.

The *cliff railway*, first operated in 1890, runs down to Lynmouth.

## Lynmouth

This picturesque town was struck by a torrential flood in 1952, caused by a freak storm over Exmoor. The town was devastated and 31 people were killed.

## North Molton

The novelist R. D. Blackmore set part of his famous book *Lorna Doone* here.

The parish church boasts a magnificent medieval pulpit, and Court Hall, built in 1533, was the home of the Earls of Morley.

## South Molton

There is hardly a street in town which does not offer the passer-by a wonderful view over the rolling hills of Exmoor.

The streets themselves are also well worth more than a casual glance for there are many fine Georgian buildings and the 15th-century church stands in an avenue of lime trees.

# Cornwall

Like a leg kicking into the Atlantic, the long, slender county of Cornwall stretches itself away from the rest of England. It is almost a severed limb, for the broad river Tamar cuts off much of Cornwall from Devon.

The single-track railway bridge built over the river by Brunel in 1859 could have signalled the end for what remained of Cornwall's Celtic identity but the social attitudes of the 1970s helped a revival of the Cornish language and traditions.

The tip of Cornwall is Land's End, the most westerly point of the English mainland, beyond which lie only the Isles of Scilly, 26 miles into the Atlantic.

So narrow is the county that it is possible to cross from Newquay, in the north-west, to Fowey, in the south-east, in little more than half an hour.

A wander into the wide-open spaces of Bodmin Moor takes a little longer. The only road across the moor runs from Bodmin to Launceston, and exploration on foot can be made from Bolventor and Altarnum.

## Tourist Information Centres
Old Railway Station, Bude, Cornwall.
Town Hall, The Moor, Falmouth, Cornwall. (0326) 312300
The Guildhall, Fore Street, East Looe, Looe, Cornwall. (Summer only) (050 36) 2072
Cliff Road, Newquay, Cornwall. (063 73) 4558/2119/2716/2822
Alverton Street, Penzance, Cornwall. (0736) 2341
The Guildhall, Street an Pol, St Ives, Cornwall. (073 670) 6297
Town Hall, St Mary's, Scilly Isles. (072 04) 536
Municipal Buildings, Boscawen Street, Truro, Cornwall. (0872) 4555

## Bude
This town was once infamous among seafarers, for from 1824 to 1874 no fewer than 80 ships were wrecked off its coast.

Today it is a favourite spot for surfing and its beaches have led to growing popularity for family holidays.

*Ebbingford Manor*, Bude's oldest house, is open Wednesday and Thursday 2.00pm to 5.30pm, Sunday July to September 2.00pm to 5.30pm.

A three-mile walk to Widemouth offers some of the most spectacular views to be found in Britain.

## Tintagel
Legend says that this is where King Arthur had his castle.

Certainly there is a romantic ruined castle, but it has nothing whatever to do with Camelot, for it was built in 1145 for the Earl of Cornwall.

Those absolutely determined to stick to the Arthurian legend will make the pilgrimage down the paths from the village to the shingle beach and Merlin's Cave.

Also helping to perpetuate a myth is King Arthur's Hall, which dates all the way back to 1933. It has 73 stained glass windows depicting Arthur's gallant knights. Open Easter to October daily 9.00am to 5.00pm.

## St Juliot
Thomas Hardy, the novelist, started his working life as an apprentice architect, and he restored the parish church here.

He even married the rector's sister, and St Juliot became the Endelstow of his book *A Pair of Blue Eyes*.

## Launceston
Parts of this market town go back to medieval days – South Gate with its pointed arches, the 13th-century castle's ramparts and what remains of an Augustinian priory.

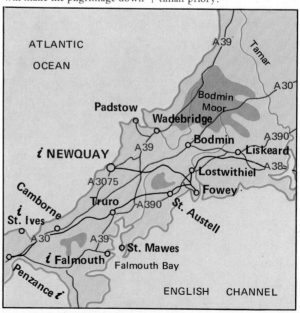

The largest font in the county sits in the Norman church of St Thomas, and there are many noted carvings in the Church of St Mary Magdalene.

## Altarnun
This village set on the edge of bleak Bodmin Moor boasts the magnificent 15th-century Church of St Nonna, the 'cathedral of the moor', as it is known to the locals.

## Bodmin
A traffic bottleneck which is worth exploring on foot.

Among the sites of Bodmin are St Petroc's, a church rebuilt in 1469, the 19th-century cattle market, the Assize Court, and the ruins of St Thomas à Becket's Chapel, dating from the 14th century.

Bodmin was once an attraction for its holy wells and the one near St Petroc's claims to have the answer to eye troubles.

Nearby is the 17th-century mansion of *Lanhydrock Park* in a wooded setting. Open March to October daily 11.00am to 6.00pm, November to March garden only 11.00am to dusk.

## Padstow
A ferry has operated from the harbour since the 15th century, crossing the estuary of the river Camel.

When he was Warden of Cornwall, *Sir Walter Raleigh* used to stay at Raleigh Court, on South Quay.

The part-Tudor and part-medieval Prideaux Place has been the home of the Prideaux family for more than 400 years.

*Padstow Bird Garden* is open daily 10.30am to 5.00pm.

South-east at Wadebridge is the *Cornish Motor Museum*. Open daily.

## St Mawgan
This delightful quiet village is set in a wooded river valley.

A fine early Christian cross stands outside the 13th-century

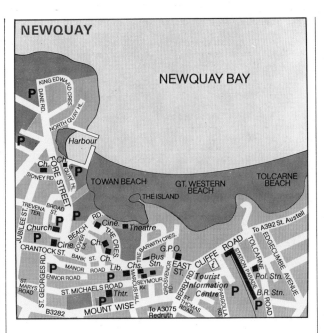

church of St Mawgan, which is rich in carvings.

## St Columb Major
The quadruple tower of the church here is 600 years old and is the finest in the county.

Every Shrove Tuesday the town becomes the setting for a hurling game with a silver-covered applewood ball.

Less than three miles south-east of town is Castle an Dinas, an Iron Age fort with three ramparts.

## St Austell
The centre of the county's important china clay industry. North of the town are large man-made mountains of sand and quartz, the effluvia of the china-clay mines.

## Newquay
A town offering not only a wealth of historical background, but also everything

that could be required of a holiday in the sun, including nine of the finest beaches in Europe.

More than a million visitors arrive each year, making it one of the top five resorts in Britain. A high sunshine record permits a long, 26-week season.

*Malibu surfboards* are available at Fistral and some other beaches, but these are not recommended for beginners.

*Trenance Gardens* is the home of the eight-acre Newquay Zoo, children's mini-railway, trampolines, tennis and bowls. There are also sub-tropical gardens and a bird sanctuary.

The town's early prosperity was boosted by pilchard fishing and there are many echoes of this trade. On Towan Headland is the *Huer's House*, where the Huer, or watchman, called out to townspeople when a pilchard shoal was sighted.

The fly promenades near the harbour are built on the sites of

ancient pilchard-curing cellars.
Porth Island has a prehistoric camp and village settlement, in addition to ancient burial mounds. There are also the cathedral caverns and banqueting hall, which can only be visited at the low spring tides.

Picturesque Elizabethan house Trerice Manor is open March to October daily 11.00am to 6.00pm.

## Perranporth
The three miles of glorious beach have made this village famous among surfers.

Students of church architecture will be fascinated by the curiosity of no less than three churches dedicated to St Piran.

The first two, built in the 6th and 12th centuries, were once buried by shifting sand. The older of the two was rediscovered in 1835.

The third St Piran's was built at nearby Perranzabuloe in 1804. The name of this town means St Piran in the Sand.

Cornish mystery plays, first performed more than 300 years ago, are still presented each year in the ancient amphitheatre of St Piran's Round.

## St Ives
This former fishing village – a brightly-coloured cluster of attractive little cottages – is now a justly famous and popular holiday resort.

The cobbled streets reach right down to the water's edge.

St Ives has been a noted artistic centre since Whistler and Sickert first came here in the 19th century. Painter Ben Nicholson, potter Bernard Leach, and sculptress Dame Barbara Hepworth have lived in the village.

The late Dame Barbara's home is now open as an *art gallery and museum*. Open Monday to Friday 10.00am to 5.00pm. There is also the *Barnes Museum of Cinematography*. Open daily 10.00am to 5.00pm.

## St Just
This pretty town is less than two miles east of the impressive rocky headland of Cape Cornwall.

## Sennen
Standing as it does a little to the west of St Just, this is England's most westerly village.

Legend has it that King Arthur defeated the Danes here and then held a banquet on the rock that later became known as Table Men.

The rock can be reached at the end of a footpath leading from the 13th-century church.

## Land's End
The most westerly point of the English mainland.

Dawn and dusk are the best times to appreciate this mass of dramatic cliffs which plummet into the Atlantic.

## Scilly Isles
These four islands are 26 miles out to sea and are reached by helicopter or ferry boat from Penzance.

The climate is delightful, making the islands an ideal place for flower-growing and the first spring flowers can be picked in November.

## Porthcurno
A good place for lovers of off-beat theatre. The open-air *Minack Theatre* is on a cliff west of the beach and is built in classical Greek style.

During the summer there are productions of Greek, Shakespearian and modern plays.

## Penzance
Palm trees and many other sub-tropical plants give this popular resort a truly exotic air.

Sir Humphrey Davy, who gave his name to his invention of the miner's safety helmet, was born here in 1778 and there is a statue of him in Market Jew Street.

The *Penlee House Museum* is open Monday to Saturday 12.30pm to 4.30pm.

## The Lizard
England's southernmost point.

The cliffs, rocks and reefs make this a far less welcoming place than Land's End.

## Falmouth
This resort has won a popularity with visitors that extends throughout the year.

*Falmouth Bay* is a noted yachting area and the beaches are excellent for bathing.

The town has a profusion of sub-tropical plants, and bananas grow in St Mary's Garden.

*Pendennis Castle* was one of Henry VIII's forts. Open April to September daily 9.00am to 5.00pm.

## Truro
The administrative heart of Cornwall, and its only cathedral city.

Truro's triple-spired *cathedral* was completed in 1910, but it occupies the site of the 16th-century parish church. The church's south aisle is, in fact, incorporated in the present building.

## Mevagissey
This tiny fishing village is a magnet for visitors, but the streets are too narrow for heavy vehicles.

In the height of the season no motor traffic is allowed and anyone wishing to enter the village must do so on foot.

Among the seagoing attractions are shark-fishing trips.

## Looe
The twin towns of East and West Looe are connected by a Victorian bridge which replaced a 13-arch structure built in the 15th century.

There is excellent bathing and the more adventurous can go on river and sea excursions, including shark-fishing.

# South Devon

On the Devon side of the river Tamar stands the large Naval city of Plymouth. The city, which incorporates Devonport, spreads itself between the Tamar and its own river, the Plym.

Extending southwards from Plymouth is a particularly mild stretch of coastal countryside known as the South Hams. On this coast is the Naval town of Dartmouth and, a few miles up the river Dart, the charming old town of Totnes.

To the east of the Dart, the famous resorts of Brixham, Paignton and Torquay line Tor Bay.

Inland, the woodlands and desolate beauty of Dartmoor sprawl between Plymouth, Tavistock, Okehampton and Widecombe.

**Tourist Information Centres**
Brixham Theatre, Market Street, Brixham, Devon. (080 45) 2861
The Quay, Dartmouth, Devon. (080 43) 2281
The Quay, Kingsbridge, Devon. (0548) 3195
Festival Hall, Esplanade Road, Paignton, Devon. (0803) 558383
Civic Centre, Plymouth, Devon. (0752) 68000
Salcombe Town Association, Shadycombe Road, Salcombe, Devon. (054 884) 2736
Vaughan Parade, Torquay, Devon. (0803) 27428
Totnes Publicity Association, The Plains, Totnes, Devon. (0803) 863168

## Plymouth

Plymouth's history dates back 900 years to William the Conqueror, and since the time of Elizabeth I. Plymouth has been one of the foremost maritime cities of the world.

Today Plymouth is a city of two distinct personalities. There is the Barbican, the original Elizabethan heart, and the striking modern city centre.

Plymouth became a naval centre during the 16th century when Sir Francis Drake and Sir Walter Raleigh made it their base for the wars with Spain. The Hoe, one of Europe's most outstanding natural promenades, is the spot from which, in 1588, Drake set out to defeat the Spanish Armada after finishing his game of bowls.

A century later, William of Orange ordered the building of the Royal Dockyard at what was later to become Devonport, a mile from Plymouth itself.

The Royal Navy has been at Devonport ever since, and the dockyard can be visited during the summer. In addition to naval vessels there are pleasure boats which take visitors around the dock to view the ships.

The ancient port of Plymouth can still be seen at the Barbican. The streets are narrow and cobbled and merchants' houses, some with three overhanging storeys, still line them.

The beautiful three-masted trading schooner *Kathleen and May* is moored at Guy's Quay. It was from this spot that the Pilgrim Fathers set sail aboard Mayflower for the New World. The voyage is commemorated by the Mayflower Stone.

In 1772 James Cook made Plymouth the starting point for his epic three-year circumnavigation of the globe.

The Hoe commands superb views over Plymouth Sound and the harbour. In the centre of a wide green on top of the Hoe is Smeaton's Tower. This

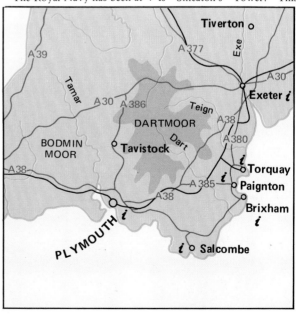

lighthouse was removed from the treacherous Eddystone Rock and erected here in 1882. The tower can be climbed during summer months.

With its long naval history it is no surprise that Plymouth continues to attract many boating enthusiasts. In addition to the sea, there are more than 15 miles of river and estuary suitable for cruising.

There is a regular car ferry service between Plymouth and Roscoff in Brittany, Northern France.

*Drake's Island* A seven-acre island in the Sound which has been fortified for 500 years. The defences were strengthened by Drake and it was garrisoned until the end of WWII. It is now an adventure training centre. Boats take visitors to the island during cruises around the harbour.

*Royal Albert Bridge* Isambard Kingdom Brunel built this famous bridge across the river Tamar to take trains across the border of Devon and Cornwall.

*Saltram House* This 18th-century mansion in Plympton has some fine rooms decorated by Robert Nash, the famous English architect. It contains many fine paintings, some by Sir Joshua Reynolds who lived nearby and was a close friend of the family. A visit to the house should include a look around the kitchen. It has a *batterie de cuisine* of 600 copper containers of all sizes on display as well as the many other implements necessary to feed the members of a grand country household. Open 24 March to end October, every day, 11.00am to 6.00pm or sunset if earlier. Last admission half an hour before closing. November to end March garden only open during daylight hours.

*Mount Edgcumbe House* A restored Tudor mansion set in a deer park overlooking Plymouth Sound. Open May to September, 2.00pm to 6.00pm,

Monday and Tuesday. Park open daily throughout the year.

*Royal Citadel* The British Army still uses the citadel but it is possible to take a tour round this 17th-century fort, which has superb views, at certain times during the day.

### Buckland
The hinterland of Plymouth is the southern edge of Dartmoor. This village is where Drake liked to spend some of his time off duty. In 1581 he bought the abbey, which was founded in 1278 and converted into a mansion in 1541. The building is now a *maritime museum*.

### Tavistock
An important market town with easy access to Plymouth. Drake was born at Crowndale Farm, a mile to the south.

### Princeton
Dartmoor's largest town, 1,400 feet above sea level was named after the Prince of Wales (who later became George IV). He gave the land for a prison to be built to hold the prisoners of the Napoleonic Wars.

The foundations of the prison were laid in 1806 and it has been here ever since.

### Widecombe in the Moor
This beautiful moorland village is known for its fair which is held on the second Tuesday in September.

The village's 14th-century church with a granite tower is known to the locals as 'the cathedral of the moors'.

### Buckfastleigh
The northern terminus of the Dart Valley Railway, run by steam enthusiasts. Every year from Easter to September they run services through a magnificent seven-mile stretch of countryside to Totnes. Ring (036 44) 2338 for times.

Nearby Buckfast Abbey was completed in 1938 and has

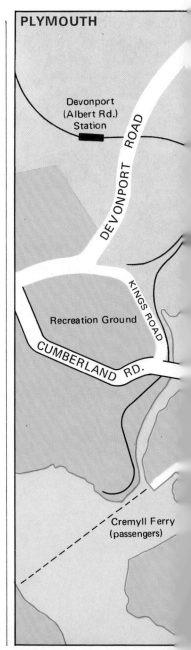

**PLYMOUTH**

Devonport (Albert Rd.) Station

DEVONPORT ROAD

KINGS ROAD

Recreation Ground

CUMBERLAND RD.

Cremyll Ferry (passengers)

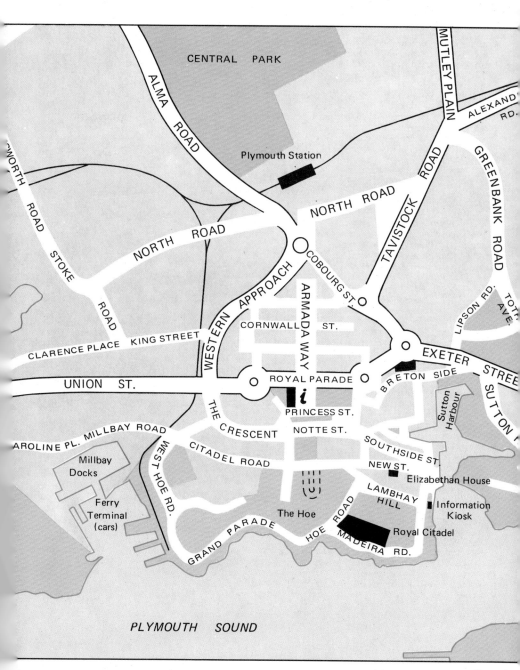

impressive modern stained glass windows. It is open when services are not being held.

## Totnes

This magnificent old town has been a borough since the 10th century.

The castle at the north end of the town dates from the 11th century, although only parts of the 13th-century keep and some walls now remain. Open March, April, October, weekdays, 9.30am to 5.30pm, Sundays 2.00pm to 5.30pm. May to September, every day, 9.30am to 7.00pm. November to February, weekdays, 9.30am to 4.00pm, Sundays 2.00pm to 4.00pm. Closed Christmas Eve, Christmas Day, Boxing Day and New Year's Eve.

The Elizabethan House in the High Street is open on weekdays in summer. Furniture and domestic articles are on show. Open May to September 10.30am to 5.30pm.

## Torquay

Devon's biggest and best-known resort. Set in high wooded hills it commands panoramic views of Torbay.

Sub-tropical trees and flowers and stuccoed villas add a Mediterranean flavour. The balmy climate makes Torquay one of the few resorts in Britain to operate all the year round.

The Victorians created Torquay and their influence is everywhere in the character of the buildings.

Kent's Cavern, a mile from the harbour, is one of the country's oldest known dwelling places. It was lived in during the last Ice Age and among the exhibits is the skull of a sabre-toothed tiger. *Torquay Museum* contains other finds from the site. Open weekdays, 10.00am to 5.00pm.

## Paignton

In Saxon times this was a tiny village half a mile from the sea.

Today it is a pretty town on this beautiful stretch of coast.

The town overlooks Torbay and offers holidays for all tastes. It has many caravan sites, holiday villages, hotels and guest houses.

The *Torbay Steam Railway* runs regular summer services from Paignton to Kingswear. *Babbacombe Model Village* occupies 14 acres of beautiful landscaped grounds. It is open daily from Easter to October.

Just outside the town is *Torbay Aircraft Museum* which has many aircraft built during the years 1924 to 1954. Open daily 10.00am to 6.00pm May to September, 10.00am to 4.00pm, October to April.

## Brixham

William of Orange landed here on 5 November, 1688, to depose James II. Since then the town has attracted visitors for more peaceful pursuits, such as fishing and simply strolling in the balmy seaside atmosphere.

Local caves date back to the Stone Age, and Roman times. Windmill Cave, discovered in 1858, is the most notable of these and is open to visitors.

Henry Francis Lyte, the poet who wrote the famous hymn *Abide With Me*, was Brixham's first vicar.

## Dartmouth

This historic town has a powerful maritime history. It is at the mouth of the River Dart, which gave its name to Dartmoor. It has been an important harbour since the Romans came to England. Since 1905 it has been the home of the Royal Naval College, an impressive building set on a hill on the south side of the river. Naval officers of the future are trained here.

The castle guarding the mouth of the river dates back to the 15th century. Open March, April, weekdays, 9.30am to 5.30pm, Sundays 2.00pm to 5.30pm. May to September,

every day 9.30am to 7.00pm. October, weekdays, 9.30am to 5.30pm, Sundays 2.00pm to 5.30pm. November to February weekdays 9.30am to 4.00pm, Sundays 2.00pm to 4.00pm.

## Kingsbridge

This busy market town is sometimes called the capital of the South Hams. It is inland at the head of the Kingsbridge estuary.

The town has some interesting historical buildings. St. Edmund's Church has a 13th-century tower. There is a 16th-century market arcade called the Shambles, which was rebuilt during the late 18th century. The 17th-century grammar school houses the William Cockworthy museum of china clay. Open weekdays in summer 10.00am to 5.00pm.

Gone fishing . . . Brixham

## Salcombe

This popular holiday resort is the most southerly town in the South Hams. It stands at the mouth of the Kingsbridge estuary. Its warm climate encourages the growth of exotic trees and plants.

Boating is popular in all the seaside and riverside towns along the coast. Salcombe is especially well favoured for this pastime.

# East Devon

Though their styles are quite different, Devon has two important cities. Vying with Plymouth in status, though far less of a big city in atmosphere, is Exeter.

This pleasant country city is an ancient port, with a lovely cathedral and a modern university. It is also an excellent centre from which to explore, with Dartmoor to the west, and some of the most typically Devonian agricultural countryside to the north and east.

The rich, red earth of this area grows the grass that feeds the cows that give the milk that make the cream that goes on the scones that accompany tea on a Devon summer's afternoon.

Though the county has little industry, Honiton is known for its lace, and Axminster for its carpets.

The river Exe, which flows through the city to which it gives its name, reaches the coast a few miles away garlanded by pretty little resorts.

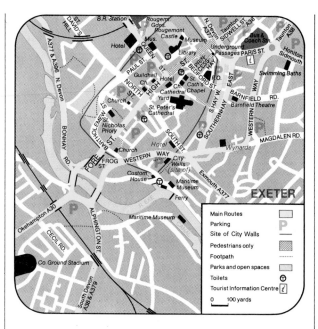

Main Routes ·
Parking — P
Site of City Walls
Pedestrians only
Footpath
Parks and open spaces
Toilets
Tourist Information Centre

0   100 yards

## Exeter

Celtic people in the second and third centuries BC settled on a plateau above the River Exe where they had good grazing for their sheep and the river for water.

The Romans came in AD 50 and built a wall around their city on the same plateau, on which now rests Exeter High Street. The remains of the Roman walls, which were built from local red sandstone, and were 10 feet wide, can still be seen at Southernhay, Northernhay and Rougemont.

The city walls were strengthened during Norman times by Athelston, the first King of England, and it was during Norman times that the two towers were added to the building of Exeter cathedral.

The cathedral is at the centre of life in the town. Physically, it forms the focal point of the beautiful Close, a green square with the Archdeacon's residence and Mol's Coffee House (now a shop) on the north-east side.

The Ship Inn, which Drake used to frequent, is in a passageway off the north-east corner of the Close. There are some fine Victorian buildings on the north side and the Chapter House is to the south.

The cathedral itself is very fine. Like Wells, the west front is decorated with many figures. Inside there is some exquisite stone carving, a fan-vaulted ceiling, a 59-ft high Bishop's throne, a minstrel's gallery and an astronomical clock.

Exeter was once a busy port. The Countess of Devon built a weir across the river in 1282, and the now-sleepy village of Topsham, four miles downstream, served as the city's main port.

The channel was cleared in 1567 and again during the 17th century, and a Customs House was built in 1681. This fine

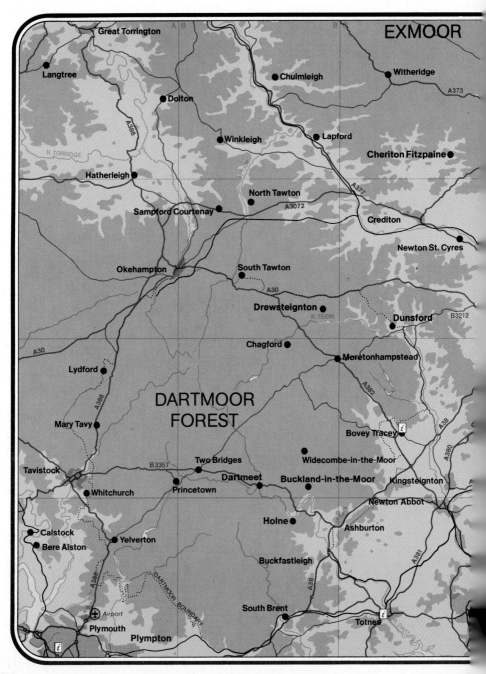

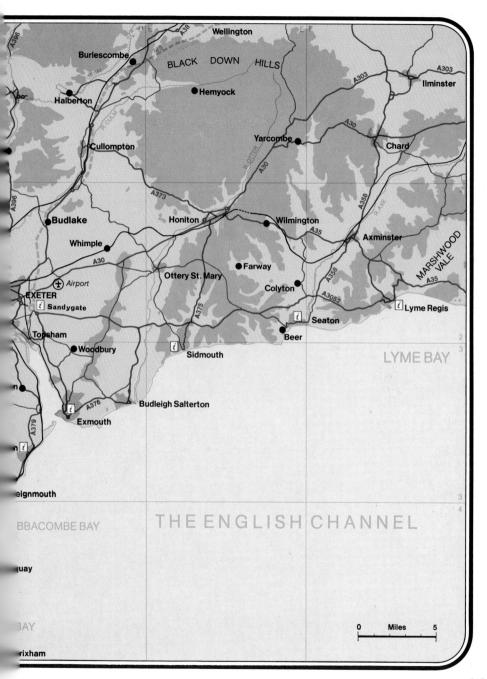

brick building remains in the canal basin and can be viewed by arrangement with HM Customs.

The old quay and warehouses now form the *Maritime Museum*. More than 700 boats from all over the world make up one of the finest collections in the country. Open daily 10.00am to 6.00pm in the summer and 10.00am to 5.00pm in the winter.

The port made Exeter an important commercial centre from early times. The Guildhall in the High Street is the most important medieval building in the town. It is said to be the oldest municipal building in England.

The Guildhall has a 15th-century hall, and the stone carved external wall of the upper storey rests on granite pillars forming an arch over the High Street pavement.

The granite for the pillars probably came from Dartmoor, for which Exeter is a touring centre.

The prehistoric hut circles, the wild landscape with its projections of granite rocks, known as tors, rising out of the hills, and the delightful rocky streams make Dartmoor worthy of its National Trust protection.

South of the city of Exeter and along the coast to the east and west are some delightful seaside towns and villages.

To the north, in Exeter's agricultural hinterland, are some of the picturesque farming villages for which Devon is famous.

The cob-walled cottages with their thatched roofs and delightful flower-filled gardens are reached along steep-sided, leafy lanes. The narrow, winding lanes run between fields of waving, golden crops, and apple orchards.

*The University* is a modern addition to Exeter's amenities. It was built in the grounds which belonged to the family who began the Reed Paper Group, and an earlier member of the family planted an arboretum of over 150 species of trees.

*Northcott Theatre*, a recent addition to the city's arts scene, was built in the University grounds.

*St Nicholas Priory* The remains of an 11th- and 16th-century Benedictine Priory, with Norman undercroft, Tudor room and 15th-century kitchen Open Tuesday to Saturday, 10.00am to 1.00pm, 2.00pm to 5.30pm.

*Tuckers Hall* The medieval guildhall of weavers, fullers and shearmen. Wagon roof and 17th-century panelling. Open June to September Tuesday, Thursday and Friday, 10.30am to 12.30pm, rest of the year Friday, 10.30am to 12.30pm.

*Medieval Aqueducts* These underground passages, entered from Princesshay, are open Tuesday to Saturday, 2.00pm to 5.00pm.

*St Mary Steps Church* contains a famous clock with figures said to represent Henry VIII. The javelin men strike the hour. The church also has a fine Norman font.

*St Mary Arches Church* The only remaining Devon church with a 12th-century double Norman arcade.

*Albert Memorial Museum and Art Gallery* in Queen Street has a permanent exhibition of paintings. Open Tuesday to Saturday, 10.00am to 5.30pm.

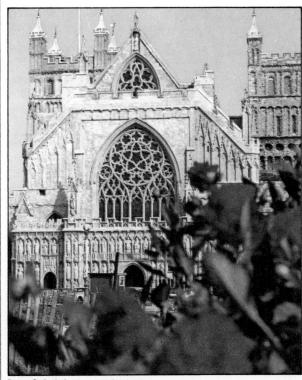

Exeter Cathedral . . . a true focal point

**Seaton**
This is the most easterly of Devon's many seaside resorts. It has a mile-long shingle beach at the foot of towering cliffs.

**Beer**
Next door to Seaton, Beer is similarly a popular seaside resort. It has the most westerly chalk cliffs of the English Channel and Beer Head is 426 ft high. A quarry near the village is where the stone was mined for Exeter Cathedral and other famous buildings.

**Sidmouth**
The Brighton of the southwest. The Regency-style houses fronting the pebble beach give this fishing village an air of elegance which the summer visitors have enjoyed for over a century. Queen Victoria stayed at the Royal Glen Hotel when she was a small child.

**Budleigh Salterton**
A quiet, restful, pretty seaside village. It still has the sea wall which figures in the painting *The Boyhood of Raleigh*, by Sir John Millais.

**Exmouth**
Still a very busy, popular estuary town. It has a harbour for fishing vessels and pleasure boats, and long, sandy beaches. There is a strong current in the sea which makes bathing unsafe. There are many entertainments for children and adults such as a zoo, swimming pool and amusement park.

**Woodbury Common**
Inland from Exmouth and off the road to Exeter is the high land to the east of the river which forms this medieval common land. It has some interesting earthworks and is a delightful walking area.

**Ottery St Mary**
On the edge of the common, has a church modelled on the cathedral in Exeter. Samuel Taylor Coleridge was born here in 1772.

**Tiverton**
The largest town on the River Exe north of Exeter. It had a wool industry which was revived in the 19th century with the addition of spinning looms.

A rich local wool merchant founded the famous Blundell's School here in 1604.

The town has two sets of almshouses, both dating back to the 16th century, called the Waldron and Greenway Almshouses.

The main church in Tiverton dates back to the 15th century, while St Peter's Church has carvings in the magnificent south porch of the ships that were used by early Tiverton merchants.

**Dawlish**
South of the Exe estuary, it is an extremely popular seaside holiday resort.

The town is not without its literary connections. Charles Dickens made it the birthplace of Nicholas Nickleby, and Jane Austen made many visits here.

The architecture of the town is part-Georgian and part-Victorian. The Lawn is a notable landscape feature of the town.

**Teignmouth**
The prosperity of this old town arose from fishing and shipbuilding. There are good beaches, a fine esplanade and many sporting and entertainment facilities.

The Ness, a huge, red, sandstone headland across the Teign stands sentinel over the river mouth and the delightful village of Shaldon, which can be reached by passenger ferry.

**Moretonhampstead**
The River Teign flows from its source on Dartmoor to the east of Moretonhampstead. Near the town are the remains of Cranbrook Castle which is an Iron Age hill fort 1,100 ft above the river Teign.

The town itself is a market town with some two-storey granite almshouses dated 1637.

From Moretonhampstead the whole of the southern half of Dartmoor can be explored. The nearest tor is Easdon Down and beyond that lies Bowerman's Nose, Hound Tor and Haytor, rocks whose imposing size and height dominate the scene.

**Chagford**
This delightful village, which was once a Stannary town, has Georgian and Tudor buildings and a fine market square at the centre. Even the local bank has a thatched roof.

**Gidleigh**
This tiny village is on the edge of an area of the Moor where the scenery becomes extremely wild and exciting. There are ancient hut circles, and in the garden of one house are the remains of an Anglo-Saxon long house and a Norman tower.

**Grimspound**
To the south of the B3212 road crossing Dartmoor from Moretonhampstead to Yelverton, this is a well-preserved group of the remains of 24 ancient stone huts. Grim was a name for the Anglo-Saxon god Woden.

**Newton Abbot**
A very important market town and railway centre. The high-speed trains between London and Penzance stop at Newton Abbot after the line runs along the Exe estuary. The proximity of such a transport system has meant that the town has developed industrially, commercially and as a main touring centre for holidays on Dartmoor, in the South Hams and in Cornwall.

# Dorset Coast

If inland Dorset has retained a flavour of Thomas Hardy's days, it is also true that the coast has a character protected by the lack of big towns, motorways or major railways, and by its own unusual geography.

The Dorset coast is shaped into three bays, separated by jutting peninsula formations. Each peninsula juts into the sea so far as to be almost an island.

In the west, from the resort of Lyme Regis, there are massive cliffs for several miles, and then a long ridge of clay and pebbles called Chesil Bank runs to the 'Isle' of Portland, famous for its stone.

The 'isle' sees the end of Lyme Bay, and the beginning of Weymouth Bay, with the resort of the same name. Then comes the 'Isle' of Purbeck, the resort of Swanage, and Poole Bay.

**Tourist Information Centres**
The Guildhall, Bridge Street, Lyme Regis, Dorset. (029 74) 2138
The White House, Shore Road, Swanage, Dorset. (092 92) 2885
The Esplanade, Weymouth, Dorset. (030 57) 5747
Publicity Office, 12 The Esplanade, Weymouth, Dorset. (030 57) 72444

## Lyme Regis
Jane Austen loved this resort and wrote and set part of the action of her novel *Persuasion* here.

The Duke of Monmouth landed at the harbour in 1685 to launch his ill-fated rebellion.

Edward I granted the town its royal title when he used the harbour, protected by a 600-ft breakwater known as The Cobb, during his battles against the French.

Lyme Regis became a holiday resort in the 18th century when sea-bathing began to be fashionable. Before this it was better-known as a haunt of smugglers.

## West Bay
Small, but popular with visitors who are attracted by the two excellent beaches. It is also noted for fishing and sailing.

The 19th-century customs house is now a cafe.

## Abbotsbury
The swannery here is the only nesting colony of mute swans in the world that is open for visiting.

The swans were originally bred to feed the Benedictine monks who founded an abbey in the 15th century.

In addition to this, the monks built the superb tithe barn. At 276 ft long, it is one of the largest in the country.

The warm climate produces an abundance of exotic plants and trees in the village's subtropical gardens. Spring is an excellent time to pay a visit for the air is heavy with the scent of magnolia.

High on the top of *Black Down Hill* stands the Hardy Monument, which celebrates Admiral Hardy, the flag captain of Nelson at the Battle of Trafalgar.

This spot makes a splendid vantage point as it commands views of miles of Dorset countryside.

## Chesil Beach
This bank of graded shingle stretches 10 miles west of Portland and is separated from the mainland by a sheltered brackish lagoon known as the Fleet.

Storms and powerful currents have swept the pebbles from along the Dorset and Devon coast and piled them on the bank. The pebbles increase in size as they go eastwards, and their colour changes from grey to brown-yellow.

The shingle makes this an excellent area for beachcombing, for the sea has in its time offered up such rarities as whales and Spanish galleons.

## Portland
The 'Gibraltar of Wessex' was Thomas Hardy's description of this narrow peninsula. It is an almost treeless rock, from whose many quarries stone has gone to enhance such buildings as St Paul's Cathedral.

Portland Castle was built by Henry VIII and still stands on the north shore. An earlier castle, built by the Normans is now a ruin.

The famous old lighthouse on Portland Bill is now used as a bird-watching station.

## Weymouth
In addition to being a most pleasing resort with excellent sandy beaches, this is the terminal for the Channel Island and Cherbourg steamers. No. 3 Trinity Street is an early 17th-century example of a pair of semi-detached houses. This style of building did not become common until the 19th century.

## Lulworth
One of the best-known tourist spots in Britain, it incorporates East and West Lulworth and the famous Lulworth Cove.

The cove can only really be appreciated on foot. The cliff top view of Man o' War Bay and the mighty limestone arch

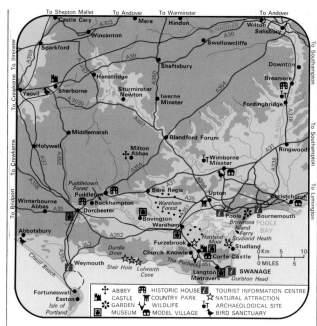

To Shepton Mallet | To Andover | To Warminster | To Andover
Castle Cary  Mere  Hindon  Wilton  Salisbury
Wincanton  Swallowcliffe
Sparkford
Shaftsbury  Downton
Henstridge  Breamore
Sherborne  Sturminster Newton  Iwerne Minster  Fordingbridge
Yeovil
Middlemarsh  Blandford Forum
Holywell  Milton Abbas  Ringwood
Puddletown Forest  Wimborne Minster
Winterbourne Abbas  Puddletown  Bere Regis  Upton  Christchurch
Bockhampton  Wareham Forest
Dorchester  Bovington  Poole  Bournemouth
Wareham  Brownsea Island  POOLE BAY
Abbotsbury  Furzebrook  Hartland Moor  Studland Heath
Church Knowle  Studland
Weymouth  Durdle Door  Corfe Castle
Stair Hole  Lulworth Cove  The Purbecks  Langton Matravers  SWANAGE
Fortuneswell  Easton  Durlston Head
Isle of Portland

To Crewkerne  To Ilminster  To Bridport  To Crewkerne
To Southampton  To Southampton  To Lymington

0 Km 5 10
0 MILES 5

✝ ABBEY  🏰 CASTLE  ❀ GARDEN  🏛 MUSEUM  🏠 HISTORIC HOUSE  ❦ COUNTRY PARK  ♦ WILDLIFE  🏘 MODEL VILLAGE  ℹ TOURIST INFORMATION CENTRE  ☆ NATURAL ATTRACTION  ⚒ ARCHAEOLOGICAL SITE  ♦ BIRD SANCTUARY

of Durdle Door is unforgettable.

There are also superb views on the road east along the ridge of the Purbeck Hills towards Steeple. But care should be taken as this is Defence Ministry land and intrusion may be unwelcome and even dangerous.

**Swanage**
Hardy described Swanage as 'lying snugly as between finger and thumb', and it is easy to see why when standing on either side of the graceful sweeping bay, looking down on a town which is one of the county's most popular resorts.

The Isle of Purbeck on which it stands is not an island in the strictest sense, although a journey to Swanage from the east can involve a ferry trip if desired.

Stone features strongly in the town, due to the generosity of John Mowlem and George Burt, who bought monuments which were to be demolished in London and transferred them to Swanage. There are so many relics of the capital city that Swanage has been described as 'Old London by the sea'.

Walking the *Dorset Coast Path*, which runs along this spectacular coastline, one can retrace the steps of the smugglers who once brought their illicit hauls ashore into quiet coves before stealing away across the fields.

*St Mary the Virgin* The town's parish church, dating from 1250.
*Town Hall* The stone-carved façade was once the front of the Mercer's Hall in London's Cheapside. It was designed by Edward Jermain, a pupil of Christopher Wren.
*Wellington Clock Tower* Another import from London. It was originally erected in Southwark in 1854 as a memorial to the Duke of Wellington, but was brought to Swanage in 1867.
*Anvil Point Lighthouse* A 19th-century lighthouse, with electric lighting, 170 ft above sea level and visible for 18 miles. Open Monday to Friday 1.00pm to sunset.
*Peveril Point* Coastguard lookout and lifeboat house.
*Durlston Country Park* The highlight here is the famous oddity, the Great Globe, a 40-ton Portland stone representation of the world, 10 ft in diameter which was placed here in 1866.
*Nature trails and walks* Marked footpaths throughout Durlston Country Park where puffins and other sea birds nest on the National Trust-owned Downland to the north. There are also many miles of footpaths and bridleways. Maps and books are available at the Tourist Information Centre.
*Water-skiing* This is permitted in the bay, seaward of the prescribed inshore area.
*Events Regatta and Carnival*, first week in August.

**Poole**
The natural harbour here is about 95 miles in diameter. Little seems to have changed since the days 200 years ago when pirates and smugglers sailed the waters.

Brownsea Island, in the harbour, covers some 500 acres and features miniature glens and hills. Open April to September daily 10.00am to dusk.

For those interested in old pubs, there are many in Poole dating from the 18th and 19th centuries. Among the most notable are the Angel and the Old Custom House, which was rebuilt in 1813 after the original had burned down.

In the 18th and 19th centuries Poole built up a flourishing timber trade with Newfoundland, Canada.

The famous *Poole Pottery* stands on the quayside. The working craft sections, shops and showrooms are open daily.

# Bournemouth

The harbour town of Poole, the green resort of Bournemouth and the old town of Christchurch adjoin each other along a broad bay.

Having grown together, they made nonsense of a county boundary which affected to separate them, and now all three are deemed to be in Dorset, though they belong less to the West than to the South.

Thus their geographical ambivalence remains, and to the advantage of the visitor: to the west, Dorset offers Thomas Hardy Country; to the east, Hampshire counters with the New Forest; offshore, the Isle of Wight adds to the considerable attractions of this south coast.

Map legend:
RACE COURSE
HISTORIC HOUSE
NOTABLE CHURCH/ CATHEDRAL
CASTLE
TOURIST INFORMATION CENTRE
HISTORIC SITE
BIRD GARDEN
MUSEUM
GARDEN

MILES
KILOMETRES

**Tourist Information Centres**
Westover Road, Bournemouth, Dorset. (0202) 291715
Caravan, Saxon Square, Christchurch, Dorset. (020 15) 4321
Arndale Centre, Poole, Dorset. (020 13) 3322
Civic Centre, Poole, Dorset. (020 13) 5151

**Bournemouth** (*map p 222*)
A large seaside resort which manages not to be spoiled in the face of popularity. It brings in more than a million visitors each year.

Its sands are seven miles long.

There are some 2,000 acres of parks and gardens, accounting for a sixth of Bournemouth's total area, two fine examples of English pier architecture and a wide choice of open air sports.

Top stars appear in the shows at the town's three theatres, and the Bournemouth Symphony Orchestra has achieved an international reputation. For something a little racier, there are casinos to tempt those with a sporting disposition.

There were once three million pine trees in Bournemouth. This number has now been considerably reduced by the ravages of time and development, but enough survive to allow the town a delightful wooded setting.

Cliffs plunge 100 ft down to the bay and there are cliff walks for the energetic. There are three lifts down to the beach for those who cannot face the steps.

A walk along the cliffs leads to Hengistbury Head and the remains of a prehistoric village. It is also an excellent point for observing bird migrations.

*Russell-Cotes Art Gallery and Museum* Victorian works of art in a domestic setting. Paintings, water-colours, sculpture, miniatures, ceramics, furniture and plate from the 17th to 20th centuries. It also houses a collection of more than 350 typewriters dating from the first commercial machine of 1873. Open Monday to Saturday 10.00am to 6.00pm.

*Rothesay Museum* The Lucas collection of early Italian paintings, in addition to pottery, English porcelain and 17th-century furniture. Victorian pictures and bygones. Important marine col-

lection. Open Monday to Saturday 10.00am to 6.00pm.
*Bournemouth Pier* Opened in 1880. Popular for fishing and has a theatre and restaurant.
*Boscombe Pier* Opened in 1889, rebuilt in 1926 and restored in 1958. Fishing in the winter only.
*Meyrick Park* A 154-acre estate of pine trees, with an 18-hole golf course, tennis courts, squash courts, bowling greens, cricket, hockey and football pitches.
*Alum Chine, Durley Chine and Middle Chine* Pleasant walks from the Westbourne and West Cliff areas down to the sea.
*Robert Louis Stevenson Memorial Gardens* Former residence of the famous author. The stonework outline of his house is still visible.
*Swanmore Gardens* Rose displays.
*Boat Trips* Passenger vessels operate summer services from both piers to the Isle of Wight and Swanage. Rowing boats and other small craft are available for hire.
*Events Daffodil Vintage Car Rally*, in April; *Hurn Airport Air Show*, in June; *Open-air painting exhibition* in Central Gardens, in June/July; *Regatta*, in August.

## Christchurch

This beautiful old town stands on the estuaries of the rivers Avon and Stour. The *priory*, which was founded in 1100, dominates the town, and was originally part of a monastery which stood on the site.

The tower is 15th-century and is 120 ft high, the nave is Norman, the transepts early English and the chancel perpendicular in style.

The entire structure is an interesting blend of styles from Saxon to Renaissance. The choir stalls are even older than those in Westminster Abbey.

Christchurch can also boast an impressive Norman Motte Bailey *Castle*, a rare example of

Yachting centre . . . Lymington

a Norman house dating back to the 12th century. An ancient mill stream and a monastery gatehouse are all within the precincts of the former castle. Open daily 9.00am to sunset.

The *Red House Museum and Art Gallery* is an 18th-century building which houses geological, local history and archaeological exhibits. It also has a herb garden. Open Tuesday to Saturday 10.00am to 5.00pm, Sunday 2.00pm to 5.00pm.

*Tucktonia*, which has miniature versions of British landmarks, towns and villages is open daily 10.00am to dusk.

## Lymington

Although better-known to travellers as the departure point for the ferries to the Isle of Wight, this ancient town is a popular yachting centre and its tidal harbour is usually packed with small craft.

## Bucklers Hard

Until the 19th century, this village was a shipbuilding centre founded by the Duke of Montagu, whose family still live in the area.

Henry Adams, who built ships for Lord Nelson, once lived in the building which is now the Master Builder's House Hotel.

A *maritime museum* recalls those romantic days, and it has models and exhibits of ships built here for Nelson's great fleet. Open daily 10.00am to 6.00pm.

The village's small landing stage is the starting point for trips on the Beaulieu River.

From Saxon to Renaissance . . . Christchurch Priory

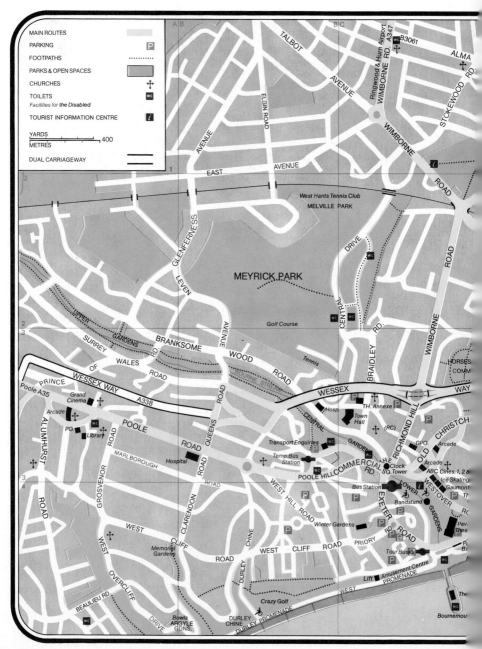

MAIN ROUTES

PARKING   P

FOOTPATHS   ............

PARKS & OPEN SPACES

CHURCHES   ✝

TOILETS   WC
*Facilities for the Disabled*

TOURIST INFORMATION CENTRE   *i*

YARDS
METRES   400

DUAL CARRIAGEWAY

A B   B C

Ringwood & Hurn Airport
WIMBORNE RD. A347   B3061
ALMA RD.
STOKEWOOD RD.
TALBOT
AVENUE
ELGIN ROAD
WIMBORNE
ROAD
AVENUE
EAST   AVENUE

West Hants Tennis Club
MELVILLE PARK

GLENFERNESS
LEVEN
AVENUE

MEYRICK PARK

DRIVE
CENTRAL RD.
WC

Golf Course

BRANKSOME
SURREY
UPPER GARDENS
OF WALES ROAD
AVENUE
WOOD
ROAD
ROAD
Tennis
BRAIDLEY RD.
WIMBORNE ROAD
HORSES COMM

WESSEX WAY
Poole A35
PRINCE
A338
WESSEX   WAY
Grand Cinema
Arcade
PO.
Library
POOLE
ROAD
QUEENS ROAD
Hospital
ROAD
MARLBOROUGH ROAD
ALUMHURST ROAD
GROSVENOR ROAD
CLARENDON ROAD
Hosp.
CENTRAL
Town Hall
(RC)
GARDENS
Transport Enquiries
Temp. Bus Station
POOLE HILL
COMMERCIAL RD.
RICHMOND HILL
GPO.
Arcade
Arcade
ABC Cines. 1, 2 &
Ice Skating
Gaumont
OLD CHRISTCH
TH. Annexe
T.H.
Clock SQ. Tower
TOWER
Bus Station
Bandstand
EXETER ROAD
WESTOVER GARDENS
RO
Pav. Thea
WEST
CLIFF
ROAD
Memorial Gardens
DURLEY CHINE ROAD
WEST CLIFF ROAD
Winter Gardens
WEST HILL ROAD
PRIORY RD.
Tour Buses
P
Amusement Centre
Lift
PROMENADE
WEST
P. Ba
WC
The
Bournemou
WEST OVERCLIFF DRIVE
BEAULIEU RD.
Bowls
ARGYLE GDNS.
WC
DURLEY CHINE
Crazy Golf
DURLEY PROMENADE

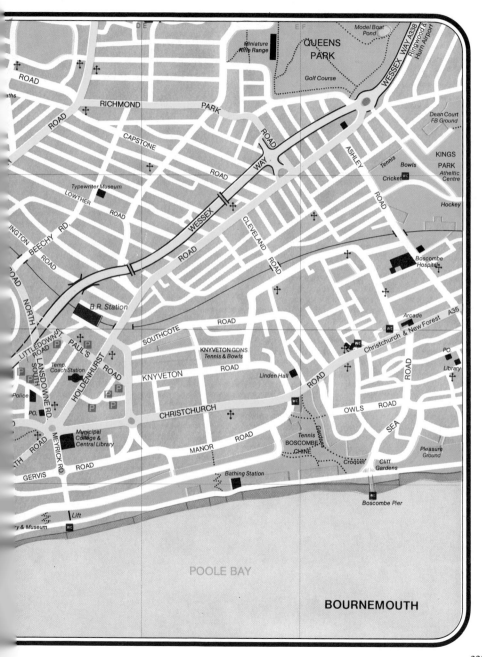

POOLE BAY

**BOURNEMOUTH**

# The New Forest

Between Bournemouth and Southampton, stretching inland for a dozen or 20 miles in places, fringed in parts by the river Beaulieu and the Hampshire Avon, lie nearly 300 square miles of unspoiled countryside.

Much of this area remains under woodland, as it has been for more than 1,000 years, with a notably wide variety of trees, though there are also stretches of heathland, often with gorse and heather.

There are drives and walks in the Forest, riding stables and even golf courses, with Lyndhurst as the natural base from which to explore.

Signposted walks start at Bolderwood, Brockhill, Blackwater, Puttles Bridge, Whitefield Moor and Wilverley.

**Tourist Information Centres**
The National Motor Museum, Beaulieu, Hampshire. (0590) 612345
Avon Valley Travel Services, 52 High Street, Fordingbridge, Hampshire. (0425) 54410
Camper Advisory Service, Main Car Park, Lyndhurst, Hampshire. (042 128) 2269

## Lyndhurst

The 'Capital of the New Forest', its administrative centre and seat of the Ancient Court of Verderers.

This body, the sole survivor of the powerful courts of Forest Laws, meets in the 17th-century Queen's House on the first or second Monday in January, March, May, July, September and November.

The Verderers' Hall itself was built in 1388 and housed the Court of Swainmote where those who broke Forest byelaws were tried.

Lyndhurst has many traffic problems, being on the Forest's main road, but it is surrounded by truly impressive woodland.

The Knightwood Oak is 600 years old and has a girth of some 21 ft.

Bolton's Bench was named after Lord Bolton who was Lord Warden of the Forest in 1688.

Campers can obtain detailed information about Forestry Commission sites from their offices at Queen's House. Camping in the Forest is allowed only on these official sites.

Lyndhurst is the home of Holidays Hill Reptillary, owned by the Forestry Commission. It has a comprehensive breeding collection of amphibians and reptiles. Open daily, daylight hours.

The Victorian Gothic parish church has ornamental work by Millais, Leighton and Burne-Jones. The churchyard contains the grave of Alice Liddell, on whom Lewis Carroll's classic *Alice in Wonderland* was based.

## Brockenhurst

There is a ford in the main street of this pleasant residential village.

A yew tree in the churchyard is believed to be more than 1,000 years old.

Ober Water Walk is a peaceful walk along a forest stream.

## Burley

Famous as a meeting place for huntsmen. The Queen's Head Inn has an impressive display of hunting trophies.

## Ringwood

On the Avon, this is an excellent centre for trout fishing.

The Duke of Monmouth was captured nearby as he fled towards the coast after his ill-fated rebellion in 1685.

## Moyles Court

The 17th-century manor, from which this village takes its name, has a colourful and tragic history.

It was the ancestral home of the Lisle family, until Alice Lisle was hanged by Judge Jeffreys for sheltering a fugitive of the Monmouth Rebellion.

After this, the house became a ruin. It has now been restored and is used as a school. Alice Lisle is buried in the churchyard at Ellingham, a mile away.

The village itself is typical of the New Forest, and has a ford and ponies and cattle roaming freely.

## Fordingbridge

The church here dates from the 13th century and has five carvings from the 15th century.

*Fordingbridge Show and Steam and Vintage Rally* is held over three days at Netley Marsh every July.

## Rockbourne

The excavated site of a *Roman villa* containing 70 rooms is half a mile south of this attractive village.

There is one long street in the town, lined by beautiful Tudor and Georgian houses and thatched cottages. At one end is a farm which incorporates a manor house dating from the 13th century.

## Breamore

A triangular-shaped Tudor village with a fine Saxon church

New Forest ponies . . . an idyllic scene

believed to have been built in the 10th century.

Breamore, pronounced Bremmer, is a fine place for walking. Numerous footpaths, bridleways and tracks cover the undulating downland and there are memorable views over the Avon Valley to Salisbury.

*Breamore House* was completed in 1583 and the Hulse family have lived there for 200 years. There is a collection of art, furniture and tapestries.

It also houses the *Breamore Countryside and Carriage Museum,* which has implements of all types, tracing the development of agricultural machinery. Open Easter to September daily except Monday and Friday 2.00pm to 5.00pm.

## Minstead

*Sir Arthur Conan Doyle*, creator of Sherlock Holmes, is buried outside the village's 13th-century church.

The *Rufus Stone* is a mile north-west and marks the spot where William II, known as Rufus because of his red hair, was killed by an arrow fired by Walter Tyrell.

This hunting incident in 1100 was presumed to be an accident, but many doubt it.

When William's younger brother Henry heard of the death, he dashed to Winchester and seized the treasury. He was proclaimed king by the barons, thus pre-empting the claims of his eldest brother Robert of Normandy.

Minstead's Furzey Gardens stretch for eight acres, with an ancient cottage and a craft gallery.

## Hythe

The flying-boat services of Imperial Airways used to depart from this small town on Southampton Water, on their way to all parts of the British Empire. The company is now part of British Airways.

The *Marine Life Centre aquarium* on the pier is open May to September daily 10.00am to 5.30pm.

## Beaulieu

The famous home and estate of Lord Montagu, with its fine abbey, Palace House and renowned motor museum.

The abbey was originally Cistercian, founded in 1204 by King John and later destroyed by Henry VIII. The Great Gatehouse, with its vaulted rooms, was rebuilt in 1872 and is now Lord Montagu's home, Palace House.

The abbey's refectory has been rebuilt to become the parish church, while the lay dormitory is now a restaurant.

Lord Montagu founded his *National Motor Museum* in 1952 in honour of his father, the second Baron Montagu of Beaulieu who was a famed pioneer motorist.

The collection is now the most comprehensive in the world, with more than 200 vintage and veteran cars, in addition to cycles and motor cycles.

There are also exhibitions of motoring from 1895 to modern times. Open daily 10.00am to 5.30pm.

The village itself and the surrounding area has its own scenic attractions. A mile west of Beaulieu is Hatchet Gate, a charming spot beside a pond and mill house.

Beaulieu Heath, to the south, is fine walking country with impressive views.

# Southampton

Where Poole Bay ends, the channel called The Solent passes behind the Isle of Wight as far as Southampton Water. This deep inlet meets the mouths of several rivers, including the Meon, the Itchen and the Test.

The Solent and Southampton Water are always alive with yachts and dinghies, but the town which watches over them is England's main port for ocean-going passenger ships.

Southampton is a large and interesting town, and a base from which to explore the stretch of Hampshire countryside spreading inland towards Romsey and Winchester.

**Southampton**
The town's past, present and future is inextricably bound up with the sea, its continuing source of prosperity since the Middle Ages.

Armies sailed from its waters for the Crusades, the Hundred Years War, and the Napoleonic campaigns. The Pilgrim Fathers even stopped here on their way from Lincolnshire to Plymouth, and early Italian ships traded from the port.

This old tradition of sea-bound commerce has expanded over the centuries into the giant passenger and container services for which the city is now world-famous. The liner Queen Elizabeth II moors here.

Southampton is a city which reflects the beauty of Southern England, and is a cosmopolitan centre.

Although 20th-century development, made necessary by cruel wartime bombing and the need to expand the docks, may obscure much of the city's ancient past, there is still much to see.

Catchcold Tower, Arundel Tower and the Bargate, all features of the city's imposing fortifications, are good examples.

The city has more than 1,000 acres of parks, gardens, playing fields and open spaces.

By the Royal Pier is Mayflower Park, home of

Southampton's International Boat Show.

The sports-minded are well catered for. The sports centre at Bassett covers 300 acres with athletics and cycling tracks, two golf courses and one of the best artificial ski slopes in England.

The indoor sports hall at St Mary's has a wide range of facilities, plus an Olympic standard pool.

For those just wishing to watch, Southampton is the home of Hampshire County Cricket Club, and Southampton Football Club have just won promotion back to the Football League First Division.

*The Mitchell Museum* Dedicated to R. J. Mitchell, designer of the WWII fighter plane. Open Tuesday to Saturday 10.00am to 4.30pm, Sunday 2.00pm to 5.00pm.

*Maritime Museum* In the Wool House. Includes models of great ships. Open Tuesday to Saturday 11.00am to 12.00pm, 2.00pm to 5.00pm, Sunday 2.00pm to 5.00.pm.

*The Bargate* Local history including D-Day embroidery. Open Tuesday to Saturday 11.00am to 12.00pm, 1.00pm to 5.00pm, Sunday 2.00pm to 5.00pm.

*God's House Tower* Archaeological museum including Post-Roman European pottery, artifacts from Roman port

**Tourist Information Centres**
Canute Road (opposite Dock Gate 3), Southampton, Hampshire. (0703) 20438/20494
Above Bar Shopping Precinct, Southampton, Hampshire. (0703) 23855 Ext 615

One of the many . . . Palmerston Park

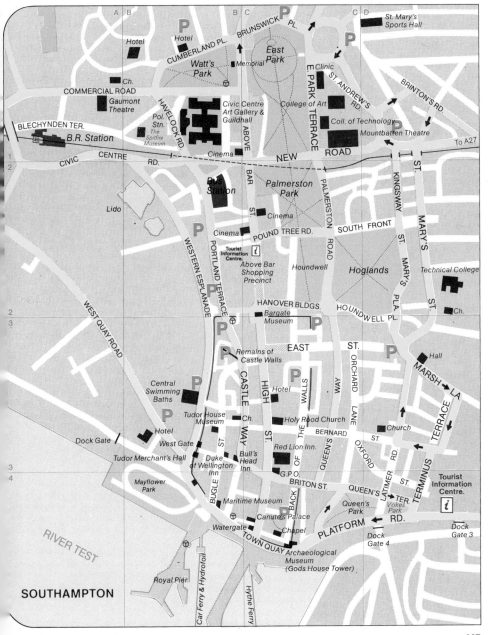

SOUTHAMPTON

at Clausentum and from Romano-British site at Nursling. Open 1st Saturday of each month, 11.00am to 1.00pm, 2.00pm to 5.00pm.

*Tudor House* Furniture, decorative arts, paintings of the town, musical instruments. Open Tuesday to Saturday 11.00am to 5.00pm, Sunday 2.00pm to 5.00pm.

*Southampton Art Gallery* Permanent collection of British paintings from 1750 to 1794, Old Masters and French art from 1800 to the 1930s. Open Tuesday to Saturday 11.00am to 5.45pm, Sunday 2.00pm to 5.00pm.

*St Michael's Church* Dates from Norman times and has an 800-year-old black marble font from Tournai. The 19th-century spire is a landmark for ships in Southampton Water.

*Red Lion Inn* The oldest pub in Southampton, dating from the 12th century.

*Duke of Wellington* Another old pub, with a building dating from the 15th and 16th centuries.

*Sports* Golf; football; cricket; tennis; bowls; ski slope; putting; canoeing; gymnastics; basketball; badminton; squash; sauna; solarium; ten pin bowling; ice skating; fishing; sea angling.

*Events* Southampton Boat Show, in September; Southampton Show, in July; Southampton Regatta, in summer.

## Hamble

Yachting centre on the river Hamble. Also noted for the excellent crab and lobster dishes available at local restaurants.

A small part of the 12th-century priory, built by the Benedictines is still standing. It was rebuilt by William of Wykeham as the parish church in the 13th century.

In 1971 thousands turned out at Hamble to welcome home yachtsman Chay Blyth at the end of his non-stop voyage around the world in an east-west direction.

## Botley

Old houses line the wide main street of this village, which nestles at a high point of the river Hamble. It is, however, still navigable for pleasure craft.

There is a memorial to William Cobbett, the 19th-century author whose *Rural Rides* carried him to this pleasant spot.

## Romsey

The 10th-century abbey here is a famous landmark. It was enlarged into a church by the Normans in the 12th century and sold for £100 at the Dissolution.

*King John's House*, built between 1230 and 1240, and once belonging to the abbey, is open March to October Tuesday, Thursday, Friday and Saturday.

Broadland, an 18th-century house in a fine park, both having been remodelled by Capability Brown, was once Lord Palmerston's home.

It is now the home of Lord Mountbatten and is where the Queen and Prince Philip spent part of their honeymoon in 1947.

## Hursley

This village consists of one street of Tudor buildings. Richard, the son of Oliver Cromwell, and lord of the Manor of Hursley, is buried in the church.

There is a monument to Cromwell senior under the tower of the present church building.

## Twyford

Alexander Pope, the poet and satirist, made an engaging start to his career when he was expelled from the local school for lampooning his teacher.

Another famous figure to spend some time in this delightful village was Benjamin Franklin, the American statesman and part-author of the Constitution.

During his period in England as agent for Pennsylvania he stayed at Twyford House and there he wrote parts of his famous autobiography.

## Bishop's Waltham

This small town in the heart of the Hampshire strawberry-growing country, is noted for its 12th-century Bishop's Palace.

The palace was part of the See of Winchester, which lies to the north-west. During the Civil War, it was vigorously defended by the Royalist forces, but was damaged when Cromwell's army overpowered the defenders.

The palace is open weekdays 9.30am to 7.00pm, Sunday 2.00pm to 7.00pm.

The Old Granary is a 200-year-old building now used as a *craft workshop*. Open Monday to Saturday 9.30am to 5.30pm.

River Hamble . . . Chay Blyth's destination

# Winchester

The capital of Saxon England is today a small and largely unspoiled city in the middle of rural Hampshire.

While the southern part of Hampshire has it great maritime cities, the middle of the county has only small towns and villages, agriculture, horticulture, and prosperous commuter dwellings towards the north and in the direction of London.

From Winchester, it is about 20 miles to Salisbury Plain, and a lesser distance in the opposite direction to the North Downs – low, but sometimes steep chalk hills, with grassy slopes, which stretch into Sussex and Kent.

**Tourist Information Centre**
The Guildhall, Winchester, Hampshire. (0962) 68166/65406 (Saturday)

**Winchester** (*map p 230*)
There are 2,000 years of history in this magnificent city. It was one of the largest towns in England during Roman times. King Alfred reigned here and succeeding kings held their courts in Winchester until the 13th century.

The city contains buildings of every period since the 12th century, and has lovely Queen Anne and Georgian architecture. The focal point is the High Street, now pedestrianized, dominated by a 15th-century cross and statue to King Alfred. The imposing Victorian Guildhall is nearby.

At one end of the High Street stands the 13th-century Westgate. Like Kingsgate, this is one of the original five city gates. It was once a prison, but is now a museum tracing Winchester's history.

The city's crowning glory is the cathedral. At 556 ft it is one of the longest in Europe and stands next to the site of an earlier Anglo-Saxon church.

A 15-minute walk from the compact city centre will take the visitor along a riverside footpath to the Hospital of St Cross – one of the finest medieval almshouses in England.

Winchester College is just outside the city, and was founded in 1382 by Bishop William of Wykeham. The school chapel contains the original wooden vaulting.

*Cathedral* Built by the Normans to replace the Anglo-Saxon church on an adjacent site, it was consecrated in 1093, having taken 23 years to build.

In the Middle Ages, pilgrims to Canterbury broke their journey to visit St Swithun's shrine in the cathedral. They slept in Pilgrim's hall, which is next to the cathedral.

Splendid tombs enclose the bones of such notables as King Canute, Izaak Walton and Jane Austen.

The Old Deanery, in the Close, has a 13th-century entrance and 15th-century windows.

*Castle* Little remains of William the Conqueror's fortress, from which Empress Mathilda escaped in a coffin in the 12th century. Most of it was destroyed in the Civil War but the 13th-century Great Hall can still be seen.

The Hall was the meeting place of the first English parliaments, and the scene of many famous trials – including some held by the notorious Judge Jeffreys in 1685. It is the home of the Arthurian Round Table, which recent tests have dated at around 1335.

*Hyde Abbey Gateway* The remains of Hyde Abbey, burial place of King Alfred.

*Hospital of St Cross* Founded in 1136, the oldest functioning charitable institution in England.

The Brothers still wear black or red gowns with a silver cross and medieval cap. As in the days of old, all visitors may ask for, and receive, the traditional Wayfarer's Dole of bread and ale.

*St Catherine's Hill* Site of an Iron Age settlement, with good views over Winchester and the Itchen Valley.

## Alresford

A delightful small town on the bank of the River Alre, a tributary of the Itchen.

It is also the starting point of the Mid-Hants Watercress Line, a *steam railway* which runs along the eight miles of track to Ropley. It operates on weekends and Bank Holidays from May to October.

Admiral Rodney, who defeated the Spanish off Cape St Vincent in 1780 and the French off Dominica two years later, is buried at Alresford churchyard.

Many French prisoners of the Napoleonic Wars were kept at the town and many are also buried at the church.

## Chawton

Jane Austen's last home before her death in 1817. The house is now a *museum* with many relics of the novelist and her family. Open April to October, Wednesday to Sunday 11.00am to 4.30pm.

## Selbourne

Gilbert White, the naturalist, was born and lived here. Little has changed since he was the local curate in the 1750s.

His house is now a memorial museum and library devoted to him, and to Captain Oates, who died in Antarctica, while on Scott's tragic expedition, and Frank Oates, an explorer of Central Africa. The museum is open March to October Tuesday to Sunday 12.00pm to 5.30pm.

## Basingstoke

Unless enthralled by endless office and apartment blocks, visitors can safely ignore the centre of this concrete and steel new town and devote themselves instead to the charms of the surrounding areas.

At the nearby village of Basing, under threat of development, is Basing House. This ruined Tudor palace underwent a two-year siege in the Civil War. Among the prisoners taken was Inigo Jones, the architect. Open April to October, Tuesday to Saturday 2.00pm to 5.30pm.

Wellington Country Park, at nearby Stratfield Saye, is the home of the Duke of Wellington, with woods, parkland, sailing, fishing, riding, nature trails and picnic areas.

## Burghclere

Home of the Sandham Memorial Chapel. Built in 1926, its walls are covered with *Stanley Spencer* murals depicting war scenes from the Salonica front in the 1914–18 war.

Kingsclere and Watership Down are nearby.

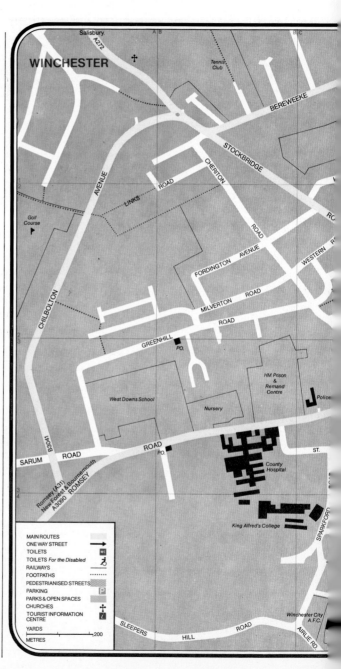

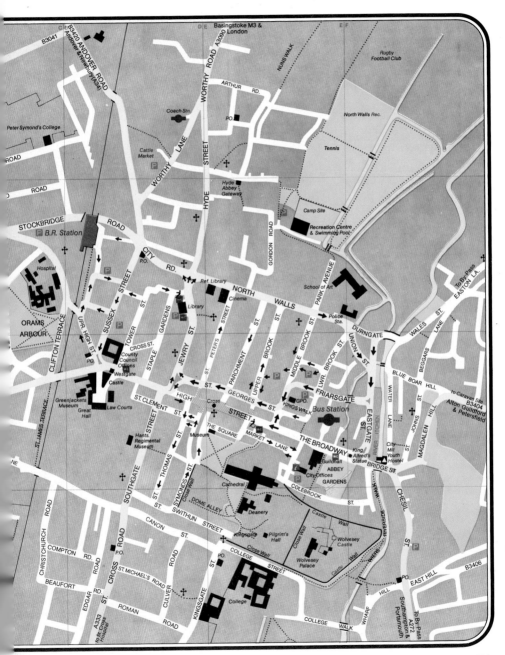

# Portsmouth

Hampshire has two big cities, both of great maritime importance, and only a few miles apart.

As Southampton is to passenger shipping, so the neighbouring city of Portsmouth is to Naval shipping. Portsmouth also faces the Isle of Wight, at the point where the Solent gives way to the channel, known as Spithead.

The city is surrounded by interlocking towns, along a coastline of jigsaw complexity. A peninsula which accommodates the towns of Fareham and Gosport forms one side of Portsmouth Harbour. Across the harbour is the city of Portsmouth itself, merging into the resort of Southsea. Beyond Portsmouth and Southsea lies the resort of Hayling Island, linked to the mainland by a road to Havant. East of Hayling Island is Chichester Harbour and the resorts of Sussex.

Portsmouth is an excellent base from which to explore the Meon Valley, what remains of the Forest of Bere, and the neighbouring areas of Sussex.

## Portsmouth (map p 234)

The first home of the Royal Navy and a city forever linked with Lord Nelson.

Today, more than 175 years later, visitors can retrace the footsteps of this great sea-faring man as he embarked for Trafalgar aboard his flagship *Victory*.

The ship has been lovingly preserved as 'the proudest sight in Britain', and the sight of her, full colours flying, on the anniversary of Nelson's death still brings a lump to the throat.

East and west Portsmouth is flanked by natural harbours. Portsmouth Harbour itself is fringed with jetty, wharf and crane to serve the warships at anchor.

Langstone Harbour, to the east, has been designated an area of scientific interest. This is the centre for fishermen, yachtsmen, skin-divers and bird-watchers. It also includes a nature reserve.

Old Portsmouth has many fine period buildings, particularly the 17th- and 18th-century houses on Lombard Street.

An integral part of Portsmouth is Southsea, at the end of the town. This is an unashamedly noisy English seaside holiday resort, with four miles of beaches.

*HMS Victory and Portsmouth Royal Naval Museum* Nelson's famous flagship, containing many relics of the great man, his officers and crew. Open weekdays 10.30am to 5.30pm, Sunday 1.00pm to 5.00pm.

*Dickens Birthplace Museum* The Georgian house in Old Commercial Road, where the author was born in 1812. Open weekdays 10.30am to 5.30pm, Sunday 1.00pm to 5.00pm.

*Southsea Castle* Built by Henry VIII in the 16th century as part of his coastal defence scheme. It is now a museum of Portsmouth's military history. Open weekdays 10.30am to 5.30pm, Sunday 1.00pm to 5.00pm.

*Royal Marines Museum*, at Eastney. The 312 years of Royal Marine history are illustrated. Open Monday to Friday 10.00am to 4.30pm, weekends 10.00am to 12.30pm.

*Round Tower and Point Battery* A medieval tower commanding the entrance to Portsmouth Harbour.

*Fort Widley* Built by Lord Palmerston in 1868, this is one of the remarkable Victorian fortresses which encircle Portsmouth. Open April to September daily 2.00pm to 6.00pm.

*Eastney Pumping Station and Gas Engine House* Contains Boulton and Watt reciprocal steam pumps which were installed in 1887, Crossley Gas Engines of 1904 and other interesting historic pumping equipment. Open April to September daily 2.00pm to 6.00pm, steaming at weekends.

*Cathedral Church of St Thomas à Beckett* Founded in the 12th century, with original transepts and chancel.

*Garrison Church* Remains of the ancient hospital Domus Dei, founded in 1212. Charles II married Catherine of Braganza here.

*Sports* Golf; athletics; bowls; ten-pin bowling; swimming; yachting; sailing; tennis; putting.

*Events* Portsmouth Festival, in May; Navy Days, Summer Bank Holiday weekend; Southsea Show, in August.

### Hayling Island

A hugely popular holiday centre. The island divides the tidal waters of Langstone and Chichester Harbours. It is connected to the mainland by a bridge at Havant.

The island is about four miles square and flat, which boosts the summer temperature above the average for the mainland area.

There is magnificent sailing on the Chichester side of the island.

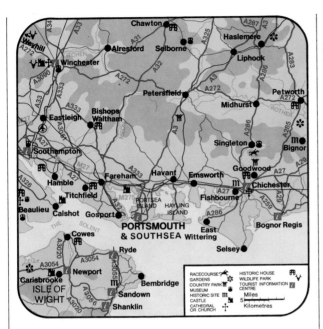

## Fareham

Many interesting Georgian buildings.

*Portchester Castle*, near the town, is a Norman castle on the site of a Roman fort. Open weekdays 9.30am to 5.30pm, Sunday 2.00pm to 5.30pm.

## Titchfield

This little town was once a seaport, but today it is two miles from the mouth of the Meon, across the marshland of Titchfield Haven.

There is much of historical interest here. Titchfield Abbey, dissolved in 1536, was later adapted as a home by the Earl of Southampton. He named it *Place House*.

It was under this roof that Charles I spent his last night as a free man in 1647.

Place House has been ruined since 1781 and is open weekdays 9.30am to 5.30pm, Sunday 2.00pm to 5.30pm.

## Wickham

The birthplace in 1324 of William of Wykeham, who was to become Chancellor of England and founder of Winchester College and New College, Oxford.

The mill here was built in 1813 with timbers taken from the captured American frigate *Chesapeake*.

## West Meon

A compulsory stopping point for all cricket enthusiasts.

This was the home of Thomas Lord, who later moved to St John's Wood in London where he opened a cricket ground, Lord's. Today it is the headquarters of world cricket and a revered centre for students and players of the game.

Lord died in 1832 and is buried in the West Meon churchyard. One of his 'neighbours' is the slightly less beloved figure of Guy Burgess, a Soviet spy and defector.

Each piece of flint in the church walls is of equal size, giving it an almost perfect finish.

## East Meon

Izaak Walton, 17th-century author of *The Compleat Angler*, fished the Meon here and thought highly not only of the waters, but of the outstanding village under and through which they flow.

The trout fishing here is still outstanding and very popular.

## Liphook

*Bohunt Manor* has a woodland garden with a collection of more than 100 ornamental ducks, geese and golden pheasants. Open April to September weekdays 9.00pm to 5.30pm.

## Hambledon

The spiritual home of cricket, although it may not actually be the birthplace of the game, in spite of local claims.

However, there is no doubt that this village and its famous cricket club had a profound influence on the development of the game.

The club was founded in 1760 and gradually developed the laws of the game, many of which are unchanged today. The team, which played on Broadhalfpenny Down, two miles from the village, was powerful enough to defeat teams representing all of England.

Players used to drink at the nearby Bat and Ball inn after matches.

Opposite the pub is a monument to Hambledon Cricket Club.

## Petersfield

Queen Elizabeth Country Park, near the town, has miles of marked trails and footpaths. There are also guided walks and exhibitions at the park centre. Open March to September 10.00am to 6.00pm.

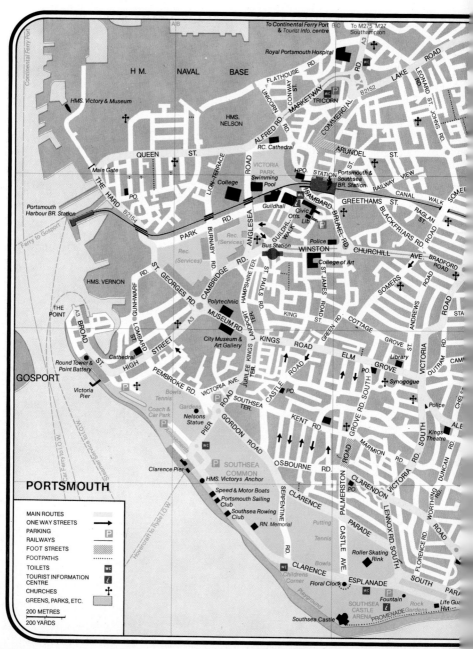

PORTSMOUTH

| | |
|---|---|
| MAIN ROUTES | |
| ONE WAY STREETS | → |
| PARKING | P |
| RAILWAYS | |
| FOOT STREETS | |
| FOOTPATHS | |
| TOILETS | WC |
| TOURIST INFORMATION CENTRE | i |
| CHURCHES | † |
| GREENS, PARKS, ETC. | |

200 METRES
200 YARDS

# Isle of Wight

This holiday island can be reached from Portsmouth, Southampton and Lymington – by ferry, hovercraft and hydrofoil.

The island is three or four miles from the English mainland, 13 miles wide and 23 miles long, and well known for Cowes, with its regatta, the small ports of Yarmouth and Ryde, and the resorts of Sandown, Shanklin and Ventnor. The inland town of Newport is the island's 'capital'.

The Isle of Wight is notable for its mild and sunny climate, its hydrangeas and sub-tropical plants, its blue-clay gorge called Blackgang Chine, the multi-coloured sands of Alum, and a long chalk ridge which ends at a formation called The Needles.

### Ryde

Most visitors arrive on the Island here, by ferry or hovercraft from Portsmouth.

There are six miles of excellent sandy beaches, backed by splendid woods and gardens.

Ryde has a pier stretching half a mile out to sea, making it the second longest in Britain. It was built in 1813 and an electric railway added 67 years later was among the first in the world.

There is a regular train service from the pierhead to Shanklin, with a bus connection to Ventnor.

Seaview is two miles east and has a *flamingo park*, with geese, peacocks, and cranes. Open June to September weekdays 10.30am to 6.00pm, Sunday 2.00pm to 6.00pm.

### St Helens

The houses, cottages and shops in this charming village are beautifully grouped around the green. Many buildings are Georgian.

### Bembridge

With its wide harbour, Bembridge is among the Island's favourite yachting centres.

This quiet village has splendid beaches with safe swimming at low tide.

The *lifeboat station* is open for visits from Spring Bank Holiday to September Wednesday and Thursday 2.00pm to 4.00pm.

Bembridge also has a *windmill*, which is open from Spring Bank Holiday to September weekdays 10.00am to 5.00pm, Sunday 7.00am to 6.00pm.

### Brading

*Osborn-Smith's Wax Museum* is housed in the only timber-framed house on the Island. It is also the oldest building on the Island, dating back to 1499. Open daily 10.00am to 5.00pm.

The 12th-century *church* is noted for the wooden monuments to the Oglander family,

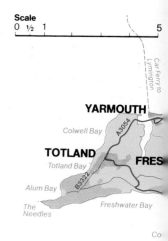

who still live at *Nunwell House* and have done since 1607. The house, with its dolls museum, is open from Spring Bank Holiday to September daily except Thursday 11.00am to 5.30pm.

The village stocks and whipping post are kept in the old town hall, along with the old bear-baiting ring.

There is also a Roman villa with fine examples of mosaic floors. Open Spring Bank Holiday to September weekdays 10.00am to 5.30pm, Sunday 10.30am to 5.30pm.

### Sandown

Sandown Bay, sheltered by Culver Cliff, has five miles of sweeping sandy bay.

It is among the most popular resorts on the Island and is also the home of the *Isle of Wight Museum of Geology*, which is open Monday to Saturday 10.00am to 5.00pm.

### Newchurch

A delightful inland village with old houses and a church dating back to Saxon times.

### Shanklin

This town at the southern end of Sandown Bay has held the

THE SOLENT

Car Ferry & Hydrofoil To Southampton

Hovercraft

COWES
Gurnard

Thorness Bay

Norris Castle

EAST COWES
Osborne House

B3325

B3321

A3021

Fishbourne

Car Ferry To Portsmouth

Passenger Ferry to Portsmouth

Hovercraft to Southsea

Stn.
Stn.

RYDE

SPITHEAD

Puckpool

Seaview

Northwood

A3020

Parkhurst Forest

A3054

Wootton Bridge

A3054

B3330

Newtown

Havenstreet

St. Helen's

Shalfleet

A3054

B3330

B3395

Bembridge

Newbridge

B3401

NEWPORT

Carisbrooke Castle

Arreton

Brading

Whitecliff Bay

Calbourne

A3056

Newchurch

A3055

Brighstone Forest

B3323

Gatcombe

Medina

A3020

A3056

Stn.

SANDOWN

Mottistone

Shorwell

Lake

Brighstone

Yafford

Godshill

A3020

Stn.

SHANKLIN

A3055

B3327

Chale Green

Wroxall

A3055

Bonchurch

Whitwell

Chale

St. Lawrence

VENTNOR

Blackgang Chine

Niton

St. Catherines Lighthouse

THE UNDERCLIFF

---

British sunshine record more times than any other resort.

It sits on the cliff top while a mile of golden beach lies sheltered below with its popular facilities for bathing, boating and sea angling.

Shanklin Old Village is a rare treat with quaint thatched cottages, and The Crab – one of the prettiest pubs on the Island.

The walk from the village through Shanklin Chine to the beach is delightful for it passes through a cleft in the cliff with overhanging trees, plants, ferns and a cascading stream.

John Keats the poet found the climate here much to his liking and the scenery so inspiring that he lived in Shanklin for many years. Keats Green, a spacious cliff-top promenade commemorates his association with the town.

### Luccombe Village

This delightful hamlet has a picturesque chine and a good viewpoint.

### Godshill

This village on a steep hill has a group of magnificent thatched cottages and an early 15th-century church, from which the place takes its name.

The church has many noteworthy paintings and effigies.

The Godshill *model village* and *natural history collection* are both open from April to October daily 10.00am to 5.30pm.

Many tea gardens cater for the throngs of summer visitors.

### Wroxall

The ruins of Appuldurcombe House, formerly a classical 18th-century mansion, are just outside the village. Although the house is now only a shell, the grounds laid out by Capability Brown are still there for strolling.

### Bonchurch

Another old village, complete with a superb duckpond and a tiny Norman church.

Nearby are the solid and respectable Victorian villas

237

where Charles Dickens, William Makepeace Thackeray and Thomas Macaulay stayed during their visits.

## Ventnor

The only town on the southern side of the Island, standing on the edge of St Boniface Down.

Its position makes this the warmest of the resorts and it is known as the 'Madeira of England'.

Much of the town is built on a series of terraces which snake up to the top of the Down – at 785 ft the highest point on the Isle of Wight. It effectively shelters the town and the beach from any winds.

The *Botanic Gardens* have an excellent display of roses – and a museum devoted entirely to the age-old seaside practice of smuggling. Open daily 10.00am to one hour before sunset.

## Niton

Noted for Catherine's lighthouse below the cliffs, which warns shipping of the dangers of this coastline.

The lighthouse stands at the end of Undercliff — a six-mile ledge suitable for cars or walkers, to the west of Ventnor.

Undercliff was formed long ago by landslides and is brightened by palm trees, myrtles and cork trees.

The lighthouse is open to the public at the discretion of the Keeper in charge from 1.00pm to an hour before sunset. No visitors are permitted during fog or on Sundays.

## Chale

The church here has a 15th-century tower. Nearby is the path leading to the dramatic-sounding *Blackgang Chine*, a cleft in the face of the cliff.

It was once used by a band of notorious local smugglers – the Black Gang from whom it is believed to have taken its name.

The path leads deep down into the chine with crags, precipices and sandstone rocks of many colours. From the observation peak there are magnificent views along the south-west coast to the *Needles* and *Needles Lighthouse*. There is also a museum and bazaar. Open daily in summer. Floodlit at night.

## Shorwell

Yet another near-perfect little village, with thatched cottages.

Shorwell boasts an inn with a garden, dovecote, ducks, weeping willows and a brook that actually babbles.

The church dates from the 15th century and has interesting carved pew heads which are set at differing angles, thus creating the illusion that the church is full of worshippers.

Nearby is *Yafford Mill*, a beautifully-restored 18th-century water mill in the centre of a small nature reserve.

On show are the Yafford seals, ornamental wildfowl, rare cattle, sheep and pigs, and a unique collection of farm machinery and tools. There is also a children's play area. Open Easter to October weekdays 10.00am to 6.00pm, Sunday 12.00pm to 6.00pm.

## Brightstone

Once pronounced Brixton, this place has been a winner of the Isle of Wight's Best-Kept Village competition. It is easy to see why.

It is a series of charming cottages standing in clean streets and beautifully-tended small gardens. The partly Norman church has a 14th-century tower.

Grange Chine and Chilton Chine are a mile south and there are magnificent walks over Brightstone Down.

## Mottistone

A delightful spot with a grey stone Tudor manor house and a tree-lined churchyard. The church dates back to the 12th century, but was restored in the 19th century.

Students of archaeology can go much further back in history, for there is a path by the lych gate leading to the Long Stone, a pillar which is part of a long barrow dating from between 2000 and 3000 BC.

## Compton Bay

An excellent sandy beach, set below a splendid cliff-top road with fine views of the sea and of Compton Down.

Nearby is Hanover Point, Brook Bay and the charming village of Brook.

## Freshwater Bay and Peninsula

The Bay is a charming resort at the tip of Compton Bay, set in a sandy dip between the chalk cliffs. At low tide, a cave can be explored. The local church is of outstanding interest for it has a most unusual thatched roof and was built only in 1908.

The peninsula comes to an abrupt end with the massive chalk stacks known as the *Needles*.

Tennyson Down, which leads to the Needles, is named after *Lord Tennyson*, the poet, who liked to take a walk here every day from his home at Freshwater.

His house, called Farringford, is now a hotel. Tennyson lived there for 14 years from 1853 and wrote *Maud* and *Idylls of the King* while in residence.

## Alum Bay

The cliffs here are famous for their multi-coloured layers which produce the Bagshot sands which have 12 distinct shades.

Unavoidably, much of the natural beauty has been eroded by commercialization, with tea rooms, souvenir stalls and even an Alpine chairlift.

The colours – white, grey, yellow, orange, blue, brown,

Cowes . . . home of the Royal Yacht Squadron

beige, red and many more – are the end result of a geological fault which runs right through the Isle of Wight.

### Totland

Totland Bay and neighbouring Colwell Bay can both offer good sands and safe bathing.

Totland is also the home of Island Glass, a fascinating one-man glassware factory with goblets, vases and jewellery on show. Open Monday to Friday 9.30am to 5.30pm.

### Yarmouth

Of all the Island's many resorts, this is the most Continental-looking, bustling with yachts, sights and sounds.

The small *castle* here was built in 1545 by Henry VIII. It is open weekdays 9.30am to 5.30pm, Sunday 2.00pm to 5.30pm.

The ferry from Lymington docks here and it is probably the prettiest and most picturesque way of arriving on the Island.

### Newtown

This ancient borough's prosperity disappeared with the receding sea. All that remains to remind visitors of the past glories is the Old Town Hall.

This 18th-century National Trust building has been restored and is open Easter to September Wednesday, Thursday and Sunday 2.30pm to 5.00pm.

Also of interest is the old stone church.

To the north there is a *nature reserve* and trail running through an unspoiled tidal estuary. This is owned by the National Trust which has succeeded admirably in saving much of the Island's 60 miles of coastline from urban development.

### Calbourne

Another unspoiled village set at the foot of a ridge of downland.

It is noted for Winkle Street, a superb row of ancient stone cottages, thatched and tiled. The village church is 12th- to 13th-century and has some particularly interesting brasses.

### Newport

The Island's capital, lying in its heart. This bustling market town is at the head of the navigable part of the river Medina and has many interesting features.

The beautiful Guildhall was designed by John Nash. Among many other historic buildings are the Grammar School (1614) in which Charles I stayed while conferring with the Roundheads about the Treaty of Newport, the ancient Chantry House (1449), and God's Provident House (1710).

The remains of a *Roman villa* were discovered in the town in 1926. Open June to September

daily except Thursday 10.30am to 4.30pm.

*Carisbrooke Castle*, one of the most famous in England, is only a mile from the centre of Newport. The present castle was begun early in the 11th century. Charles I was imprisoned here in 1648 and was taken to the mainland and execution.

The castle, which is the official residence of the Island's Governor, is open weekdays 9.30am to 5.30pm, Sunday 2.00pm to 5.30pm.

*Parkhurst Forest* to the north-west covers 1,000 acres and is near Parkhurst Prison, one of Britain's top security jails.

### Cowes

This is really two distinct entities – Cowes and East Cowes, separated by the river Medina.

Cowes is, of course, the home of British *yachting* and the headquarters of the Royal Yacht Squadron.

The Squadron operates from *Cowes Castle*, which was built by Henry VIII. Outside are 22 brass guns, ready to fire Royal Salutes and start the races.

The ruined castle was built by John Nash. Norris Castle, an 18th-century house not open to the public, is north of the town.

A floating bridge across the harbour leads to East Cowes, where the first hovercraft was designed and built. It is also the bus ferry terminal connecting with Southampton.

A mile south-east is *Osborne House*, the favourite home of Queen Victoria. She died there in 1901.

The state and private apartments are furnished as they were in Victoria's time. Swiss Cottage, a play house built for the royal children, contains the Queen's writing table and her collection of porcelain.

Osborne House is open Easter to mid-October Monday to Saturday 10.00am to 5.00pm.

# West Sussex and Brighton

Between the little festival city of Chichester and the Regency resort of Brighton lie a string of well-known seaside towns.

Chichester itself is a few miles from the open sea, on a deep inlet and harbour. Then come Bognor Regis, Littlehampton, Worthing, Shoreham and Hove, the latter merging into Brighton.

Inland, but only a few miles from the coast, the South Downs curve through the county. A long-distance footpath along the Downs starts just across the Hampshire border at Buriton and runs through the whole of West Sussex, into East Sussex, ending at Eastbourne and Beachy Head.

Further inland, beyond the Downs, rural Sussex has become very much commuter country, though country life survives, and there is still a market-town character to important centres like Horsham.

## Chichester

This picturesque cathedral city was an important tribal settlement long before the Romans arrived.

When the Romans had gone, the Saxons took over and it was given to Cissa, son of the chieftain Aella. The new ruler called his domain Cissa's Caester.

Chichester is a city in a most attractive setting for it is surrounded by golden fields, woods and salt marshes, and it is dominated by the spire of the cathedral.

The harbour is one of the largest semi-enclosed stretches of tidal water in Britain and is an obvious magnet for yachtsmen and other small boat users.

There are many fine 18th-century houses, particularly around St Martin's Square and the Pallant area.

The *cathedral* was begun in 1091 by the Norman Bishop Ralph and it has a beautiful soaring nave, a magnificent window in the transept, and a graceful tapering spire 277 ft high.

There is also a 15th-century market cross in the city and many long stretches of the Roman wall.

St Mary's Hospital is a group of almshouses founded in 1158, and is now the setting for a Summer Festival of plays. The almshouses are open Tuesday to Friday 11.00am to 12.00pm, 2.00pm to 5.00pm.

The *Festival Theatre* was built in 1962 and has now established an international reputation as the home of the famous Chichester Festival which annually presents classical and modern plays with the world's leading actors.

Two miles west of the city is *Fishbourne Roman palace*, the largest Roman excavation in England. It was occupied from the 1st to 4th centuries and many magnificent mosaic pavements remain. Open March to November daily 10.00am to 5.00pm.

*Weald and Downland Open Air Museum* is six miles north of Chichester at Singleton. Historic buildings from the Weald and Downland area of Kent, Sussex, Surrey and Hampshire have been re-erected here.

The exhibits include a 15th-century farmhouse, 18th-century granary, and a 19th-century forge. There is also a woodland trail and picnic area. Open March to September daily except Monday 11.00am to 6.00pm, October Wednesday and weekends 11.00am to 5.00pm, November to March Sunday only 11.00am to 4.00pm.

## Bognor Regis

George V convalesced here in 1928, after which the Regis was added to the town's name.

It began life as a Saxon village, developing into a medieval fishing port and, from 1790, into a fashionable resort.

There are five miles of good sand, sea fishing, a pier and even a holiday camp.

## Goodwood House

Home of the Duke of Richmond and Gordon. The superb 18th-century building contains fine furnishing, tapestries, porcelain, and an important collection of paintings by Van Dyck and Stubbs.

Open Sunday and Monday from May to September, also Easter Sunday, and on Tuesdays in August.

The estate includes the beautiful racecourse which is set on the downs above the house. It is here that the famous Goodwood meeting is held.

## West Dean

Flint and half-timbered houses adorn this charming village in the valley of the river Lavant. There is a *botanical garden* boasting fine displays of azaleas, magnolias and rhododendrons. Open March to September, Sunday 2.00pm to 7.00pm.

Dominating the town . . . Arundel Castle

from its mighty battlements down to the river Arun.

The flag of the Duke of Norfolk, Earl Marshal of England, flies from the castle tower. Next door to this awesome building is the 14th-century church of St Nicholas and the Roman Catholic cathedral of St Philip Neri.

There is a strong catholic influence in Arundel for the Norfolks are one of England's premier RC families. Indeed, St Nicholas' is unique in being one-quarter catholic, while the other three-quarters remain Protestant.

The 1100-acre park is always open, but cars, motor cycles, bikes and dogs are barred. The park contains a delightful cricket ground, for the game was the late duke's passion. Each season the tourists play their first fixture here, against the Duchess of Norfolk's XI.

The castle is open Easter to October Monday to Friday 12.00pm to 5.00pm.

Potters Museum of Curiosity has an unusual collection of small stuffed animals in nursery rhyme tableaux. Open daily 10.30am to 1.00pm, 2.15pm to 5.30pm.

*Arundel Museum and Heritage Centre* relates the history of the town. Open March to September weekdays 10.30am to 1.00pm, 2.00pm to 5.00pm, Sunday 2.00pm to 5.00pm.

*Arundel Wildfowl Reserve*, north of the castle, has a variety of swans, ducks and geese from all over the world. Open summer 9.30am to 6.00pm, winter 9.30am to dusk.

*Fontwell Park racecourse*, four miles west, has 14 National Hunt meetings every year.

## Chilgrove
Excellent spot for walks along the downland, including Bow Hill which is the site of an Iron Age hill fort. Kingley Vale has a yew wood which is said to be the burial ground of Danes killed in battle.

## The Hartings
Home of Emma Hamilton, mistress of Lord Nelson. Uppark, which was her house, is a Queen Anne mansion on the downs a mile south of the hamlets. Owned by the National Trust, it is open March to September Wednesday, Thursday and Sunday 2.00pm to 6.00pm.

## Pulborough
This village on the Arun offers some of the best boating and fishing in all of Sussex.

## Parham House
An Elizabethan mansion with walled garden and deer park,

and a church on the lawn. Little has been altered since Tudor times. Open Easter to October Wednesday, Thursday and Sunday, house 2.00pm to 5.30pm, gardens 1.00pm to 6.00pm.

## Bignor
A village famous as the site of one of the largest *Roman villas* in Britain. There are exceptionally fine mosaics. Open April to October daily 10.00am to 6.30pm.

## Bury
John Galsworthy, author of the *Forsyte Saga* lived and died at Bury House. Turner painted the walks along the Arun, which are still as they were in the picture.

## Arundel
The Norman *castle* dominates the landscape here, with the town seemingly tumbling away

## Littlehampton
This ancient port at the Arun's mouth is now a noted family holiday resort and yachting centre.

The old harbour has a salty tang about it and there is a great

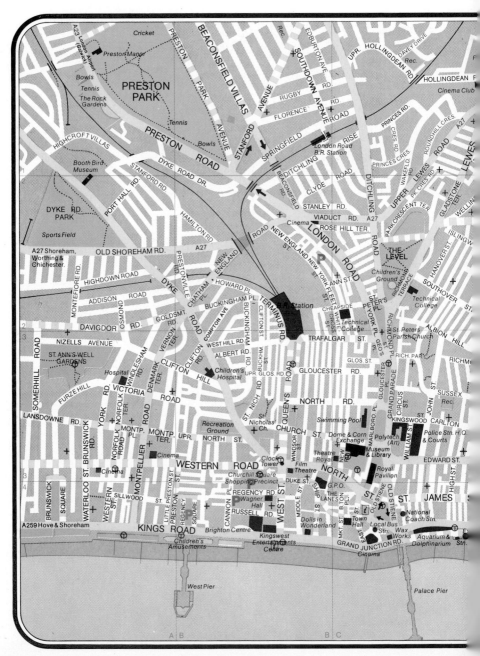

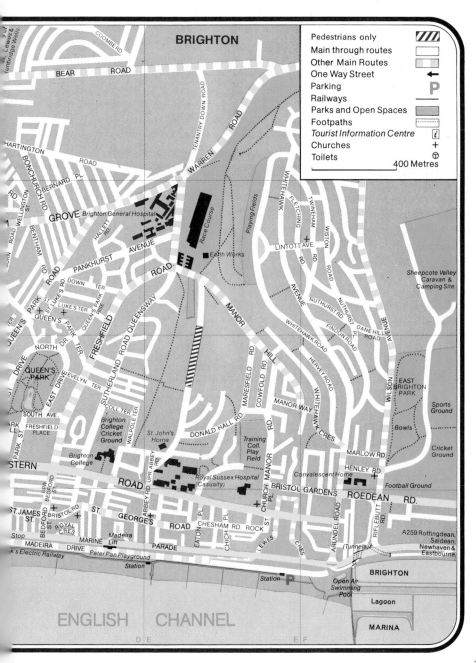

BRIGHTON

| Pedestrians only | ▨ |
| Main through routes | |
| Other Main Routes | |
| One Way Street | ← |
| Parking | P |
| Railways | — |
| Parks and Open Spaces | |
| Footpaths | ⋯ |
| *Tourist Information Centre* | ℹ |
| Churches | + |
| Toilets | ⊕ |

400 Metres

COOMBE RD.
BEAR ROAD
TENANTRY DOWN ROAD
WARREN ROAD
HARTINGTON ROAD
BONCHURCH RD.
BERNARD PL.
GROVE  Brighton General Hospital
WELLINGTON RD.
BENTHAM RD.
HALLETT RD.
AVENUE
Race Course
Earth Works
Playing Fields
WHITEHAWK
FLETCHING RD.
TWINEHAM RD.
WISTON RD.
LINTOTT AVE.
PANKHURST ROAD
ROAD
DOWN TER.
ST. LUKE'S RD.
ST. LUKE'S TER.
QUEEN'S PARK RISE
FRESHFIELD
SUTHERLAND ROAD  QUEENSWAY
MANOR
HILL
AVENUE
NUTHURST RD.
NUTHURST PL.
DANE HILL ROAD
FINDON ROAD
WHITEHAWK ROAD
HERVEY ROAD
Sheepcote Valley Caravan & Camping Site
QUEEN'S PARK TER.
NORTH DR.
EAST DRIVE
EVELYN TER.
QUEEN'S PARK
COLL. TER.
WALPOLE TER.
MARESFIELD RD.
COWFOLD RD.
MANOR WAY
WHITEHAWK CRES.
WILSON
EAST BRIGHTON PARK
Sports Ground
Bowls
Cricket Ground
SOUTH AVE.
FRESHFIELD PLACE
Brighton College Cricket Ground
St. John's Home
DONALD HALL RD.
Training Coll. Play Field
MARLOW RD.
HENLEY RD.
Convalescent Home
Football Ground
Brighton College
UPR. BEDFORD ST.
ROAD
ABBEY RD.
UPR. ABBEY RD.
Royal Sussex Hospital (Casualty)
CHURCH
MANOR RD.
BRISTOL GARDENS
ROEDEAN RD.
ARUNDEL ROAD
RIFLEBUTT RD.
STERN
ST. JAMES ST.
BEDFORD ST.
BRISTOL RD.
ST. GEORGE'S ROAD
ROYAL CRES.
EATON PL.
CHESHAM PL.
CHICH. RD.
ROCK
LEWES ST.
CRES.
A259 Rottingdean, Saldean, Newhaven & Eastbourne
BRIGHTON
Stop
MARINE
Madeira Lift
PARADE
MADEIRA DRIVE
k's Electric Railway
Peter Pan Playground
Station
Station
Open Air Swimming Pool
Lagoon
MARINA
ENGLISH   CHANNEL

D E
E F

expanse of green between the Edwardian and Victorian sea-front houses and the sandy beach.

A funfair sits at one end of the long promenade and there is an interesting 18-hole golf course just across the river mouth, which is reached by ferry.

### Selsey

Selsey Bill is the southernmost point of Sussex and offers excellent views of the coastline and the Isle of Wight.

The monastery, established by St Wilfred in AD 681, later became a cathedral, but the site is now under the waves.

### West Wittering

Once a tiny fishing village, this has been transformed into a 'tasteful' holiday resort.

Cakeham Manor, now in ruins, was once a palace of the bishops of Chichester.

Nearby East Wittering has bungalows and chalets and a beach at low tide.

### Worthing

A flourishing seaside resort with good beaches, safe bathing, a pier and a four-mile promenade studded with concert halls and theatres.

The town started life as a fishing hamlet, but in 1798 Princess Amelia, the youngest daughter of George III, visited it. She liked the place and her good opinion was enough to attract the crowds.

### Steyning

The old gabled houses are a feature of this medieval town. An eccentric local legend has it that the town was founded in the 8th century when St Cuthman who was ambitiously attempting to push his invalid mother from Devon in a wheelbarrow, lost a wheel here and decided to stay on to build a wooden church.

Steyning Round Hill commands a superb view over the Adur Valley.

### Bramber

This village was once the provincial capital of William the Conqueror and an important port on the Adur.

A 76-ft piece of the old Norman castle wall is all that remains of those exciting days.

The bells in the 13th-century church tower were cast in 1536.

### Ditchling Beacon

At 813ft, this is the highest point of the South Downs and it offers walkers magnificent views of the countryside for miles around.

At the village of Ditchling, just over two miles to the north, there is a 16th-century house given by Henry VIII to Anne of Cleves.

### Shoreham-by-Sea

An ideal spot for small-boat sailors, the town lies at the busy mouth of the river Adur. The long beach stretches westwards all the way to Worthing.

### Brighton (*map p 242*)

This one-time tiny fishing village rose to fame in 1750 when a resident named Dr Richard Russell published a book extolling the magical effects of sea air and salt water. The book was widely read and, more to the point, believed.

A few years later the wayward Prince of Wales – later to become George IV – was attracted by the health-giving properties. He lived in the exotic iron-domed *Pavilion*, which is perhaps Brighton's best-known attraction.

The town's rich historical and architectural heritage derives from the Regency period. The town owes not only the graceful buildings, but also its pervading sense of fun, to those days.

Many dignified examples of Regency architecture can be found along the sea front and in the older parts of town.

Particularly notable are the windows and balconies in the

244

terraces, crescents and squares including Regency Square. There is a Georgian manor in Preston Park.

Reminders of the years before the stylish Regency bucks made Brighton famous can still be found.

The fascinating series of byways, known as The Lanes, are a step back to the days of the old fishing village of Bright-helmstone. The tightly-packed houses in these narrow, twisting passages were fishermen's cottages in the 17th century. Today they are mainly antique shops.

Brighton has three open-air swimming pools and two piers. The aquarium stands beside the famous Palace Pier. Just about the only thing the town lacks is a sandy beach – Brighton is all pebbles.

The town is only marginally less busy in the winter these days, for the massive new Conference Centre attracts delegates from all over the country.

*Royal Pavilion* The creation and seaside home of the Prince Regent. This dazzling palace was started in 1787 by Henry Holland, and rebuilt from 1815 by John Nash, in the style of the moghul palaces and mosques of India. On his succession, George IV lavished vast sums on the Chinese interior. The 23 State Rooms are still furnished in the original style, and include the King's Apartments, Banqueting Room and Great Kitchen. Open summer daily 10.00am to 8.00pm, winter 10.00am to 5.00pm. The Regency Exhibition is held from July to September.

*Royal Crescent* Facing the sea west of Kemp Town, it was built from 1799 and is faced in distinctive mathematical tiles.

*St Peter's Parish Church* Splendid example of the Gothic Revival style, designed in 1824 by Sir Charles Barry, architect of the House of Commons.

*St Nicholas Church* The town's

The Lanes . . . originally an old fishing village

14th-century mother church, containing several interesting monuments and a superbly-carved Norman font.

*Volks Electric Railway* One of the first in Britain, running 1½ miles along the front from the aquarium to Black Rock swimming pool.

*Preston Manor* This fine house, with the original furnishings, retains the atmosphere of a country gentleman's house from the time of George II. Open Wednesday to Saturday 10.00am to 5.00pm, Sunday 2.00pm to 5.00pm.

*Events Brighton Arts Festival*, in May; *Brighton Carnival*, in July and August; *Brighton Expo*, in August; *Seafront Art Exhibition*, daily during summer; *Royal Automobile Club Veteran Car Run*, from Hyde Park, London, to Madeira Drive, Brighton, in November.

## Hove

A resort inextricably linked with Brighton. There are many good parks and gardens, including a scented garden in St Ann's Well.

Palmeira Square can boast a fine floral clock, something that is sadly disappearing from many towns in England.

All Saints Church was designed in 1890 and is a superb structure containing a carved high altar and screen.

## Plumpton

This pretty village is best-known as the home of an attractive racecourse.

*Plumpton Place*, the 16th-century moated manor, was magnificently restored in the 1920s by Edward Lutyens.

Royal connections are never far away in this part of the county, for on the downs to the south is a V-shaped plantation of trees, put there to celebrate Queen Victoria's Golden Jubilee in 1887.

## Lewes

The county town of East Sussex, with 1,000 years of history. A Norman castle ruin, medieval streets and many Georgian buildings provide a visually exciting mixture. The castle is open from April to October daily 10.00am to 5.00pm, closed Sunday in winter.

Lewes Racecourse is northwest, and so is Mount Harry, the scene in 1264 of the Battle of Lewes when the barons under Simon de Montfort defeated Henry III.

## Rottingdean

Rudyard Kipling once lived here, in a house on the Green. He eventually left because of the interference of sightseers.

The village is also the home of Roedean, the ultra-exclusive public school for girls.

# East Sussex

The administrative county of West Sussex meets its sister East Sussex near Brighton, but the difference in their characters becomes more pronounced beyond Beachy Head. At this point, the coastline curves into Pevensey Bay, presenting the visitor with a further group of Sussex resorts before reaching its conclusion at Dungeness, in Kent.

This group includes the peaceful town of Eastbourne, the small resort of Bexhill, the adjoining resorts of St Leonard's and Hastings, the latter of great historical import, and finally Rye.

Inland, Lewes is the county town. It is an agreeable small town, rich in history and quite dramatically set into the Downs. Many houses in Lewes have tiled upper façades, a style characteristic to the county, and elsewhere in East Sussex weather-boarding is a typical mode of building.

## Tourist Information Centres
Memorial Hall, Langton House, High Street, Battle, East Sussex.
De La Warr Pavilion, Marina, Bexhill, East Sussex. (0424) 212023
3 Cornfield Terrace, Eastbourne, East Sussex. (0323) 27474
Shopping Precinct, Terminus Road, Eastbourne, East Sussex. (0323) 27474
Lower Promenade, Grand Parade, Eastbourne, East Sussex. (0323) 27474
4 Robertson Terrace, Hastings, East Sussex. (0424) 424242
Car Ferry Terminal Car Park, Newhaven, East Sussex. (079 12) 4970
The Downs, Sutton Road, Seaford, East Sussex. (0323) 892224

## Eastbourne
A very popular resort, with miles of sandy beaches. The town is gracefully planned with tree-lined streets and is sheltered by the 575 ft high Beachy Head.

Eastbourne rises on the downland slopes to the west, but is mainly at sea level, reaching eastwards across a broad plain to Pevensey and Norman's Bay.

In Saxon times, King Alfred owned the Royal Manor of Bourne, which was bought by three Sussex families in 1555. It was then known as East Bourne. By the end of the 18th century the land belonged to the Gilbert and Cavendish families. When George III's children stayed here in 1780, the town's popularity as a resort became established.

The rising prosperity of the Industrial Revolution encouraged William Cavendish, later the Seventh Duke of Devonshire, and John Gilbert to launch the town's real development.

The town covers more than 11,356 acres, several hundred of which are preserved as parks, gardens and open spaces. These include the Manor Gardens, Gildredge Park, Hampden Park, Princes Park and Motcombe Park.

The *Carpet Gardens* on the sea front are world-famous.

There is fishing, an amusement arcade, showbar, and a glass-animal workshop on the *pier*.

The *Congress Theatre* and the *Devonshire Park Theatre* offer a variety of entertainment.

Each June the *Colgate Women's International Tennis Championships* attract the world's top players, and cricket is played during the season at Saffrons Cricket Ground.

*Tower 73* A restored martello tower built as part of the defence during the Napoleonic wars. It houses material on the construction and history of the

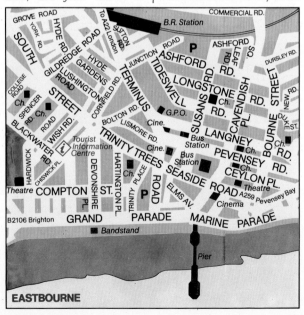

EASTBOURNE

tower. Open Easter to September daily 10.00am to 5.30pm.

*Royal National Lifeboat Museum* Britain's first permanent lifeboat museum. Open Easter to September daily 10.00am to 4.00pm.

*Towner Art Gallery* An 18th-century manor house set in beautiful public gardens. 19th- and 20th-century British painters, and temporary exhibitions. Open weekdays 10.00am to 5.00pm, Sunday 2.00pm to 5.00pm.

*St Mary's* The town's parish church. Saxon origins, rebuilt by the Normans.

*All Souls* 19th-century church in Byzantine style.

*Pilgrims* 14th-century half-timbered house.

*Lamb Inn* Pub dating back to the 13th century. An underground tunnel once used by smugglers linked this inn with St Mary's Church.

*Redoubt* Bowls, tennis, putting, crazy golf, aquarium and the Treasure Island Play Centre for children.

*Sports* Angling; boat fishing; archery; badminton; tennis; swimming; bowls; county cricket; football; golf; putting; miniature golf; croquet; sailing; squash; sea cruises; motorboat and speedboat trips; hang-gliding at Beachy Head.

## Beachy Head

Among the highest cliffs on the south coast. It towers 534 ft above the sea and has a lighthouse at its foot, beaming 16 miles into the Channel.

For those willing to brave the sea breezes, an open-top bus runs here from Eastbourne and back.

Between Beachy Head and Birling Gap – a strange cleft in the South Downs – on the cliff is Belle Tout – the old lighthouse.

## Westdean

*Charleston Manor,* a mile north of this mellow village, is a pleasing combination of Norman, Tudor and Georgian styles. It was once owned by a man named Cerlestone, who was William the Conqueror's Cupbearer. Gardens open daily 11.00am to 6.00pm, house by written application to the Manor.

## Alfriston

A picturesque village in the Cuckmere valley full of old houses. Outside the *Star Inn* is a wooden figure believed to be the figurehead from a 17th-century Dutch ship wrecked in the Channel.

To the south of the village is the tiny church of *Lullington,* only 16 ft square.

At *Drusillas Corner,* nearby, is *Drusilla's Zoo,* open daily 11.00am to 6.00pm.

The *Valley Wine Cellars* are also here and the vineyards are open to the public. Ring (032 182) 532 for details.

## Wilmington

Looking out over this small village is the mysterious *Long Man of Wilmington,* on Windover Hill. 231 ft high, he holds a staff in each hand, and some say that he is guarding the gates of hell. Although he was first recorded in 1779, he may well date back to the 6th century.

There is a ruined 12th-century priory. The yew tree in the churchyard is over 1,000 years old.

## Seaford

Some medieval houses still remain in the old town. There are magnificent views of the *Seven Sisters* – the spectacular 500-ft high chalk cliffs – from Seaford Head, where there are also the remains of a pre-Roman camp.

## Newhaven

This is a busy cross-Channel port, with a beach and a shingle bank. The town became known as New Haven in 1579 when a freak storm altered the course of the river Ouse and diverted it here from Seaford.

## Michelham Priory

An Augustinian priory founded in 1229 around a moat. It has been restored and the gatehouse dates from 1385. Open March to October daily 11.00am to 5.30pm.

## Heathfield

A Sunday market is held by the Crown Inn.

The *Merrydown Wine Company* operates from Horam, and wines and cider are produced. The vineyards are open to the public. Ring (043 53) 2254 for details.

## Burwash

*Rudyard Kipling* lived half a mile south of this village at *Bateman's,* where he wrote *Puck of Pook's Hill* and *Rewards and Fairies.* It is a Restoration period house. Open March to October daily except Friday 2.00pm to 6.00pm, Monday to Thursday 11.00am to 12.30pm from June to September.

## Sheffield Park

Garden and five lakes owned by the National Trust, laid out in 18th century. Open March to September Tuesday to Saturday 11.00am to 7.00pm Sunday 2.00pm to 7.00pm, October to November Tuesday to Saturday 11.00am to 5.00pm Sunday 2.00pm to 5.00pm.

The *Bluebell Railway* runs from the Park to Horsted Keynes, five miles away. There are 20 steam trains. Open January, February, March, April, November and December weekends, May and October Wednesday and weekends, June to September daily.

## Bodiam

Near the biggest hop farm in Britain, the Guiness estate, is the ruined *Bodiam Castle,* built in 1386 to discourage French raiders from sailing up the river Rother. Owned by the National Trust open March to October daily 10.00am to 7.00pm, November to March Monday to Saturday 10.00am to sunset.

## Rye

Once an important port, Rye is now several miles from the sea, which began to recede in the 16th century.

*Henry James* the novelist lived at *Lamb House*, from 1898 until his death in 1916. Owned by the National Trust, it is open March to October, Wednesday and Saturday 2.00pm to 6.00pm.

The *Church of St Mary* dating back to 1120 has a clock with Quarter Boys who chime the hour.

In Mermaid Street is the famous *Mermaid Inn* – the town's largest medieval building. Smugglers used to drink here as late as the 18th century.

## Winchelsea

This attractive town is set on the opposite hill to Rye, and was submerged in the 13th century. A new town was built by Edward I to a regular grid plan.

## Hastings

This is not, as is popularly believed, the site of the Battle of Hastings at which the Norman Conquest got so successfully under way. That event took place a few miles away at Battle.

In spite of this, Hastings is a thriving and deservedly popular resort and was one of the original Cinque Ports.

The east end of the town is where to find the spirit of old Hastings, for there narrow winding streets, lined with timbered houses, tumble down to the old harbour area.

The harbour is a magnet for lovers of fresh fish, for the day's catch is unloaded straight from the boats on to the beach and then sold. Plaice, codling, crab and lobsters are among the possibilities offered to the many buyers.

Hastings' centre is mainly Victorian, but has a number of good Regency buildings in addition to modern shops and offices.

To the west is the sister town of St Leonards, which was laid out early in the last century. This is the place for small hotels and boarding houses.

Near to the 13th-century Hastings Castle are *St Clement's Caves*, which cover an area of three miles. Needless to say, these have for centuries been popular with smugglers. Open daily 10.00am to 5.30pm.

The *Hastings Embroidery*, depicting almost a century of English history from the Conquest, is on permanent display in the Town Hall.

The last of the Hastings Luggers built for sail can now be seen at the Fishermen's Museum. Open daily except Friday 10.00am to 12.00pm, 2.30pm to 5.00pm.

*Yew Tree Farm* at Westfield is a vineyard open to the public. Ring (0424) 752501 for details.

## Beauport Park

There are 900 acres of fine woodland in which is set a splendid Georgian mansion, once the residence of the Governor of Quebec, General James Murray. The house is now an hotel.

## Battle

This town stands on the site of the Battle of Hastings in 1066.

It was here that Harold's army were tricked into believing that the Normans were running away and were then defeated as they chased after them.

It was William's solemn vow that he would build an abbey on the spot if he won. He fulfilled his promise and *St Martin's Abbey* was built and then consecrated in 1094.

It was duly dissolved by Henry VIII and is now partly a girls' school. However, the grounds and some other buildings are still open daily 10.00am to 5.00pm.

## Bexhill

More than half the population of this resort are retired, so the pace is somewhat more leisurely than at Eastbourne or Brighton.

However, Bexhill can boast a fine entertainment complex, the *De La Warr Pavilion*, overlooking the beach. It has a theatre, ballroom, concert hall, sun terraces and restaurants.

## Pevensey

The famous *castle* dominates everything in this attractive village. It is now a ruin and covers 10 acres. Open daily 10.00am to 5.00pm.

The village of Pevensey has many interesting old houses. For example, *Mint House* was built around 1340 on the site of a Norman mint. This is now a museum, including rooms which were once the haunt of smugglers. Open Easter to September weekdays 11.00am to 5.00pm, Sunday 2.00pm to 5.00pm.

## Herstmonceux

Housed in the *castle* is the *Royal Greenwich Observatory*. The surrounding area is dotted with four large aluminium telescopes, the most famous being the *Isaac Newton Telescope* – built in 1967 and one of the most powerful in the world. The observatory and gardens are open March to October Monday to Friday 2.00pm to 5.30pm weekends 10.30am to 5.30pm.

## Berwick

Murals painted by *Duncan Grant*, *Vanessa Bell* and *Quentin Bell* from 1941 to 1942 decorate the walls of the church of St Michael and All Angels in this small village.

# Kent Coast

They may only be made of chalk, but the White Cliffs of Dover are for millions of visitors, and more especially for returning exiles, the physical embodiment of England.

Dover itself is an important port for channel traffic, and it is surrounded by towns with a place deep in both the history and the heart of English life: Folkestone, Deal, Sandwich, Ramsgate, Margate and Whitstable.

A few miles inland is a town with perhaps the greatest of all claims to historical importance – Canterbury, dominated by the foremost of all Anglican churches.

Further inland, the North Downs spread themselves through the north and east of the county, and there are hop gardens near the brewing town of Faversham.

**Tourist Information Centres**
Pierremont Hall, Broadstairs, Kent. (0843) 68399
22 St Peters Street, Canterbury, Kent. (0227) 66567
Time Ball Tower, Sea Front, Deal, Kent. (030 45) 61161 Ext. 263
Townwall Street, Dover, Kent. (0304) 205108
Portakabin, A2 Diversion, Whitfield, Dover, Kent.
Town Hall, Dover, Kent. (0304) 206941
The Precinct, Folkestone, Kent. (0303) 53840
Council Offices, 1 Richmond Street, Herne Bay, Kent. (022 73) 66031
Marine Terrace, Margate, Kent. Thanet (0843) 20241/1
The Ramsgate District Office, Queen Street, Ramsgate, Kent. Thanet (0843) 581261
1 Tankerton Road, Whitstable, Kent. (0227) 272233

## Hythe

This quiet and pleasant seaside town was once a port of great importance to the British defences. It was named as one of the Cinque Ports during the Middle Ages and had special responsibility in warding off invaders from Europe.

The threat of invasion from Napoleon resulted in the construction of the Royal Military Canal, during the early years of the 19th century. Now the canal is a focal point in the town. It is lined with trees and flowers and is the scene of a water pageant held biennially during August.

For those who are interested in the ghoulish there are 2,000 human skulls and 8,000 thigh bones to be seen in the crypt of St Leonard's Church. They date from between 1200 and 1400, and are similar to bones found in Spitalfields Market in London.

The Norman castle at nearby Saltwood has a number of distinctions. In 1170 four knights spent a night in the castle before going on to Canterbury to murder Thomas à Becket, Archbishop of Canterbury, the following day. The castle was damaged during an earthquake in the 16th century.

## Ashford

Inland from Hythe up the river Stour is Ashford. The town has a shopping centre, some medieval houses and some industry. It is a good touring centre for the North Downs and there is a vineyard open to the public at Little Whatmans, Biddenden, Ashford, Kent. Telephone R A Barnes, Biddenden Vineyards Ltd. (0580) 291237.

## Folkestone

With nearby Dover, this is one of the south's major Channel ports with frequent ferries travelling to and from France.

Unlike Dover, it is also a holiday town in its own right. The picturesque harbour is in the Old Town where there is a network of fascinating cobbled streets.

William Harvey, the man

On the top of the white cliffs . . . Dover Castle

249

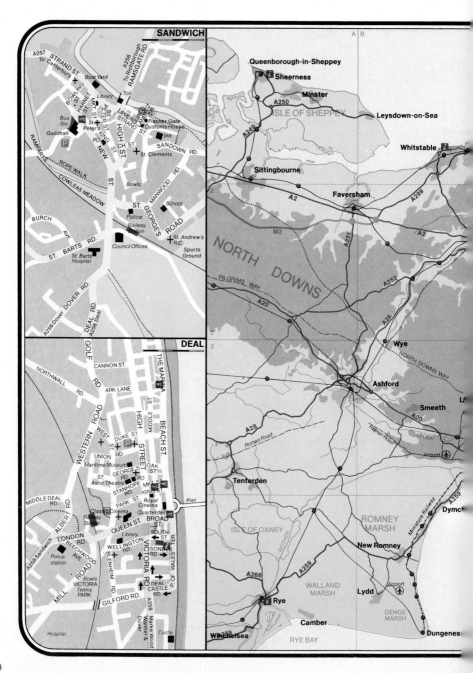

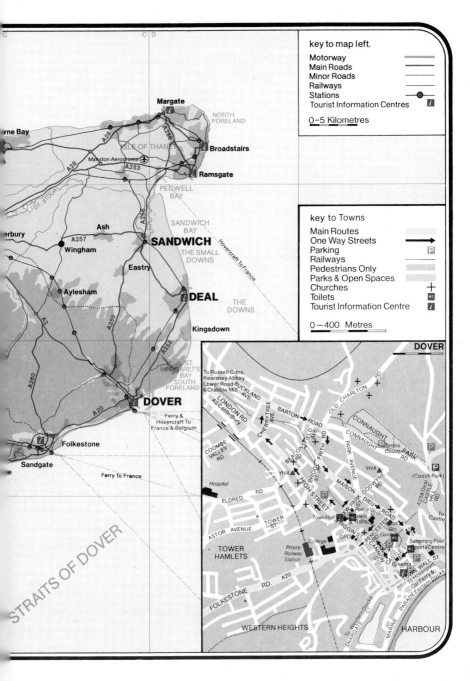

key to map left.

Motorway
Main Roads
Minor Roads
Railways
Stations ●
Tourist Information Centres 𝑖

0-5 Kilometres

key to Towns

Main Routes
One Way Streets →
Parking P
Railways
Pedestrians Only
Parks & Open Spaces
Churches +
Toilets WC
Tourist Information Centre 𝑖

0-400 Metres

Margate 𝑖

NORTH
FORELAND

ISLE OF THANET
Broadstairs
Manston Aerodrome ✈
A253
Ramsgate

ne Bay
A28
A28
FGT. STOUR
A253

PEGWELL
BAY

SANDWICH
BAY

Ash
A257
Wingham
SANDWICH

THE SMALL
DOWNS

Eastry

DEAL

erbury
Aylesham

THE
DOWNS

A2
A259
A258
Kingsdown

ST.
MARGARET'S
BAY
SOUTH
FORELAND

DOVER

A20
Ferry &
Hovercraft To
France & Belgium

Folkestone 𝑖

Sandgate

Ferry To France

STRAITS OF DOVER

Hovercraft To France

DOVER

To Russell Gdns.
Kearsney Abbey
Lower Road
& Crabble Mill

To Canterbury

LONDON RD.

BUCKLAND
AVE.

BARTON ROAD

OLD CHARLTON RD.
CONNAUGHT RD.

CHERRYTREE AVE.

CONNAUGHT
PARK

Tennis
Courts

COOMBE
VALLEY
RD.

BEACONSFIELD RD.

FRITH RD.

PARK AVENUE

CONNAUGHT RD.

YHA

(Coach Park)
P

Hospital

ELDRED RD.

YHA

HIGH STREET

BRIDGE ST.

MAISON

GODWYNE RD.

CASTLE HILL RD.

To
Castle

A258 Deal

ASTOR AVENUE

TOWER
ST.

NEW PARK DIEU ROAD

MAISON

Police Coll.

Town Hall

BIGGIN ST.

Bowls
Gdns

GPO

PERCESTER

Bus
Stn.

Gardens

Swimming Pool
Sports Centre

TOWER
HAMLETS

Priory
Railway
Station

College

CANNON ST.

CASTLE ST.

Cinema

TOWN WALL ST.

FOLKESTONE RD.

A20

To Hovercraft
Car Ferry &
Eastern Docks

MARINE PARADE

SNARGATE ST.

WESTERN HEIGHTS

To Western Docks

HARBOUR

251

who discovered how blood circulates, was born in Folkestone in 1578. There is a memorial window to him in the Church of St Mary.

## Dover (map p 251)

The area around Dover has earned the name 'Gateway of England' through its position at the most south-easterly point of England. Dover, as the principal Channel port, has aptly been termed Key to the Gate.

In spite of extensive war damage and massive rebuilding, Dover still has a generous share of beautiful old buildings. Much of its antiquity has been carefully preserved and this is evident in such ancient buildings as the *Maison Dieu* which was founded in 1203 as a hostel for pilgrims.

The building is now part of the Town Hall buildings, and houses a collection of arms and armour on loan from Buckingham Palace. Open Monday to Friday, 9.00am to 4.00pm and Saturday 10.00am to 12.00 noon.

The *earthen fortifications* on the Eastern Heights were created in the Iron Age. They were later adapted and improved by the Romans who also built a lighthouse, known as the Pharos, here. The beacon is one of the most complete Roman buildings in England.

The *Roman Painted House* was unearthed off Market Street as recently as 1971. It contains Roman wall paintings of brilliant design and colour. Open 10.00am to 5.00pm except Mondays. Admiralty Pier is the longest Marine Walk in the world (4,041 ft) and it offers excellent fishing.

From the pier there is an excellent view of the white cliffs and the 13th-century *castle*. It is well worth the climb to the castle for the panoramic view. The keep was built by Henry II in the 12th century, and the castle is open daily, May to Sep-

'The Weavers', Sandwich . . . part of a 16th-century legacy

tember, 9.00am to 7.00pm, March and October, weekdays 9.30am to 5.30pm, Sunday 2.00pm to 5.30pm, November to February, weekdays 9.30am to 4.00pm, Sunday 2.00pm to 4.00pm.

## Deal (map p 250)

It is a common sight in Deal to see anglers returning from boats, beach or pier with a fine catch of fish. The beach is lined by fleets of fishing boats.

A day spent on the beach swimming or sunbathing has the additional interest of being a point from which to see large ships passing inshore of the treacherous Goodwin Sands, which are five miles out.

Old Deal can be found around Middle Street where tiny lanes run back from the seafront, crowded with 18th-century cottages.

Deal and Walmer castles once

formed part of Henry VIII's coastal defence system. The one at Deal now has a small museum with Iron Age weapons and early pottery. Both castles are open to the public, May to September, daily, 9.30am to 7.00pm, October and March, weekdays 9.30am to 5.30pm, Sunday 2.00pm to 5.30pm. November to February, 9.30am to 4.00pm, Sunday 2.00pm to 4.00pm, April, daily 9.30am to 5.30pm.

Walmer Castle is the official residence of the Lord Warden of the Cinque Ports.

*Time Ball Tower* was used for sending semaphore messages to London during the Napoleonic Wars. It stands at what was once the entrance to the Navy Yard.

Julius Caesar made his initial invasion of England from the beach between Deal and Walmer in 55 BC.

## Sandwich (*map p 250*)

Of the Cinque Ports chosen by Edward the Confessor, this was the most important. However, the sea is now two miles away and the prosperous market-garden town is best-known for having some of Britain's finest golf courses.

The town centre has changed little since the Domesday survey of 1081, and the main feature is the number of half-timbered houses. These are the legacy of the many Flemish weavers who arrived in Kent in the 16th century.

The Guildhall is 400 years old and contains Cinque Port relics. It is open daily.

The Barbican is a medieval tower gate where those wishing to cross the river Stour still have to pay a toll.

St Bartholomew's Hospital is a group of almshouses dating from 1227, the exterior of which is accessible.

Roman ornaments and glass can be seen at Richborough Castle, an early Roman fort. Access at any time.

## Ramsgate

This pleasant town is usually compared with its great rival, Margate. This is unfortunate, for Ramsgate has a totally different atmosphere.

Although it is a major yachting centre and marina, it manages to retain the look and feel of a small fishing port.

There is a hovercraft terminal at Ebbsfleet, on Pegwell Bay, a mile south. Here also is a replica of the Viking long ship Hugin, which was sailed from Denmark in 1949 to mark the 1500th anniversary of the raiders on this shore.

## Broadstairs

Miles of sand in a series of attractive small bays contribute to the enduring charm of this town.

The old town stands around the jetty and it is here that Charles Dickens walked during his breaks from writing *David Copperfield*. His castellated home was called Fort House, but it has since been re-named Bleak House.

Broadstairs holds a *Dickens Festival* every mid-June.

## Margate

This is a very popular seaside holiday resort. It has a huge amusement park called Dreamland, which incorporates a ballroom and a cinema. There are also superb sands, floral gardens, a pier and lido.

The first bathing machines were introduced at Margate back in the mid-18th century.

Visitors who prefer a quieter resort might choose nearby Westgate.

## Whitstable

The leading oyster port in England. It has been famous for this delicacy since Roman times.

This beautiful little town has a wealth of old streets, inns and shipyards.

## Canterbury

This ancient city had already been occupied for 350 years when the Romans arrived in AD 43. It had been the settlement of the Belgae tribe, but the invaders turned it into the fortress camp of Durovernum.

The city is dominated by the beautiful *cathedral*, which is the Mother Church of Anglicans all over the world.

The first cathedral was built in AD 597 in the town known to the Saxons as Cant-wara-byrig, which means the borough of the men of Kent. Nothing now survives of that cathedral which was built for the baptism of King Ethelbert of Kent by St Augustine.

The cathedral which today attracts millions of visitors was begun in 1067. It has been the goal of pilgrims since the murder of Thomas à Becket, the Archbishop of Canterbury, in 1170. Henry II had carelessly wished the 'turbulent priest' out of his way, and four knights had taken him at his word. Henry was later to walk barefoot to the cathedral in penance.

The shrine to which the Pilgrims walked, which commemorated the murder of Becket, was destroyed during the reign of Henry VIII and the Dissolution of the Monasteries. The stained glass that has survived, however, is amongst the finest in the world.

The cathedral has many items of artistic and historical interest. The 12th-century choir is very beautiful, as is its 12th-century screen. The Trinity Chapel houses the tombs of Henry IV and Edward, the Black Prince.

Pilgrims came from all over the world to visit the shrine of Becket. Those who came from abroad are said to have taken the path that is now the North Downs Way, which now offers walkers splendid views of fields, hop gardens and sea.

People also came from other towns in England, like the pilgrims in Chaucer's *Canterbury Tales*.

A walk around the old lanes of the town leading to the cathedral can be very rewarding. The old houses overhang the streets.

The ruins of *St Augustine's Abbey* near the cathedral have some Saxon and Norman remains.

The town walls, built on Roman foundations, were constructed during the 13th and 14th centuries, and can still be seen. The *museum* at the West Gate, the only surviving gate in the walls, houses exhibits of weaponry and is open to the public on weekdays, from 10.00am to 5.00pm.

To the north of Canterbury is the new University of Kent. In contrast to the old buildings of the town centre and the cathedral, the university has modern, interesting buildings.

# The Medway

As the North Sea coast curls into the Thames estuary, the Isle of Sheppey (once occupied by the Dutch Navy) guards the mouth of the river Medway.

On the Medway, the naval town of Chatham merges into Rochester and Gillingham. Then the river leads the visitor inland to Maidstone, a large market town, Tonbridge, a smaller market town, and the spa of Royal Tunbridge Wells.

This attractive town, where the waters can still be drunk, lies at the heart of The Weald, an area in which fruit, nuts and hops stake Kent's claim to be 'The Garden of England'.

### East Grinstead

Near to the source of the Medway, and just over the Kent border into West Sussex, is East Grinstead, an admirable starting point for exploring The Weald.

The primeval *forest* which covered most of this area of ancient England remains in a few places such as Ashdown Forest which can be reached easily from East Grinstead.

In the town, Sackville College is an outstanding example of Jacobean building. It was founded by the Earl of Dorset in 1619 as a home for the poor and disabled.

### Royal Tunbridge Wells

This is without doubt one of Britain's most elegant towns. In Regency times it was a serious rival to Bath as a spa resort. It was frequently visited by fashionable society.

Many parts of town have remained from those gracious days. For example, the Pantiles is a colonnade of 18th-century shops shaded by magnificent lime trees.

At the far end of the parade is Bath Square where Lord North discovered medicinal springs in 1606. These springs eventually earned the town its title of Royal.

On the western edge of town at Eridge are Bowles Rocks, a 70-ft outcrop of sandstone which is used to train mountaineers. Nearby is High Rocks, which has been a popular picnic spot since the 17th century.

There is a vineyard which can be visited at Priory Farm, Lamberhurst, Tunbridge Wells. Telephone K. McAlpine, 089 278 286 for details.

### Bidborough

This has been named as Kent's best-kept village on two occasions and it is not difficult to see why. There are also magnificent views over the Weald and the North Downs.

### Hever Castle

This moated manor house beside the river Eden was where Anne Boleyn spent her girlhood. A group of single-storey Tudor-style houses were built around the moat in 1903 when the castle was bought by the Astor family. Open Easter to September Tuesday, Wednesday, Friday and Saturday 1.30pm to 6.00pm.

### Tonbridge

One of Kent's main hop-growing centres, and a pleasant market town on the Medway.

Much of the town's fame rests on its famous public school, founded in 1553 by a former Lord Mayor of London. *Jane Austen's* father was a teacher here and one of the school's most famous pupils was *Colin Cowdrey* who became one of the world's finest cricketers.

The river offers good facilities for fishing and there are motor cruisers for hire.

### Penshurst

*Penshurst Place* dominates everything in the village. It was the birthplace in 1554 of Sir Philip Sidney the poet, courtier and soldier. His family has lived here for some 400 years. Open Easter to September daily except Monday and Friday 2.00pm to 6.00pm.

Down in the village itself is the original Leicester Square, enclosed by timbered and tile-hung Tudor cottages. The square was named after the Elizabethan Earl of Leicester.

### Chiddingstone

A magnificent Elizabethan village, kept in immaculate order by the National Trust.

The name comes from the ancient chiding stone which stands near the 19th-century Gothic castle. It was here that annoying chattering women were once chided by the rest of the villagers.

## Chartwell

Once the country home of Sir Winston Churchill, which still attracts many visitors, both to the gardens and the museum with its many souvenirs of the great man's life. Owned by the National Trust open March to November weekends 11.00am to 6.30pm, Tuesday, Wednesday and Thursday 2.00pm to 6.30pm.

There is an impressive bronze statue of Churchill in the nearby town of Westerham.

## Sissinghurst

The castle here was once a prison for 3000 French prisoners of the Seven Years War. It later became the home of writer and poet V. Sackville-West and her husband Sir Harold Nicolson. Owned by the National Trust, the gardens and turret of the castle are open March to October, Monday to Friday 12.00pm to 6.30pm, weekends 10.00am to 6.30pm.

## Maidstone

The original Meddestane of the Domesday Book and still a busy Medway market town.

The 14th-century palace was a residence of the Archbishop of Canterbury until 1538. A *museum of carriages* is opposite the palace. Open Monday to Saturday 10.00am to 1.00pm, 2.00pm to 5.00pm.

*All Saint's Church* is the largest in Kent. The 3-acre *Kentish Vineyards* at Wateringbury is open to the public. Ring (0622) 812655.

## Chatham

This was an almost totally unknown village until Elizabeth I ordered it to be developed into a naval base.

There is still an important and famous Royal Navy Dockyard here, which includes a base for refitting nuclear submarines.

## Upnor

The ruined *castle* here dates

Rochester Cathedral

from 1561. It was built as a fortress to defend Chatham from attack by sea. However, it proved unsuccessful when the Dutch sailed unmolested up the Medway in 1667.

The local fishermen have clearly defined rights and the Whittington Stone marks the limits of their operations.

## Rochester

This cathedral city was a centre of Belgic civilization before the Romans, who later built a fortified camp here which developed into a walled city.

The *cathedral* was founded by King Ethelbert, the Saxon, but the building which stands today is Norman and contains an outstanding library. This includes Textus Roffensis (1115 to 24) and Coverdale's Bible (1535).

The magnificent West Door is the only surviving example in England of a column-figure doorway. It is believed that the late Norman stone figures, defaced by Cromwell's men, are Henry I and Queen Matilda.

Among the tombs are those of St William of Perth, who was murdered in 1201, and Bishop Walter de Merton, founder of Merton College, Oxford.

Rochester and much of the surrounding countryside is synonymous with Charles Dickens. He spent his childhood here and he mentions the town in many of his books.

*Eastgate House Museum* is five minutes walk from here, and just over the Medway at Strood there are boat trips from the pier. Open daily except Friday 2.00pm to 5.30pm.

Pleasure craft dot the waters during the summer months and the Medway Regatta is held in July.

## Gravesend

The point in the Thames Estuary where ships bound for London must take on a pilot to guide them the rest of the way. The ships pass close by the shore and the pilots' cutters can be seen scurrying back and forth throughout the day.

## Sheerness

The main town on the Isle of Sheppey. It has been a naval centre since the time of Charles II.

After the Battle of Trafalgar, Nelson's body was brought to the pier here. Opposite is the Royal Fountain, a naval inn.

255

# Surrey

For all its reputation as a commuter county, Surrey does have its share of open country, especially where the North Downs broaden into what is colourfully described as the Hog's Back, just to the east of Guildford.

This prosperous and pleasant town is the nearest that Surrey can manage to a city, since the county's more thoroughly urban stretches were swallowed by Greater London.

Surrey survives as a house-and-garden county: there is a lovely 19th-century house and rose garden, in National Trust hands, at Polesden Lacey; Winkworth Arboretum near Godalming; Birdworld Zoological Gardens near Farnham; the Royal Horticultural Society Garden at Wisley; and Savill Gardens not far from Windsor, which is across the Berkshire border.

Map legend:
HISTORIC HOUSE
BIRD GARDEN
VIEWPOINT
MUSEUM
GARDENS
COUNTRY PARK
ARCH. SITE
N. DOWNS WAY
CHURCH
PICNIC SITE
ART GALLERY
TOURIST INFORMATION CENTRE
VINEYARD

**Tourist Information Centres**
Farnham Locality Office, South Street, Farnham, Surrey. (048 68) 4014
Civic Hall, Guildford, Surrey. (0483) 67314

## Guildford

Surrey's ancient capital has almost certainly been a borough for 1000 years, if not longer. The first explicit reference to such status was made in 1131, but the presence of a Saxon mint indicates a much earlier date.

The famous 1683 clock on the Guildhall is probably the city's most photographed and painted object. It was made by John Aylward after the guilds had refused him permission to open a shop. After he presented it to the Guildhall he was allowed to open his shop.

Guildford has several noteworthy buildings, including the cathedral and Guildford House. There are two theatres – the Yvonne Arnaud and the Bellerby. Concerts given by the Guildford Philharmonic Orchestra take place at the Civic Hall from September to May.

*Cathedral of the Holy Spirit* The first Anglican cathedral to be built on a new site in the south of England since the Reformation. It was consecrated in 1961.

*Castle* Only the preserved keep of the ruined 12th-century castle remains. The grounds contain flower beds, a bowling green and a bandstand.

*Guildford House* A 17th-century house with features including finely-decorated plaster ceilings. There is also an art gallery which holds many special exhibitions throughout the year. Open Monday to Saturday, 11.00am to 5.00pm.

*Guildford Museum* Archaeology and the history of Surrey. Examples of Wealden iron work and various articles associated with Lewis Carroll. There is also a needlework collection. Open Monday to Saturday, 11.00am to 5.00pm.

*St Mary's* Guildford's oldest ecclesiastical building, dating from Saxon times. The tower is late-Saxon, although the rest is Norman to 13th-century.

*Brass Rubbing Centre* Replicas of

256

monumental brasses can be seen and rubbed.

*Sports Centre* Three swimming pools, badminton, netball, cricket, archery, golf, boxing, fencing, table tennis, keep fit, gymnastics, trampolining.

*River trips* 1½-hour boat trips from Guildford or Farncombe Boathouses. 45-minute trips to St Catherine's Lock and back. Rowing boats, punts and canoes for hire.

*Events Surrey Hard Court Tennis Championships*, in May; *Surrey County Show* at Stoke Park, Spring Bank Holiday; *Guildford Show* at Stoke Park, in August/September; *Surrey Antiques Fair*, in October; *Torchlight Procession and Bonfire*, in November.

## Ewhurst

The church here has a fine Norman doorway. Walkers meet in the village before climbing the 813 ft of Pitch Hill, a mile to the north.

## Godalming

This town has a great sense of history, with winding streets, old half-timbered houses and inns.

One of the latter, the King's Arms, had Peter the Great as a guest in 1698. Czar Alexander and King Frederick William of Prussia dined there together in 1816.

The famous public school of Charterhouse is on the outskirts of town.

*Winkworth Arboretum* is three miles south-east. It is 99 acres of hillside planted with rare shrubs and trees.

## Witley

Home of one of England's oldest pubs. The White Hart is 600 years old and hung with tiles and built on to a hunting lodge used by Richard II.

## Elstead

This charming little village stands on the banks of the Wey

and has a 14th-century church, a bridge with five arches and a Georgian watermill. Nearby the ruins of *Waverley Abbey* are 850 years old and inspired Sir Walter Scott's novel of the same name.

## Frensham

The Great Pond is one of the largest lakes in southern England, and the Little Pond is also quite big. They are excellent for sailing, fishing and birdwatching.

The local church claims to have a genuine medieval witch's cauldron, belonging to a Mother Ludlam, who lived in a cave.

## Farnham

Surrey's most westerly town, and one of the most attractive and unspoilt in the country.

The Pilgrim's Way from Winchester to Canterbury enters Surrey here and traces can still be found on the Hog's Back.

Farnham was the birthplace in 1763 of the author of *Rural Rides*, William Cobbett. The house is now a pub called The Jolly Farmer.

The town's *castle* was built in the 12th century and until 1927 it belonged to the bishops of Winchester. It is now used as a residential college for the Centre of International Briefing, but the Norman keep is open to the public.

*Bird World* at nearby Holt Pound has nearly 1000 birds free flying and housed in large flights and paddocks. Open daily 9.30am to 6.00pm.

## Bagshot Heath

Travellers used to fear venturing on to the heath, for it was a notorious haunt of highwaymen, and other desperadoes.

These days it is a peaceful place, although the adjacent *Bisley Common* is the national centre for marksmen.

## Virginia Water

This lovely woodland lake is 1½ miles in length and is part of Windsor Great Park. The lake was created in George III's time when old marshy streams were dammed.

In 1958 a 100-ft totem pole was put up to celebrate the centenary of British Columbia.

The waters of the lake are a favourite spot for coarse anglers and wildfowl enthusiasts.

## Runnymede

Traditionally, the birthplace of English democracy. This broad meadow on the banks of the Thames is the spot where King John was finally bullied into signing Magna Carta.

There is much American involvement here, for the domed temple at Coppers Hill is a *Magna Carta Memorial* erected by the American Bar Association.

Further up the hill is the John F. Kennedy Memorial, standing on an acre of ground given to the United States.

At the top of the hill is the Air Forces Memorial, commemorating 20,000 airmen who died in WWII and have no known grave.

## Wisley Gardens

The Royal Horticultural Society's 300-acre estate, with magnificent walks among rock gardens blooming with heather and alpine shrubs. Although these gardens are a big attraction for visitors, they also have a practical and academic use.

Experimental work is conducted here on new varieties and there is a training centre for prospective young gardeners.

## Shere

Silent Pool is one mile west of this charming North Downs village. Legend says that a peasant girl drowned after being frightened by King John while bathing there. It is widely believed to be haunted.

# A day out of London

For those wishing to escape from the city, the following is a list, arranged in alphabetical order under county, of just some of the places which can be visited quite easily in a day.

**AVON**
Bath (p 190–2)

**BEDFORDSHIRE**
Bedford (p 36)
Luton (p 35)
Shuttleworth Collection, (p 36)
Whipsnade Park Zoo (p 35)
Woburn Abbey (p 35)

**BERKSHIRE**
Cliveden (p 17)
Courage Shire Horse Centre (p 17)
Eton (p 17)
Maidenhead (p 17)
Mapledurham House (p 17)
Reading (p 17)
Royal Windsor Safari Park (p 16)
Stoke Poges, a peaceful village 6 miles north-east of Maidenhead
Stratfield Saye House, a 17th-century house open daily in summer, except Fridays, 8 miles south of Reading
Savill Garden (p 16)
Windsor (p 16)

**BUCKINGHAMSHIRE**
Beaconsfield (p 28)
Hughenden Manor (p 28)
Milton's Cottage (p 28)
Penn (p 28)
West Wycombe (p 28)

**CAMBRIDGESHIRE**
Anglesey Abbey (p 41)
Cambridge (p 38–9)
Ely (p 40–1)
Haddenham Farmland Museum, open first Sunday of each month 2.00pm to dusk, 6 miles south-east of Ely
Newmarket (p 37)

Peterborough (p 41–2)
Stretham Beam Pumping Engine (p 41)
Thorney Wildlife Park, open daily in summer 10.00am to 6.00pm, 5 miles north-east of Peterborough
Wansford Steam Centre, open at weekends in summer 2.00pm to 5.30pm, 8 miles west of Peterborough
Wildfowl Trust, open daily 9.30am to 5.30pm, 6 miles north of Peterborough

**EAST SUSSEX**
Alfriston (p 247)
Battle Abbey (p 248)
Bodiam Castle (p 247–8)
Brighton (p 244–5)
Devil's Dyke, a local beauty spot near Brighton
Drusilla's (p 247)
Firle Place, open in summer Wednesday and Thursday 2.15pm to 5.30pm, 4 miles south-east of Lewes
Great Dixter, open in summer daily except Monday 2.00pm to 5.00pm, 9 miles north-west of Rye
Hastings (p 248)
Lewes (p 245)
Michelham Priory (p247)
Preston Manor (p 245)
Rottingdean (p 245)
Rye (p 248)
Wilmington (p 247)
Winchelsea (p 248)

**ESSEX**
Audley End (p 44)
Clacton (p 47)
Colchester (p 46)
Layer Marney Tower, open in summer Tuesday, Thursday and Sunday 2.00pm to 6.00pm, 8 miles south-west of Colchester
New Linton Zoological Gardens, open daily 10.00am to 7.00pm, 5 miles north-east of Saffron Walden
Paycocke's House (p 47)
Saffron Walden (p 44)
Southend (p 44)
Thaxted Guildhall and Church, 5 miles south-east of Saffron Walden

**GLOUCESTERSHIRE**
Chedworth Roman Villa, open daily, 7 miles north-east of Cirencester
Cirencester (p 183)

**HAMPSHIRE**
Marwell Zoological Park, rare animals in 200 acres of enclosures, 6 miles south-east of Winchester
Winchester (p 229)

**HERTFORDSHIRE**
Ayot St Lawrence (p 33–4)
Hatfield (p 33)
Knebworth (p 34)
St Albans (p 29–32)

**ISLE OF WIGHT** (p 236–9)

**KENT**
Allington Castle, open daily 2.00pm to 4.00pm, 2 miles north-west of Maidstone
Aylesford Priory, open daily 10.00am to 5.00pm, 3 miles north-west of Maidstone
Broadstairs (p 253)
Canterbury (p 253)
Chartwell (p 255)
Chiddingstone Castle (p 255)
Chilham, a picturesque village, 5 miles south-west of Canterbury
Ellen Terry Museum, Smallhythe, open daily in summer except Tuesday and Thursday 2.00pm to 6.00pm
Fleur de Lis Heritage Centre, Faversham, open weekdays 9.30am to 5.00pm
Folkestone (p 249–52)
Hever Castle (p 255)
Howletts Zoo Park, Bekesbourne, open daily 10.00am to 6.00pm
Knole, open Wednesday to Saturday in summer 11.00am to 5.00pm, 8 miles east of Westerham
Leeds Castle, open in summer Tuesday, Wednesday, Thursday and Sunday 1.00pm to 5.00pm, 5 miles east of Maidstone
Maidstone (p 255)
Owl House, Lamberhurst, open Monday, Wednesday,

Thursday and Friday
11.00am to 6.00pm
Penshurst Place (p 254)
Port Lympne Wildlife Sanc-
tuary, open daily 10.00am to
6.00pm, 8 miles west of
Folkestone
Rochester (p 255)
Romney Hythe and Dym-
church Railway (p 259)
Tenterden, attractive town
Tunbridge Wells (p 254)
Westerham, old Kentish
market town

## NORFOLK
Banham International Motor
Museum, open in summer
10.30am to 6.00pm.
Banham Zoo (p 60)
Bressingham Gardens and
Steam Engine Museum
(p 259)
Diss, a pleasant country town
Grimes Graves (p 60)
Kilverstone Wildlife Park
(p 60)
Thetford (p 59)

## OXFORDSHIRE
Banbury (p 25–6)
Blenheim Palace (p 26)
Broughton Castle (p 26)
Compton Wynates (p 25)
Deddington Castle (p 26)
Oxford (p 21–4)
Rousham House (p 26)
Woodstock (p 26)

## SUFFOLK
Bury St Edmunds (p 54)
Clare Country Park, country
park with castle ruins 10
miles north-west of Sudbury
Easton Farm Park, open
Wednesdays and Sundays in
summer 10.30am to 6.00pm,
7 miles north of Woodbridge
Framlingham Castle, open
daily, 12 miles north of
Woodbridge
Helmingham Hall, moated
house open in summer on
Sundays 2.00pm to 6.30pm,
9 miles north of Ipswich
Ickworth House (p 54)
Ipswich (p 52)
Lavenham (p 52)
Long Melford (p 52)
Museum of East Anglian Life
(p 53)
Norton Bird Gardens, open
daily in summer 11.00am to
7.00pm, 7 miles north-east of
Bury St Edmunds
Orford Castle (p 55)
Saxtead Green Windmill
(p 56)
Sudbury (p 52)
Woodbridge (p 55)

## SURREY
Aldershot, a military town 5
miles north-east of Farnham
Bird World Zoological Gar-
dens (p 257)
Farnham (p 257)

Godalming (p 257)
Polesden Lacey, 19th-
century house, open in
summer daily except Monday
and Friday 2.00pm to 6.00pm
Ripley, a coaching village of
half-timbered houses
Winkworth Arboretum
(p 257)

## WARWICKSHIRE
Stratford-upon-Avon
(p 164–5)

## WEST MIDLANDS
Coventry (p 156)
Kenilworth Castle (p 162)
Warwick (p162–3)

## WEST SUSSEX
Arundel (p 241)
Bluebell Railway (p 247)
Chichester (p 240)
Chichester Harbour (p 240)
Cuckfield, market town dat-
ing from Middle Ages
Fishbourne Roman Palace
(p 240)
Goodwood House (p 240)
Sheffield Park House (p 247)
Wakehurst Place, open daily
10.00am to 5.00pm, 5 miles
north-east of Cuckfield
Weald and Downland Open
Air Museum (p 240)

## WILTSHIRE
Salisbury (p 184)

# Travellers' Information

Whether you are travelling by rail, road or air, the following list of phone numbers should help you have a better, easier journey.

## BY ROAD

### Express coach services
Call your local coach station or company. In London, call either Kings Cross (01) 837 7373 or Victoria (01) 730 0202.

### Motoring
The following centres will provide information on road conditions within a 50-mile radius of each city.
Birmingham (021) 246 8021
Bristol (0272) 8021
Leeds, Bradford, Sheffield and Doncaster (0532) 8021
London (01) 246 8021
Manchester and Liverpool (061) 246 8021
Newcastle and Teesside (0632) 8021
Southampton (0703) 8021

### Weather
Check what the weather will be like by phoning the appropriate city listed below.
*East Midlands*
Lincoln (0522) 8091
Nottingham (0602) 8091

*London* (01) 246 8091
*North West*
(061) 246 8092 (coast)
(051) 275 8091
*Northumbria* (0632) 8091
*South East*
Essex (01) 246 8096
Hampshire/Isle of Wight (0703) 8091
Kent (01) 246 8098
Sussex (01) 246 8097
*West Country*
Bristol (0272) 8091
Gloucester (0452) 8091
*West Midlands*
Birmingham (021) 246 8091
Gloucester (0452) 8091
*Yorkshire*
Leeds (0532) 8091
Sheffield (0742) 8091
*Enquiries* (01) 836 4311

## BY RAIL

For rail information, call your local station. In London, call the following phone numbers for the area specified.
East Anglia (Fenchurch Street or Liverpool Street) (01) 283 7171
Midlands, North West, and Lakes (Euston, Marylebone or St Pancras (01) 387 7070
South East (Victoria or Waterloo) (01) 928 5100
West Country and parts of

West Midlands (Paddington) (01) 262 6767
Yorkshire, Northumbria and parts of East Midlands (King's Cross) (01) 837 3355

## BY AIR

For air information, phone the relevant number below.
Birmingham (021) 743 4272
Bournemouth (02016) 2975
Carlisle flight information via Newcastle (0632) 860966/862191
East Midlands (0332) 810552
Exeter (0392) 66151
Isle of Man (062 482) 3311
Isles of Scilly (072 04) 677
Leeds/Bradford (097 37) 3271 (North East Airlines) (097 37) 5650 (Dan-Air) (097 37) 3251 (Servisair)
Liverpool (051) 427 4101
London (Heathrow) (01) 759 4321
(01) 759 3131 (BEA)
Luton (0582) 36061
Manchester (061) 437 5233
Newcastle (0632) 860966
Newquay (06374) 270
Norwich (0603) 49783
Penzanze (0736) 3871
Plymouth (0752) 78002/76865
Southampton (042 126) 3681
Teesside (032 573) 2811

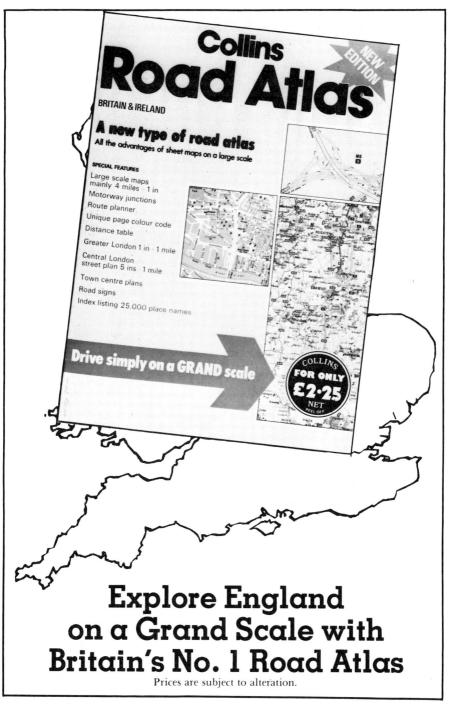

# Useful Addresses

## ACCOMMODATION AND TRAVEL TRADE

**Association of British Travel Agents**
53 Newman Street
London W1
(01) 580 8281

**British Federation of Hotel and Guest House Associations**
23 Abingdon Street
Blackpool
(0253) 24241

**British Hotels, Restaurants and Caterers' Association**
13 Cork Street
London
W1X 2BH
(01) 499 6641/5

**British Motels Federation Ltd**
10 Bolton Street
London W1
(01) 499 2002

**British Resorts Association**
23 Midhurst Avenue
Westcliff-on-Sea
(0702) 40563

**London Tourist Board**
26 Grosvenor Gardens
London SW1
(01) 730 0791

**Young Men's Christian Association**
National Council
640 Forest Road
London E17
(01) 520 5599

**Young Women's Christian Association**
2 Weymouth Street
London
W1N 4AX
(01) 636 9722

**Youth Hostel's Association**
Trevelyan House
8 St Stephen's Hill
St Albans
AL1 2DY
(0727) 55215

## CAMPING AND CARAVANNING

**Camping Club of Great Britain and Ireland Ltd**
11 Lower Grosvenor Place
London
SW1W 0EY
(01) 828 1012/7

**Caravan Club**
East Grinstead House
East Grinstead
RH19 1UA
(0342) 26944

**Motor Caravanners Club**
29 Wimbledon Park Road
London
SW18 5SJ
(01) 874 1929

**National Caravan Council Ltd**
43–45 High Street
Weybridge
(Weybridge) 51376

## CAR HIRE

**Avis Rent A Car**
Reservations
Trident House
Station Road
Hayes
(01) 848 8733

**Godfrey Davis (Car Hire) Ltd**
Davis House
129 Wilton Road
London SW1
(01) 834 8484 (Car Rental)
(01) 834 6701 (Chauffeur Driven)

**Hertz Rent A Car**
Head Office (Administration)
1272 London Road
London SW16
(01) 679 1777

## TRANSPORT

**Automobile Association**
Fanum House
Basingstoke
(0256) 20123

**British Airports Authority**
2 Buckingham Gate
London
SW1E 6JL
(01) 834 6621

**British Airways**
Intercontinental Flights
Reservations
West London Terminal
Cromwell Road
London SW7
(01) 370 5411

**British Caledonian Airways**
Gatwick/Crawley
Reservations
(0293) 30331 or (01) 668 4222
London Airport, Gatwick
Reservations
(01) 668 4222

**British Railways Board**
Headquarters
222 Marylebone Road
London NW1
(01) 262 3232

**British Road Federation**
26 Manchester Square
London W1
(01) 935 0221/2445

**Civil Aviation Authority**
Aviation House
129 Kingsway
London WC2
(01) 405 6922

**London Transport**
55 Broadway
London SW1
(01) 222 1234

**National Bus Company**
25 New Street Square
London EC4
(01) 583 9177

**Royal Automobile Club**
London Head Office
83–85 Pall Mall
London SW1
(01) 839 7050

**Transport Trust**
11 Great Marlborough Street
London W1
(01) 437 6155

## WATER ORGANISATIONS

**British Waterways Board**
Melbury House
Melbury Terrace
London NW1
(01) 262 6711

**Central Water Planning Unit**
Reading Bridge House
Reading
Berkshire
(0734) 57551

**Inland Waterways Amenity Advisory Council**
122 Cleveland Street
London W1
(01) 387 7973

**Inland Waterways Association**
114 Regents Park Road
London NW1
(01) 586 2510/2556

**National Water Council**
1 Queen Anne's Gate
London
SW1H 9BT
(01) 930 3100

**River Thames Society**
2 Ruskin Avenue
Kew
Richmond
Surrey
(01) 876 1520

**Thames Passenger Services Federation**
Westminster Pier
London SW1

**Water Space Amenity Commission**
1 Queen Anne's Gate
London
SW1H 9BT
(01) 930 3100

## TOURIST BOARDS

**British Tourist Authority**
64 St James's Street
London SW1
(01) 629 9191

**English Tourist Board**
4 Grosvenor Gardens
London
SW1W 0DU
(01) 730 3400

**Cumbria**
Ellerthwaite
Windermere
Cumbria
LA23 2AQ
(09662) 4444

**East Anglia**
*(Cambridgeshire, Essex, Norfolk, Suffolk)*
14 Museum Street
Ipswich
Suffolk
1P1 1HU
(0473) 214211

**East Midlands**
*(Derbyshire, Leicestershire, Lincolnshire, Northampton-shire, Nottinghamshire)*
Bailgate
Lincoln
LN1 3AR
(0522) 31521

**Heart of England**
*(Gloucestershire, Hereford and Worcester, Shropshire, Staffordshire, Warwickshire, West Midlands)*
The Old Bank House
65 High Street
Worcester
WR1 2EW
(0905) 29511

**London**
*(Greater London Area)*
26 Grosvenor Gardens
London
SW1W 0DU
(01) 730 3450

**Northumbria**
*(Cleveland, Durham, Northumberland, Tyne and Wear)*
Prudential Building
140–50 Pilgrim Street
Newcastle upon Tyne
Tyne and Wear
NE1 6TQ
(0632) 28795

**North West**
*(Cheshire, Greater Manches-ter, Lancashire, Merseyside)*
Last Drop Village
Bromley Cross
Bolton
Greater Manchester
BL7 9PZ
(0204) 591511

**South East**
*(East Sussex, Kent, Surrey, West Sussex)*
Cheviot House
4–6 Monson Road
Tunbridge Wells
Kent
TN1 1NH
(0892) 33066

**Southern Tourist Board**
*(Hampshire, East Dorset, Isle of Wight)*
The Old Town Hall
Leigh Road
Eastleigh
Nr Southampton
Hampshire
SO5 4DE
(0703) 616027/8

**Thames and Chilterns**
*(Bedfordshire, Berkshire, Buckinghamshire, Hertford-shire, Oxfordshire)*
8 The Market Place
Abingdon
Oxfordshire
OX14 3HG
(0235) 22711

**West Country**
*(Avon, Cornwall, Devon, parts of Dorset, Isles of Scilly, Somerset, Wiltshire)*
Trinity Court
Southernhay East
Exeter
EX1 1QS
(0392) 76351

**Yorkshire and Humberside**
*(Humberside, North York-shire, South Yorkshire, West Yorkshire)*
312 Tadcaster Road
York
YO2 2HF
(0904) 707961

# Guide Services

In many towns and cities throughout the country, guided tours are available. These are listed below, in alphabetical order. They are arranged for individuals, but tours for groups can be organised. A name of a contact from whom further details can be obtained is given.

## AVON

**Bath (p 190–2)**
Mr J. Clifton
Dept. of Leisure and Tourist Services
Pump Room
Tel: (0225) 28411

Cdr. G. Cronin
Parade Guides of Bath
Norman House
The Normans
Bathampton
(0225) 66884

**Bristol (p 193–6)**
Publicity and Information Manager
City Corps of Guides
Colston House
Colston Street
(0272) 26031

## CAMBRIDGESHIRE

**Cambridge (p 37–9)**
Tours Assistant
Tourist Office
Wheeler Street
(0223) 58977/53363

**Ely (p 40–1)**
Mr J. Blunt
24 St Mary's Street
(0353) 3311

## CHESHIRE

**Chester (p 137–8)**
Joan Houghton
Town Hall
(0244) 40144

**Daresbury (p 137)**
Kenn Oultram
Clatterwick Hall

Little Leigh
Northwich
(0606) 891303

**Nantwich (p 134)**
Richard Stretton
Information Centre
Beam Street
(0270) 63914

## DEVON

**Plymouth (p 209–10)**
Miss J. Gunn
Tourist Information Centre
Civic Centre
(0752) 68000

**Torbay (p 212)**
Mr J. B. Newton
Shorelands
Clennon Drive
Paignton
(0803) 550295/25659/36888

## DORSET

**Bournemouth (p 220–1)**
Mrs T. Barringer
Dept. of Tourism
Westover Road
(0202) 291715

## EAST SUSSEX

**Brighton (p 244–5)**
Resort and Conference Dept.
Marlborough House
Old Steine
(0273) 29801

**Hastings (p 248)**
Tourism and Recreation Officer
Information Centre
(0424) 424242

**Lewes (p 245)**
Nicky O'Reilly
Lewes District Council
187 High Street
(079 16) 71797/71600

## ESSEX

**Colchester (p 46–7)**
Heather Pushman
Tourist Information Centre
4 Trinity Street
(0206) 46379

## GLOUCESTERSHIRE

**Cheltenham (p 177)**
Gill Osborne
Information Centre
Municipal Offices
The Promenade
(0242) 22878

**Gloucester (p 181–2)**
Mrs M. Turner
Robincroft
Reservoir Road
Tuffley
(0452) 24715

## GREATER MANCHESTER

**Manchester (p 130–3)**
Mr R. J. Brall
T.H.B. Holidays
30 York Place
Edinburgh
(031) 556 0948

## HAMPSHIRE

**Portsmouth (p 232)**
Mr B. C. Thomas
City Museum and Art Gallery
Museum Road
(0705) 811527

**Southampton (p 226–8)**
Tim Whitehead
Tourism and Publicity Officer
Civic Centre
(0703) 23855

**Winchester (p 229)**
Miss J. Urry
Guildhall
The Broadway
(0962) 68166

## HERTFORDSHIRE

**St Albans (p 29–32)**
Mrs Clark
Tours Secretary
48 Abbey Avenue
(0727) 56078

## HUMBERSIDE

**Kingston upon Hull (p 95)**
Mr J. Bradshaw
Town Docks Museum
(0482) 27625/224316

## KENT

**Canterbury (p 253)**
Margaret Coomber
Owaissa
Clapham Hill
Whitstable
(0227) 272536

**Rochester (p 255)**
Mr T. J. Hogarth
Tourist Information Centre
85 High Street
(0634) 43666

## LANCASHIRE

**Blackpool (p 127)**
Mr D. Hurrell
10 Loxley Place
(039 14) 75586

**Lancaster (p 126–7)**
Mrs Tyson
Lancaster City Museum
Market Square
(0524) 64637

## LEICESTERSHIRE

**Leicester (p 67–8)**
Mr E. Stacey
Leicester City Council
New Walk Centre
Welford Place
(0533) 54992

## LONDON (p 4–15)

Dundas Guides
135 Notting Hill Gate
London W11
(01) 229 6267/9
or (01) 229 3208

Guide Booking Services
8 Danehurst Street
London SW6
(01) 736 7572

International Booking
Service
Mrs E. Arnold
17 Melcombe Court
Dorset Square
London NW1
(01) 723 4285
or (01) 203 3613

London Transport Guide
Agency
Mrs Gaythwaite
Private Hire Office
55 Broadway
London SW1
(01) 222 5406

London Walks
139 Conway Road
London N14
(01) 882 2763

L.T.G. Travel
18 Blenheim Road
London SW20
(01) 542 4355

Offbeat Tours of London
66 St Michael's Street
London WC2
(01) 262 9572

## NORFOLK

**Norwich (p 57–9)**
Mrs P. M. Petersen
14 Tombland
(0603) 20679/23445

## NORTH YORKSHIRE

**York (p 92–4)**
Mr W. Maxwell
Tourist Information Centre
De Grey Rooms
Exhibition Square
(0904) 21756/7

Mrs Anne Horsley
Enrichment Travel
53 Skeldergate
(0904) 52232

Mr R. Richardson
West Yorkshire Road Car Co.
Ltd.
Barbican Road
(0904) 24161

## OXFORDSHIRE

**Oxford (p 21–4)**
Mrs J. Turner
Information Centre
St Aldgate's Chambers
St Aldgate's
(0865) 48707/49811

## SHROPSHIRE

**Shrewsbury (p 139–42)**
Mrs R. Barker-Jones
Information Centre
The Square
(0734) 52019

## SOUTH YORKSHIRE

**Sheffield (p 81–2)**
Keith Cheetham
Publicity Dept.
Town Hall
(0742) 734130

## TYNE AND WEAR

**Newcastle upon Tyne
(p 107–9)**
Miss B. Stephenson
Central Library
Princess Square
(0632) 610691

## WARWICKSHIRE

**Stratford upon Avon
(p 164–5)**
Guide Friday Services
32 Henley Street
(0789) 69888/9

## WEST MIDLANDS

**Coventry (p 156)**
Miss Gillam
Information Centre
36 Broadgate
(0203) 20084

## WEST SUSSEX

**Chichester (p 240)**
Alastair de Watteville
Kenway Tours
Fordwater Lane
(0243) 527212

## WILTSHIRE

**Salisbury (p 184)**
Information Officer
District Council
10 Endless Street
(0722) 4956

# Bicycle Hire

In many towns throughout the country, it is possible to hire a bicycle. The following is a list, arranged in alphabetical order of the county, of shops where bicycles can be rented.

## AVON

**Bath Bike Hire & Coastal Concessions**
72/74 Walcot Street
Bath
Tel: (0225) 62546

## CAMBRIDGESHIRE

**Ben Hayward**
69 Trumpington Street
Cambridge
(0223) 52294

**Cycloan**
4 Coniston Road
Cambridge
(0223) 46976

**J. Dyson**
77 Norwich Street
Cambridge
(0223) 54805

**J. Howes**
46 Regent Street
Cambridge
(0223) 50350

**Reids Cycles**
68 Victoria Road
Cambridge
(0223) 54009

**University Cycles**
93/95 King Street
Cambridge
(0223) 311560

## CHESHIRE

**Roy Vernon & Sons**
208 Stockport Road
Timperley
Altrincham
(061) 980 3069

## CORNWALL

**Langdon Cycle Shop**
20 St Mary's Street
Truro
(0872) 2207

**Robert Horne**
Kemyl Vean
3 Laregan Hill
Penzance
(0736) 2653

**Silly Cycles**
Wesley Yard
Newquay
(063 73) 2455

## CUMBRIA

**Ghyll Side Cycle Shop**
Bridge Street
Ambleside
(096 63) 3592

**John Peel Garage**
Market Place
Cockermouth
(0900) 822113

**Keswick Cycle Hire**
Pack Horse Court
Keswick

**Lakeland Cycles**
104 Stricklandgate
Kendal
(0539) 23552

**Rent-a-Bike**
Langdale View
117 Craig Walk
Bowness-on-Windermere
(096 62) 2878

**Windermere & Grasmere Cycle Hire**
Black and White Snack Bar
Grasmere
(096 65) 403
and

8 High Street
Windermere
(096 62) 5553

## DERBYSHIRE

Bicycles can be hired in the Peak District. For further information, contact:

**The Peak District National Park Office**
Aldern House
Baslow Road
Bakewell
(062 981) 2881

**Derbyshire County Council**
County Offices
Matlock
(0629) 3411

## DEVON

**Mac's Cycles**
100 Fore Street
Heavitree
Exeter
(0392) 54304

**Plymouth Camping Hire Centre**
107 North Hill
Tavistock Road
Plymouth
(0752) 21881

## DORSET

**Cy-Sales**
644 Wimbourne Road
Winton
Bournemouth
(0202) 515880

**Harveys**
59 Poole Road
Westbourne
Bournemouth
(0202) 761550

**Shepherds Cycles**
319 Ashley Road
Parkstone
Poole
(0202) 742180

# WEDGWOOD VISITOR CENTRE SPANS TWO CENTURIES

You can see potters and decorators at work making Wedgwood for today. You can see the first wares Josiah Wedgwood made when he founded his famous firm in 1759–and hundreds of unique and beautiful pieces made in the years between. Two centuries of Wedgwood history and development

are set out before you. You can also see a film in colour depicting Wedgwood's heritage, design and manufacture.

After visiting the souvenir shop you can relax in the refreshment lounge.

The Visitor Centre is open 9am to 5pm Monday to Friday. (The last complete tour is at 3.15pm.) Parties of 12 or more are advised to book in advance but groups of two or three are always welcome. Contact our Tours Supervisor by letter or telephone (Barlaston 3218) for further information and to make a reservation for your visit.

**Wedgwood**

Barlaston, Stoke-on-Trent, Staffordshire, England.

## EAST SUSSEX

**Cronins Garage**
1 St John's Road
Hove
(0273) 732350

**Rentabike**
Silverdale Road Garage
Silverdale Road
Eastbourne
(0323) 34549

**R. J. Search & Sons**
97 London Road
Bexhill
(0424) 213299

**Stubberfields**
12 South Street
Eastbourne
(0323) 30795

**Tutt Brothers**
Clinton Lane
Seaford
(0323) 893130

## ESSEX

**Coastal Concessions**
'Rent-a-Cycle'
Garage opposite Butlin's
Holiday Camp
Clacton
(0225) 62546 (Head Office)

**Lexden Cycles**
West Berholt
(0206) 240474

**Oxley Hill Farm**
Layer Road
Abberton
Colchester
(0206) 66422

## GLOUCESTERSHIRE

**Mr T. W. Morris**
Manor House Antiques
The Square
Stow-on-the-Wold
(0451) 30379

**A. Williams & Co. (Cycles)
Ltd.**

8/14 Portland Street
Cheltenham
(0242) 52291 or 54796

## HAMPSHIRE

**Jim Osborne**
80 Gregson Avenue
Bridgemary
Gosport
(032 92) 80181

**Chesil Cycle Depot**
3 Chesil Street
Winchester
(0962) 63703

**Payne's Picnics**
12 Carisbrooke Road
Rowner
Gosport
(032 92) 86499

**Peter Hansford**
The Cycle Shop
Bridge Road
Park Gate
Southampton
(048 95) 3249

**Renham Cycles**
3 St Denys Road
Portswood
Southampton
(0703) 556470

## HEREFORDSHIRE

**Little & Hall**
48 Broad Street
Ross-on-Wye
(0989) 2639

**P.G.L. Holidays**
Station Street
Ross-on-Wye
(0989) 4211
(winter period only)

## HUMBERSIDE

**Dale Hire**
Forge Garage
St John's Street
Bridlington
(0262) 78031

## ISLES OF SCILLY

**The Cycle Shop**
St Mary's

## ISLE OF WIGHT

**A. W. Baker**
16 Carisbrooke Road
Newport
(098 381) 4227

**Newshams**
31 Sandown Road
Lake
Sandown
(098 384) 2783

**Parkes of Ryde**
Castle Garage
John Street
Ryde
(0983) 62752

**Vectis Products**
The Broadway
Totland Bay
(098 383) 2455

## KENT

**Andy Cycles**
156 London Road
Dover
(0304) 204401

**Calor and Tool Hire Centre**
7 Portland Road
Hythe
(0303) 67954

**Coastal Concessions**
'Rent-a-Cycle'
Bottom of Chair Lift
Seafront
Folkestone
(0225) 62546 (Head Office)

**F. C. Couchman**
8 Station Approach
Tonbridge
(0732) 353569

**Smiths**
5 Sevenoaks Road
Otford
(830) 2517

268

## LEICESTERSHIRE

**Julie's Cycle Shop**
216 Clarendon Park Road
Leicester
(0533) 707936

## LINCOLNSHIRE

**Lincoln Cycling Centre**
69 Canwick Road
Lincoln
(0522) 25803

**Ward & Son**
36 High Street
Skegness
(0754) 2936

## LONDON

**Bell Street Bikes**
73 Bell Street
London NW1
(01) 724 0456
and
28 St John's Road
London SW11 1PW
(01) 223 7700

**Beta Bikes**
275 West End Lane
London NW6 1QS
(01) 794 4133

**Geoffrey Butler Cycles**
9 South End
Croydon CR10 1BE
(01) 688 5094

**Hira-Bike Ltd.**
Vine House
11 Balfour Mews
London W1Y 5RJ
(01) 499 3085

**Rent-a-Bike**
Kensington Student Centre
Kensington Church Street
London W8
(01) 937 6089

**Savile's Cycle Store Ltd.**
97/99 Battersea Rise
London SW11 1HW
(01) 228 4279

## NORFOLK

**Dodgers**
128 Cambridge Street
Norwich
(0603) 22499

**Rent-a-Bike**
The New Inn
Roughton
Nr. Cromer
(0263) 76389

**Scott Cruiser Ltd.**
Rent-a-Bike
Norwich
(0603) 713489

**Smith**
The Street
Corpusty
Nr. Holt

## NORTHAMPTONSHIRE

**Newlec Cycles**
117/119 St James Road
Northampton
(0604) 51996

## NORTHUMBERLAND

**Chappells' Cycle Dealers**
17a Bridge Street
Berwick-upon-Tweed
(0289) 6295

## NORTH YORKSHIRE

**Brian Shannon**
171 Boroughbridge Road
Acomb
York
(0904) 791610

**Coastal Concessions**
'Rent-a-Cycle'
Butlin's Holiday Camp
Filey
(0225) 62546
(Head Office)

**Craven Cycles**
51 Belmont Street
Skipton
(0756) 5932

**The Dales Centre**
Craven Cottage
44 Main Street
Grassington
Nr. Skipton
(0756) 752205

**Freedom of Ryedale**
8 Bondgate
Helmsley
(043 92) 282

## NOTTINGHAMSHIRE

**National Trust East
Midlands**
Regional Office
Clumber Park
Worksop
(0909) 81341
Contact Head Warden

## OXFORDSHIRE

**Denton Cycles**
194 Banbury Road
Oxford
(0865) 53859

**North Oxford Bike Shop**
North Parade Avenue
Oxford

**Penny Farthing**
27 George Street
Oxford

**Robinson's Cycles**
46 Magdalen Road
Oxford
(0865) 49289

## SHROPSHIRE

**Border Holiday Tours**
11a St John's Hill
Shrewsbury
(0743) 65150

## SOMERSET

**Coastal Concessions**
'Rent-a-Cycle'
The Lido
Seafront
Minehead
(0225) 62546 (Head Office)

**Quantock Rent-a-Bike**
Rowford Cottage
Cheddon Fitzpaine
Taunton
(082 345) 248

**West Country Rent-a-Bike**
Merriott
Crewkerne
(0460) 72401

*STAFFORDSHIRE*

**Hub of England Cycle Hire**
Y.H.A. Midland Region
116 Birmingham Road
Lichfield
(054 32) 22279

**Roy Swinnerton**
69 Victoria Road
Fenton
Stoke-on-Trent
(0782) 47782

**Scotia Sports Centre**
Scotia Road
Tunstall
Stoke-on-Trent
(0782) 812008

*SUFFOLK*

**Countryman Leisure Ltd.**

Main Street
Leiston
(0728) 830250

**Holiday Leisure and Hire
Services Ltd.**
329 Whapload Road
Lowestoft
(0502) 64759

**Ranelagh Road Cycles**
Ranelagh Road
Ipswich
(0473) 50610

*TYNE AND WEAR*

**Sander Bros. Cycle Corner**
6a Brighton Grove
Newcastle-upon-Tyne
(039 67) 35045

*WARWICKSHIRE*

**Hirabike—Stratford Marine**
Clopton Bridge
Stratford-upon-Avon
(0789) 69669

**Knotts**
Greenhill Street
Stratford-upon-Avon

*WEST SUSSEX*

**Coastal Concessions**
'Rent-a-Cycle'
Opposite the Tourist
Information Centre
Coastguard Road
Littlehampton
(0225) 62546 (Head Office)

**R. C. Floyds Ltd.**
31 Surrey Street
Littlehampton
(090 64) 3957

**Mr Reeks**
20 Broadwater Way
Worthing
(0903) 32550

*WILTSHIRE*

**C. F. Haines & Son**
8 Water Lane
Salisbury
(0722) 4915

*WORCESTERSHIRE*

**T. L. Kemp (Broadway)**
'Cycle Hire Centre'
39 High Street
Broadway
(038 681) 2458

# COLLINS
# HANDGUIDES

The most beautiful introductory guides to Natural History ever published

## Alan Mitchell & John Wilkinson

### Collins Handguide to the
# TREES
## of Britain and Northern Europe

Trees are one of the glories of the English landscape. But none of us can claim familiarity with them until we can give them names. Here is a clear and simple guide to 125 of our native trees and to the commonest and most prominent of the introduced trees of parks and gardens.

The book is portable, compact, beautifully illustrated and easy to use. The text is simply written, without unnecessary technicalities. It is an ideal companion for any walk in the country, in town parks and gardens and the perfect introduction for anyone who has ever wondered, "Which tree is that?"

*Illustrated throughout in full-colour.*
**£1.95** *limpback*
**£3.95** *hardback*

## Martin Woodcock & Hermann Heinzel

### Collins Handguide to the
# BIRDS
## of Britain and Europe

All bird-watching begins with identification. We can only appreciate the rich and varied bird life around us when we can tell the different species from each other and name them. Here is a clear and simple guide to 122 species of our commoner birds.

Like the other volume in the series this book is beautifully illustrated and the text is clear and simple, giving all the basic information you need about the appearance, habits and habitats of the birds.

Each volume in the HANDGUIDE series has a lively introduction, an illustrated contents list and an index with both English and Latin names.

*Illustrated throughout in full-colour.*
**£1.95** *limpback*
**£3.95** *hardback*

*Prices are subject to alteration*

271

# Steam Trains

Attractions for steam buffs are growing all over England. They range from locomotives on show in sheds and museums, to railway routes operated entirely by steam. The following is a list, in alphabetical order of county, of the railway preservation societies in England.

## BEDFORDSHIRE (p 35–6)

**Leighton Buzzard**
Pages Park Station
Billington Road
Tel: (052 53) 3888
March to September
Sundays

## BUCKINGHAMSHIRE (p 27–8)

**Quainton**
Quainton Road Station
Nr. Aylesbury
(01) 422 9964
Selected times in the summer

## CAMBRIDGESHIRE (p 37–42)

**Nene Valley Railway**
Wansford Station
(0780) 782021
Easter to October Sundays,
March to September
Saturday

## CUMBRIA (p 116–125)

**Lakeside and Haverthwaite Railway**
See page 125 for detailed information

**Ravenglass and Eskdale Railway**
See page 123 for detailed information

## DERBYSHIRE (p 71–75)

**Dinting Railway Centre**
See page 73 for detailed information

## DEVON (p 204–17)

**Dart Valley Railway**
See page 210 for detailed information

**Torbay and Dartmouth Railway**
See page 212 for detailed information

## DURHAM (p 100–6)

**Darlington North Road Station Railway Museum**
See page 101 for detailed information

**North of England Open Air Museum**
See page 106 for detailed information

## EAST SUSSEX (p 244–8)

**Bluebell Railway**
See page 247 for detailed information

## ESSEX (p 43–9)

**Stour Valley Railway Preservation Society**
Chappell & Wakes
Colne Station
Selected times in the summer

## GLOUCESTERSHIRE (p 177–83)

**Dean Forest Railway Society**
Parkend
Sundays, May to October
Saturday afternoons

**Dowty Railway Preservation Society**
Northway Lane
Ashchurch
Nr. Tewkesbury
Sunday afternoons

**Winchcombe Railway Museum**
23 Gloucester Street
(0242) 602257
July to August Sundays,
Easter Spring and Summer
Bank Holidays

## HAMPSHIRE (p 224–35)

**Mid-Hants Railway (The Watercress Line)**
See page 229 for detailed information

## HEREFORD AND WORCESTER (p 166–76)

**Severn Valley Railway**
See page 168 for detailed information
'Steam in Hereford'
Bulmer Cider Factory
Whitecross Road
(0432) 6182
March to September
weekends

## ISLE OF WIGHT (p 236–9)

**Isle of Wight Railway Company**
Havenstreet Station
Nr. Ryde
(0983) 882204
May to September Sundays,
July to August Thursday
afternoons

## KENT (p 254–5)

**Kent and East Sussex Railway**
Tenterden Station
(058 06) 2943
Easter to October weekends,

272

July to September daily,
November to December
Sundays

**Romney, Hythe and
Dymchurch Railway**
New Romney
(067 93) 2353
Easter to September daily

**Sittingbourne and Kemsley
Light Railway**
(0795) 24899
Easter to October weekends

*LANCASHIRE (p 126-9)*

**Bury Transport Museum**
See page 133 for detailed
information

**Steamtown Railway
Museum**
See page 126 for detailed
information

*LEICESTERSHIRE
(p 67-70)*

**Cadeby Light Railway**
Cadeby Rectory
Nr. Market Bosworth
(0455) 290462
2nd Saturday in each month

**Great Central Railway**
Great Central Road
Loughborough
(0509) 216433
Weekends and Bank
Holidays

**Shackerstone and Bosworth
Railway**
Shackerstone Station
Nr. Market Station
Easter to October weekends
and Bank Holidays

*MERSEYSIDE (p 135-6)*

**Steamport Southport**
Derby Road
(0704) 30693
Weekend afternoons, May to
September daily

*NORFOLK (p 57-62)*

**Bressingham Steam
Museum & Gardens**
Bressingham Hall
Diss
(0379) 88386
May to September Sundays
and Thursdays

**North Norfolk Railway**
Sheringham
(0263) 822045
March to October daily

*NORTH YORKSHIRE
(p 89-99)*

**Derwent Valley Railway**
Layerthorpe Station
York
(0904) 58981
Train leaves 2.30pm daily
except Saturday May to
September

**National Railway Museum**
See page 93 for detailed
information

**North York Moors Railway**
See page 97 for detailed
information

*OXFORDSHIRE (p 18-26)*

**Great Western Society**
See page 20 for detailed
information

*STAFFORDSHIRE
(p 144-9)*

**Chasewater Light Railway**
Chasewater Pleasure Park
Nr. Brownhills
(021) 523 8516
April to September 2nd and
4th Sundays in each month

**Foxfield Light Railway**
Dilhorne
Nr. Cheadle
(088 93) 4669
April to September Sundays
and Bank Holidays

*SOMERSET (p 197-203)*

**East Somerset Railway**
Cranmore Railway Station
(074 988) 417
Daily

**Somerset and Dorset
Railway**
Museum Trust
Washford Station
Nr Watchet
Weekends and Bank
Holidays

**West Somerset Railway**
The Railway Station
Minehead
(0643) 4996
All year

*SURREY (p 256-7)*

**Brockham Museum Trust**
Brockham Pits
April to September
3rd Sunday in each month

*TYNE AND WEAR (p 107-9)*

**Bowes Railway**
Springwell
Nr Gateshead
(0632) 461847
Weekends

*WEST MIDLANDS (p 150-8)*

**Birmingham Railway
Museum**
See page 152 for detailed
information

*WEST YORKSHIRE
(p 185-8)*

**Middleton Railway**
Tunstall Road
Leeds 11
Weekends and Bank
Holidays

**Worth Valley Railway**
See page 85 for detailed
information

# Wildlife Parks

The following is a list of some of England's safari and wildlife parks, arranged in alphabetical order by county.

## BEDFORDSHIRE

**Whipsnade Park Zoo**
See page 35 for detailed information.

**Woburn Wild Animal Kingdom**
See page 35 for detailed information.

## BERKSHIRE

**Royal Windsor Safari Park**
See page 16 for detailed information.

## CHESHIRE

**Bridgemere Wildlife Park**
Nantwich
(093 65) 223
Exhibits include: rare species of deer; otters; foxes; wolves; puma; leopards; waterfowl; birds of prey and foreign birds. Car and coach park; café (farm house cooking); refreshment kiosk; souvenir and gift shop; picnic area.
Open March to 31 October 10.30am to dusk.

## CUMBRIA

**Lowther Wildlife Country Park**
See page 118 for detailed information.

## DERBYSHIRE

**Riber Castle Wildlife Park**
Matlock
(0629) 2073
Exhibits include: pine marten; polecats; wild boar and lynx.

Car and coach park; café; souvenir and gift shop; model railway; pony rides; playground; life-size models of prehistoric creatures.
Open daily 10.00am to 6.30pm in summer, 10.00am to 4.00pm in winter.

## DEVON

**Dartmoor Wildlife Park**
Sparkwell
Nr Plymouth
(075 537) 209
Exhibits include: deer; badgers; foxes; squirrels; wild cats; wolves; ornamental pheasants; peafowl and birds of prey. Large car park; coach park; café; refreshment kiosk; souvenir and gift shop; donkey rides.
Open daily 10.00am to dusk.

## COUNTY DURHAM

**Lambton Pleasure Park**
See page 106 for detailed information.

## EAST SUSSEX

**Heathfield Wildlife and Country Park**
Hailsham Park
Heathfield
(043 52) 4656/4748
Exhibits include: chimps; camels; deer; bison; llama; racoons; monkeys; zebras and birds.
Car and coach park; restaurants; café; refreshment kiosks; souvenir and gift shop; children's corner; picnic areas; car museum.
Open daily 10.00am to 6.00pm.

## ESSEX

**Mole Hall Wildlife Park**
See page 44 for detailed information.

## HAMPSHIRE

**Marwell Zoological Park**
Colden Common
Winchester
(096 274) 206
Exhibits include: Siberian and Sumatran tigers; Scimitar horned oryx; zebras; a variety of antelope; cheetahs; leopards; jaguars; lynx and European bison.
Car and coach parks; café; refreshment kiosk; souvenir and gift shop; children's zoo; picnic area.
Open daily 10.00am to 6.00pm in summer, 10.00am to dusk in winter.

**Weyhill European Wildlife Park**
Nr Andover
(026 477) 2252
Exhibits include: muntjac; Fallow, Read and Roe deer; Arctic and Red foxes; wild boar; badgers; stoats; polecats; bears; monkeys and wolves. Car and coach parks; refreshment kiosk; souvenir and gift shop; children's corner; picnic area.
Open daily 10.30am to 6.00pm in summer, 10.30am to 4.00pm in winter.

## HEREFORD AND WORCESTER

**West Midlands Safari Park**
Spring Grove
Bewdley
(0299) 402114
Exhibits include: lions; tigers; giraffes; antelope; zebras; white rhinos; baboons; wolves; bears; monkeys; sea lions. Car and coach parks; restaurant; refreshment kiosks; souvenir and gift shop; children's corner; pony rides during summer; picnic area and kennels.
Open March to November daily 10.00am to 7.00pm or dusk.

## KENT

**Howletts Zoo Park**
Bekesbourne
Nr Canterbury
(022 778) 440
Exhibits include: first bred
Honey badger and Clouded
leopard in the world; largest
collection of tigers in the
world; first bred Siberian
tiger in Great Britain; largest
collection of gorillas in Great
Britain. Large car park; tea
tent; gardens; picnic area.
Open daily 10.00am to
6.00pm or dusk.

**Port Lympne**
Hythe
(0303) 60618
Exhibits include: tigers;
leopards; wolves; cheetahs;
black rhino; antelope;
gazelle and monkeys.
Large car park; refreshment
kiosk and picnic areas.
Open daily 10.00am to
6.00pm or dusk.

## MERSEYSIDE

**Knowsley Safari Park**
See page 136 for detailed
information.

## NORFOLK

**Kilverstone Wildlife Park**
See page 60 for detailed
information.

**Norfolk Wildlife Park and
Pheasant Trust**
See page 59 for detailed
information.

## OXFORDSHIRE

**Cotswold Wildlife Park**
See page 25 for detailed
information.

## SOMERSET

**Cricket St Thomas Wildlife
Park**
See page 201 for detailed
information.

## STAFFORDSHIRE

**Drayton Manor Park and Zoo**
Nr Tamworth
(0827) 68481/2
Exhibits include: lions;
leopards; puma; bears; sea
lions; llamas; wallabies;
penguins; pelicans.
Car and coach parks;
souvenir and gift shop; children's corner; amusement
park; aerial cabins and picnic
area.
Open Easter to October daily
10.30am to 7.00pm.

## SUFFOLK

**Suffolk Wildlife and Country
Park**
See page 56 for detailed
information.

## WILTSHIRE

**Lions of Longleat**
See page 184 for detailed
information.

# Tourist Information Centres

The following is a list of all the Tourist Information Centres in England, listed alphabetically. The sign of a bed denotes centres offering a Tourist Accommodation service. An (L) after the county shows that only detailed local information is supplied, an (R) shows that regional and local information is given, and an (N) shows that information on the whole country is available.

**Abbey Town** *Cumbria* (L)
Holm Cultram Abbey
☎ (09656) 654

**Abingdon**/*Oxfordshire* (N)
8 Market Place
☎ (0235) 22711 🛏

**Alfreton** *Derbyshire* (L)
Alfreton Library, Severn Square
☎ (077 383) 3199

*Alnwick *Northumberland* (L)
The Shambles, Northumberland Hall
☎ (0665) 3120

**Alston** *Cumbria* (L)
The Railway Station
☎ (049 83) 696 🛏

*Ambleside *Cumbria* (R)
Old Courthouse, Church Street
☎ (09663) 2582 🛏

**Amesbury** *Wiltshire* (L)
Redworth House, Amesbury,
Nr Salisbury
☎ (098 02) 3255 🛏

*Appleby *Cumbria* (L)
The Moot Hall, Boroughgate
☎ (0930) 51177 🛏

**Arundel** *West Sussex* (R)
61 High Street
☎ (0903) 882268/882419

**Ashbourne** *Derbyshire* (R)
13 Market Place
☎ (033 55) 3666 🛏

**Askrigg** *North Yorkshire* (L)
The Market Place, Askrigg,
Nr Leyburn
☎ Bainbridge (096 95) 441 🛏

**Aylesbury** *Buckinghamshire* (L)
County Hall, Walton Street
☎ (0296) 5000 Ext 308

**Banbury** *Oxfordshire* (L)
Borough House, Marlborough Road
☎ (0295) 52535 Ext 250

**Barnard Castle** *Co. Durham* (R)
43 Galgate
Weekend : Witham Hall,
Market Place
☎ (083 33) 3481

**Barrow-In-Furness** *Cumbria* (R)
Civic Hall, Duke Street
☎ (0229) 25795

**Barton-upon-Humber**
*Humberside* (L)
Baysgarth House, Baysgarth Park
☎ (0469) 32333

**Bath** *Avon* (N)
Abbey Churchyard
☎ (0225) 62831 (Enqs.)
60521 (Accom.)

**Battle** *East Sussex* (L)
Memorial Hall, Langton House,
High Street

**Beaulieu** *Hampshire* (L)
The National Motor Museum
☎ (0590) 612345

**Bedford** *Bedfordshire* (L)
Town Hall, St Pauls Square
☎ (0234) 67422 Ext 250

**Bedford** *Bedfordshire* (L)
The Museum, The Embankment
☎ (0234) 53323

**Bellingham** *Northumberland* (L)
Council Offices
☎ (066 02) 238 🛏

*Berwick upon Tweed
*Northumberland* (N)
Castlegate Car Park
☎ (0289) 7187 🛏

**Beverley** *Humberside* (R)
The Hall, Lairgate
☎ (0482) 882255

**Bexhill** *East Sussex* (R)
De La Warr Pavilion, Marina
☎ (0424) 212023 🛏

*Bideford *Devon* (L)
The Quay
☎ (023 72) 77676 🛏

**Birkenhead** *Merseyside* (R)
Birkenhead Library, Borough Road
☎ 051-652 6106

**Birmingham** *West Midlands* (R)
110 Colmore Row
☎ 021-235 3411/2

**Birmingham** *West Midlands* (N)
Information Bureau, National
Exhibition Centre
☎ 021-780 4141 🛏

**Blackburn** *Lancashire* (R)
Tower Block, Town Hall
☎ (0254) 55201 Ext 214 or
53277

**Blackpool** *Lancashire* (R)
Central Promenade
☎ (0253) 21623 🛏

**Blackpool** *Lancashire* (R)
Blackpool Hotel & Guest House
Association Ltd.
87a Coronation Street
☎ (0253) 21891 🛏

**Bognor Regis** *West Sussex* (R)
Belmont Street
☎ (024 33) 23140

**Bolsover** *Derbyshire* (L)
Bolsover Library, Church Street
☎ Chesterfield (0246) 823179

**Bolton** *Greater Manchester* (R)
Town Hall
☎ (0204) 22311 Ext 211/485

*Boston *Lincolnshire* (L)
Assembly Rooms
☎ (0205) 62354

**Bournemouth** *Dorset* (N)
Westover Road
☎ (0202) 291715 🛏

*Bovey Tracey *Devon* (L)
Lower Car Park, Bovey Tracey,
Newton Abbot
☎ (0626) 832047

*Bowness-on-Windermere
*Cumbria* (L)
The Glebe
☎ (096 62) 2244 Ext 43 🛏

**Bracknell** *Berkshire* (L)
38 Broadway
☎ (0344) 50111

**Bradford** *West Yorkshire* (R)
Central Library, Princes Way
☎ (0274) 33081

**Bradford** *West Yorkshire* (R)
City Hall
☎ (0274) 29577 Ext 425

*Brampton *Cumbria* (L)
Allison Pottery & Studio,
32/34 Main Street
☎ (069 77) 2685

*Bridlington *Humberside* (N)
Garrison Street
☎ (0262) 73474/79626 🛏
Winter address : The Spa
☎ (0262) 78255/6/7

**Brigg** *Humberside* (L)
Glanford Borough Council,
Bigby Street
☎ (0652) 52441

**Brighton** *East Sussex* (N)
Marlborough House,
54 Old Steine
☎ (0273) 23755; 26450 (weekends)

*Brighton *East Sussex* (L)
Seafront, Kings Road
☎ (0273) 26540 (weekends)

**Bristol** *Avon* (N)
Colston House, Colston Street
☎ (0272) 293891

*Brixham *Devon* (R)
Brixham Theatre, Market Street
☎ (08045) 2861

**Broadstairs** *Kent* (L)
Pierremont Hall
☎ Thanet (0843) 68399

**Bromsgrove** *Worcestershire* (L)
47/49 Worcester Road
☎ (0527) 31809

**Bromyard** *Herefordshire* (L)
Council Offices, 1 Rowberry Street
☎ (088 52) 2341

**Brough** *Cumbria* (L)
The One Stop Shop, Brough.
Nr Kirkby Stephen
☎ (093 04) 260 🛏

**Bude** *Cornwall* (L)
Old Railway Station

*Budleigh Salterton *Devon* (L)
3 Fore Street
☎ (039 54) 2311

**Burnham-on-Sea** *Somerset* (L)
Berrow Road
☎ (0278) 782377 Ext 43/44 🛏

*Burnsall *North Yorkshire* (L)
Burnsall Car Park, Burnsall,
Nr Skipton (During winter months
open weekends only)
☎ (075 672) 295

**Burton-upon-Trent**
*Staffordshire* (R)
Town Hall
☎ (0283) 45369 🛏

*Bury St. Edmunds *Suffolk* (N)
Abbey Gardens.
Winter address : Thingoe House.
Northgate Street
☎ (0284) 64667 🛏

**Buxton** *Derbyshire* (N)
St Ann's Well, The Crescent
☎ (0298) 5106 🛏

**Cambridge** *Cambridgeshire* (N)
Wheeler Street
☎ (0223) 58977; 53363
(weekends)

**Canterbury** *Kent* (L)
22 St Peters Street
☎ (0227) 66567 🛏

**Carlisle** *Cumbria* (R)
Old Town Hall, Green Market
☎ (0228) 25396/25517 🛏

**Castle Donington**
*Derbyshire* (L)
East Midlands Airport
☎ Derby (0332) 810621

**Castletown** *Isle of Man* (L)
Commissioners' Office.
Parliament Square
☎ (062 482) 3518

**Chard** *Somerset* (L)
Taylors Travel, Fore Street
☎ (046 06) 4414

**Cheadle Hulme**
*Greater Manchester* (R)
Oak House, 20 Station Road
☎ 061-486 0283

**Cheddar** *Somerset* (R)
The Library, Union Street
☎ (0934) 742769

**Cheltenham Spa**
*Gloucestershire* (N)
Municipal Offices, Promenade
☎ (0242) 22878/21333 🛏

**Chester** *Cheshire* (N)
Town Hall
☎ (0244) 40144 Ext 2111 🛏

**Chesterfield** *Derbyshire* (R)
Central Library, Corporation Street
☎ (0246) 32047/32661

**Chichester** *West Sussex* (L)
Council House, North Street
☎ (0243) 82226

*Christchurch *Dorset* (R)
Caravan, Saxon Square
☎ (020 15) 4321

*Church Stretton *Shropshire* (L)
Shropshire Hills, Church Street
☎ (069 42) 2535

**Cirencester** *Gloucestershire* (N)
Cotswold Publicity Association,
Corn Hall, Market Place
☎ (0285) 4180 🛏

**Clacton on Sea** *Essex* (R)
Amenities & Recreation
Department, Town Hall,
Station Road
☎ (0255) 25501

**Clacton on Sea** *Essex* (R)
Central Seafront
☎ (0255) 23400 🛏

**Cleethorpes**
*Humberside* (R)
Alexandra Road
☎ (0472) 67472/66111 🛏

**Clitheroe** *Lancashire* (R)
Church Street
☎ (0200) 25566 🛏

**Coalville** *Leicestershire* (L)
Coalville Library,
60/62 New Broadway Precinct
☎ (0530) 32093

*Cockermouth *Cumbria* (R)
Riverside Car Park
☎ (0900) 822634 🛏

**Colchester** *Essex* (N)
4 Trinity Street
☎ (0206) 46379 🛏

**Congleton** *Cheshire* (R)
Market Square
☎ (026 02) 71095 🛏

*Coniston *Cumbria* (L)
Main Car Park
☎ (096 64) 533 🛏

*Corbridge *Northumberland* (L)
Vicars Pele Tower
☎ (043 471) 2815 🛏

**Coventry** *West Midlands* (N)
36 Broadgate
☎ (0203) 25555/20084/
51717 🛏

*Cranbrook *Kent* (R)
Cranbrook Tourism & Craft
Information Centre, Vestry Hall
☎ (058 04) 2538 🛏

**Crewe** *Cheshire* (R)
Crewe & Nantwich Borough
Council, Delamere House,
Delamere Street
☎ (0270) 583191 🛏

*Cromer *Norfolk* (R)
North Lodge Park
☎ (0263) 2497

*Danby *North Yorkshire* (L)
Danby Lodge National Park Centre
Lodge Lane, Danby, Whitby
(During winter months open
weekends only)
☎ Castleton (028 76) 654 🛏

**Darlington** *Co. Durham* (R)
Darlington District Library,
Crown Street
☎ (0325) 69858/62034

*Dartmouth *Devon* (L)
The Quay
☎ (080 43) 2281

**Dawlish** *Devon* (R)
The Lawn
☎ (0626) 863589

**Deal** *Kent* (L)
Time Ball Tower, Sea Front
☎ (030 45) 61161 Ext 263

*Dedham *Essex* (L)
C.P.R.E. Countryside Centre,
Duchy Barn, Dedham, Colchester
☎ Colchester (0206) 323447 🛏

**Derby** *Derbyshire* (R)
Reference Library, Central Library,
The Strand
☎ (0332) 31111 Ext 21856;
46572 (weekdays 17.00-
19.00 & Sats)

**Doncaster** *South Yorkshire* (R)
Doncaster Central Library,
Waterdale
☎ (0302) 69123

276

# Guide to British Relais Routiers

The Collins/Dunlop Guide with details of around 300 value-for-money restaurants, inns and hotels in the U.K.

only **95p**

All prices are subject to alteration

**Dover** *Kent* (N)
Townwall Street
☎ (0304) 205108

*****Dover** *Kent* (N)
Portakabin, A2 Diversion,
Whitfield

**Dover** *Kent* (N)
Town Hall
☎ (0304) 206941

**Douglas** *Isle of Man* (N)
13 Victoria Street
☎ (0264) 4323

**Droitwich** *Worcestershire* (L)
Norbury House, Friar Street
☎ (090 57) 2352

**Dudley** *West Midlands* (R)
39 Churchill Precinct
☎ (0384) 50333

**Dunstable** *Bedfordshire* (L)
Queensway Hall, Vernon Place
☎ (0582) 603326

**Durham** *Co. Durham* (N)
13 Claypath
☎ (0385) 3720

**Eastbourne** *East Sussex* (N)
3 Cornfield Terrace
☎ (0323) 27474

**Eastbourne** *East Sussex* (L)
Shopping Precinct, Terminus Road
☎ (0323) 27474

*****Eastbourne** *East Sussex* (L)
Lower Promenade, Grand Parade
☎ (0323) 27474

**East Grinstead** *West Sussex* (L)
East Court, College Lane
☎ (0342) 23636

*****Egremont** *Cumbria* (L)
Lowes Court Gallery,
12/13 Main Street
☎ (0946) 820693

**Ely** *Cambridgeshire* (L)
24 St Mary's Street
☎ (0353) 3311

**Exeter** *Devon* (N)
Civic Centre, Dix's Field
☎ (0392) 77888 Ext 2297

*****Exmouth** *Devon* (R)
Alexandra Terrace
☎ (039 52) 3744

**Falmouth** *Cornwall* (L)
Town Hall, The Moor
☎ (0326) 312300

**Farnham** *Surrey* (L)
Farnham Locality Office,
South Street
☎ Godalming (048 68) 4014
Ext 214/5

**Faversham** *Kent* (L)
Fleur de Lis Heritage Centre,
Preston Street
☎ (079 582) 4542

*****Felixstowe** *Suffolk* (N)
No. 2 Dock Gate, Felixstowe Docks
☎ (039 42) 78359

**Felixstowe** *Suffolk* (R)
91 Undercliff Road West
☎ (039 42) 2126/3303

*****Filey** *North Yorkshire* (L)
John Street
☎ Scarborough (0723) 512204

*****Fleetsbridge** *Dorset* (L)
Camper Advisory Service,
Camping Reception & Information
Centre, Fleetsbridge, Poole
☎ Poole (020 13) 85436

**Fleetwood** *Lancashire* (R)
Marine Hall, Esplanade
☎ (039 17) 71141

**Folkestone** *Kent* (N)
Harbour Street
☎ (0303) 58594

*****Folkestone** *Kent* (L)
The Precinct
☎ (0303) 53840

**Fordingbridge** *Hampshire* (L)
Avon Valley Travel Services,
52 High Street
☎ (0425) 54410

**Fowey** *Cornwall* (R)
Toyne Carter & Co Ltd,
1 Albert Quay
☎ (072 683) 3274

**Gateshead** *Tyne & Wear* (R)
Central Library,
Prince Consort Road
☎ (0632) 773478

*****Glastonbury** *Somerset* (R)
7 Northload Street
☎ (0458) 32954

*****Glenridding** *Cumbria* (L)
Beckside Car Park,
Glenridding, Penrith
☎ (085 32) 414

**Gloucester** *Gloucestershire* (L)
Gloucester Leisure Centre,
Station Road
☎ (0452) 36498/36788

*****Grange over Sands**
*Cumbria* (L)
Victoria Hall
☎ (044 84) 4331

**Grasmere** *Cumbria* (L)
Broadgate Newsagency
☎ (096 65) 245

**Great Yarmouth** *Norfolk* (R)
Dept of Publicity,
14 Regent Street
☎ (0493) 4313/4

*****Great Yarmouth** *Norfolk* (R)
Marine Parade
☎ (0493) 2195

**Guildford** *Surrey* (R)
Civic Hall
☎ (0483) 67314

**Guisborough** *Cleveland* (L)
Chapel Beck Gallery,
10/12 Fountain Street
☎ (028 73) 35240

**Hailsham** *East Sussex* (R)
Hailsham Library, Western Road
☎ (0323) 840604

**Halifax** *West Yorkshire* (R)
The Piece Hall
☎ (0422) 68725

**Haltwhistle** *Northumberland* (L)
Council Offices, Sycamore Street
☎ (049 82) 351

**Harrogate** *North Yorkshire* (N)
Royal Baths Assembly Rooms,
Crescent Road
☎ (0423) 65912

*****Hartlepool** *Cleveland* (N)
Victory Square
☎ Hartlepool 68366
Winter address : Leisure & Amenities
Department, Civic Centre
☎ (0429) 66522

*****Harwich** *Essex* (R)
Parkeston Quay
☎ (025 55) 6139

**Hastings** *East Sussex* (R)
4 Robertson Terrace
☎ (0424) 424242

*****Hawkshead** *Cumbria* (L)
Main Car Park
☎ (096 66) 525

**Haworth** *West Yorkshire* (R)
Mill Hey, Nr Keighley
(During winter months open Sats,
Suns & Weds)
☎ (0535) 42329

**Hazel Grove**
*Greater Manchester* (R)
Civic Hall, London Road,
Hazel Grove, Stockport
☎ 061-456 4195

**Hebden Bridge**
*West Yorkshire* (N)
1 Bridge Gate
☎ (042 284) 3831

**Hemel Hempstead**
*Hertfordshire* (L)
Pavilion, Marlowes
☎ (0442) 64451

**Henley-on-Thames**
*Oxfordshire* (L)
West Hill House, 4 West Street
☎ (049 12) 2626

**Hereford** *Herefordshire* (N)
Trinity Almshouses Car Park
☎ (0432) 68430

**Herne Bay** *Kent* (L)
Council Offices, 1 Richmond Street
☎ (022 73) 66031

**Hertford** *Hertfordshire* (L)
Vale House, Cowbridge
☎ Hertford 54977

**Hexham** *Northumberland* (N)
Manor Office
☎ (0434) 5225

**High Wycombe**
*Buckinghamshire* (R)
Wycombe District Council,
Queen Victoria Road
☎ (0494) 26100

**Hinckley** *Leicestershire* (R)
Hinckley Library, Lancaster Road
☎ (0455) 35106/30852

**Horncastle** *Lincolnshire* (L)
Town Hall, Boston Road
☎ (065 82) 3513

*****Hornsea** *Humberside* (R)
The Floral Hall
☎ (040 12) 2919

**Hove** *East Sussex* (R)
Town Hall, Church Road
☎ (0273) 775400

**Hull** *Humberside* (N)
Central Library, Albion Street
☎ (0482) 223344

**Hull** *Humberside* (N)
Corporation Road, King George
Dock, Hedon Road
☎ (0482) 702118

**Hunstanton** *Norfolk* (R)
Le Strange Terrace
☎ (048 53) 2610

**Huyton** *Merseyside* (R)
Municipal Buildings,
Archway Road
☎ 051-489 6000

**Ilfracombe** *Devon* (R)
The Promenade
☎ (0271) 63001

**Ilkeston** *Derbyshire* (L)
Ilkeston Library, Market Place
☎ (0602) 303361 Ext 289

**Ipswich** *Suffolk* (N)
Town Hall, Princes Street
☎ (0473) 55851

**Ironbridge** *Shropshire* (L)
The Iron Bridge Tollhouse
☎ Telford (0952) 882753

**Jarrow** *Tyne & Wear* (R)
Jarrow Hall, Church Bank
☎ (0632) 892106

**Kendal** *Cumbria* (N)
Town Hall
☎ (0539) 23049 Ext 253

**Kenilworth** *Warwickshire* (L)
The Library, 11 Smalley Place
☎ (0926) 52595

*****Keswick** *Cumbria* (R)
Moot Hall, Market Square
☎ (0596) 72645
Winter address : Council Offices,
Main Street

**Kettering** *Northamptonshire* (R)
Information Centre,
Public Library, Sheep Street
☎ (0536) 82143/85211

*****Kingsbridge** *Devon* (R)
The Quay
☎ (0548) 3195

**King's Lynn** *Norfolk* (R)
Town Hall, Saturday Market Place
☎ (0553) 61241

**Kington** *Herefordshire* (L)
Council Offices, 2 Mill Street
☎ (054 43) 202

**Kirkby** *Merseyside* (R)
Municipal Buildings, Kirkby,
Liverpool
☎ 051-548 6555

**Kirkby Lonsdale** *Cumbria* (L)
The Art Stone (Kirkby Lonsdale)
Ltd., 18 Main Street
☎ (0468) 71603

*****Knaresborough**
*North Yorkshire* (L)
Market Place

**Knutsford** *Cheshire* (R)
Council Offices, Toft Road
☎ (0565) 2611

**Lancaster** *Lancashire* (N)
7 Dalton Square
☎ (0524) 2878

**Laxey** *Isle of Man* (L)
Commissioners Office, New Road
☎ (0624) 86241

**Leamington Spa**
*Warwickshire* (L)
Southgate Lodge,
Jephson Gardens
☎ (0926) 311470/27072
Ext 216

**Ledbury** *Herefordshire* (R)
St Katherines, High Street
☎ (0531) 2461/3429

**Leeds** *West Yorkshire* (N)
Central Library, Calverley Street
☎ (0532) 462453/4

**Leek** *Staffordshire* (L)
18 St Edward Street
☎ (0538) 385509/385181

**Leicester** *Leicestershire* (N)
12 Bishop Street
☎ (0533) 20644

**Leominster** *Herefordshire* (L)
Leominster Library, South Street
☎ (0568) 2384

**Lewes** *East Sussex* (L)
187 High Street
☎ (079 16) 6151 Ext 57

**Leyburn** *North Yorkshire* (L)
Central Garage, Market Place
☎ (096 92) 3103

**Lichfield** *Staffordshire* (R)
9 Breadmarket Street
☎ (054 32) 52109

**Lincoln** *Lincolnshire* (N)
90 Bailgate
☎ (0522) 29828

**Lincoln** *Lincolnshire* (L)
City Hall, Beaumont Fee
☎ (0522) 32151

**Littlehampton** *West Sussex* (R)
Council Offices, Church Street
☎ (090 64) 6133

**Liverpool** *Merseyside* (N)
187 St Johns Centre, Elliot Street
☎ 051-709 3631/8681

**London** *SW1* (N)
London Tourist Board,
26 Grosvenor Gardens
☎ 01-730 0791

**London** *SW1* (N)
London Tourist Board
Adjacent Platform 15,
Victoria Station
☎ 01-730 0791

**London** *SW1* (R)
British Tourist Authority
'Welcome to Britain' Tourist
Information Centre,
64 St James's Street
☎ 01-629 9191
Telex : 21231

**London Tower of London** (R)
London Tourist Board
Tourist Information Centre,
Tower of London
☎ 01-730 0791

**London Heathrow**
*Underground Station* (R)
London Tourist Board, Tourist
Information Centre,
Underground Station, Heathrow
Airport
☎ 01-730 0791

**London Harrods** (R)
London Tourist Board, Tourist
Information Centre,
Harrods, Knightsbridge, SW1
☎ 01-730 0791

**London Selfridges** (R)
London Tourist Board,
Oxford Street, W1
☎ 01-730 0791

**London** *City of London* (L)
St Paul's Churchyard, EC4
☎ 01-606 3030 Ext 6456/7

*****London** *Greenwich* (L)
King William Walk, Cutty Sark
Gardens, SE10
☎ 01-858 6376

**London** *Hillingdon* (R)
Civic Centre, High Street,
Uxbridge, Middlesex
☎ Uxbridge 0600

**London** *Richmond* (L)
Old Richmond Town Hall,
Hill Street, Richmond, Surrey
☎ 01-892 0032

**London** *Thamesmead* (L)
Harrow Manor Way, SE2
☎ 01-310 5223/4

**London** *Tower Hamlets* (L)
88 Roman Road, E2
☎ 01-980 3749

**London** *Twickenham* (L)
58/60 York Street, Twickenham,
Middlesex
☎ 01-892 0032

**Long Eaton** *Derbyshire* (L)
Long Eaton Library,
Tamworth Road, Long Eaton,
Nottingham
☎ (060 76) 5426/7

**Longtown** *Cumbria* (L)
21 Swan Street, Longtown, Carlisle
☎ (022 879) 201

*****Looe** *Cornwall* (L)
The Guildhall, Fore Street,
East Looe
☎ (050 36) 2072 🛏

**Loughborough** *Leicestershire* (R)
John Storer House, Wards End
☎ (0509) 30131

**Louth** *Lincolnshire* (L)
East Lindsey District Council,
Area Office, Town Hall, Eastgate
☎ (0507) 2391

**Lowestoft** *Suffolk* (N)
The Esplanade
☎ (0502) 65989 🛏

**Lowestoft** *Suffolk* (L)
Town Hall, High Street
☎ (0502) 62111

*****Ludlow** *Shropshire* (L)
13 Castle Street
☎ (0584) 3857

**Luton** *Bedfordshire* (R)
25 George Street
☎ (0582) 413237

**Luton** *Bedfordshire* (L)
Central Library, Bridge Street
☎ (0582) 32629

**Lyme Regis** *Dorset* (R)
The Guildhall, Bridge Street
☎ (029 74) 2138

*****Lyndhurst** *Hampshire* (R)
Camper Advisory Service.
Main Car Park
☎ (042 128) 2269

**Lynton & Lynmouth** *Devon* (R)
Lee Road
☎ (059 85) 2225 🛏

*****Lytham St Annes** *Lancashire* (R)
The Square
☎ (0253) 725610

**Mablethorpe** *Lincolnshire* (R)
Foreshore Office,
Central Promenade
☎ (052 13) 2496

**Macclesfield** *Cheshire* (R)
Town Hall
☎ (0625) 21955 Ext 114/5

**Maidenhead** *Berkshire* (R)
Central Library, St Ives Road
☎ (0628) 25657

**Maidstone** *Kent* (L)
The Gatehouse, Old Palace Gardens
☎ (0622) 671361

**Malvern** *Worcestershire* (N)
Winter Gardens, Grange Road
☎ (068 45) 4700 🛏

**Manchester**
*Greater Manchester* (R)
Town Hall
☎ 061-236 3377 Ext 433

**Manchester**
*Greater Manchester* (R)
County Hall Extension, Piccadilly
Gardens
☎ 061-247 3694

**Manchester**
*Greater Manchester* (R)
Manchester International Airport
☎ 061-437 5233

**Margate** *Kent* (R)
Marine Terrace
☎ Thanet (0843) 20241/2
Teletourist: (0843) 291540

**Market Harborough**
*Leicestershire* (L)
Market Harborough Library,
53 The Square, Market Harborough,
Leicester
☎ (0858) 2649

**Maryport** *Cumbria* (L)
Maryport Maritime Museum,
1 Senhouse Street
☎ (090 081) 3738 🛏

**Matlock Bath** *Derbyshire* (R)
The Pavilion
☎ (0629) 55082 🛏

**Melton Mowbray**
*Leicestershire* (R)
Melton Carnegie Museum,
Thorpe End
☎ (0664) 69946

**Mere** *Wiltshire* (R)
The Square, Mere, Warminster
☎ (074 786) 341 🛏

**Middlesbrough** *Cleveland* (R)
125 Albert Road
☎ (0642) 245750/245432
Ext 3580 🛏

*****Millom** *Cumbria* (L)
The Folk Museum,
St Georges Road
☎ (0657) 2555

**Milton Keynes**
*Buckinghamshire* (L)
7 Wetherburn Court, Bletchley
☎ (0908) 76311

**Milton Keynes**
*Buckinghamshire* (L)
Milton Keynes Development
Corporation, Wavendon Tower,
Wavendon
☎ (0908) 74000

**Milton Keynes**
*Buckinghamshire* (L)
6 Church Street, Wolverton
☎ (0908) 312581

**Minehead** *Somerset* (R)
Market House, The Parade
☎ (0643) 2624 🛏

**Morecambe** *Lancashire* (R)
Marine Road Central
☎ (0524) 414110/417120
Ext 249

**Moreton-in-Marsh**
*Gloucestershire* (L)
Council Offices
☎ (0608) 50881

**Morley** *West Yorkshire* (L)
Leeds City Council, Town Hall,
Morley, Leeds
☎ (0532) 535541

**Nantwich** *Cheshire* (R)
Crewe & Nantwich Borough
Council, Beam Street
☎ (0270) 63914 🛏

**Nelson** *Lancashire* (R)
19/23 Leeds Road
☎ (0282) 692890

*****Newark-on-Trent**
*Nottinghamshire* (R)
The Ossington, Beast Market Hill
Winter address:
The Palace, Appletongate
☎ (0636) 71156 🛏

**New Brighton** *Merseyside* (R)
The Pier
☎ 051-639 3929

**Newbury** *Berkshire* (L)
Newbury District Council
Wharf Road
☎ (0635) 42400/44000

**Newcastle upon Tyne**
*Tyne & Wear* (N)
Central Library, Princess Square
☎ (0632) 610691 🛏

*****Newhaven** *East Sussex* (R)
Car Ferry Terminal Car Park
☎ (079 12) 4970 🛏

**Newport** *Isle of Wight* (N)
21 High Street
☎ (098 381) 4343 🛏

**Newquay** *Cornwall* (N)
Cliff Road
☎ (063 73) 4558/2119/2716/
2822 🛏

**Northampton**
*Northamptonshire* (N)
21 St Giles Street
☎ (0604) 34881 Ext 404/537;
32054 (Sats 10.00-12.30) 🛏

**Norwich** *Norfolk* (N)
14 Tombland
☎ (0603) 20679/23445 🛏

**Nottingham**
*Nottinghamshire* (N)
18 Milton Street
☎ (0602) 40661

**Nuneaton** *Warwickshire* (L)
Nuneaton Library, Church Street
☎ (0682) 384027/8

**Oakham** *Leicestershire* (R)
Oakham Library, Catmos Street
☎ (0572) 2918

**Oldham** *Greater Manchester* (R)
Greaves Street
☎ 061-620 8930 🛏

**Onchan** *Isle of Man* (L)
Onchan Village Commissioners
Office, 79 Main Road
☎ Douglas (0624) 22311/5564

*****Oswestry** *Shropshire* (R)
Caravan, Babbinswood,
Nr Whittington
☎ Whittington Castle (069 187)
488 🛏

**Otley** *West Yorkshire* (L)
Council Offices, 8 Boroughgate
☎ (094 34) 2241/2

**Oxford** *Oxfordshire* (N)
St Aldates
☎ (0865) 48707/49811 🛏

**Paignton** *Devon* (R)
Festival Hall, Esplanade Road
☎ (0803) 558383

**Peel** *Isle of Man* (R)
Town Hall, Derby Road
☎ (062 484) 842341

*****Penrith** *Cumbria* (L)
Robinsons School, Middlegate
☎ (0768) 4671 Ext 33 🛏

**Penzance** *Cornwall* (N)
Alverton Street
☎ (0736) 2341 🛏

**Pershore** *Worcestershire* (L)
37 High Street, Pershore,
Worcester
☎ (038 65) 2442

**Peterborough**
*Cambridgeshire* (N)
Town Hall, Bridge Street
☎ (0733) 63141 🛏

**Peterborough**
*Cambridgeshire* (R)
Central Library, Broadway
☎ (0733) 69105

**Peterlee** *Co. Durham* (R)
Arts & Information Centre,
The Upper Chare
☎ (0783) 864450

**Pickering** *Yorkshire* (L)
North York Moors Railway,
The Station
☎ (0751) 72508 🛏

**Plymouth** *Devon* (N)
Civic Centre
☎ (0752) 68000

*****Plymouth** *Devon* (N)
Ferry Terminal, Millbay Docks
☎ (0752) 68000

**Poole** *Dorset* (R)
Arndale Centre
☎ (020 13) 3322 🛏

**Poole** *Dorset* (R)
Civic Centre
☎ (020 13) 5151 🛏

*****Pooley Bridge** *Cumbria* (L)
Eusemere Lodge Car Park,
Pooley Bridge, Penrith
☎ (085 36) 530 🛏

*****Portbury** *Avon* (N)
Gordano Services, M5 Motorway,
Bristol
☎ Pill (027 581) 3382 🛏

**Port Erin** *Isle of Man* (L)
Commissioners Office,
Station Road
☎ (062 483) 2298

**Port St Mary** *Isle of Man* (L)
Town Hall, Promenade
☎ (0624) 832101

*****Portsmouth & Southsea**
*Hampshire* (N)
Continental Ferry Terminal,
Mile End Quay
☎ (0705) 819688 🛏

**Portsmouth & Southsea**
*Hampshire* (R)
Castle Buildings, Southsea
☎ (0705) 26722 🛏

**Portsmouth & Southsea**
*Hampshire* (L)
Civic Information Centre,
Civic Offices, Guildhall Square
☎ (0705) 834092/3

**Preston** *Lancashire* (R)
Town Hall, Lancaster Road
☎ (0772) 53731 🛏

**Prudhoe** *Northumberland* (L)
Council Offices, South Road
☎ (0661) 32281

**Ramsey** *Isle of Man* (L)
Town Hall, Parliament Square
☎ (0624) 812228

**Ramsgate** *Kent* (R)
The Ramsgate District Office,
Queen Street
☎ Thanet (0843) 581261

**Ramsgate** *Kent* (L)
South East England Tourist Board,
International Hoverport
☎ Thanet (0843) 57115 🛏

*****Ravenglass** *Cumbria* (R)
Car Park, Ravenglass & Eskdale
Railway Station
☎ (065 77) 278 🛏

**Reading** *Berkshire* (R)
Civic Offices
☎ (0734) 55911

**Redcar** *Cleveland* (R)
Zetland Shipping Museum,
Esplanade
☎ (064 93) 71921

**Redditch** *Worcestershire* (R)
Kingfisher House
☎ (0527) 60806

*****Reeth** *North Yorkshire* (L)
Swaledale Folk Museum

*****Richmond** *North Yorkshire* (R)
Friary Gardens, Queens Road
☎ (0748) 3525
Winter address: Swale House,
Frenchgate
☎ (0748) 4221 🛏

**Rickmansworth** *Hertfordshire* (L)
17/23 High Street
☎ Rickmansworth 76611

*****Ripon** *North Yorkshire* (R)
Market Place
☎ (0765) 4625

**Rochester** *Kent* (L)
85 High Street
☎ Medway (0634) 43666

**Ross-on-Wye** *Herefordshire* (N)
20 Broad Street
☎ (0989) 2768 🛏

**Rothbury** *Northumberland* (L)
United Auto Services Ltd.,
Malting Yard, High Street,
Rothbury, Morpeth
☎ (0669) 20358

**Rugby** *Warwickshire* (L)
Rugby Divisional Library,
St Matthews Street
☎ (0788) 2687/71813

**Runcorn** *Cheshire* (R)
57 Church Street
☎ (092 85) 76776/69656

*****Ryde** *Isle of Wight* (R)
Western Gardens, Esplanade
☎ (0983) 62905 🛏

**Rye** *East Sussex* (L)
Council Offices, Ferry Road
☎ (079 73) 2293/4

**St Albans** *Hertfordshire* (N)
37 Chequer Street
☎ (56) 64511 🛏

**St Ives** *Cornwall* (R)
The Guildhall, Street an Pol
☎ (073 670) 6297 🛏

**Salcombe** *Devon* (R)
Salcombe Town Association,
Shadycombe Road
☎ (054 884) 2736 🛏

**Salisbury** *Wiltshire* (N)
Endless Street
☎ (0722) 4956 🛏

**Salisbury** *Wiltshire* (L)
Fisherton Street
☎ (0722) 27676/4432

**Sandown** *Isle of Wight* (R)
The Esplanade
☎ (098 384) 3886/4641 🛏

**Scarborough** *North Yorkshire* (N)
St Nicholas Cliff
☎ (0723) 72261 🛏

**Scilly, Isles of** (R)
Town Hall, St Mary's
☎ Scillonia (072 04) 536 🛏

**Scunthorpe** *Humberside* (N)
Scunthorpe Central Library,
Carlton Street
☎ (0724) 60161 🛏

**Seaford** *East Sussex* (L)
The Downs, Sutton Road
☎ (0323) 892224

*****Seahouses** *Northumberland* (R)
Main Car Park, Seafield Road
☎ (0665) 720774 🛏

*****Seaton** *Devon* (R)
The Esplanade
☎ (0297) 21660 🛏

*****Settle** *North Yorkshire* (R)
Town Hall, Market Place
☎ (072 92) 3617 🛏

**Shanklin** *Isle of Wight* (R)
67 High Street
☎ (098 386) 2942/4334 🛏

**Sheerness** *Kent* (N)
Bridge Street Car Park,
Nr Sheerness Docks, Sheppey
☎ (079 56) 5324 🛏

*****Sheerness** *Kent* (L)
Swale District Council, Sea Front
☎ (079 56) 2395

**Sheffield** *South Yorkshire* (R)
Civic Information Office,
Surrey Street
☎ (0742) 734760

*****Sheringham** *Norfolk* (N)
Station Car Park, Station Road
☎ (026 382) 4329 🛏

**Shrewsbury** *Shropshire* (N)
The Square
☎ (0743) 52019 🛏

*****Sidmouth** *Devon* (R)
Esplanade
☎ (039 55) 6441

**Silloth** *Cumbria* (L)
Central Garage, Waver Street
☎ (0965) 31276

**Skegness** *Lincolnshire* (R)
Tower Esplanade
☎ (0754) 4821 (summer),
4761 (winter)

**Skegness** *Lincolnshire* (R)
Council Offices, North Parade
☎ (0754) 5441

**Solihull** *West Midlands* (L)
Library Theatre Box Office
Homer Road
☎ 021-705 0060

**Southampton** *Hampshire* (N)
Canute Road (opposite
Dock Gate 3)
☎ (0703) 20438/20494 🛏

**Southampton** *Hampshire* (L)
Above Bar Shopping Precinct
☎ (0703) 23855 Ext 615

**Southend-on-Sea** *Essex* (R)
Civic Centre, Victoria Avenue
☎ (0702) 49451 🛏

**Southend-on-Sea** *Essex* (R)
Pier Hill
☎ (0702) 44091 🛏

**Southport** *Lancashire* (R)
Cambridge Arcade
☎ (0704) 33133/40404 🛏

**South Shields** *Tyne & Wear* (L)
South Foreshore
☎ (0632) 557411

**Southwaite** *Cumbria* (N)
M6 Service Area,
Southwaite, Carlisle
☎ (069 93) 445 🛏

**Southwold** *Suffolk* (L)
Waveney District Council,
Town Hall
☎ (0502) 722366

**Spalding** *Lincolnshire* (R)
Ayscoughfee Hall,
Churchgate
☎ (0775) 5468 🛏

**Spilsby** *Lincolnshire* (L)
Council Offices, 41b High Street
☎ (079 02) 2301

**Stafford** *Staffordshire* (L)
Borough Hall, Eastgate Street
☎ (0785) 3181 Ext 244

**Stamford** *Lincolnshire* (R)
Council Offices, St Mary's Hill
☎ (0780) 4444 🛏

**Stockport** *Greater
Manchester* (R)
9 Princes Street
☎ 061-480 0315

**Stoke-on-Trent** *Staffordshire* (L)
Central Library,
Bethesda Street, Hanley
☎ (0782) 21242/25108/23122/
263568

**Stratford upon Avon**
*Warwickshire* (N)
Judith Shakespeare's House,
1 High Street
☎ (0789) 3127/66175/
66185 🛏

**Stroud** *Gloucestershire* (L)
Council Offices,
High Street
☎ (045 36) 4252

**Sudbury** *Suffolk* (L)
Sudbury Library, Market Hill
☎ (078 73) 72092/76029 🛏

*****Sutton Bank** *North Yorkshire* (L)
National Park Centre,
Sutton Bank, Sutton,
Nr Helmsley
☎ (084 56) 426 🛏

**Swadlincote** *Derbyshire* (I.)
Swadlincote Library, Civic Way,
Swadlincote, Burton-upon-Trent
☎ Burton-upon-Trent
(0283) 217701

**Swanage** *Dorset* (R)
The White House, Shore Road
☎ (092 92) 2885 🛏

**Swindon** *Wiltshire* (L)
32 The Arcade,
David Murray John Building,
Brunel Centre
☎ (0793) 30328/26161 Ext 518

**Tamworth** *Staffordshire* (L)
Municipal Offices, Church Street
☎ (0827) 3561

**Taunton** *Somerset* (N)
Taunton Area Library,
Corporation Street
☎ (0823) 84077/53424 🛏

*****Teignmouth** *Devon* (R)
The Den
☎ (062 67) 6271 Ext 207

**Tenbury Wells**
*Worcestershire* (L)
Leominster District Council,
Teme Street, Tenbury Wells
☎ (0584) 810465

*****Tenterden** *Kent* (L)
Town Hall, High Street
☎ (058 06) 3572 🛏

*****Tewkesbury** *Gloucestershire* (L)
The Crescent, Church Street
☎ (0684) 295027 🛏

**Thetford** *Norfolk* (L)
Ancient House Museum,
White Hart Street
☎ (0842) 2599

*****Thirsk** *North Yorkshire* (L)
Thirsk Museum, 16 Kirkgate
(During winter months open
weekends only)

*****Thornton Cleveleys**
*Lancashire* (R)
Victoria Square
☎ (039 14) 3378 🛏

**Torquay** *Devon* (N)
Vaughan Parade
☎ (0803) 27428

*****Totnes** *Devon* (L)
Totnes Publicity Association
The Plains
☎ (0803) 863168

**Truro** *Cornwall* (L)
Municipal Buildings,
Boscawen Street
☎ (0872) 4555 🛏

**Tunbridge Wells** *Kent* (L)
Information Bureau, Town Hall
☎ (0892) 26121 Ext 163

**Tynemouth** *Tyne & Wear* (R)
Grand Parade
☎ North Shields (089 45) 70251

**Ulverston** *Cumbria* (L)
The Centre, 17 Fountain Street
☎ (0229) 52299

**Upton upon Severn**
*Worcestershire* (L)
69 Old Street
☎ (068 46) 2318 🛏

*****Ventnor** *Isle of Wight* (R)
34 High Street
☎ (0983) 853625 🛏

*****Walsingham** *Norfolk* (L)
Shirehall Museum, Common Place
☎ (032 872) 510

**Walton-on-Thames** *Surrey* (L)
Elmbridge Borough Council
Town Hall, New Zealand Avenue
☎ Walton-on-Thames 25141

*****Walton on the Naze** *Essex* (L)
Mill Lane
☎ Frinton-on-Sea (066 478)
5542 🛏

**Warrington** *Cheshire* (R)
80 Sankey Street
☎ (0925) 36501

**Warwick** *Warwickshire* (L)
Court House, Jury Street
☎ (0926) 42212

**Wellington** *Somerset* (L)
Bowermans Travel Agency Ltd.,
6 South Street
☎ (082 347) 2716

*****Wells** *Somerset* (R)
Town Hall, Market Place
☎ (0749) 72552 🛏

**Welwyn Garden City**
*Hertfordshire* (R)
Council Offices, The Campus
☎ Welwyn Garden City 24411

**Weston-super-Mare** *Avon* (N)
Beach Lawns
☎ (0934) 26838 🛏

**Wetherby** *West Yorkshire* (L)
Council Offices, 24 Westgate
☎ (0937) 62706/9

*****Weymouth** *Dorset* (R)
The Esplanade
☎ (030 57) 5747 🛏

**Weymouth** *Dorset* (R)
Publicity Office,
12 The Esplanade
☎ (030 57) 72444 🛏

**Whitby** *North Yorkshire* (R)
New Quay Road
☎ (0947) 2674 🛏

**Whitehaven** *Cumbria* (N)
Market Place
☎ (0946) 5678 🛏

*****Whitley Bay** *Tyne & Wear* (R)
Promenade
☎ (0632) 524494

**Whitstable** *Kent* (L)
1 Tankerton Road
☎ (0227) 272233

**Widnes** *Cheshire* (R)
Municipal Buildings, Kingsway
☎ 051-424 2061

**Wigston Magna** *Leicestershire* (L)
Wigston Magna Library,
Bull Head Street
☎ Leicester (0533) 887381

**Wincanton** *Somerset* (L)
The Library, 7 Carrington Way
☎ (0963) 32173 🛏

**Winchester** *Hampshire* (N)
The Guildhall
☎ (0962) 68166; 65406 (Sats.) 🛏

**Windermere** *Cumbria* (R)
Victoria Street
☎ (096 62) 4561 🛏

*****Windsor** *Berkshire* (R)
Windsor Central Station
☎ Windsor 52010 🛏

**Withernsea** *Humberside* (L)
Grand Pavilion
☎ (096 42) 2284 🛏

**Woking** *Surrey* (L)
Council Offices
☎ (048 62) 5931

**Woodall** *South Yorkshire* (N)
Woodall Service Area,
M1 Motorway Northbound,
Harthill, Nr Sheffield
☎ Eckington (Derbys) (024 683)
4055 🛏

**Woodhall Spa** *Lincolnshire* (L)
East Lindsey District Council Offices,
Stanhope Avenue
☎ (0526) 52461

*****Woodhall Spa** *Lincolnshire* (L)
Caravan Site Office, Jubilee Park,
Stixwould Road
☎ (0526) 52448

*****Woolacombe & Morthoe**
*North Devon* (L)
Hall '70 Beach Road
☎ (027 187) 553 🛏

*****Wooler** *Northumberland* (R)
Padgepool Place Car Park
☎ (066 82) 602 🛏

**Worcester** *Worcestershire* (R)
Guildhall
☎ (0905) 23471

**Workington** *Cumbria* (L)
Carnegie Theatre & Arts Centre,
Finkle Street
☎ (0900) 2122

**Worthing** *West Sussex* (L)
Town Hall, Chapel Road
☎ (0903) 204226 🛏

**Worthing** *West Sussex* (R)
Marine Parade
(During winter months open
weekends only)
☎ (0903) 35934

*****Yarmouth** *Isle of Wight* (R)
The Quay
☎ (0983) 760015 🛏

**York** *North Yorkshire* (N)
De Grey Rooms, Exhibition Square
☎ (0904) 21756 🛏

# Come in and see us sometime
## Anytime.
## And almost anywhere.

Because now there are more than 400 Tourist Information Centres throughout England, with friendly staff to help you make the most of your leisure time. Each centre offers detailed local – and often regional – information, while larger centres have additional information on the country as a whole. All of them can be identified by this sign:

All the centres hold details of local accommodation. Centres showing this sign will book rooms for personal callers:

'*Where to Stay*' and other Tourist Board publications are also available at most Tourist Information Centres.

Even in your own home town there may be a Tourist Information Centre which can help you with holiday information before you set out.

You'll find lots of holiday ideas and advice on accommodation wherever you see this sign.

The Tourist Information directory, showing all of the centres, is obtainable free from your local Tourist Information Centre or from the English Tourist Board, 4 Grosvenor Gardens, London SW1 0DU.

# Index

# Y

## Town maps

## Area maps